RHETORIC *&* POWER

STUDIES IN RHETORIC/COMMUNICATION
Thomas W. Benson, Series Editor

RHETORIC & POWER

The Drama of
Classical Greece

NATHAN CRICK

The University of South Carolina Press

© 2015 University of South Carolina

Cloth edition published by the University of South Carolina Press, 2015
Paperback edition published in Columbia, South Carolina 29208
by the University of South Carolina Press, 2018

www.sc.edu/uscpress

Manufactured in the United States of America

27 26 25 24 23 22 21 20 19 18   10 9 8 7 6 5 4 3 2 1

Library of Congress Cataloging-in-Publication Data
can be found at http://catalog.loc.gov/.

ISBN 978-1-61117-981-1 (paperback)
ISBN 978-1-61117-396-3 (ebook)

This book was printed on recycled paper with
30 percent postconsumer waste content.

To William, Dean, Sofia, and Leo, may you each find your own Ithaca

CONTENTS

Chapter 9

Chapter 10

SERIES EDITOR'S PREFACE

Nathan Crick's *Rhetoric and Power: The Drama of Classical Greece* tells the story of how rhetoric emerged as a theory and practice in the centuries leading to Aristotle's *Rhetoric*. Crick examines in detail a series of foundational texts in Greek thought based on an understanding of the difference between violence and power, and of the fundamental relation of rhetoric with power. These earlier texts were serving cultural, aesthetic, and intellectual projects of their own, which Crick honors by refusing to regard them as simply struggling to articulate what was later to become rhetorical theory. At the same time, Crick shows how these early texts prepared the intellectual ground for rhetoric as it did emerge, under changing political and cultural conditions, as a discipline in its own right.

Each chapter explores in detail a key text in Greek thought: Homer's *Iliad*, the *logos* of Heraclitus, Aeschylus's *The Persians* and *Prometheus Bound*, surviving fragments of Protagoras, Gorgias's *Helen*, the history of Thucydides, Aristophanes's *The Birds*, Plato's *Protagoras*, Isocrates's "Nicocles," and Aristotle's *Rhetoric*. The chapters serve as both readings of the chosen text and theoretical explorations of the growing store of resources for thinking about power and symbolic action. In addition Crick gives us a highly informative tour of modern classical scholarship and a lucid, dramatic sketch of the centuries of Greek history from Homer to Aristotle and beyond. Nathan Crick's *Rhetoric and Power* is an exciting story of early Greek history and thought and a compelling exposition of the theory of rhetoric.

THOMAS W. BENSON
Series Editor

ACKNOWLEDGMENTS

It was at the end of my senior year in high school when I first encountered Plato. My grandparents Leo and Elsie Conti had a beautiful wood bookcase at the top of their stairs whose contents had remained unopened for decades. Until that year, I had never really paid any attention to these books, treating them as background in a house that I always considered filled with antiques. A stately, stucco home built in the Tuscan style, it was the product of the labor of my great-grandfather who came to the United States from Italy as a teenager, alone, and who built the house in Springfield, Massachusetts, with his own hands after founding a masonry business. Naturally, such a home, filled with decades of artifacts and memories, was a perfect place for a child to ransack for props for imaginative play, particularly in the basement with its fireplace, its potato cellar, its furnace, and its piles of dusty boxes and pickling jars. And it was good for stories, too. Sometimes, when Leo Conti was in the mood, he would corner the grandchildren and make them listen to him praise the Romans for their invention of the arch and their general possession of that rare character trait that Leo called "fire in the belly." Then he would challenge us to try to punch him in his sizable belly or try to squeeze his giant hand until he gave in—something which not even my older cousins who joined the military could ever actually make him do. One thing Leo never did was give in.

As I was going off to college, however, I felt the urge to take something else with me from that house along with my fond childhood memories. So I took two books, *You Can't Go Home Again,* by Thomas Wolfe, and *The Last Days of Plato,* a paperback which included the *Apology, Crito,* and *Phaedo.* The first book was a sprawling exploration of the upheavals of American society during the 1920s and 1930s, before and after the stock market crash which crushed the illusion of unending prosperity and forced American artists like Wolfe into literary exile as they attempted to envision a new future for the country. The second was a dramatization of philosophy in action, of a life acted according to principle in a time of war, greed, and hypocrisy. It was a vivid demonstration that ideas are weapons, that virtue is emancipatory, and that artists are the educators of history. When I read both books that summer, I did not understand much about literary criticism or the nuances of Platonic dialectic, nor did I care to. I read those books for one simple reason—because they were artifacts that found their way somehow into my family's biography, linking that place of my childhood to a larger cosmos of which I, too, would eventually have some part to play. I was ready to expand my imagination beyond the confines of my safe, rural upbringing to catch a glimpse of the possibilities of life and death, of tragic suffering and comic adventure.

The impulse that led me to take *The Last Days of Plato* off of that bookcase at the top of the stairs is not so different from what drove my grandfather to tell stories about the Romans. We look to the drama of ancient history to give us license to imagine possibilities that we often close off in our own lives once our childhood fantasies subside. When I told a good friend of mine (also an academic) that I was writing about Classical Greece, he remarked that such a project would be "like taking a trip to some beautiful island somewhere where everything is different yet somehow the same." Of course, it goes without saying that this beautiful island was also the scene of plagues, burning cities, executions, slavery, and military conquest—but to the modern imagination, it is a beautiful island nonetheless. And we cannot ever seem to abandon this beautiful island. Time and time again, there are movements within academic disciplines of all types to simply abandon the classics as irrelevant and to concentrate on cutting-edge modern scholarship, only to find that we ended up back where we started. Then there is a call for a revival of some tendency that was first articulated in a classical author, and the cycle starts all over again. The reason is plain. Whenever we seem to have run out of inspiration, energy, passion, or hope, we always turn to the past for rejuvenation. Like a child exploring a grandparent's basement, we always locate undiscovered objects that stimulate the imagination with sudden possibilities.

Although I am forever grateful to the lasting influence of my family, this book was not the product of an accidental reading of Plato's dialogues. It was in large part the result of the Fates guiding me to John Poulakos, who I can confidently say possesses that "fire in the belly" that would have impressed Leo Conti. John's primary goal as an advisor is simply to inspire a love of wisdom in his students, an unabashed passion for ideas that are validated not by their popularity but by their power and their virtue. In a university environment that judges authority by the length of one's list of secondary sources, it is truly emancipatory to be mentored by one who cares as little for popularity as does Socrates on trial. I am forever grateful to have crossed paths with someone who combines the intellect of Athena with the creativity of the Muses.

My other source of inspiration has been the graduate students with whom I have been fortunate to work at Louisiana State University. Indeed, much of this book has been composed in the context of conversations with them in the classroom, in my office, over coffee, at the bar, and strolling down the sidewalks of cities in happy avoidance of NCA panels. Special thanks are thus in order. Ryan McGeough challenged me to step up to the plate when I was an insecure assistant professor. Rya Butterfield was the first to trust that I had anything to teach her, and in exchange for my labors she introduced me to the tradition of classical rhetoric in China. Joseph Rhodes, when not playing the role of Hippocleides, was a constant source of enthusiastic provocation and loyal friendship, and to him I owe my acquaintance with the likes of Joshua, Amos, and Isaiah. Bryan Moe has invited me into the garden of Epicurus for a lunch of bread, cheese, and wine, and I shall always take courage from David Tarvin, who has taught me not to be ashamed of wearing a washbasin on my head when the time comes to sally forth. Each of them in their own way helped teach me what was important and what was not in the classical tradition.

The Greeks had a saying, which they repeated unendingly, that one should count no man happy until he is dead. I tend to be of the Aristotelian school, however, believing that the end of living is not to die but to live well and to be thankful for one's time on earth. I have been blessed with a good life because I have been surrounded by good people. And if this book manages to act as an excuse for other good people to share space and time together in noble discourse, then it will have accomplished its goal. And maybe someday, if one copy is lucky, it will end up shoved in a bookcase at the top of the stairs to be discovered by a curious grandchild with fire in her belly.

Introduction

(A crag in the Caucasus. Enter Power and Violence with Prometheus captive. Also, Hephaestus.)

POWER: Here is the world's edge, a blank Scythian tract. No trace of anyone. And now, Hephaestus, you must fulfill the duty the father saddled with you—to lash this criminal to the high crags with unbreakable shackles made of adamantine. For it was your very own ward, all empowering fire, that he stole and gave to mere mortals. For such a crime the gods require punishment, and he must learn to honor Zeus and quell his love for humans.

HEPHAESTUS: Power and Violence, you've done what Zeus required of you, and nothing holds you here. As for me, I've little heart for lashing a kindred god to this stark cliff in harshest winter. Yet I've got to find just such resolve, for he who slights the Father's commands cloaks himself with danger.

Wise son of Themis, giver of sound counsel, it's neither your will nor mine that I fix you in unbreakable bronze bonds far from all men here on this crag. You'll hear no human voice, nor see a human shape. The sun's fierce fire will singe your fair skin, and you'll be glad each time night draws its starry robe between the sun and you, but the sun will be grimly back each dawn.

And this cycle shall be endless, for nobody yet born can free you from it. This is what you get for loving humans overmuch. A god like you should know to fear the gods' wrath; instead you gave humans more than their due.

Therefore you shall stand sentinel on this drear rock, sleepless, your knee unbent. What moans you make will bring you no relief, for Zeus's heart is hard: one who wears power newly wears it harshly.[1]

The Greek poet Aeschylus opens *Prometheus Bound* with a striking scene—the figure of the Titan Prometheus being dragged by Power (*Kratos*) and Violence (*Bia*) to the desolate cliffs of Scythia, with the pathetic figure of Hephaestus trailing behind, lugging chains and blacksmith tools. Zeus, newly crowned tyrant of Olympus, has given the command to punish Prometheus for having thwarted his plan to blot out the human race and "install another, new race to replace them" (165). Against this plan, Aeschylus tells us, only Prometheus dares to stand, driven by an impulse to save "humans from utter destruction" by bestowing upon them the gifts of the arts, thereby bringing them out of the darkness of brutality and ignorance and into the sunlight of civilization and intelligence (165). Zeus by no means punishes Prometheus because he perceives the newly empowered humans to be a threat; he resents, rather, Prometheus's affront to his absolute rule. Hephaestus, chafing at his responsibility to fasten Prometheus to the rocks, sums it up succinctly: "Zeus's heart is hard: one who wears power newly wears it harshly" (158). Power mocks such expressions of pity and commands unwavering obedience. Hephaestus does as he is told, and Prometheus stoically endures his punishment. Violence stands mute until the deed is done, supervising the scene with a cold and piercing gaze. Not Violence, then, but Power speaks. Power commands. Power dominates the stage.

When Power appears in Aeschylus's play, a fifth-century Greek audience would have immediately recognized him as a representative of tyranny. Here, in dramatic depiction, is the milieu of fear, suspicion, and oppression which follows the installment of a tyrant, a ruler who "is harsh, not open to argument, suspicious of his friends, not accountable to others for his actions, and above the law."[2] For the Greeks, Power and Violence were not fictional characters played by famous actors; they represented the very real faces of people they had known, hated, and feared. And so it is today, as C. J. Herrington demonstrates in his description of the play:

[*Prometheus Bound*] presents a study of tyranny *in action,* and its effects on victims and agents alike, which has no parallel at all in ancient literature, and foreshadows the methods of twentieth-century totalitarianism . . . We see here a political offender whose will must be broken by the regime at all costs, by isolation from all fellow-beings, by torture, by chaining, and even by psychological means . . . ; the too-familiar callous police-agents,

Power and his female colleague Violence, who in a modern production might appropriately be clothed in neat black uniforms and jackboots; the gentle, non-political technician, Hephaistos, pressed in to misuse his skills for the regime's infamous purposes; and finally the high-ranking Party official, Hermes, who does not dirty his own hands with violence, but proceeds like an expert brainwasher, alternating between threats and confidential appeals to reason. These parallels between the ancient play and the modern prison seem to confirm the fact that in the *Prometheus Bound* Zeus' regime is being represented as an odious tyranny—not only by the criteria of the ancient Greek city-state, but also by the standards of all democratic societies in all ages.[3]

We are today familiar with detailed analyses of the structure of power, particularly after passing through two world wars in the twentieth century. Yet it was the Greeks who initiated this inquiry into power. For Aeschylus, as for many other artists, intellectuals, politicians, and citizens of his age, power is not simply something to use or to suffer the effects of; it was a concrete object to observe, criticize, investigate, and define. Today we can learn from the results of this inquiry, for although the mechanisms of power have changed in the modern era, power itself remains as it always was on the stage of Aeschylus: something which moves bodies to action.

What is particularly notable about the Classical Greek inquiry into power is that it always ended up placing power in relationship to speech. For instance, although *Prometheus Bounds* opens with Power and Violence as the central actors, they both are quickly moved off stage to let others speak *about* Power. William Matthews writes: "Power is the play's nub. As ever, those who have it use it against others partly to prove they have it, and partly because they can. But those who don't have power have speech (and, because of Prometheus, humans have the power to write speech down). And this play teems with boasters, taunters, whiners, monologists, phrasemakers, and filibusterers."[4] As Matthews indicates, by making power the play's nub, it cannot help but also make speech rather than violence the medium by which power is channeled, disclosed, resisted, and transformed. After all, once Prometheus is shackled to the rock through the instruments of violence, there is little else for direct physical force to do other than torture his immortal body. Power must therefore be enacted through the communication of words and meanings that move other bodies to action through their own voluntary will and judgment.

One way to understand the meaning of the play, then, is to view it as Prometheus's quest for a kind of power which is not only capable of resisting tyranny, but also of resisting it without direct access to *bia,* the physical means of violence. For Prometheus, this means exploiting his capacity for rational and persuasive speech, the capacity which provides its possessor an unexpected source of power. First, speech bestows the ability to win allies by making the listener suffer *pathos* in the immediate present. Speaking to Io (another victim of Zeus's tyranny, who was turned into a bull to cover Zeus's amorous affair), Prometheus acknowledges, "It's well worth the effort to moan and lament for your harsh fate if you can win a tear from your listener" (179). Second, speech gives one the ability to command others when expressed with authority, in this case the authority to communicate "forethought" (which is the literal translation of his name, *Prometheus*) and thus guide present action by referencing knowledge of future consequences. The only reason Zeus pays any attention to Prometheus, after all, is because his words prophesy the future and give him *kratos*. The play thus implies that Prometheus, for all his suffering, still possesses a kind of rhetorical power that can challenge institutional power. It suggests that there is more than one power in the world than tyranny, and that even when the formal representatives of power exit the stage, power may still reside in those left behind as long as they possess the capacity of speech and its ability to constitute and command an audience.

But what is the nature of that power that the character of Power represents? We get a clue from the fact that Power was traditionally paired with Violence in myth. Long before Aeschylus, Hesiod, the poet of archaic Greece, identified Power (*Kratos*) and Violence (*Bia*) as the winged servants of Zeus who "have no home apart from Zeus, nor seat nor path, except the one to which he leads them."[5] In Greek political usage, too, *bia* and *kratos* referred to the tools of a political regime in which "violence is used to maintain social order, and invasion and plunder are legitimate means of acquiring economic capital."[6] However, although both could refer to bodily strength, *bia* was usually restricted to denoting a "specific act of violence," most notably that of rape, whereas *kratos* denoted "a kind of master/slave relationship and to 'mastery' itself, as well as to victory."[7] To possess *bia* was to possess the means of coercion and fabrication which allowed one to directly control and dominate aspects of one's environment through physical manipulation, but to have *kratos* was, in James Oliver's words, to be able to make "the final decision with binding force" (57). Whoever has the *kratos* not only has the ability to speak but to speak words that others are obliged to translate into deeds.

Violence thus differs from power because it uses direct force, whether through the body or through a tool, to move or modify things and people without the mediation of symbolic action. As Hannah Arendt defines it, violence "is distinguished by its instrumental character," often taking the forms of material tools "designed and used for the purpose of multiplying natural strength until, in the last stage of their development, they can substitute for it."[8] Accordingly, the character of Violence is not presented as a person but as an implement, an object manipulated by Zeus to drag the Titan to the crag. But so, too, are the tools of Hephaestus used as implements, as are most of the gifts given humankind by Prometheus. What else but organized and methodological forms of violence is Prometheus referring to when he brags that he taught humans to yoke beasts, to ride chariots, to sail ships, to build houses, and to mine metals? All of these are tools for magnifying human strength, that purely physical capacity with which we are all born. Violence is thus more than simply one person striking another in anger; it involves the whole sphere of instrumental means used to directly alter one's environment without explicit need for speech. Violence breaks stone, but it also builds temples; violence shatters bone, but it also splints a leg; violence ends a life, but it also feeds a family.[9] The key point is simply that violence is a mute (but potentially rationally directed) direct physical manipulation of material for an end; it is not a form of expression but a component of *technē*, the art of fabrication, of making and unmaking through conscious method.

But Prometheus himself is a master of *technē*. Hence we discover the irony of the opening scene of the play—the Titan who bestowed the gifts of the arts to humankind now finds those same arts being used against him, affixing him eternally to the wall of the crag at the edge of the known world. Prometheus, the one who gave humans the gifts of fire, of metallurgy, and of pharmacy, cannot heal himself because he is bound with metal fetters to a cold stone. And even his capacity for forethought does not help him. Indeed, Power explicitly mocks him that the "gods were wrong to name you Forethought" because of his current predicament, indicating that the capacity to predict future events but remain powerless to change them is more of a curse than a blessing (161). When the chorus arrives, it thus says what is on everyone's mind: "So why lavish all your gifts on humans when you can't take prudent care of yourself? Once you've shucked off these bonds I think you'll be no less powerful than overweening Zeus" (345). Yet it is unclear what "power" Prometheus can draw upon in his current state. He appears doomed to wallow in his own self-pity for time eternal.

Yet there is one art (*technē*) which he gave to humans which is neither a form of prophecy nor of violence. This is the art of communication, in this case specifically the art of written communication. In his list of gifts to humans, Prometheus remarks that "I taught them numbers, the most useful tool, and writing, the mother of memory" (341). Although only a small mention in a long list, it nonetheless carries great significance, for none of the other arts could be successfully integrated into a society without a capacity to communicate and to write. Prometheus observes "how befuddled humans were before I aided them, how witless before I taught them to think and to solve problems. . . . For they had eyes but couldn't see, and ears but couldn't hear. They stumbled the length of their lives through a purposeless blur like the ragged shapes of dreams" (335). Eric Havelock thus asks: "What is the hallmark of his Promethean gifts? It is his ability to articulate meaningful language. His prelinguistic condition is in the poet's vision viewed from the perspective of his present command of communication; and the one is seen as a caricature of the other, a wordless dream life like that of the gibbering ghosts in the Homeric Hades, blind, deaf, and dumb."[10] Communication thus brings us out of the dream world into the light of shared reality, with oral communication producing the capacity to coordinate the activities of political life and written communication allowing one to record those activities and organize them into a coherent system of social organization.

For our purposes, the most important Promethean insight is that the gift of communication also produces power. This sense of power as something both common and communicative emerges in a closer look at the interaction between the characters in *Prometheus Bound*. For instance, it is highly significant that Aeschylus presents Violence as brute and speechless physical coercion; she stands mute in the dialogue, her only role to haul the body of Prometheus to Scythia so that Hephaestus can do his work.[11] However, Power is more complicated than Violence because Power speaks. In speaking, his word becomes deed through the medium of voluntary action. Power directs action from a distance through command. His speech is brief and impatient. Power says that he possesses a "stubborn will and changeless mood" and wastes no "energy on impossible tasks" (159, 161). Power thus exists only in action, specifically in the enactment of will through the actions of bodies (including his own) without direct recourse to violence. It is therefore significant that Power speaks only to Hephaestus and not to Prometheus. An impatient taskmaster, Power mocks Hephaestus's expressions of pity while urging him to work faster and hammer harder. And Hephaestus obeys.

Power, then, is neither rooted in divine will, nor physical strength, nor material resources, although all of these things can contribute to power; for power is the capacity to facilitate coordinated activity. As Arendt defines it, power is simply "the human ability not just to act but to act in concert."[12] Similarly, Foucault defines power as "relationships between 'partners'" which represent "an ensemble of actions that induce others and follow from one another."[13] Building from these definitions, power is a capacity to act in concert through communicative understanding, using available resources, technologies, and mediums, to overcome resistance in pursuit of an imagined good. Rhetoric therefore stands in relationship to power as a facilitator and medium. Rhetoric produces power when it creates the capacity to act in concert through the medium of symbolic action; it undermines power when it dismantles the same capacity in others, and it transforms power when it shifts from one form of collective action to another in response to contingencies and possibilities.

Prometheus thus uses rhetoric to accrue power when he speaks in order to facilitate actions in others which serve to accomplish his ends. This occurs as soon as Prometheus discovers that he, too, has access to power despite his bodily immobilization due to a weakness in Zeus's plan. Zeus commands Power to drag Prometheus to "the world's edge, the blank Scythian tract" where there is "No trace of anyone," clearly intending to cut Prometheus off from any contact and therefore render him powerless (157). Unfortunately for Zeus, the Scythian tract at the world's edge is a veritable crossroads. No sooner do Power and Violence exit the stage than Oceanus comes rolling up in a winged car full of his daughters, only to be replaced by Io (who would later give birth to whole generations of people, and whose eventual progeny including Heracles, the one who killed the bird who fed on Prometheus's liver every day). Instead of being condemned to solitude, Prometheus's suffering now appears in full public view, and his gift for prophecy transforms from an impotent capacity to a rhetorical resource which he can use to persuade others. Not only does he tell Io what she should do to help him, but he also exploits his newfound leverage with Zeus, who wants to extract from Prometheus the meaning of his prophesy (told to Io) that Zeus "shall make a marriage that will ruin him" (184). Characteristic of tyranny, in which no secret goes unheard, Hermes quickly arrives on the scene to command Prometheus to tell him what will bring Zeus "down from his throne of power" and to "tell it straight, with no riddling" for he knows "full well that Zeus means business" (191). Yet Prometheus rebuffs him with scornful words, "Spoken with swagger and puffed up with pride, as befits a lackey to the gods. . . . Now scurry back the very way you came, for there's nothing you will learn from me" (191). Hermes, a young God, makes boastful threats that are mocked and rebuffed. Far from appearing the embodiment of power, Hermes finds himself in a state of powerlessness. Indeed, he complains to Prometheus that "you mock me as if I were a child" (193). When Power was present, Prometheus was silent; against Hermes, he uses words as weapons, reducing the messenger to the status of a whining child. Indeed, in making Hermes flee the scene embarrassed, it is Prometheus who has power, not Hermes.

And what gives him power is rhetoric, the art of crafting the persuasive word. Although likely not given the name *rhêtorikê* until the late fifth or early fourth century B.C.E., the fundamentals of what came to be rhetoric was already in place by the time of Aeschylus. As Andrew King remarks, it was during these decades that it came to be widely recognized that it "is Rhetoric (the art of persuasive communication) that builds and sustains configurations of power."[14] It was also widely seen as an art which developed as an alternative to tyrannical power. In fact, rhetoric had a historical connection with tyranny at its origin in 466 B.C.E. as a *technê logon,* an "art of words." Disseminated in the form of portable "handbooks" in which ordinary citizens could learn the basics of speech writing and oratory, this art of words was designed to teach citizens the skills in public speaking to argue their cases in the courts which had were set up to distribute the land confiscated from the tyrants. Despite their unornamented style and simple form as small books on papyrus bought or borrowed in the marketplace, these handbooks were symptomatic of a shift in the structure of power away from tyrannical rule backed by sovereign violence and toward popular democracy grounded in competitive persuasion.[15] For Prometheus to use rhetoric rather than violence to resist the tyranny of Zeus would have been only appropriate given the political circumstances and democratic virtues of his age.

Yet one of the provocative aspects of the play is that the speech of Prometheus seems to characterize him not just as a potential liberator but also as a prospective tyrant himself. On the one hand, one can easily interpret Prometheus as an embodiment of the capacity for political speech which had become the primary medium of power in the Greek democracies of the time. Havelock, for instance, identifies Prometheus as an "arch-sophist" who was punished for introducing to human beings the arts of communication which made possible the formation of a new structure of power, *demokratia.*[16] For Havelock, the sin of Prometheus was simply to attend to "the process of verbal communication between men and between groups of men which made the democracy workable; and that fierce play of ideas and emotions of which words were media."[17] Havelock locates in Prometheus the seeds of what he calls the "liberal temper of Greek politics" which stood in opposition to the tyrannical rule of Zeus. In this liberal social organization, "organs of political power are so framed as to express as far as possible some conformity with the thesis that a common mind exists, that the common men are best judges of their own political interests, that political wisdom is empirical and pragmatic, and that men are naturally more inclined to co-operate than to fight, and that divergent personal opinions can be negotiated to the point of effective decision."[18] The punishment and possible emancipation of Prometheus thus represented the way that tyrannical forms of power backed by the means of violence had to acknowledge and give way to power based in unfettered political communication.

On the other hand, one can also identify Prometheus as a new kind of tyrant, the very embodiment of a demagogue. That is because, for audiences more familiar with the methods of tyranny, Prometheus may not have been understood so sympathetically. They would have known that the standard Greek method of tyranny was to rally support against the old regime by aligning oneself with the masses and posing as their liberator (despite almost always emerging from the established landowning aristocracy).[19] Richmond Lattimore describes the general tyrant as someone who "posed as a representative of the underprivileged and won and used their support, but generally got his position by unconstitutional means."[20] Those who wish to see the *Prometheus* as a simple portrayal of tyranny versus civilization thus miss what Michael Gagarin sees as one of the central themes of the play—that those who rebel, in stubborn arrogance, in their *ethos* as a resister "often become quite similar to the tyrant against whom they are rebelling."[21] In this reading, Prometheus is simply following the playbook of benevolent tyrants like Peisistratus, who gained power in Athens from 560 to 527 B.C.E. by bestowing gifts upon the people without necessarily integrating them into the political structure.[22]

What Aeschylus actually intended Prometheus to represent is lost to history. The two parts of the play which were said to have completed the *Prometheia* trilogy, *Prometheus Unbound* and *Prometheus the Fire-Bearer,* exist only in tantalizing fragments (although these fragments do seem to indicate, in Kenneth Burke's words, that "Zeus and Prometheus mellowed").[23] Even more problematically, today it remains unclear whether the play was even written by Aeschylus in the early fifth century B.C.E. or was a later production by an imitator or even his son.[24] But in many ways this ambiguity is fitting, for Prometheus appears to us today much in the same way that all revolutionary orators do—as provocative unknowns whose speech asks us to believe, to sympathize, and to act without having access to the full story. As in real political and social life, we must make our judgments about Prometheus on the basis of his rhetorical performances alone, hoping that the drama of history redeems the choices that we make in the face of uncertainty, fear, and desire. Interpreting the significance and character of the figure of Prometheus as represented in the play thus gives us an opportunity to explore the possible relationships between rhetoric and power. Imagining Prometheus as both a liberator and a tyrant brings to light the complex relationship between rhetoric and power which makes it impossible to label rhetoric as either an unalloyed good or an absolute evil.

Whenever rhetoric reveals itself to be an artistry of power capable of radical transformations in the political and social order, it is characterized simultaneously as democrat and demagogue, capable equally of emancipation and domination—which is precisely the reason we must understand the complex relationships between rhetoric and power if we are not to make the wrong judgments. Fortunately, we have the advantage of having learned from the drama of the ancient Greek experience with rhetoric and power. We have learned that rhetoric denaturalizes power and makes it appear as product of human choice, artistry, and action. And we have learned that, by using persuasion to gather together a group and its resources and to mobilize it for cooperative action, rhetoric discloses to us that power is the capacity to act in concert based on some prior level of shared communicative understanding made possible by symbols. Based on the original insights of the Greeks in conversation with contemporary rhetoricians and philosophers, this book therefore advances the theses that any discussion of rhetoric must be grounded in a conception of power; that rhetoric functions as a medium of constituting, resisting, and transforming power through the construction and dissemination of symbolic forms; that the characteristic forms and scope of rhetoric in any age are contingent on the state of means and media available for public communication; that all major works of art in any age can be understood in part as rhetorical responses to widespread problems, concerns, and possibilities; that any particular rhetorical act can be used to disclose a potentially universal rhetorical method; that we can best use historical artifacts to understand the relationship between rhetoric and power by dramatizing how they functioned within the crises and struggles of their time; and that we can only truly learn from these artifacts when we see them as common expressions of our shared humanity.

The drama of Classical Greece is in many ways a drama of rhetoric itself. What draws us to this history time and again is thus not that the Greeks were superior in character, virtue, or action to the inhabitants of other ancient cultures. We rightfully celebrate the achievements in art, science, philosophy, and politics which are its noblest legacy, but Greek culture was also a patriarchal society built on a slave economy that celebrated violence as a legitimate means to subjugate rival cities and foreign peoples. But anyone who demands purity from their exemplars is better off with propaganda than with history. What makes the drama of classical Greece so instructive is that it was a drama that the Greeks themselves narrated, argued about, fought over, reflected on, and recorded in their rhetoric. We have only a miniscule portion of that rhetorical history, yet the few objects that remain give us a window into a culture that lived to argue, to condemn, to praise, to rally, to reason, to object, to envision, to persuade, all for the goal of displaying beauty, objectifying virtue, and constituting power in such a way that would leave behind a memorial not only of deeds and things but of words and ideas. To step into this culture is thus to step out of our own and to inhabit, through the imagination, a realm of possibilities that all too often we have foreclosed. It is only through drama that rhetoric lives, and it is only when rhetoric lives that we challenge ourselves and others to make a better world.

CHAPTER 1

Homer's *Iliad* and the
Epic Tradition of Heroic Eloquence

But Thetis answered, warning through her tears,
"You're doomed to a short life, my son, from all you say!
For hard on the heels of Hector's death your death
must come at once—"

"Then let me die at once"—
Achilles burst out, despairing—"since it was not my fate
to save my dearest comrade from his death!
. . . No, no, here I sit by the ships,
a useless, dead weight on the good green earth—
I, no man my equal among the bronze-armed Achaeans,
not in battle, only in wars of words that others win.
. . . Despite my anguish I will beat it down,
the fury mounting inside me, down by force.
But now I'll go and meet that murderer head-on,
that Hector who destroyed the dearest life I know.
For my own death, I'll meet it freely—whenever Zeus
and the other deathless gods would like to bring it on!
. . . But now, for the moment, let me seize great glory! —
and drive some woman of Troy or deep-breasted Dardan
to claw with both hands at her tender cheeks and wipe away
her burning tears as the sobs come choking from her throat—

they'll learn that I refrained from war a good long time!
Don't try to hold me back from the fighting, mother,
love me as you do. You can't persuade me now."[1]

The most eloquent speeches in Homer's *Iliad* have almost nothing to do with the traditional concerns of deliberative or forensic rhetoric. King Agamemnon, who rules the invading Greek armies, does not put forward complex political policies in a parliamentary forum, and no jury listens to formal speeches of prosecution and defense concerning violations of a written legal code. Instead, larger-than-life characters like Achilles step forward to pronounce sovereign decisions that reveal their strength of virtue and their commitment to heroic action even in the face of the certain death that Fate hands them. In the example above, Achaean armies have been hoping the greatest warrior of the Greek army will return to the field of battle. This speech announces his return. After having withdrawn from the fight due to indignant rage at Agamemnon for having spitefully taken Achilles's concubine, Achilles finally has reason to fight again. His loyal friend Patroclus has just been brutally killed by the Trojan hero, Hector. Despite warnings from his mother, Thetis, about his imminent doom, Achilles will not be persuaded; the time for "words" is over. Now the only words that will come from the mouth of Achilles will be directed toward the men he will mercilessly slaughter and the women who will weep for them.

Here, then, is an example of epic oratory intended to encourage not a prudent judgment through persuasive appeal but to disclose the power of virtuous character through eloquence. Achilles has nothing in common with the courtroom lawyer or the political representative who attempts to size up contingent situations, identify the key points at issue, and use plain speech to move a particular audience of democratic citizens to throw their support behind a particular perspective on a matter of shared concern. Achilles has only contempt for common people and their common concerns; he would just as willingly cut their heads off or enslave them as talk to them. His concern is with his own place in the drama of history as a hero, as a superhuman embodiment of the greatest virtues of humankind. A lawyer or politician looks in the eyes of his or her audience with hand extended; Achilles looks to the height of Olympus, the abode of the gods, with arms outstretched. The former wishes to alter the course of human affairs through the medium of collective action; the latter wishes to live out his destiny with the greatest possible personal courage and nobility. The only reason to speak, for Achilles, is to show himself for who he is—the greatest Greek warrior to ever have lived.

Only through epics like the *Iliad* do we encounter such oratory at its best. Achilles in actual life might be closer to a psychopathic monster, but in the *Iliad* he becomes a hero for whom we cheer, even as he is bathing in rivers of blood.

This is because heroes of the ancient oral epics were not intended to represent actual people but rather to embody certain virtues pushed to their ultimate limits in action. We follow Achilles in order to see what happens when rage meets courage, just as we journey with Odysseus in the *Odyssey* to see a true tactician at work. The magnitude of Achilles's slaughters does not detract from the nobility of his character. He is noble simply because he enacts violent retribution for the death of a friend even at the price of his own life. His speech therefore exists to tell us what true loyalty meant in archaic Greece—to sacrifice everything one has for the sake of another's honor and legacy and to enact vengeance upon those who have dishonored it. By poetically threading together a series of such speeches delivered by a panoply of heroes, the Greek epic supplied the ethical and normative ground for Greek unity and power. Undoubtedly there would always be a time when Greek soldiers would ask themselves: "What would Achilles say and do?" The degree to which a group of soldiers exhibited power was thus contingent on their answering the question in the same way.

The nature of heroic eloquence therefore cannot be understood apart from the place and function of the oral epic in archaic Greek culture. Preserved in literate form in the *Iliad* and the *Odyssey*, the oral epic represented more than simply a sweeping narrative of a mighty past in which great heroes performed superhuman deeds against worthy enemies. More important is the manner in which epic "content" is experienced as an oral performance within an oral culture that requires a constant retelling of stories to maintain its shared history and traditions. As Eric Havelock has argued, the epic must therefore be considered "not as an act of creation" but as "the total active reminding, recalling, memorializing, and memorizing, which is achieved in epic verse."[2] Thus, even though Homer likely composed the written version of the epic in the late eighth century B.C.E., he did not create it out of nothing. The oral composition had been preserved for several centuries in Greek cultural memory, and his writing it down was done not to replace the oral performances but to provide them with a common point of reference. Portions of this epic were then retold by wandering bards to oral communities who would gather together to hear ancient tales of heroism and struggle, and these epic stories created a sense of continuity between generations past and present while providing a sense of community among the scattered villages and cities of the rugged Greek landscape.

Rhetorically, then, the function of the epic was not to advocate this or that judgment but to provide examples of eloquence which validated the central ethical and practical norms of a culture through beautiful and passionate speeches given by men and women of superior character. By "eloquence," then, I do not mean simply a fine case of argument or speech. I mean what Thomas Cole refers to as "a combination of volubility, native gift for holding the attention of an audience, and a mind well-stocked with accurate memories and sound counsels."[3] Eloquence has more a poetic and less an instrumental quality about it, concerned as it is more with the flowing forth and display of one's character than with achieving any particular goal through the means of persuasion. Eloquence thus has a natural affinity for aristocracy insofar as kings like Achilles had the luxury not to be bothered with the motives of other people. For Achilles, what mattered was that he spoke and acted with excellence and virtue in the face of opposition, come what may. In archaic Greece, such eloquence must have provided a rare feast of words for people whose lives were hard. Delivered by the poets, examples of epic eloquence captured their attention, lifted them out of their ordinary struggles, and for a moment allowed them to inhabit the lives of epic heroes who embodied the best of Greek culture and thereby established the shared standard of action to which all aspired to imitate.

Disclosed in epic eloquence is thus the power of speech in its most elementary form—its capacity to facilitate collective action by creating a shared experience of admiration of and loyalty to a set of heroes and their virtues. Wherever members of the group have congregated to constitute and reinforce shared memories of greatness that establish models for imitation and reaffirm a moral order, heroic eloquence is not far behind. Eloquence thus forms the basis for power in any culture and forms the beginning of an inquiry into the relationship between rhetoric and power. If rhetoric at its fullest development represents an art of facilitating collective judgment in moments of crisis and contingency, eloquence in its earliest and fullest expression represents the capacity for poetic speech to bind people together in such a way that they identify themselves as a collective. Paradoxically, aristocratic eloquence therefore provides the shared basis of cultural power out of which the art of rhetoric emerges as a means of democratic persuasion, deliberation, and advocacy.

In the age of Achilles, eloquence was the rare possession of a true aristocrat. Before democracies appeared in Greece and rhetoric became the art of the engaged citizen, Greece was a heroic, aristocratic culture in which the exhibition of powerful speech was the privilege of the few. It was aristocratic because it was a "rule by the best," meaning those nobles with "good breeding" who owned the land on which others labored and had a respect for tradition;[4] and it was "heroic" because it was a society that defined an individual by public actions, not by his or her inner thoughts or private character. As Alasdair MacIntyre writes: "A man in heroic society is what he does."[5] A heroic society thus tends to be aristocratic by nature insofar as it relies on a continuity of tradition controlled by fixed hierarchies in which everyone "has a given role and status within a well-defined and highly determinate system of roles and statuses."[6] The oral tradition of epic eloquence was a natural fit for this kind of culture, for through its repeated performances it memorialized the "best" words and deeds (usually of its kings) for both the aesthetic pleasure and the normative order of the community.

What made Greece unique as a heroic culture can in many ways be accounted for by the accident of geography. Unlike Egypt or Mesopotamia, civilizations based on expansive river valleys that allowed for hierarchical systems of governance across a wide swath of easily traversable, fertile land, Greece was a mountainous region broken up into a multitude of separate small planes, river valleys, and islands which encouraged the development of individual cities and villages dominated by a king or a small group of aristocratic landowners. Moreover, the temperate climate allowed people to live relatively comfortably without a great deal of resources and to build open-air gathering places for festivals and communal events. Through Homer's description, we catch a glimpse into the ideal of one of these kingdoms in the scene that the god Hephaestus etches into the Shield of Achilles:

> And he forged a king's estate where harvesters labored,
> reaping the ripe grain, swinging their whetted scythes.
> Some stalks fell in line with the reapers, row on row,
> and others the sheaf-binders girded round with ropes,
> three binders standing over the sheaves, behind them
> boys gathering up the cut swaths, filling their arms,
> supplying grain to the binders, endless bundles.
> And there in the midst the king,
> scepter in hand at the head of the reaping-rows,
> stood tall in silence, rejoicing in his heart.
> And off to the side, beneath a spreading oak,
> the heralds were setting out the harvest feast,
> they were dressing a great ox they had slaughtered,
> while attendant women poured out barley, generous,
> glistening handfuls strewn for the reapers' midday meal. (18: 640–50)

Laid out before the reader's eyes, the heroic ideal shines. Looking at his shield's surface, Achilles could witness everyone performing their role with excellence within an autonomous king's estate—the harvesters reap the grain, the sheaf-binders gird round with ropes, the boys gather the swaths, the heralds set out the feast, the attendant women pour out barley, and the King stands in silence, rejoicing in the peace and harmony of his rule.

Rhetoric did not exist as a conscious art in this society. As Cole defines it, a rhetorical consciousness is one that "recognizes the possibility and necessity of communicating a single message in different ways."[7] But in Homer's Greece there was no gap between thought, speech, and action. In a heroic, oral culture bound tightly by tradition, word and deed were inseparable, so even a great speaker like Agamemnon did not adapt his message to his audience. There would only exist what Cole refers to as the "power or ability (eloquence) of a naturally effective speaker" who expresses his or her thoughts and feelings in a forceful and charismatic manner.[8] What we take for granted today would thus be considered dishonorable: "the capacity to detach oneself from any particular standpoint or point of view, to step backwards, as it were, and view and judge that standpoint or point of view from the outside. In a heroic society there is no 'outside' except that of the stranger."[9] As we see in Homer, there is never a time that any of the heroes (who themselves could be that King supervising the harvest) say anything other than what he thinks or thinks anything other than what he wishes to say. They are men of action, and for them to do anything other than follow their impulses is not so much to deceive as to be a coward.

In heroic culture, fate, not technique, determines the course of history, just as character, not success, is the mark of excellence. We thus encounter heroic elements of culture wherever we collectively confront fate with character. The purpose of a hero is to act heroically, not necessarily to achieve practical success or even necessarily to avoid complete destruction. The opposite of a heroic culture, then, is a bureaucratic culture, which fixes manageable problems through impersonal procedures. Today, in our bureaucratic culture, we still label those rare people "heroes" who sacrifice their lives to save others, even if they do not succeed; in Homeric culture, this was not an exceptional event but a general expectation. Because nobody could ever tell what Fate and the gods had in store, the best one could do was die with honor. Consequently, the whole system of *paideia* in heroic society, or what Jaeger calls "cultural education which aims at fulfilling an ideal of man as he ought to be," was focused on cultivating a sense of excellence (*arête*) which held physical and moral virtues like discipline, duty, and courage in highest regard.[10] This is why Achilles represents the heroic ideal. He not only "fulfills the true harmony of the highest powers of both body and mind," but he also heroically faces death with courage in the defense of Greek culture and power.[11]

The Trojan warrior Hector equals Achilles in his heroic attitude toward fate. In the climactic scene, Achilles finally reaches Hector and chases him three times around the city walls, with Hector fleeing because he knows that he is no match for Achilles in a face-to-face encounter. Then Athena, a patron of Achilles, appears in the guise of Hector's brother Deiphobus and calls on him to face Achilles together, side-by-side. Believing in the illusion, Hector turns to confront Achilles only to find his brother vanished, causing him to cry aloud:

> My time has come!
> At last the gods have called me down to death.

I thought he was at my side, the hero Deiphobus—
he's safe inside the walls, Athena's tricked me blind.
And now death, grim death is looming up beside me,
no longer far away. No way to escape it now. This,
this was their pleasure after all, sealed long ago—
Zeus and the son of Zeus, the distant deadly Archer—
though often before now they rushed to my defense.
So now I meet my doom. Well, let me die—
but not without struggle, not without glory, no,
in some great clash of arms that even men to come
will hear of down the years! (22: 350–60)

No coordinated military strategy or personal fighting skill could have saved Hector from his fated death at the hands of Achilles. There is only one choice he can make—to die forgotten as a coward or to die in a great clash of arms that all will remember.

His speech thus becomes a performance of heroic eloquence designed as his own eulogy to be retold in epic narrative. The epic therefore sustained the ideals and traditions of heroic culture through an oral performance of ancient speeches that immortalized the actions of these heroes and used them as models for *paideia*. Consequently, epic poetry always had three central interrelated elements which helped sustain heroic culture: "a conception of what is required by the social role which each individual inhabits; a conception of excellences or virtues as those qualities which enable an individual to do what his or her role requires; and a conception of the human condition as fragile and vulnerable to destiny and to death, such that to be virtuous is not to avoid vulnerability and death, but rather to accord them their due."[12] It was in his ability to embody these conceptions in a passionate and immersive oral performance that gave the Homeric poet his unique power. Through rhythmic voice, dramatized action, and ritualistic dance, the Homeric poet created in his audience a total experience whose primary function was to sustain tradition. Havelock describes the nature of this power:

The Homeric poet controlled the culture in which he lived for the simple reason that his poetry became and remained the only authorized version of important utterance. He did not need to argue about this. It was a fact of life accepted by his community and by himself without reflection or analysis. . . . But this could not be published or communicated except in performance, and he was very conscious of his virtuosity. . . . To control the collective memory of society he had to establish control over the personal memories of individual human beings. This in effect meant that his poetry was

a mechanism of power and of personal power. He was the medium of the
Muse, and the grandson of the goddess Mnemosune, whose spell he wove.[13]

Homeric poetry was a mechanism of power because it created the shared narratives, virtues, and habits that allowed the scattered population spread across
a multitude of individual Greek cities and villages to think, feel, and act collectively. In this way, the epic tradition did not simply reflect aspects of Greek
culture; it constituted Greek culture itself.

The cultural function of the epic explains one of the notable features that
often bewilder modern readers who treat the oral epic as if it were a nineteenth-
century novel written to be encountered by a private consciousness. Instead of
intimate psychological disclosures punctuated by lively dramatic encounters,
one finds long excurses on how to sacrifice to the gods (1: 550), how to arrange
soldiers by clan (2: 430), how to unwind after a battle (10: 660), how to mix
a drink for a guest (11: 740), how to build a funeral pyre (23: 290), how to race
chariots (23: 350), and how to grieve for your dead son (23: 200). Yet these
lengthy descriptions of the proper and right way to perform everyday tasks
form the core of the epic's original cultural function as what Havelock calls a
"tribal encyclopedia."[14] Whereas a written encyclopedia separates material into
distinct categories to give precise detail about topics unfamiliar to its reader,
an oral tribal encyclopedia blends together every familiar aspect of a culture
in order to reinscribe its normative practices through repetition. The rare feast
of heroic eloquence was certainly a pleasure for the audience, but it was only
pleasurable insofar as it emerged out of a longer narrative that immersed an
audience within a shared cultural milieu that reflected their common rituals,
relationships, speech patterns, and skills.

The finest expression in the *Iliad* of its character as a tribal encyclopedia
appears in the remarkable Book 18, "The Shield of Achilles." After hearing of
the death of Patroclus, Achilles decides to return to battle to avenge his friend.
But Achilles lacks armor, Hector having torn it from the dead body of Patroclus. Fortunately, Achilles has friends in high places, and his goddess mother
Thetis asks the smith god Hephaestus to craft him a shield. But this is no ordinary shield; blazoned upon it is a panorama of snapshot images of Greek life.
Pausing from the narrative of the battle, Homer spends half of Book 18 simply
describing the shield. One particular scene stands out:

> And he forged on the shield two noble cities filled
> with mortal men. With weddings and wedding feasts in one
> and under glowing torches they brought forth the brides
> from the women's chambers, marching through the streets
> while choir on choir the wedding song rose high

and the young men came dancing, whirling round in rings
and among them flutes and harps kept up their stirring call—
women rushed to the doors and each stood moved with wonder.
And the people massed, streaming into the marketplace
where a quarrel had broken out and two men struggled
over the blood-price for a kinsman just murdered.
One declaimed in public, vowing payment in full—
the other spurned him, he would not take a thing—
so both men pressed for a judge to cut the knot.
The crowd cheered on both, they took both sides,
but heralds held them back as the city elders sat
on polished stone benches, forming the sacred circle,
grasping in hand the staffs of clear-voiced heralds,
and each leapt to his feet to plead the case in turn.
Two bars of solid gold shone on the ground before them,
a prize for the judge who'd speak the straightest verdict. (18: 570–90)

This episode is entirely self-contained. Homer provides us no further background and no conclusion. We are offered a mere glimpse into an event frozen in time when the joy of a wedding celebration was juxtaposed with the public hearing of a quarrel. The purpose of each description is simply to reveal and celebrate the proper manner in which each event was performed according to accepted cultural practices. In the wedding scene, we bear witness to the ritual of celebrating multiple weddings simultaneously as a community event, bringing the festivities through the streets for all to see; in the marketplace, we find the proper way of resolving a quarrel over a killing, with the murderer offering payment to the family of the victim whose right it is to refuse, while elder judges compete for making the straightest verdict. The stories lack introductions and conclusions not because of the need to generate suspense but because such things are irrelevant; what matters is that a part of cultural tradition has been given poetic expression to the delight of those already immersed in it.

One of the reasons for the difficulty of modern readers is that the power of this poetic expression is impossible to convey through the printed word. Essential to the epic is the oral style in which it is performed. For oral performance is not simply about the ear, as if it could be understood through a recording. An oral performance of an epic is a whole-body experience in which a rhapsode would embody the spirit of each character in such a way that engaged the whole sensorium of the audience. In Homeric poetry, "a whole series of motor reflexes throughout the entire body was enlisted to make memorization and future recall and repetition more effective."[15] A few of these techniques are readily identifiable. First, there is always a rhythmic and musical quality to

epic speech that makes verse its natural medium of expression. Second, epic
narratives tend to rely heavily on additive structure in which the use of "and"
emphasizes a succession of events in consequence rather than any elabora-
tion of complex causation. Third, stock phrases, common epithets, and grandiose adjectives are consistently associated with certain characters and events
in order to amplify characteristics of the narrative and to help the bard recall
plot sequence as well as who and what are significant. Fourth, descriptions
of events or people often make use of metaphors which speak to the familiar
environment and everyday practices of the audience. Lastly, epic narratives
usually circle around some major conflict in which individuals clash with others in physical, verbal, and intellectual combat as a test of their virtue.[16] These
characteristics assist the poet to give an unscripted oral performance and invite
the audience to engage fully and actively in the unfolding story.

But the Homeric epic was not simply a vehicle for cultural education; it was
also was an aesthetic event valued for its own sake, a work of art which used
eloquence to convey images of such beauty and force that it raised the imagination and feeling to new heights. Few passages in Homer compare in terms of
sheer visceral energy to the description of Achilles at the height of his bloody
rampage through Trojan lines in search for Hector. Achilles becomes even more
than just a great human warrior—he is "something superhuman," a "raging,
wild" embodiment of pure force (20: 505, 530). In this scene, the Homeric poet
is not concerned with inculcating a community in the proper practices of war.
Quite the opposite. Achilles at this point is raging beyond the point of natural
human limits and threatens to violate the very laws of the gods through wanton
slaughter. And so here the poet goes into ecstasies:

> Achilles now
> like inhuman fire raging on through the mountain gorges
> splinter-dry, setting ablaze big stands of timber,
> the wind swirling the huge fireball left and right—
> chaos of fire—Achilles storming on with brandished spear
> like a frenzied god of battle trampling all he killed
> and the earth ran black with blood. Thundering on,
> on like oxen broad in the brow some field hand yokes
> to crush white barley heaped on a well-laid threshing floor
> and the grain is husked out fast by the bellowing oxen's hoofs—
> so as the great Achilles rampaged on, his sharp-hoofed stallions
> trampled shields and corpses, axle under his chariot splashed
> with blood, blood on the handrails sweeping round the car,
> sprays of blood shooting up from the stallions' hoofs
> and churning, whirling rims—and the son of Peleus

charioteering on to seize his glory, bloody filth
splattering both strong arms, Achilles' invincible arms— (20: 550–65)

No complex description here, and no intricate subordinate clauses to explain
what is happening. Image follows image, each subsequent passage building the
momentum of the one that preceded it. And Homer saves the most graphic
metaphor for last. In previous accounts of battle, he had often used images of
lions and storms and waves, but now he calls for the image of a ball of fire
which has accumulated in one of the deep gorges in the Greek hills after consuming the splinter-dry timber of the summer heat. In the metaphor, timber
represents the bodies and the brush the blood, the latter covering the body of
Achilles in bloody filth as he crushes his opposition underfoot. No subtlety here
to be analyzed for its symbolism. Achilles stands for the raw natural force let
loose upon a helpless opposition who waits to have their livers split open, their
eyes pierced with lances, and their guts impaled on a spear shaft. One can only
imagine the collective energy produced on hearing the story told with passionate intensity on a dark night around a fire, built upon a high ground overlook-
ing the expanse of the Aegean Sea.

   Yet the epic cannot dwell long on such scenes of superhuman brutality.
The function of the Greek epic is not to wallow in sensuous barbarism, but to
highlight the complex relationship between mortal heroism and divine law. As
Jaeger explains, the "entire poem is filled with the same purpose—to justify
the ways of God to man. The poet holds the supreme deity to be an omniscient
power, far above all the thoughts and efforts of mortal men: a spiritual power,
whose essence is thought; a power infinitely superior to the blind passions
which make men sin and entangle them in the net of *Até* [ruin]."[17] From this
perspective, the *Iliad* is about the rage of Achilles, and how this rage produces
contradictory effects which lay the foundation for tragedy. On the one hand,
rage propels Achilles into superhuman feats that are inspiring and noble even
in their brutality. On the other hand, this rage, first directed toward Agamemnon and then at Hector, causes him to isolate himself from his community and
then break the divine laws which prohibited violating the dead body of a worthy opponent and preventing its proper burial. So when he denies burial rights
to Hector, and instead drags his dead body around the city and then leaves it
outside of his tent, face down in the dust to be eaten by dogs, the God Apollo
complains to Zeus: "That man without a shred of decency in his heart / His
temper can never bend and change—like some lion / going his own barbaric
way, giving in to his power, / his brute force and wild pride as he swoops on
the flocks of men to seize his savage feast. Achilles has lost all pity!" (24: 50).
Despite the courage in his noble character which makes him an enduring
symbol of the heroic individual, the rage of Achilles has also made him into a

monster, someone incapable of functioning within a human community without completely destroying it.

The final encounter between Achilles and King Priam of Troy thus sets the stage for a final burst of heroic eloquence which announces Achilles's return to humanity. Priam has disguised himself and slipped past Greek lines to appeal directly to Achilles for the body of his son, Hector. Although bringing with him great treasures in payment, he also does an extraordinary act—he kisses the hands of the man who killed his son. This act finally breaks the wall which has kept Achilles isolated from any sense of human compassion or pity, and it brings forth a final moment of eloquence:

> Those words stirred within Achilles a deep desire
> to grieve for his own father. Taking the old man's hand
> he gently moved him back. And overpowered by memory
> both men gave way to grief. Priam wept freely
> for man-killing Hector, throbbing, crouching
> before Achilles' feet as Achilles wept himself,
> now for his father, now for Patroclus once again,
> and their sobbing rose and fell throughout the house.
> Then, when brilliant Achilles had had his fill of tears
> and the longing for it had left his mind and body,
> he rose from his seat, raised the old man by the hand
> and filled with pity now for his gray head and gray beard,
> he spoke out winging words, flying straight to the heart:
> "Poor man, how much you've borne—pain to break the spirit!
> What daring brought you down to the ships, all alone,
> to face the glance of the man who killed your sons,
> so many fine brave boys? You have a heart of iron.
> Come, please, sit down on this chair here . . .
> Let us put our griefs to rest in our own hearts,
> rake them up no more, raw as we are with mourning.
> What good's to be won from tears that chill the spirit?
> So the immortals spun our lives that we, we wretched men
> live on to bear such torments—the gods live free of sorrows. . . ."
> (24: 590–610)

Characteristic of heroic eloquence, he speaks "winged words" which fly "straight to the heart." There is no calculation, no reflection, no time to craft an artistic response designed to persuade a particular audience. His words burst from him and go straight into the heart of his listener, causing both to weep freely in recognition of each other's pain. Thus Achilles does what he has been incapable of doing through the entire epic—he acknowledges both the emotional existence of another person and the existence of a divine will that supersedes his own. Achilles, the superhuman ball of fire capable of destroying anybody in his path, has tempered his brute force in recognition of divine law which sanctions and regulates the power of a community. The eloquent retelling of this moment through epic narrative preserves its wisdom for generations to follow, creating a model for cultural imitation which provided the foundation for Greek power that would rise to unforeseen heights in the centuries to follow.

The rhetorical legacy of Homer is to provide cultural exemplars of such eloquence spoken by men and women of *arête,* of "superlative ability and superiority," who meet Fate with character.[18] Such exemplars, embedded within an epic narrative and given expression through oral performance, also show how speech and power are integrally related. As Havelock indicated, the true source of "power" in archaic Greece was not any individual aristocrat or king, but the Homeric poet who traveled from village to village, performing different scenes within the epic tradition that constituted Greek culture at large. The individual leaders of any particular city or village certainly had *kratos* (the power of the commanding word) insofar as tradition, lineage, resources, and education bestowed upon them this authority; but for a whole culture to have *dynamis* (the power to act upon an opposing force) required a basis of common virtues, understanding, desires, and practices. It was the Homeric tradition which gave power to Greece as a collective group, and which allowed them to act together with people they had never met because they shared a common poetic heritage which inculcated them with the same values and laws and expectations. Undoubtedly, the model of reconciliation provided by Achilles and Priam cause more than one blood feud to be resolved by the donation of gifts and the gracious kissing of the hand of one's enemy.

When looking for echoes of the heroic tradition of eloquence in contemporary culture, one is tempted simply to look to examples in popular film and media. Yet despite the never-ending conveyor belt of heroes dumped on popular culture, the function of heroic eloquence remains intimately tied to the oral tradition. Historically, at the time of Homer, writing existed, but only in the form of what Havelock calls "craft literacy," used mostly by aristocrats or lawmakers who composed public announcements, "in which the public inscription is composed as a source of referral for officials and as a check upon arbitrary interpretations."[19] When Homer finally compiled a written version of the epic, it had existed in purely oral form for over a century, and his putting it on paper was likely meant less for "publication" than simply for record and standardization. In other words, what Homer produced was not a novel to be read but a script to be performed. Homer undoubtedly knew that the power of the epic came not through its words but through what Havelock describes as "the hypnotic pleasure of the performance, which placed the audience under the minstrel's control, but was itself the ready servant of the paideutic [educational] process."[20] The oral performance thus broke the spell of individuality and immersed a collective within an entire field of experience that carried with it the weight and power of tradition.

This is why epic performances of heroic eloquence are not *seen* in the theater, *heard* on the radio, or *read* in a book; they are *experienced* with others in oral settings which reenact heroic moments that reinscribe the normative practices of a face-to-face community. However, the media provide innumerable examples of eloquence that provide the "content" for the "form" of expression. For instance, Homer's rich version of the Greek epic provides a content for rhapsodic form. But so, too, does a highlight reel for a professional football game provide the content for a high-school player's reenactment of a heroic clash of titans in the locker room. A radio talk show provides the narrative that a middle manager performs with exuberance in the lunchroom, and a historical novel provides an example of courageous action that a parent narrates to a child. In each case, someone has chosen to play the role of a rhapsode, pulling material from history (however recent) to bring to life moments of eloquence within an oral performance intended to create a sense of community validated by the heroic actions of others. These performances form the basis of power in any social group, no matter how interpenetrated it is by contemporary media. Heroic eloquence is not a dead tradition. It is reborn anew during every moment of adolescence when children gather together and one steps forward to say "remember when." These are rhapsodes in training, and the eloquence they imitate lays the ground for common practices and virtues which make possible the development of a rhetorical culture.

CHAPTER 2

Heraclitus and the
Revelation of *Logos*

> It is impossible to step twice into the same river. Upon those that step into the same rivers different and different waters flow. They scatter and gather, come together and flow way, approach and depart.[1]

As the sixth century B.C.E. was coming to a close, Heraclitus of Ephesus (ca. 544–470) attempted to do what Achilles could not do—defeat the river. For despite his panoply of man-killing skills, Achilles was helpless against the force of the river-god Xanthus when it rose up in anger against him. Achilles had incited its rage by choking its waters with the blood and bodies of Trojans, causing Xanthus to take human form and deliver this warning: "All my lovely rapids are crammed with corpses now, / no channel in sight to sweep my current out to sacred sea— / I'm choked with corpses and still you slaughter more, / you blot out more! Leave me alone, have done— / captain of armies, I am filled with horror!" (*Iliad* 21: 245–50). When Achilles continues his rampage, Xanthus hurls the entire force of the river against him, slamming the hero's shield and forcing him to cling to the roots of a tree, which topples down upon him and sends him into a whirlpool from which he struggles to escape: "So the relentless tide kept overtaking Achilles, / yes, for all his speed—gods are stronger than men" (21: 298). Only through the intervention of Hera, who commands Hephaestus to ignite the hordes of corpses in the river and thus subdue Xanthus by fire, does Achilles escape death to fight on.

Yet the same river that had the power to defeat Greece's most celebrated warrior is rendered powerless against Greece's most obscure philosopher. This

is because Achilles mounted frontal assaults against an opponent with winged
words and heroic deeds alone, meaning that he had to retreat when met with an
equal or greater counterforce. Heraclitus, by contrast, had the capacity to challenge the river in a way that Achilles did not. Through the power of a new kind
of word, Heraclitus emerged victorious neither through martial violence nor
heroic character, but through a kind of linguistic exorcism that stripped away
the aura of transcendent divinity that gave the river its power. This new kind
of word was the prophetic aphorism. Derived from the Greek *aphorizein,* "from
the horizon," aphorisms are compressed poetic statements which, by provoking acts of thinking and inquiry, bring near to us what appears at first glance
to be far away; and an aphorism is prophetic when its words bring into view
some aspect of divine or cosmological will or law that was previously with-
held or concealed.[2] More than simply a clever phrase or beautiful expression, a
prophetic aphorism represented a form of rhetorical expression, a compact and
easily transportable linguistic weapon that would unleash indeed new energies
in the mind.

Against this new technology (*technē*) of the word, even the river had no
defense. This is because Heraclitus's aphorism undermined the very ground on
which the river acquired its power. For the river was only capable of speaking and acting with authority based on the traditional Greek assumption that
the river possessed an eternal and unchanging essence deserving of our pious
respect. From this perspective, Xanthus rages not so much out of indignation
for the death of the Trojans but for the sheer fact that their blood and bodies
prohibit the normal flow of the currents out to sacred sea. It is Achilles's disruption of continuity which so offends the river god, less so the hero's pitiless
slaying of mortals. Yet through a single prophetic aphorism, Heraclitus shows
all of these assumptions to be false. The river, he says, is no permanent habitat
of a god; it is an ever-changing flux of different waters which scatter and gather,
come together and flow away, approach and depart. What does it matter, then,
if Achilles turns water to blood and chokes its normal channel with a tangle of
floating bodies? He simply has shown what was true all along—that the river is
always changing and has no enduring power over the minds and will of men.

Of course, the false assumption about the stability of the river is only a
symptom of what Heraclitus saw as a larger disease within Greek culture—
namely, the uncritical acceptance of Homeric religious traditions with all of
its archaic beliefs, rituals, idols, and shrines. Rather than use the resources of
human intelligence to investigate the nature of the rational universe, these
worshippers spend their time performing sacrifices to nonexistent gods. As
Heraclitus sees it, they "vainly purify themselves with blood when they are
defiled with it, which is like someone who has stepped in the mud using mud to
wash himself. Anyone who has observed a person doing this would think him

mad. And in their ignorance of the true nature of gods and heroes they pray to the statues, which is like someone chatting to a house."[3] In the pitiless judgment of Heraclitus, this type of behavior is all that can be expected of most human beings, whose dominant character trait is the uninformed arrogance to assume that their personal perspective on the world reflects that of the gods. What they do not know is that, just as "donkeys would prefer refuse to gold," and "pigs prefer filth to clean water," so too are human beings "thought as foolish by a supernatural being as a child is by a man."[4] For Heraclitus, most people differ only in degree from pigs or donkeys, preferring as they do to talk to houses and call themselves sane while they cover their bodies with blood and boast of their piety.

Heraclitus undermines the integrity of tradition, however, not to abandon us to chaos but to prophesy an emergent order to come. His purpose in dissolving the integrity of the river or the virtues of heroic culture was therefore not to produce skepticism but to open people's ears to a new harmony revealed through the flux of appearances. A second aphorism thus acts as a balance to the first: "Listening not to me but to the Logos it is wise to agree that all things are one."[5] With this aphorism, Heraclitus moves from destructive skeptic to oracular prophet, or what Kierkegaard calls that "individual who spies the new in the distance, in dim and undefined contours," who "does not possess the future" but "has only a presentiment of it."[6] For like all prophets, Heraclitus does not speak for himself but for a higher law, principle, or authority; and although only he alone can interpret and communicate this law (however incompletely), he speaks in the hope that others will acquire the ears to hear until they are able to truly listen and thereby understand.

That Heraclitus spoke with a prophetic voice is further evidenced by the Logos being not merely a material law of nature but a divine law of the cosmos. For Heraclitus, the Logos represented a unified spiritual order intended to supplant the anthropomorphic polytheism of archaic Greek culture. According to Jaeger, it was only through his effort to disclose the laws of this divinity that "we understand his justification for introducing himself as a prophet. The *logos* according to which everything occurs, though it still remain hidden from mankind, is the divine law itself. . . . This theological aspect makes very clear how profoundly the law of Heraclitus differs from what we mean when we speak of a 'law of nature.'"[7] The reason Heraclitus referred to this divine law as *logos* is because, in common speech, *logos* referred variously to story, speech, reason, and logic, with perhaps the most accurate synonym being an "account," or "that which sets forth what a thing was or is."[8] By the Logos, then, Heraclitus meant the definitive account of everything which *is,* the all-encompassing world order that in turn could be communicated to others through the power of the word. By creating a *logos* for the Logos, Heraclitus therefore sought to challenge the archaic belief that human fate was determined by the inaccessible will of a multiplicity of impulsive gods and replace it with a belief in a cosmos guided by the rational and accessible laws of a single ordering principle that could reveal to human intelligence the unified order underlying the flux of becoming.

The aphorisms of Heraclitus are thus brought into the sphere of the rhetorical insofar as they were consciously designed as prophetic provocations to shock Greek culture from its Homeric slumber and awaken it to the possibilities of a new order. Although Heraclitus was able to discern only the dim outlines of what was to come, of one thing he was sure—that the age in which ancient convention dictated the thoughts and actions of families, communities, and nations was giving way to an order in which the thinking and speech of the individual was sovereign when it was spoken with truth. For Heraclitus was not alone in his efforts. He was part of a whole movement in Greek intellectual thought, including both philosophers and poets, that was challenging the norms of conventional oral culture on all fronts. Jaeger explains:

> The boldness with which these philosophers applied pure independent logic to the current conception of the universe is parallel to the courage of the Ionian poets in voicing their emotions and opinions on human life in their own age. Both ventures are based on the growing power of the individual. At this stage logic appears to work like an explosive. The oldest authorities shake and fall under its impact. Nothing is correct but that which *I* can explain to myself on conclusive grounds, that for which *my* thought can reasonably account. . . . Yet in this victory of the rational I over traditional authority, there is latent a force which is to triumph over the individual: the concept of Truth, a new universal category to which every personal preference must yield.[9]

Heraclitus can thus defeat the river because, for him, the river is a symbol of a dying authority whose power is based on the blind acceptance of an attractive lie. But the truth of the river is disclosed through the aphorisms of Heraclitus, and before that truth it must yield. The gods recede into history to make way for the Logos announced by the individual who can comprehend its laws, speak truth to illegitimate power, and make way for the legitimate power to come.

With Heraclitus, then, we first glimpse the possibility of rhetoric as a medium for challenging and transforming power. Whereas Homeric eloquence was a medium for maintaining and propagating power, the prophetic character of Heraclitus's speech was designed to do the opposite. Not only did its explicit content condemn conventional beliefs and practices for their narrowness, pettiness, and hypocrisy while pointing to the existence of a more rational order behind appearances, but the manner of its expression was revolutionary. For the aphoristic form stimulated that most dangerous of all things—*thinking*. By compressing complex logical thought within paradoxical poetic form, the aphorism stimulated the individual to inquire into appearances and pursue the truth wherever that truth might lead. For to think means more than to use the capacities of the mind to deliberate, solve problems, or make judgments; it means to abstract an issue from its immediate context, to reflect upon it with oneself, and to follow it wherever the unfettered activity of the mind, without consideration of consequences and without concern for established authority, might lead. With the aphorisms of Heraclitus, we thus find expressed the core of the rhetorical motive—to craft a *logos* designed to remake the structure of power according to a vision of a higher order which commands the authority of truth.

In the sixth century B.C.E., along the coast and islands of Ionia, the Logos revealed itself to the prodigious mind of Heraclitus. An aristocrat born to the noblest family in Epheseus, a powerful city which contained the shrine of Artemis, Heraclitus had available to him all the privileges and luxuries of his class; yet he chose to abandon all of it in pursuit of the Logos. Establishing a model for oracular philosophers and prophets through the ages, Heraclitus withdrew into solitude out of contempt for the obtuseness of the common people, the hypocrisy of admired sages, and the incompetence of tyrants and democrats alike. His goal: to search out the true order of things through independent rational inquiry. And this is what he discovered: "Of the Logos which is as I describe it men always prove to be uncomprehending, both before they have heard it and when once they have heard. For although all things happen according to this Logos men are like people of no experience, even when they experience such words and deeds as I explained, when I distinguish each thing according to its constitution and declare how it is; but the rest of men fail to notice what they do after they wake up just as they forget what they do when asleep" (194). As revealed to Heraclitus, the Logos is an active force, a fire, consuming and remaking people and things by its own autonomous logic: "This world-order did none of gods or men make, but it always was and is and shall be: an ever living fire, kindling in measures and going out in measures."[10] Yet despite this fire surrounding and penetrating the lives and experiences of human beings, most people ignore its presence by fixing their attention on familiar idols or objects. Consequently, "although the Logos is common the many live as though they had a private understanding."[11] Confident in their own limited perspective and unconcerned with their interconnectedness with others, the representatives of the "many" thus remain numb to anything beyond their immediate self-interest. It is this narrowness of vision, this solipsism of mind, this lack of perspective and of curiosity that is the root of human arrogance and stupidity; it is what makes people think that they can control fate with soldiers and assemblies when in fact all of those things will be fuel to the divine fire which burns eternally through history.

However, Heraclitus's dedication to writing a book that might wake them up revealed his faith that all was not lost, even when that book fell on so many deaf ears that it earned him the nickname "The Obscure." For if humanity was condemned to the shadow world of dream, then his writing would never land on fertile ground and his labor would be in vain; but Heraclitus did nothing in vain. His purpose was to translate his wonder at the Logos into a speech capable of revealing its nature through a thoughtful investigation into appearances. As Arendt describes the process by which Heraclitus penned his aphorisms, "wonder has led to thinking in words; the experience of wonder at the invisible manifest in the appearances has been appropriated by speech, which at the same time is strong enough to dispel the errors and delusions of our organs for the visible, eyes and ears, are subject to unless thinking comes to their help."[12] The purpose of constructing a *logos* of the Logos is therefore less to articulate the physical laws of the universe and more to wake up the sleepwalkers, to shock them out of their communal dream, to disrupt their traditional interpretation of appearances, and to inspire the thinking which can make them aware of the fire which is burning all around them.

What made this faith possible was precisely that a growing number of Greeks at the end of the sixth century B.C.E. were ready to *think*. For Greek culture suddenly appeared to them like Heraclitus's river. In ages past, tradition had assured them that the currents of history would always return to their customary channels despite occasional upheavals that temporarily blocked its flow or flooded its banks. But as the fifth century B.C.E. approached, the possibility appeared that the cumulative effects of subsequent upheavals might be to carve a new channel and thus change the entire nature of the river. This is the radical implication of the proposition that one cannot step twice into the same river. Heraclitus does not merely give creative expression to the mundane idea that no two experiences are alike. He speaks not to our subjective experience *with* the river but with our objective knowledge *of* the river itself. For Heraclitus, it is not *we* who are different, but the *river;* and it is different because the "river" as we know it is not a transcendent entity but simply the sum total of existing forces at any one time. As the currents change and different waters flow, different "rivers" come into existence. The same goes for Greece. As populations change, technology advances, wisdom accumulates, and power transforms, a new "Greece" emerges out of the cumulative interaction of its parts as guided by the laws of Logos, laws which neither preach "such it is" nor "thou shalt not" but rather state "thus it occurs." Caught up in these changes that the authority of tradition could no longer predict or control, more and more Greeks were willing to listen to this Logos of which Heraclitus spoke.

After centuries of relative continuity and tradition, then, Greek life was undergoing dramatic changes that were gradually waking people from their somnambulism. Most of these changes were centered in Athens, where the reforms of Solon in 594 B.C.E. had set tendencies in motion that would eventually produce the Athenian democratic empire. Specifically, Solon had staved off a veritable civil war between the aristocracy and the peasants by forgiving debts, forbidding selling Athenians into slavery, and redistributing land to small farmers in a way that finally gave them a sense of self-determination. Furthermore, he had replaced a two-tiered hierarchy of rich and poor with a four-tiered class distinction, which expanded opportunities for participation in political assemblies and law courts. These reforms were continued even under the "enlightened" tyranny of Pisistratus, who rose to power by providing farm equipment to peasants, investing in public works projects, and encouraging the production of olive oil as a trading commodity and the primary source of Athenian wealth. Finally, the mature form of democracy was instituted by Cleisthenes around 508 B.C.E. following the oppressive rule of Pisistratus's son, Hippias. Cleisthenes gained support among the masses by promising dramatic democratic reforms that instituted a complex system of political divisions based around neighborhood "demes" (*demoi*) through which male citizens directly participated in the running of government free of the constraints of class and tribal loyalties.[13] The sixth century thus saw the rapid ascent of Athens from a large village into a vibrant cosmopolitan center whose power grew proportionally to the degree to which its free peasants took on the roles of landowner and citizen and the extent to which those new citizens began developing the political habits by which they could act in concert without the need for a tyrant or king to command them.[14]

Although Heraclitus lived on the other side of the Aegean Sea as an aristocrat in Ephesus, he was uniquely situated to feel the effects of the changing political and cultural currents. From the years leading up to his birth, from 546 B.C.E., the seaports along Ionia had enjoyed considerable prosperity and security under the largely benign rule of the Persian Empire.[15] In 500 B.C.E., however, Ephesus became the center of revolutionary activity as former tyrant-turned-freedom-fighter Aristagoras rallied support for an Ionian revolt against Persian rule in the name of democracy, notably gaining initial support from Athens, which supplied the twenty ships that were a major factor in the initial victories against the Persian forces in 499 B.C.E. Although the revolt eventually was crushed and Aristagoras killed in 493 after six years of fighting, the Athenian support of the Ionians had set in motion forces that would eventually lead to full-scale war between Persia and mainland Greece.[16] As Herodotus put it: "These ships were the beginning of evils for Greeks and barbarians."[17] Heraclitus was witness to all of these changes, thus putting him in a position to be keenly aware of the shifting currents of power at this dramatic juncture in Western history. But he saw these currents driven not by the heroic acts of courageous revolutionaries but by the logic of an underlying intelligent world order making itself apparent through the strife, war, and conflict.

Heraclitus responded to this situation in a very un-Homeric manner. Instead of stepping forward within a gathering of kings to deliver wise counsel through eloquent speech like the loyal Nestor, Heraclitus retreated into the shrine of Artemis to write and publish a book filled with prophetic aphorisms about nature (*physis*). But his strategic choice did not merely reflect a personal character which preferred a life of contemplative solitude to that of political community; it was also indicative of the widespread changes in Greek culture brought about by new communication technology and rising literacy rates. Although sixth-century Greece largely remained on oral culture, the availability of lightweight papyrus which could be used to publish "books" (in the form of scrolls) expanded the audience for and the diversity of written works. For in the Homeric age, the idea of "publishing" in a contemporary sense did not exist. Writing was primarily a means of record-keeping, lawmaking, and long-distance communication by kings and aristocrats. It was the Presocratic philosophers, specifically Anaximander (ca. 611–547), who introduced the radical notion of the authorial "I" into Greek culture. According to Harold Innis, Anaximander "was the first to write down his thoughts in prose and publish them, thus definitely addressing the public and giving up the privacy of his thought. The use of prose reflected a revolutionary break, an appeal to rational authority in the influence of the logic of writing."[18] With Anaximander, the idea of the single-authored "book" was introduced into the Greek world, thus making possible the dissemination of individual perspectives to any and all literate Greeks who could then spread its words through subsequent oral performance.[19]

Yet Heraclitus's choice to communicate his thoughts in writing rather than speech reflects more than a desire to utilize the book as a means of mass communication; it also shows how he used the medium itself as the message. As Marshall McLuhan has argued, the use of the written word on its own, quite irrespective of its content, releases the individual from the tribal bonds formed in the oral community, thereby "giving to its user an eye for an ear, and freeing him from the tribal trance of resonating word magic and the web of kinship."[20] What he means is that writing allows us to encounter language as a fixed visual object—and hence a matter for the eye—whose meaning can be interrogated by an individual apart from the social experience which accompanies oral communication for the ear. Havelock describes the basis for this affect in the simple act of being able to "look again" at language: "Refreshment of memory through written signs enabled a reader to dispense with most of that emotional identification by which alone the acoustic record was sure of recall. This could release psychic energy, for a review and a rearrangement of what had now been written down, and of what could be seen as an object and not just heard and felt. You could as it were take a second look at it."[21] It was this newfound capacity to look again not only at language but at the conventional rituals, beliefs, and appearances of the world that Heraclitus attempted to exploit through his own writing.

One deceptively simple aphorism of Heraclitus communicates the powerful effect that the new medium could have on an individual consciousness: "I searched out myself."[22] Through these four words, Heraclitus introduces an entirely new way of understanding one's relationship to oneself and the universe. First, he asserts that the individual has the capacity for self-investigation, which would be almost incomprehensible for those immersed in the communal existence of a strictly oral culture. Second, he opens up the possibility that there is some form of universal knowledge which can be acquired through self-investigation despite the obvious difference between the finitude of human experience and the breadth and complexity of universal knowledge. He thus provides a new model for humanistic philosophical inquiry centered upon the ideal of the enlightened individual who could investigate the truth of the Logos by reflecting upon the appearances of the world through the power of rational thought pursued in solitude.

According to Jaeger, this humanism was the great novelty of Heraclitus's doctrine in comparison with other philosophers of his time. Whereas many of them, like Parmenides, had "lost sight of human life in the vast pattern of nature," Heraclitus "held that the human soul with all its emotions and sufferings was the center of all the energies of the cosmos."[23] The Logos, in other words, was not only common to all things in the physical world but also interpenetrated every aspect of human experience and consciousness. The individual could search himself and find the truth precisely because "cosmic phenomena happened through him . . . and for him. He believed that all his acts and words were only the effect in him of nature's power, although most men did not realize that they were merely the instruments wielded by higher order."[24] Caught up in the constant chatter of oral culture, most people shunned solitude because for they had never learned to be alone with themselves in the search for something greater than themselves. Heraclitus opened the possibility that an inquiry pursued in solitude was not a sign of madness but a mark of genius, a noble and even courageous effort to use the power of the mind to grasp some aspect of the world order that coursed through human experience.

With Heraclitus, then, a new capacity is bestowed upon human beings— the capacity to *think*. According to Arendt, thinking refers to a very particular activity of mind which sets it apart from the actions of will or the processes of judgment which constitute most of our everyday cognitive experiences.

Whereas we pursue objects of our desire through actions of will and decide upon which rules to apply in situations of choice through the processes of judgment, thinking isolates us from the demands of the immediate situation in order that we might dwell upon the meanings of things in order to understand them.[25] Whereas the objects of will are the things desired and the objects of judgment are the decisions to be made, the objects of thinking are simply what Arendt calls "thought-objects," or those objects which "come into being only when the mind actively and deliberately remembers, recollects, and selects from the storehouse of memory whatever arouses interest sufficiently to induce concentration."[26] Homeric heroes, for instance, are not celebrated for their thinking but for their willing and judging, as when their will propels them into battle but their judgment tells them when they must retreat. For them, to dwell upon thought-objects for their own sake is to spend idle time in fantasy when one should be speaking eloquently and acting courageously. When Heraclitus celebrates thinking he thus introduces a new kind of hero capable of penetrating the secrets of the Logos and then revealing them to a human civilization in need of enlightenment.

For this new kind of hero, solitude is not a vice but a virtue. This is because, as the aphorism of Heraclitus conveys, thinking is only possible when one pursues the truth in conversation with oneself or the imagined voice of another. In other words, thinking requires one to be able to split oneself in half, as it were, so that there is a sense of what Arendt calls the "two-in-one" in the thinking consciousness. The distinction between loneliness and solitude is thus based on whether one has the capacity to create this duality within oneself. Arendt writes that "thinking, existentially speaking, is a solitary but not a lonely business; solitude is that human situation in which I keep myself company. Loneliness comes about when I am alone without being able to split up into the two-in-one, without being able to keep myself company."[27] For those unable to split themselves up, loneliness becomes a kind of exile in which the world seems a wasteland because it is stripped of the possibility of shared experience. But for the thinker who can contemplate the thought-objects of the soul through multiple conversations with imagined others, there is not the pain of loneliness in which nothing is worthwhile but joy of solitude in which there are infinite truths to discover. Heraclitus writes, for instance, that "you would not find out the boundaries of the soul, even by traveling along every path: so deep a measure does it have."[28] This is the ecstatic expression of a man who has experienced infinite satisfaction in revealing new pathways of the soul by searching out himself in solitude through the act of thinking.

That Heraclitus would communicate his discoveries through aphoristic form only reveals the depth of his commitment to provoking thinking in Greek culture. This is because the paradoxical and incomplete nature of aphorisms shocks people into a state of thinking in order to dwell upon the meaning of the thought-object for its own sake. As McLuhan observes, whereas detailed argumentation satisfies the passive need for easily digestible packages, those "who are concerned in pursuing knowledge and seeking causes will resort to aphorisms, just because they are incomplete and require participation in depth."[29] Friedrich Nietzsche explains this phenomenon in his own aphoristic style:

> *The effectiveness of the incomplete.*—Just as figures in relief produce so strong an impression on the imagination because they are as it were on the point of stepping out of the wall but have suddenly been brought to a halt, so the relief-like, incomplete presentation of an idea, of a whole philosophy, is sometimes more effective than its exhaustive realization: more is left for the beholder to do, he is impelled to continue working on that which appears before him so strongly etched in light and shadow, think it through to the end, and to overcome even that constraint which has hitherto prevented it from slipping forth fully formed.[30]

The aphorism thus appeals to those who wish to be challenged precisely because they crave the stimulation of inquiry and hence want to only be given enough of the "relief" that gives them a clue to its hidden meaning. Heraclitus himself conveys the motive behind decoding the aphorism when he says of phenomena that "the real constitution is accustomed to hide itself" and that "an unapparent connection is stronger than an apparent one."[31] For him, that which is embedded within and behind appearances is stronger, more real, and also more fascinating to contemplate then those things which come to us fully formed and visible.

Moreover, for Heraclitus, the form of the aphorism reflects nature itself, which appears to our senses as a kind of figure in relief whose account of its real constitution—the Logos—remains hidden until an active thinking about appearances can reveal its nature to the mind (*nous*) and disclose it to others in speech (*legein*). The word "appearances" (*phainomena*) here is not meant to be contrasted with "realities" but with those things that do not show themselves. Things that "appear," Arendt notes, "are meant to be seen, heard, touched, tasted, and smelled, to be perceived by sentient creatures endowed with appropriate sense organs."[32] For Heraclitus, appearances are not realities, to be sure, but they not deceptions or punishments either. They are rather the way that nature reveals itself to us through those partial disclosures in a way which seems to make the non-apparent apparent, the invisible visible. Arendt remarks that "another early word for the invisible in the midst of the appearances is *physis*, nature, which according to the Greeks was the totality of all things that were not man-made and not created by a divine maker but that had come into being by themselves; and of this *physis* Heraclitus said that 'it likes to hide itself,' namely behind the appearances."[33] But even *physis* is not itself the same as the Logos. When we encounter appearances we discern some aspect of *physis* and create an account of nature through reasoned argumentation and logic; the Logos thus represents the one true account whose apprehension equals wisdom. As he writes: "The wise is one thing, to be acquainted with true judgment, how all things are steered through all."[34] The Logos thus represents the one true judgment that steers all things in nature despite the fact that natural appearances often come to us conflicted, confused, and contradicted.

What sets Heraclitus apart from all other Greek philosophers of his age is his insistence that one must go *through* appearances to discover the Logos rather than (as suggested by Parmenides) fleeing from the senses and retreating to a kind of solipsistic Reason. For Heraclitus, the Logos represents harmony, and harmony only comes about through a sounding-together of opposites. In all appearances, then, "there is a back-stretched connection, as in the bow and the lyre."[35] The methodological consequence of this attitude is that all appearances are deserving of inquiry, even those of violence, death, and conflict. Whereas the Homeric mind might see in such appearances the judgment of the gods, Heraclitus perceives the hidden harmonies of the Logos. Displaying the critical objectivity that is the mark of the philosopher, Heraclitus does not take painful appearances personally, for "it is necessary to know that war is common and right is strife and that all things happen by strife and necessity."[36] Nor does the appearance of prosperity mean that one is blessed, but only lucky; for "war is the father of all and King of all, in some he shows as gods, others as men; some he makes slaves, and others free."[37] In each case, Heraclitus shows how contradictions in appearances reveal the nature of the world-order to one capable of discerning invisible harmonies through thinking.

With respect to existing structures of power, this worldview represented the height of impiety; but to those with artistic sensibility, it represented liberation. This is because the philosophy of Heraclitus was in many ways the translation of the spirit of play into a principle of nature itself. For those in power, nothing was more threatening than the uninhibited spirit of play which took nothing for granted, respected no restriction on the imagination, and was prepared to dismantle and reconstruct anything for no other reason than to experiment with new ideas, new forms, and new materials. But for those with aesthetic sensibilities who wished to explore the nature of possibility, nothing was more stirring. Predictably, then, it is Heraclitus to whom Nietzsche looks for inspiration in the Greek world:

For him all contradictions run into harmony, invisible to the common human eye, yet understandable to one who, like Heraclitus, is related to the contemplative God. . . . In this world only play, play as artists and children engage in it, exhibits coming-to-be and passing away, structuring and destroying, without any moral additive in forever equal innocence. And as children and artists play, so plays the ever-living fire. It constructs and destroys, all in innocence. Transforming itself into water and earth, it builds towers of sand like a child at the seashore, piles them up and tramples them down. From time to time it starts the game anew. An instant of satiety—and again it is seized by its need, as the artist is seized by the need to create. Not *hybris* but the ever self-renewing impulse to play calls the world into being.[38]

For Heraclitus as for Nietzsche, artistic play and philosophical thinking are not opposites but counterparts within the creative process. For the Logos need not simply represent some abstract logical formula or natural law; it also represents a method of invention which can be revealed only to one capable of thinking for oneself beyond the boundaries of convention. Nietzsche goes on: "Only aesthetic man can look thus at the world, a man who has experienced in artists and in the birth of art objects how the struggle of the many can yet carry rules and laws inherent in itself, how the artist stands contemplatively above and at the same time actively within his work, how necessity and random play, oppositional tension and harmony, must pair to create a work of art."[39] From the perspective of Heraclitus, this work of art is the world in which human beings lived, and as a work of art it can be constantly broken and remade by the will of its creator; but the nature of this divine will can nonetheless be discerned by one capable of philosophical inquiry free from the pieties of power.

Of course, if the influence of Heraclitus was confined to offending traditional sensibilities while stimulating idle thinking about the universe, he would be of little to no relevance to an inquiry into the nature of rhetoric. But the Logos was not merely a vehicle for the play but also the basis of a new form of power. For what soon becomes apparent through his aphorisms is that Heraclitus is actually prophesying the coming of a whole new political and social order in which the relationship between rhetoric and *logos,* rather than eloquence and tradition, would determine the structure of power. For in Heraclitus we catch a glimpse, for the first time, of a universal conception of law which transcends both personality and culture, is capable of being comprehended through sustained inquiry into appearances, and can be applied to human affairs when used as a universal premise in rational, persuasive speech. Heraclitus formulates this new order of power in this way: "Those who speak with sense must rely on what is common to all, as a city must rely on its law, and with much greater reliance. For all the laws of men are nourished by one law, the divine law; for it has as much power (*kratei*) as it wishes and is sufficient for all and is still left over."⁴⁰ Within this structure of power, it becomes the responsibility of the citizens and rulers alike to follow the "one law," the Logos, no matter what challenges they must face and what strife befalls them. As he says, "the people must fight on behalf of the law as though for the city wall."⁴¹ For Heraclitus, this is where true power lies—the power to act in common through the guidance of the Logos as disclosed to and by those with the capacity for thinking and for rational speech.

This conception is rhetorical because it creates a new model for political advocacy, deliberation, and judgment. In the oral tradition of Homeric eloquence, an audience evaluated a person's speech by how well it perpetuated traditional practices and exhibited accepted virtues such that character (*ethos*) became one of the most important persuasive qualities of a speaker. In the age of Heraclitus, however, the reliability of character was being eroded in the same way as the banks of the river. What matters is not the relationship between a speaker's character and a communal tradition, both of which represent constantly changing appearances, but rather with the relationship between a particular account and its truth, which exists in a more stable realm of logical reason (*logos*) which can be discerned by the individual mind. The historical context in which *logos* rose to prominence in Greece is described by John Dewey, who effectively shows how Heraclitus's discovery of the Logos was continuous with the tendencies already ongoing in Greek political culture:

> In Athens not merely political but legal issues were settled in the public forum. Political advancement and civic honor depended more upon the power of persuasion than upon military achievement. As general intellectual curiosity developed among the learned men, power to interpret and explain was connected with the ability to set forth a consecutive story. To give an account of something, a logos, was also to account for it. The logos, the ordered account, was the reason and the measure of the things set forth. Here was the background out of which developed a formulated theory of logic as the structure of knowledge and truth.⁴²

Following Dewey's narrative, we can see how Heraclitus, with his characteristically prophetic insight, was able to identify the characteristics of the coming age by interpreting the underlying tendencies of the appearances around him. What he saw was that the sleepwalkers still gripped by the Homeric worldview would soon be shocked into a new state of wakefulness by a new kind of speaker, one who did not only use poetic eloquence to entrance them with beauty but also used logical persuasion to command them with truth.

In short, the essential characteristic of these new kinds of speakers would be their desire to challenge an inherited *mythos* with a rational *logos,* thus breaking the spell of the rhapsode and emancipating individual thinking and judgment about common affairs. They would therefore share Heraclitus's goal to, as Eduard Zeller puts it, "set in the place of a mythological world a world of ideas built up by the strength of independent human thought, the *logos,* which could claim to explain reality in a natural way."[43] In practice, this meant not only changing the content of speech but also its form of expression. The traditional epic style of persuasion relied on the ability of orators to embed themselves within a mythic narrative, a *mythos,* by proving he or she was a person of great and noble character capable of crafting great words and performing great deeds continuous with the heroic examples from the distant past. The new "logical" style of persuasion required a speaker to construct a rational argument, a *logos,* which responds to problematic appearances by showing how a certain principle or law not only can sufficiently account for those appearances but can also indicate a possible path through them. For this new type of speaker, sheer strength of heroic character was an insufficient guide for judgment; what was required was a preliminary act of thinking in which a reflective dwelling on appearances would produce a true *logos* quite independent of one's personality or cultural heritage.

What Heraclitus actually prophesized in his aphorisms was therefore less the coming of the divine Word as one might think of the Kingdom of God; it was rather the coming of a social order in which the authority of *mythos* gave way to that of *logos* in the context of collective human actions and judgments. In practice, this meant that the representative agent of political power would cease to be the rhapsode or poet who celebrates and transmits the virtues of heroic tradition, and would instead be the *rhêtor,* or the citizen-orator who advances motions in a democratic assembly. Undoubtedly, of course, Heraclitus likely had just as much contempt for the *rhêtors* of his day as he did for the rhapsodes insofar as they probably did not speak with what he believed to be sufficient forethought; yet the fact that these *rhêtors* eschewed appeals to *mythos,* and attempted to persuade a gathering of citizens to act in concert based on the presumed validity of a reasonable account, shows that they had already begun to listen to the Logos to the extent that it was affecting their patterns of speech. For these *rhêtors* believed, just as much as Heraclitus did, that the *logoi* they articulated in the assemblies were common to all and representative of laws for which the citizens should fight as for their city walls.

Rhetoric becomes a genuine possibility in the Greek imagination with the revelation of the Logos. This is because rhetoric is not simply synonymous with any and all persuasion. Persuasion is a ubiquitous consequence, often accidental or unintended, of all forms of symbolic communication which affect changes in another person's attitude or behavior. In contradistinction, rhetoric represents a coherent system of rationally derived methods whereby persuasion occurs because another mind or group of minds has come to accept a speaker's *logos* as credible, practical, virtuous, and true. As Cole has argued, Homeric eloquence is not yet rhetoric because it lacks a *logos* which is detachable from the person speaking and can be examined on its own account or reproduced by another person. With rhetoric, however, "verbalization, argumentation, and the marshaling of facts and evidence are inextricably bound together in a process whose aim is the creation of ever better discourse."[44] In other words, rhetoric has for its goal the invention and iteration of a *logos* which can stand on its own and whose improvement is a collective rather than merely an individual responsibility. Thus, whereas excellence in Homeric eloquence is always a highly personal affair, excellence in rhetoric "can just as easily lie in a new figure of thought as in a new discovery or proof, or a new scientific or mathematical discovery."[45] Of course, rhetoric serves a function different from philosophy or science insofar as its immediate goal is the resolution of a problematic situation rather than the discovery of metaphysical truth or natural laws; but it welcomes any discoveries in any field of thought which give it resources to produce new and better accounts capable of predicting and controlling the flux of historical events in which we are immersed.

In this way, the thinking Heraclitus tried to stimulate through his prophetic aphorisms was also an indirect form of political action. Only by pausing to acknowledge and think about the Logos were the Greeks able to eventually conceive of a political discourse grounded in the authority of a logical account rather than a poetic rendition. By creating finely crafted poetic statements which shocked people out of their sleepwalking, Heraclitus paralyzed habitual patterns of thought and behavior and disabled the structures of power they supported, thus making it possible to contemplate new forms of power which might emerge in place of the old. And in the context in which Heraclitus was writing, this act of stopping and thinking perhaps was the most revolutionary action of all; for as Arendt observes, "when everybody is swept away unthinkingly by what everybody else does and believes in, those who think are drawn out of hiding because their refusal to join in is conspicuous and thereby becomes a kind of action."[46] Heraclitus was the paradigmatic iconoclast, one who withdrew from a life of action in order to contemplate it and perhaps even paralyze it. Yet he did so not to reject action but to produce a more thoughtful action. The point, for Arendt, is that "whenever I transcend the limits of my own life span and begin to reflect on this past, judging it, and this future, forming projects of the will, thinking ceases to be a politically marginal activity."[47]

For Heraclitus, thinking was the only thing that could save Greece from being completely washed away by the currents of history.

In spite of the venerable tradition of opposing philosophical thinking to rhetorical persuasion, then, the subsequent development of rhetoric into a recognized art throughout the next two centuries actually was the practical recognition of the importance of thinking as applied to the sphere of politics. This does not mean that all rhetorical acts were thoughtful; undoubtedly, much that was spoken in the assembly could easily be mistaken for the mutterings of sleepwalkers or the rantings of mud-spattered madmen. Nor does it mean that rhetoric at its best ever met the Heraclitean standards of "pure" thinking; but this was only because political actors recognized that mobilizing the will and judgment of an audience required more than just stimulating the unfettered play of the mind. As important as thinking was to emancipating individuals from the bonds of habitual tradition in order that they could apprehend and interpret a *logos* on its own merits, political *rhêtors* knew they still required the motivational resources of *mythos* to translate thinking into action. They thus demonstrated a practical, if implicit, recognition of the maxim Jaeger adapts from Kant: "Mystical thought without the formative *logos* is blind, and logical theorizing without living mystical thought is empty."[48] Rhetoric as an art attempted to draw from the resources of both *logos* and *mythos* in order to open our eyes to a world filled with meaning and give rational direction to our deepest impulses.

This effort to transform the nature of power by drawing on rational and mythic resources remains at the core of almost any successful rhetorical endeavor. As Reinhold Niebuhr pointed out, even the most enlightened speaker in contemporary society requires the integration of *logos* and *mythos* in a single discourse. On the one hand, "mythic descriptions of reality, though always inexact in describing detailed and historical fact, have the virtue of giving men a sense of depth in life."[49] Like the Homeric epics which allowed members of a culture to feel part of a shared and meaningful history, mythic narratives express what Niebuhr calls the "vertical tendencies in culture which refer to the ultimate sources of meaning in life."[50] On the other hand, appeals to *logos* provide the necessary "horizontal" understanding of the complex play of forces in modern civilization necessary to make prudent judgments. Similarly to how the Logos of Heraclitus provided a broad principle for understanding a wide spectrum of conflicting appearances, the kind of rational argumentation we today associate with scientific reasoning "may extend social impulses beyond the immediate objectives which nature prompts; it may insist upon harmony in the whole field of vital impulses; and it may reveal all the motives which prompt human action in all the consequences which flow from it so that honest error and dishonest pretensions are reduced."[51] If *logos* deflates our pretensions and shows how we are embedded within a complex system of forces which imposes upon us the burden of understanding, *mythos* assures us that human beings, acting together, nonetheless have a meaningful role to play in a historical drama which transcends our mortal life.

The aphorisms of Heraclitus prophesy this new form of discourse—that of rhetoric—by pointing to a Logos which was both rational and spiritual, both capable of bringing order to the chaos of appearances and revealing the meaning of our existence, which makes human life represent something more than that of pigs and donkeys. Of course, these aphorisms were not themselves representative of rhetoric. To the degree that they had a rhetorical function, it did not extend far beyond the provocation of thinking and the disruption of the habits that sustain existing structures of power. Yet *rhêtors* faced with imminent crises do not have the luxury of smiling at catastrophes from the safety of the shrine of Artemis; they must face up to the burden of judgment and the responsibility of will. For them, Heraclitus provides an inspiration to investigate the world of appearances and play with the logical possibilities that emerge through the act of thinking about the *logos*. This act provides new resources to blend with those of the mythic tradition toward the goal of helping even our still-awakening culture to navigate the turbulent rivers of history with its eyes wide open and its ears ready to hear.

CHAPTER 3

Aeschylus's *Persians* and
the Birth of Tragedy

MESSENGER:

O you cities of the whole land of Asia! O land of Persia, repository of great wealth! How all your great prosperity has been destroyed in a single blow, and the flower of the Persians are fallen and departed! [*to the CHORUS of royal counselors:*] Ah, me, it is terrible to be the first to announce terrible news, but I have no choice but to reveal the whole sad tale, Persians: the whole of the Oriental Army has been destroyed! . . .

CHORUS:

Otototoi! It was all in vain

that those many weapons, all mingled together,

went from the land of Asia to the country

of Zeus, the land of Hellas!

MESSENGER:

Yes, our archery was of no avail; the whole host perished, destroyed by the ramming of ships.

CHORUS:

Otototoi, you are saying

that the dead bodies of our loved ones

are floating, soaked and constantly buffeted by salt water,

shrouded in mantles that drift in the waves!

MESSENGER:

The shores of Salamis, and all the region near them, are full of corpses wretchedly slain.

CHORUS:

Raise a crying voice of woe
for the wretched fate of <our loved ones>,
for the way <the gods> have caused
total disaster! *Aiai,* for our destroyed army! . . .

QUEEN [*to the* MESSENGER]: I have been silent all this time because I was
struck dumb with misery by this catastrophe. The event is so monstrous
that one can neither speak nor ask about the sufferings it involved. Still,
we mortals have no choice but to endure the sorrows the gods send us;
so compose yourself and speak, revealing all that has happened, even if
you are groaning under the weight of the disaster. . . . [*Later, after hearing
a detailed account of the battle and the news that Xerxes remains alive:*]
Ah wretched me, our army annihilated! Ah you clear dream vision of
the night, how very plainly you revealed these disasters to me—and you
[*turning to the* CHORUS], in interpreting the dream, took it far too lightly!
All the same, since this was your firm advice, I intend first to pray to the
gods; then I will return, bringing from my palace a rich libation as a gift
to Earth and the dead. I know that this is after the event, but it is in the
hope that there may be something better to come in the future. For your
part, it is your duty, in the light of these events, to offer trusty counsel
to us who trust you; if my son comes home before I return, comfort him
and escort him home, for fear that he may add some further harm to the
harm he has suffered.[1]

On the Athenian stage in 472 B.C.E., the Queen of Persia awoke from a nightmare only to encounter a nightmare in reality. In her dream, Xerxes, her son,
the king of the Persian Empire, had attempted to yoke two beautiful women,
one Persian and one Greek, to the same chariot; but whereas the Persian was
obedient, the Greek woman rose up in rebellion, snapping the wooden yoke
and knocking Xerxes to the ground. The dream troubled the Queen precisely
because Xerxes only months earlier had departed, a vast army in tow, with
the goal of reducing the rising power of Athens to just another tribute-
paying satellite of the Persian Empire. Without news, she had waited, enduring "dreams of the night" that finally culminated in the nightmare (180).
Then, seeking solace from the dreadful appearances in her imagination, she
asked the aging counselors of Persia to interpret the dream, and they obedi-
ently assured her that, with proper supplications to the gods, "things will turn
out well for you in every way" (224). The counselors are wrong. A herald has
entered with the devastating news that the Greeks have destroyed the invading Persian forces, sending Xerxes home cloaked in ragged clothes and ruin.
No longer is hope an alternative for the Queen, only sorrow and the knowledge

that every other mother's son who journeyed to conquer a strange land will never return.

The oldest surviving Greek tragedy, Aeschylus's *The Persians* performs a delicate rhetorical balancing act—it celebrates Athenian power to an audience of Athenians by dramatizing the defeat of the enemy while at the same time eliciting their pity at witnessing the downfall of the noble and proud empire. No easy task, for just eight years prior to the play, in 480 B.C.E., Xerxes had personally led an army of half a million soldiers and twelve hundred ships to incorporate all of Greece into the Persian Empire. The invasion had united much of Greece in opposition, but the sheer size of the army had overwhelmed Greek forces at the initial battles of Thermopylae and Artemisium, defeats which allowed the Persian Army to advance unopposed into Athens and burn it to the ground. Only a strategic deception by Athenian General Themistocles, which lured the entire Persian fleet into the narrow waters of Salamis where they were cut to pieces by the waiting Greek navy, saved the Greeks from the tyranny of subjugation. When Aeschylus performed the play, the burned ruins of the Acropolis still towered over the city of Athens, left there as a memorial, and the images of devastation and death were still very fresh in the memories of its citizens—and yet the play chooses not to condemn the Persians for their barbarism but to mourn for their pain.

Aeschylus makes this dramatic choice less for his specific concern about the Persians and more for the fact that their experience illuminates something universal about the human condition. This is one of the essential characteristics of tragedy—that all human beings, no matter their race, wealth, power, or virtue, are all subject to the divine laws of justice (*dikē*) whose function is to restore balance through retribution. On the tragic stage, all names and titles are irrelevant; characters only exist as vehicles for the disclosure of justice made possible by their heroic capacity for intense suffering. In tragedy, there are no chosen ones free from the bonds of necessity; to what race we belong, which empire we are born in, and whether we achieve prosperity or endure misery, is a matter of chance. We are all as determined by the whim of fate as the two women who appear in the Queen's dream: "one, by the fall of the lot, was a native and inhabitant of the land of Greece, and the other of the Orient" (185). Accordingly, the Queen, too, represents all mothers who fear for their sons just as Xerxes represents all sons who attempt to equal and surpass the accomplishments of their fathers; and both of them are as susceptible to divine retribution as Achilles or the new Athenian Empire. What matters in tragedy is therefore not the idiosyncratic characteristics of this or that person; attention to particulars is a trope of comedy. Tragic characters are viewed from a distance. We can only see their broad outlines which make them representative of certain types of people and attitudes common to all human cultures.

It is this love of amplifying the universal characteristics of the human condition that make tragedies such grand spectacles. Hamilton writes: "Lift us to
tragic heights, we say, and never anything else. The depths of pathos but never
of tragedy. Always the height of tragedy."[2] Consequently, tragedies were the
blockbusters of their day, grand productions that stimulated all the senses to
their highest point by staging the actions of larger-than-life figures draped in
robes, speaking with booming voices, and moving to the rhythms of choral
dance. First introduced by the Athenian tyrant Pisistratus when he began the
Great Dionysia Festival in 534 B.C.E., his proximate goal was to solidify his own
power among the people by celebrating "both the poetic and the visual genius
of Athens" through *tragoidia,* "the art of all arts, embracing choral and solo
song, lyre and woodwind music, recited poetry, and costume and mask."[3] Of
course, tragedy as we now recognize it did not emerge fully formed like Athena
from the mind of Zeus. These early productions likely had minimal plot structure whose primary function was to thread together the musical performances
and visual spectacles. It was not until Aeschylus that tragedy became truly
dramatic. Hamilton observes that "until he came there was only a chorus with
a leader. He added a second actor, thus contriving the action of character upon
character which is the essence of drama."[4] After Aeschylus performed his first
play in 498 B.C.E., when he was twenty-seven years old, there would no longer
be tragedies absent heroes who entered the tragic stage free of the crushing
weight of *dikē* bearing down on their furrowed brow. Tragedies would now
promise a grand spectacle of heroic action and even greater suffering.

Yet tragedy was not simply about the spectacle itself. According to Hamilton, tragedy arises when the spirit of poetry meets the spirit of inquiry. She
writes that in Greece of the early fifth century B.C.E., people "were thinking
more and more deeply about human life, and beginning to perceive more and
more clearly that it was bound up with evil and that injustice was of the nature
of things. And then, one day, this knowledge of something irredeemably wrong
in the world came to a poet with his poet's power to see beauty in the truth of
human life, and the first tragedy was written."[5] However, one misses Hamilton's
point if she is used to validate moralistic interpretations that view tragedy as
simply punishment for arrogance and a celebration of the return of the old
order. As Nietzsche observes, aestheticians throughout the ages "never tire of
characterizing the true essence of tragedy as the struggle of the hero with faith,
the triumph of a universal moral order, or the discharge of affects induced by
tragedy; such persistence makes me think that they may not be susceptible to
aesthetic stimulation at all."[6] Tragedies are not glorified fairy tales akin to stories about prideful children who disobey their parents and are eaten by wolves
or witches. Tragedies are written for the powerful to understand the true
nature of power and its relationship to justice. Specifically, tragedy represents

an inquiry into the laws of justice in an emerging political order by dramatizing the motives of the powerful as they exceed the conventional limits of
human action, not only often to the ruin of themselves and those around them
but also to the passing age. The audience for tragedy does not condemn and
judge the hero but rather empathizes with and celebrates him, knowing that the
tragic hero has acted in accordance with necessity to shatter a decaying order
of things and reveal the laws of justice on which a new order can be built.

What gave Aeschylus unique insight into the spirit of tragedy was his direct
participation in the rapid ascendance of Greek power by having fought both
at Marathon and Salamis, two battles which saw outnumbered Greek armies
destroy the invading forces of the mighty Persian Empire. Not out of defeats,
but out of victories, came the spirit of tragedy, for it showed the Greeks that
they were better than the old Homeric gods. Hamilton observes:

> Aeschylus lived in one of those brief periods of hope and endeavor which
> now and again light up the dark ages of history, when mankind makes a
> visible advance along its destined path without fear or faltering. . . . Life was
> lived at an intenser level. Pain, terror, and anguish had sharpened men's
> spirits and deepened their insight. A victory achieved past all hope at the
> very moment when utter defeat and the loss of all things seemed certain
> had lifted them to an exultant courage. Men knew that they could do heroic
> deeds, for they had seen heroic deeds done by men. This was the moment
> for the birth of tragedy, that mysterious combination of pain and exaltation,
> which discloses an invincible spirit precisely when disaster is irreparable.[7]

If Aeschylus were a lesser man, he might have used the material of these victories to pen jingoistic propaganda that offered exaltation without pain. But what
made him a tragic poet was his grasp of the humanity of the Persians. He saw in
their suffering lessons that apply equally to the Greek experience, for he knew
that pride was not the property of the barbarian but of all those with power. By
writing the defeat of the Persians as a tragedy rather than a triumph, Aeschylus
hoped to gain wisdom rather than satisfaction so that the Greek could learn
from the suffering of their enemies about the relationship between power and
justice in the new order.

With the birth of tragedy comes the birth of something else—the possibility that rhetoric can become a new medium of power in a new world. Tragedy
announces that the resources of tradition are no longer sufficient to confront
the complex and dynamic forces of a new age, and that we must seek not just
to discover but to articulate and act upon higher values and laws if we ourselves are to avoid ruin. Tragedies amplify the suffering that comes from heroic
action, it is true, but not to paternalistically warn us against action; it does so in

order to bring about wisdom through tragic witnessing of a grand experiment that only characters of great stature can attempt. Pain is inevitable only because to test unknown limits is to inevitably crash headlong into recalcitrance. What we gain in recompense, says Kenneth Burke, is simply that "one learns by experience" such that "the suffered is the learned."[8] But if this is true, then rhetoric has a twofold relationship to tragedy. On the one hand, rhetoric reacts to tragic events by using this newfound wisdom to chart new courses of action toward higher values and ends. On the other hand, rhetoric is the necessary impetus to tragic actions insofar as it opens up new possibilities that inevitably exceed the limits of convention and habit. As evidenced by *The Persians,* great events require great art to disclose their meaning. This is the function of tragedy. But we produce tragedies not simply to entertain ourselves. Tragedies are also rhetorical when they guide our aspirations, actions, and judgments in our own lives—when we find that the tragic attitude is the only fitting response to situations of such magnitude that we must confront great suffering with greatness of character.

We turn to the *Persians* to explore the relationship between tragedy and rhetoric because it sets the bar for all tragedies to follow. In Western history, there is perhaps no more famous founding event then the triumph of the outnumbered forces of Greece over the might of the Persian Empire. Here is an event of grand proportions, the only kind fitting for the tragic stage. Xerxes, in his ambition to live up to his subjects' expectations and to outdo the accomplishments of his father, has attempted what no other Persian King has done—to create an army of close to a half-million soldiers, construct an artificial bridge across the Hellespont, and subjugate all of the forbidding and unfamiliar land of Greece. To him and to the Persian Chorus, it is a given that even the combined forces of all the Greek armies could not hope to withstand such a force in a face-to-face battle. Yet the upstart Greeks not only push back the assault but also destroy virtually the entire invading force. So incredible is this feat that the messenger can only conclude that "it was some divinity that destroyed our fleet like this, weighting the scales so that fortune did not fall out even" (345). The question of the play, then, is what wisdom can be gained from the enormity of the suffering. In the words of the Chorus: "After this, how can we, the Persian people, get the best possible outcome for the future?" (788). This echoes the essential question of tragedy: why is suffering necessary?

Unfortunately, the conventions of unimaginative literary criticism are always ready with pat answers that would satisfy any of Nietzsche's "aestheticians." As Nietzsche warns us, the voices of tradition are very persuasive: "one voice tells us that pity and fear are to be driven by these grave events to the point of discharge and hence relief, another that we are to feel elevated and inspired by the victory of good and noble principles when we see the hero being sacrificed in the name of a moral view of the world."[9] The problem with these voices is that they follow a "medical," rather than and aesthetic, interpretation of Aristotelian *catharsis* that completely ignores the relationship among tragedy, power, and justice. As Martha Nussbaum points out, *catharsis* originally referred to the clearing up, clarification, and "removal of some obstacle (dirt, or blot, or obscurity, or admixture) that makes the item in question less clear than it was in its proper state."[10] In the medical interpretation, this "obstacle" might be the fatal flaw in character or the immoral action of the hero which produced disharmony, suffering, and ruin, and the elimination of this obstacle allows the audience to purge their pity (for the admirable hero) and their fear (that this might happen to them) by finally seeing the situation with moral clarity.

One can easily see how the medical interpretation of catharsis might be applied to *The Persians*. First, Aeschylus presents a plot in which a noble character suffers a sudden turn of fate and falls from the height of glory to the depth of ignominy. When the chorus considers the fate of Xerxes, they lament that "he had available to him the tireless strength of men-at-arms and of a mixed multitude of allies. But now we are experiencing the decisive reversal of all of this by the gods in war, mightily smitten by blows struck at sea" (905). Second, the cause of this downfall appears to be a flaw in character of the tragic hero of Xerxes, who possessed that most fatal of all character traits, *hubris,* or prideful overreaching. When the ghost of his father Darius appears at the end of the play and is informed of his son's failure, he immediately accuses his son of *hubris* for thinking "he could stop the flow of the Hellespont, the divine stream of the Bosphorus, by putting chains on it, as if it were a slave" and that "he, a mortal, could lord it over all the gods and over Poseidon" (825). Third, the play seems to reaffirm the moral order in the wake of the hero's destruction, as when Darius laments that the "heaps of corpses will voicelessly proclaim to the eyes of men, even to the third generation, that one who is mortal should not think arrogant thoughts: outrage has blossomed and has produced a crop of ruin, from which it is reaping a harvest of universal sorrow" (820). Lastly, the play produces *catharsis* by assuring the audience that all has been restored to order. What could be more reassuring, after all, than the conclusion of Darius that the best advice for the Persians is "not invading the land of the Greeks, not even with a Median army still greater than before" (790)? Leaving with such wisdom, the Athenian audience was sure to sleep soundly, rocked to sleep by the gentle arms of Aeschylus.

Tragedy, however, does not rock us to sleep; it shakes us awake. Tragedy appears in the Greek world when tidal forces clashed and new powers were rising while others collapsed into memory. Nothing can be understood about tragedy until one understands this context. Walter Benjamin, for instance, completely rejects the notion that tragedy has anything to do with either the flawed character of heroes or the restoration of moral orders which the heroes dare to violate. Quite the opposite: the hero, according to Benjamin, is one who for the first time breaks the "endless pagan chain of guilt and atonement" that was characteristic of traditional oral cultures bound by the ancient rituals of their tribal gods.[11] Rather than paying penance to the tribal god, "in tragedy pagan man becomes aware that he is better than his god, but the realization robs him of speech, remains unspoken. Without declaring itself, it seeks secretly to gather its forces."[12] In other words, in tragedy, the hero realizes that the old laws of the tribal gods are no longer relevant in the new order, and that he now has the capacity to surpass that order and break those laws. But the realization leaves him speechless because there yet exists no vocabulary with which to represent the world to come; lacking speech, the hero thus gathers enough force to break and transcend those laws in the faith that something new will emerge in its place. Consequently, for Benjamin, "there is no question of the 'moral world order' being restored; instead, the moral hero, still dumb, not yet of age—as such he called a hero—wishes to raise himself by shaking that tormented world."[13] The theme of tragedy is what Benjamin calls "the birth of genius in moral speechlessness," by which he means a heroic act that, through the inspiration of genius, shakes and shatters the tormented world of a passing age without having the speech to explain, characterize, or even to defend what has occurred as a consequence of that act.[14]

The tragic hero is not out to produce suffering, of course; that is simply cruelty. The suffering happens as a consequence of a necessary act. Søren Kierkegaard writes that the tragic hero "battles for the new and strives to destroy what for him is a vanishing actuality, but his task is still not so much to destroy as to advance the new and thereby destroy the past indirectly."[15] But it is here that these heroes commit *hubris* by crossing the boundary of cosmic *dikē* which reveals itself through some kind of painful retribution. Yet even when it is the heroes who suffer, we nonetheless celebrate their suffering because it is the suffering of a great soul. Hamilton says that "the suffering of a soul that can suffer greatly—that and only that, is tragedy."[16] But this statement does not describe suffering for its own sake, as if tragedy were a form of masochism. Tragic heroes suffer greatly because they strive for great things and gain wisdom through strife.

Following Benjamin and Kierkegaard, then, the statement that justice (*dikē*) is central to tragic narratives should therefore not be interpreted in a legalistic or paternalistic sense; the justice that stands at the core of tragedy has more in common with the Heraclitean Logos than the order of conventional law embodied in maxims or codes. Whereas Homeric justice was articulated in written or unwritten legal statutes which, according to Benjamin, "determined not only men's relationships but also their relation to the gods," the Logos represented a transcendent cosmic order that defied codification and revealed itself only through the flux of often conflicting and painful appearances.[17] But each of these conceptions was nonetheless continuous with the original meaning of *dikē*, which was used to indicate both the rule of judges and the compensation given to an injured party by a guilty party in legal disputes like the one represented on the shield of Achilles. In addition, *dikē* had a connection with the other essential term of tragedy, *hubris*. According to Jaeger, "*dikē* means the due share which each man can rightly claim; and then, the principle which guarantees that claim, the principle on which one can rely when one is injured by *hybris*—which originally signifies illegal action."[18] In Homeric times, then, *hubris* was an illegitimate crossing of boundaries, such as the unauthorized taking of someone's life or property, which demanded *dikē* to restore balance between parties. The difference in tragedy is that these boundaries are not known until they are violated and thereby revealed through the suffering either of the heroes themselves or those around them. The eventual association of *hubris* with pride simply recognized that only those with extreme self-confidence had the capacity to willfully and openly cross those boundaries with the expectation that they would not be condemned for their arrogance but celebrated for their courage.

The ethical complexity of tragedy therefore derives not only from its relationship to justice but also to power. For justice is power made concrete. Justice establishes the boundaries between people, both individually and in groups, and establishes the proper pathways of action that solidify any structure of power. Yet tragic heroes are precisely those people who disrupt established power in order to reveal a new order of justice through which power can flow. Thus, on the one hand, we celebrate tragic heroes precisely because they shake a tormented world that is passing out of existence while raising themselves above the mumbling gods who no longer speak with authority or truth; and we choose to live vicariously through tragic heroes because we, too, wish to trod this world underfoot and then ascend with them to new heights that surpass the narrow vision of petty divinities in their dusty shrines. On the other hand, we fear those who brazenly challenge existing power without a clear knowledge of what is to come. For justice represents limits, and human beings cannot live without limits. Tragic heroes know no limits. Free from the constraints of tradition and law, they continue moving forward on the tide of necessity toward a new possibility even if it comes at the consequence of the suffering of themselves and others. As a result, tragic heroes often perish precisely because of the lack of will of those who purport to follow them. Despite their followers' craving for a new order of justice, sometimes they choose the familiarly of chronic oppression when faced with the prospect of enduring acute suffering.

It is in this effort to wrest meaning from great and noble suffering, whether it is the suffering of the past or the suffering yet to come, that the rhetorical significance of tragedy lies. As a form of speech which arises within crises of judgment and transformations of power, rhetoric obtains a tragic character whenever it calls for or reflects upon the overstepping of boundaries that produce inevitable suffering which carries with it the feeling of necessity. As Thomas Farrell remarks, "it is rhetoric that is given the formidable task of constructing and expressing human thought for those who would undergo the brute force of necessity, as well as for those others who would witness this fate."[19] For those who must undergo the brute force of necessity, tragic rhetoric provides the courage to endure suffering in the faith that the wisdom gained will compensate for the battles lost. For those who would witness this fate, rhetoric reveals the nature of *dikē* that appears through the suffering of others in the faith that coming possibility will be more just than the vanishing actuality. Tragic rhetoric tells us that all is not lost despite the inevitability of suffering, precisely because suffering is not an absolute finality but a limitless potentiality, a means to a higher end which transcends the finitude of individual life and the pain that accompanies it. Rhetoric is the only means of encouraging the actions and of disclosing the meanings necessary to break the boundaries of conventional power in the uncertain faith in a future possibility.

In other words, we look to rhetoric in those tragic situations in which we feel forced into an impossible choice or because we have witnessed the fate of others who made one.[20] A tragic choice is not one in which we are faced with an evil and a good path but choose the evil one; that is simply due to error, vice, or coercion. A tragic choice is one in which we are faced with two competing goods, each of which is accompanied by necessary evils. As Cornel West puts it, "the tragic consists of moral choices that must be made in the face of irreconcilable values, and especially conflicting obligations."[21] Xerxes thus faces a tragic choice when he must choose between prudence and ambition, between safely maintaining his empire at the expense of appearing a coward and mounting a grand expedition to conquer Greece at the risk of destroying the power of Persia. And Greece faces a tragic choice when it must choose between survival and freedom, between maintaining peace at the expense of subjugation and pursuing freedom at the possible price of annihilation. It is during these moments that rhetoric steps forward to chart a path that opens up new possibilities and legitimates the suffering that comes with choosing one or the other seemingly impossible course of action. Or as Farrell puts it: "rhetoric conceived tragically involves the invention of thought for characters whose options are foreclosed."[22]

Although tragedies like *The Persians* are not themselves works of rhetoric, they perform rhetorical functions insofar as they present an audience with appearances through which they can catch a glimpse of higher possibilities and confront present actualities. Aristotle speaks truly that *catharsis* is the emotional consummation of tragedy, but not if *catharsis* is taken to mean the purging of pity and fear or the medical removal of a contaminant which restores an organism to its former health. Tragic *catharsis* in an Aristotelian sense only occurs when the purging of the pity and fear we experience in the sufferings of the characters produces not relief and self-satisfaction but what Nussbaum refers to as "illumination."[23] *Catharsis* for Aristotle represents the combined effect of the pleasure of emotional release and the pleasure that comes with intellectual clarity. Far from celebrating strife, suffering, and needless conflict, tragedy presents itself as an art form perfectly suited to learning, which according to Aristotle, "is the greatest of pleasures, not only to the philosopher but also to the rest of mankind, however small their capacity for it" (*Poetics*, 1448b13). Therefore, the essential Aristotelian lesson of tragedy, according to Hamilton, is that "pain and error have their purpose and their use: they are steps to the ladder of knowledge."[24] One of the most important rhetorical functions of tragedy is therefore to ennoble our errors and give purpose to our pain and to tell us that these things are inevitable if we are to ever push past the limits of the known in search of the unknown. Tragedy tells us that "great spirits meet calamity greatly."[25] But this is a profoundly radical doctrine, for it suggests that greatness comes from shattering the conventional order in pursuit of a higher justice capable of bringing ruin upon all. No wonder that rhetoric and the tragic spirit have appeared together in history so infrequently, for their appearance suggests that the current regime of power is soon to come to its catastrophic end.

From this understanding of the radical nature of tragedy, one can see how the formulaic and conservative reading of *The Persians* actually denies its tragic nature. In the first case, the seemingly obvious choice of Xerxes as a tragic hero is inconsistent with our understanding of what makes such a hero tragic. After all, Xerxes does not stand out in the play as a unique character. The defeated King only appears at the very end of the play, and his role mostly consists of weeping and tearing his clothes. There is nothing great or noble about Xerxes on stage, only pathetic: "Hapless that I am, to have met / this dreadful fate, so utterly unpredictable! / How cruelly the God has trodden / on the Persian race! What am I to do, wretched me?" (905–10). We soon discover that Xerxes, far from being arrogant, is actually a weak-willed leader who was pressured into the invasion by his counselors. The Queen says as much to the ghost of Darius when he demands to know why this catastrophe happened: "The rash Xerxes, I should tell you, was taught this way of thinking by associating with wicked men. They said that whereas you had acquired great wealth for your children by warfare, he, from unmanliness, was being a stay-at-home warrior and doing nothing to increase the riches he had inherited. It was because he had heard taunts like that, over and over again, from the wicked men that he planned his military expedition against Greece" (753–59). Even here, Xerxes did not embark on anything that his father had not already attempted. Darius responds with characteristic parental disgust, lamenting that Xerxes has "not kept my instructions in mind" and noting that "I invaded many lands with great armies, but I never inflicted on my state such harm as this" (780). But Darius was the one who launched the first invasion of Greece in 492 B.C.E., in which he was defeated at the battle of Marathon, and had he not died he himself would have initiated a second assault. His son was merely carrying on his father's wishes to the best of his ability, and his invasion of Greece was consistent with the long Persian tradition of subjugating foreign peoples.

If Xerxes does not fit the role of tragic hero, neither does his father Darius appear the natural choice to give voice to the supposed "moral order" that is restored. The assumption that Aeschylus somehow makes the "Great King" the spokesperson for morality (despite Darius being the one who violently suppressed the Ionian revolt and initiated the first Persian invasion of Greece) derives mainly from the play allowing Darius to express the conventional tragic maxim that those with *hubris* are destined to suffer what he calls "a crowning catastrophe, in requital for their outrageous actions and their godless arrogance" (807). Yet little in the actual behavior of Darius marks him as a wise and moral exemplar. Rather, he appears as a self-satisfied blowhard with a selective memory who is all too eager to place the entire blame for the defeat on his son. Darius no sooner hears about the defeat than he immediately refers to Xerxes as a "wretched boy" without even knowing any of the details of the invasion (719). When the Queen attempts to place responsibility with the Chorus, Darius ignores her, focusing instead on Xerxes having the ambition to complete an "immense, never to be forgotten achievement" (760). This, of course, conveniently ignores the fact that his son's ambition was his own, a distortion made worse by his acting as if he had warned his son not to mount a second expedition when in fact this was his explicit intention before his death. In other words, Aeschylus allows Darius to warn his prideful son of their arrogance while showing himself to be prideful and arrogant.

One might suggest that if Xerxes is not the tragic hero, then perhaps the Chorus might be a better choice. After all, it is the Chorus that continually boasts of its own intelligence, the wisdom of its counsel, and the honor of its cause. Gagarin, for instance, suggests that the focus of dramatic action revolves around "the fall of Persia as a whole, not of Xerxes as an individual."[26] The blindness and arrogance thus belongs less to Xerxes than to the Chorus of counselors, who in turn speak for the spirit of Persia. At the beginning of the play, we hear the Chorus confident in the rule of their "bold ruler of populous Asia" who "drives his divine flock over the whole world / on both elements, trusting in commanders stout and rugged, / those who govern the land force and those at sea— / a man equal to the gods, from the race begotten of gold" (75–80). But they treat Xerxes merely as the latest instrument of Persian destiny, a destiny which pushes its leaders to impose Persian rule upon the known world through military force. They boast:

> No one can be counted on to withstand
> this great flood of men
> and be a sturdy barrier to ward off
> the irresistible waves of the sea:
> none dare come near the army
> of the Persians and their valiant host.
> For destiny long ago prevailed
> by divine decree, and imposed on the Persians
> the fate of conducting wars
> that destroy towered walls, clashes
> of chariots in battle and the uprooting of cities;
> and they have learned to cross the level expanse
> of the sea, when its broad waters
> are whitened by rough winds,
> trusting in cables made of thin strands
> and in devices for transporting an army. (87–113)

What leader could resist acting on such a destiny and still maintain legitimacy in the eyes of the people? Xerxes is trapped by the forces of historical necessity and placed in an impossible position—to preserve the empire by rejecting its presumed destiny and allowing the unchecked growth of Greek power, or to destroy the empire by following the will of the people and confronting the Greeks with all the power available to him. The choice is obvious. He must invade Greece and hope that, with the aid of overwhelming force, fate will look kindly upon him as it had to Persian kings in the past. But in this case he is simply acting on behalf of the Chorus.

This interpretation gets us closer to the rhetorical significance of the play insofar as it points to one of its key "illuminations" about the nature of the human condition—the impulse to flatter power and the need of the powerful to be flattered.[27] Like all tragedies, *The Persians* warns us of the dangers of *hubris*, but it does not take the easy way out and attribute *hubris* to (in the words of Darius) some "mental disease" unique to a single character (749). The origin of *hubris*, as dramatized by Aeschylus, is the flattery of the strong few by the weaker many, the latter whom are bolstered by the authority of tradition. The

Chorus itself recognizes this fact in the beginning of the play after it has just sung its paean to Persian power:

> But what mortal can escape
> the guileful deception of a God?
> Who is so light of foot
> that he has power to leap easily away?
> For Ruin (*Até*) begins by fawning on a man in a friendly way
> and leads him astray into her net,
> from which it is impossible for a mortal to escape and flee. (93–101)

Master flatterers themselves, the Chorus has at least enough self-awareness to begin to sense its own character flaw, which is complicity in *Até* by fawning over the powerful. And we soon see this fawning in action. When the Queen arrives they prostrate themselves in front of her and offer her wise counsel from loyal friends (175), which amounts to the reassuring lie that all will be well as long as she prays to the gods (210).

This obsequious fawning over the powerful reaches its full height when Darius returns from the underworld to give his own counsel. Once again ignoring the former King's defeat at Marathon, the Chorus is hopeful: "for he was never one to lose many men / by disastrous slaughters in war; / the Persians called him 'divine counselor', and a divine counselor / he was, for he guided the people well" (652–55). Predictably, when Darius appears, they prostrate themselves. Yet the King expresses impatience for such displays: "since it is your laments that have induced me to come up from below, speak now, not in long-winded words but putting it concisely and covering everything, setting your awe of me aside" (697–700). But the chorus cannot do so: "I am afraid to gratify your wish; / I am afraid to speak plainly, / saying things that are hard to say to a friend" (700–702). Frustrated, Darius remarks to the Chorus that "your old fear is standing guard over your mind" (703) and instead turns to his wife, begging her to stop crying and wailing and to speak plainly to him. But the Queen fails to do so either, choosing instead to flatter her former husband, "whose fortunate fate surpassed all mortals in bliss" because he did not live to see the fortunes of Persia ruined (710). In his quest for plain speaking, Darius receives only the silence of toadies and the fawning of an obedient and grieving wife.

Showing his mastery of the dramatic form, Aeschylus uses the interaction between Darius, the Queen, and the Chorus to reveal to the Greeks the nature of the flattery which leads to the downfall of empires. In his portrayal, the entire system is corrupt from top to bottom. For it soon becomes clear that Darius was not really sincere, and that the Queen and the Chorus are giving him precisely what he wants. As soon as he hears of Xerxes's defeat, he immediately rushes to judgment and replaces the Queen's initial description of her son as "bold Xerxes" with his own epithet, "wretched boy" (717–19).[28] The Queen is quick to pick up on what Darius wants to hear—that the destruction of the Persian army has nothing to do with his own legacy, the tradition of Persia, or the counsel of his trusted Chorus and has everything to do with an arbitrary act of divine retribution to punish the arrogance of a single man. In other words, Darius is looking for a scapegoat, as he makes clear in the following exchange with the Queen.

> DARIUS: And how did a land army of that size manage to get across the water?
> QUEEN: He contrived means to yoke the strait of Helle, so as to create a pathway.
> DARIUS: He actually carried that out, so as to close up the mighty Bosporus?
> QUEEN: It is true. Some divinity must have touched his wits.
> DARIUS: Ah, it was a powerful divinity that came upon him, to put him out of his right mind!
> QUEEN: Yes, one can see by the outcome what a disaster he managed to create. (720–26)

As it turns out, of course, the "divinity" that touched his wits was the advice of his counselors, the example of Darius, and the mythology of the indestructible Persian Empire. Yet when the Queen manages to suggest as much through "plain speech," Darius completely ignores her, preferring instead to think himself blameless and wise. And on his exit back to the underworld, the Chorus returns to true form and does their duty with a kingly farewell: "What a great and good life we enjoyed / in our well-run city, when our old / never-failing, never-harming, invincible king, / godlike Darius, ruled the country!" (853–56). But when he disappears, the only thing he leaves behind is a wasteland of suffering and pain.

However, the problem with focusing on the dangers of flattery is that it turns the *Persians* into a morality play about the dangers of flattery; it does not perform the essential function of tragedy, which is to reveal the nature of justice through an act of *hubris* by a tragic hero who shakes a tormented world. But that hero exists in the play; it is the Greeks themselves. It is the Greeks who dared not only to challenge the military force of the mighty Persian Empire but also the very structure of justice and power they represented. Their only extended characterization occurs in the interaction between the Queen and the Chorus prior to learning of the Persian defeat. The Queen knows nothing about Greece, Athens, or its people, and asks the Chorus to inform her:

QUEEN: Do they have such great numbers of men in their army?

CHORUS: And an army of quality that is already done the Medes a great deal of harm.

QUEEN: Why, are they distinguished for their wielding of the drawn bow and its darts?

CHORUS: Not at all; they use spears for close combat and carry shields for defense.

QUEEN: And what else apart from that? Is there sufficient wealth in their stores?

CHORUS: They have a fountain of silver, a treasure in their soil.

QUEEN: And who is the shepherd, master and commander over their host?

CHORUS: They are not called slaves or subjects to any man.

QUEEN: How can they resist an invading enemy?

CHORUS: Well enough to have destroyed the large and splendid army of Darius.

QUEEN: What you say is fearful to think about for the parents of those who have gone there. (235–45)

All we need to know about our tragic hero is in these lines. The Greeks, and more specifically the Athenians, have committed *hubris* by violating the traditional boundaries of the vanishing actuality. In short, they have upended the traditional political order by choosing to act in voluntary cooperation with other citizens rather than follow the dictates of the one or the few. Combined with their skill in close combat and their newfound resources of silver found in a mine near Athens prior to the Persian invasion, these elements gave the Greeks the power to act the tragic hero in pursuit of a future possibility despite the suffering that would ensue, which the perceptive Queen immediately recognizes.

Yet the Greeks defeated the Persians. So where does the tragedy lie? Certainly, one can point to the obvious suffering of the Greek soldiers who died and the Athenian population for being forced to leave their city to complete destruction in order to save themselves. But it is to slip back into formulaic thinking to assume that tragedies must only result in the death or suffering of the tragic hero. Tragedy is not about the suffering of a specific person, but suffering itself. There is plenty of suffering in *The Persians,* but the suffering we care about belongs not to the Queen, the Chorus, Xerxes, or Darius, but to the mothers of the noble and guiltless soldiers and sons and fathers who were slaughtered on the altar of Persian pride. A soldier himself, Aeschylus had great respect for other soldiers, including the ones he fought against, and the play goes to great length to praise them. Here is the Messenger giving the news: "all those Persians who were in their bodily prime, outstanding in courage, notable for high birth, and who always showed the highest degree of loyalty to the person of the King, have perished shamefully by a most ignoble fate" (440–44). And Aeschylus goes into great detail about this fate. In a voice reminiscent of the *Iliad*, he identifies many Persian commanders by name and describes their deaths in detail. One example: "Artembares, the commander of ten thousand and horse, is being pounded against the rugged shores of Sileniae; Dadaces, commander of a thousand, was struck by a spear and took an effortless leap out of his ship; and the excellent Tenegon, a noble of the Bactrians, now wanders around the wave beaten island of Ajax" (300–310). But then Aeschylus increases the suffering even more in this vivid account that only an eyewitness could produce:

> At first the streaming Persian force resisted firmly, but when our masses of ships were crowded into a narrow space, they had no way to come to each other's help, they got struck by their own side's bronze-pointed rams, they had the whole of their oarage smashed, and the Greek ships, with careful coordination, surrounded them completely and went on striking them. The hulls of our ships turned keel-up, and the sea surface was no longer visible, filled as it was with the wreckage of ships and the slaughter of men; the shores and reefs were also full of corpses. Every remaining ship of the Eastern armada was being rowed away in disorderly flight; meanwhile the enemy were clubbing men and splitting their spines with broken pieces of oars and spars from the wreckage, as if they were tunny or some other catch of fish, and a mixture of shrieking and wailing filled the expanse of the sea, until the dark face of night blotted it out. (412–30)

There is no great glory here, only pathetic death, the ruthless and bloody slaughter of once noble men who had gone to war in loyalty to the King and the spirit of Persia. The Persian soldiers do not even have the privilege of having a spear thrust of Achilles slice open their liver in face-to-face combat; they simply flounder like fish in a shallow pond, waiting for their spines to be broken with a club made from the wreckage of their own ship. Certainly, the mothers who hear of such a fate will suffer greatly for the remainder of their sad lives; but so, too, must Aeschylus live with this image seared in his imagination until his own death. The dead at least have the luxury of dying and thereby of forgetting; it is the living who must endure the constant reminders of pain through the curse of memory.

The tragedy of *The Persians* is therefore not that Xerxes boldly pursued a path that was already laid before him; the tragedy derives from the Greeks daring to resist what seemed to be the inexorable movement of necessity and thereby bringing down suffering upon everyone. For in overstepping what appeared to be the established moral and political order, hundreds of thousands of noble Persian sons had to die an ignominious death while tens of thousands of Greek citizens had to be responsible for and bear witness to their slaughter. In this suffering, however, the new order of justice is revealed, an order Aeschylus put in the mouth of the Chorus after the exit of the Queen (for the Chorus only speaks the truth when they are alone):

> Not long now will those in the land of Asia
> remain under Persian rule,
> nor continue to pay tribute
> under the compulsion of their Lords,
> nor fall on their faces to the ground
> in awed obeisance; for the strength of the monarchy
> has utterly vanished.
> Nor do men any longer keep their tongue
> under guard; for the people
> have been let loose to speak with freedom,
> now the yoke of military force no longer binds them.
> In its blood-soaked soil
> the sea-washed isle of Ajax
> holds the power of Persia. (584–95)

This is the new order of justice which has been revealed through the appearances of suffering brought about by an act of *hubris* on the part of the Greeks. From now on, power will not come from a monarch who monopolizes the tools of violence and forces his subjects to hold their tongue and prostrate themselves before authority; power will come from the free speech of citizens standing on their own feet and deliberating over how to act in concert in pursuit of possibilities. But this is simply to say that the Greeks will develop power through the medium of rhetoric.

The possibility of rhetoric as a medium by which power is challenged, destroyed, created, and transformed is first disclosed in tragedy. The Homeric heroes had shown the possibility of eloquence to reveal the strength of character and to embody the virtues of an oral culture. Heraclitus had challenged this order with the aphorism, which paralyzed action and liberated the mind to dwell upon the nature of Logos through thinking. The accomplishment of Aeschylus is to unite these two tendencies in Greek culture into a single aesthetic form. Tragic heroes do not simply act but also reflect and speak; their action, in effect, becomes an inquiry into the nature of the Logos by disrupting power and revealing the nature of justice through the conflict of appearances. Whereas philosophers like Heraclitus gaze upon the flux of the world and dwell upon its meaning, tragic heroes burst headlong into this flux to create even more turmoil in the wordless faith that a new possibility will reveal itself through the ruins of the vanishing actuality. But what makes their action rhetorical, and not simply impulsive, is that it follows and is followed by eloquent speeches which justify their actions through the invocation of new purposes, principles, or passions. This is the rhetorical significance—not only to confront power and the order of justice, but to do so with *logos,* an "account."

Rhetoric and tragedy are therefore inextricably bound in history and in practice whenever we see possibilities of power tempting us just beyond the limits of conventional justice. The tragic sense is that which pierces the veil of appearances and shows us a glimpse of the new within the structure of the old, and the art of rhetoric is the means by which we articulate and direct others toward these possibilities. Richard Weaver concludes that "without rhetoric there seems no possibility of tragedy, and in turn, without the sense of tragedy, no possibility of taking an elevated view of life."[29] On the one hand, without rhetoric, tragedy is impossible because we would neither be able to motivate ourselves or others to tragic action nor be able to express the meanings of those actions even if they occurred. On the other hand, without tragedy, we would always be trapped within the existing order of justice and never be able to see beyond the constraints of existing power. We would be forever locked within the Homeric order, continually reproducing the same through our epic narratives of old.

The tragic spirit is not thus confined to the stage, the theater, or the novel. Indeed, we encounter tragedy more often in our rhetoric than in our arts. Rhetoric finds its habitation in the situations of struggle, suffering, and hope which constantly punctuate the drama of history. The creative artist can always wrest a happy ending out of even the worst of circumstances; but the political rhetor must always confront the brute realities of suffering and the possibility of failure. Tragedy provides the rhetor a way of rousing courage in the face of painful necessity and finding meaning when confronted with seemingly meaninglessness suffering. To those who must endure suffering or bear witness to those who do, these words of Aeschylus shall always ring true: "Even in our sleep, pain which cannot forget, falls drop by drop upon the heart, until in our own despair, against our will, comes wisdom, through the awful grace of God."[30] For this is the solace of all those who shake a tormented world in the faith that divine justice will be revealed through the suffering which the Logos has decreed to be the necessary price of wisdom and of freedom.

CHAPTER 4

Protagoras and the
Promise of Politics

A human being is the measure of all things, of those things that are, that
they are; and of those things that are not, that they are not.1

If the mark of a tragic hero is an act of *hubris* that confidently oversteps the
established boundaries of justice and power, then Protagoras might appear to
be one of the most tragic of all the Greeks. Surpassing even the pride of Achilles, Protagoras boldly wrested from the gods that most sovereign of all authority—to determine and measure "all things" (*pantôn chrêmatôn*). Protagoras thus
carried to its limit the humanistic tendency already present in Heraclitus. For
Heraclitus had also used variations of the word measure (*metron*) in his aphorisms, referring in his case to an act of appropriate proportion or ordering; but
this measurement was not done by human beings but by the Logos.[2] Heraclitus had thus deposed the Homeric gods but had concentrated their authority
within a single impersonal world order that, while potentially intelligible to
human cognition, nonetheless remained a sovereign principle and law. Protagoras eradicated the last vestiges of supernaturalism when he declared the
human being (*anthrôpos*), both individually and collectively, the measure of
that existence. For him, there was no distinction between Logos and *logos,*
between a divine and merely human account of things; human accounts (*logoi*)
were all that we possessed. But if that was the case, then it would seem that all
established boundaries could be potentially called into question and rendered
nonexistent by an act of will. For aspiring tragic heroes eager to shatter the

existing order, the words of Protagoras might be reassuring—the opportunities for *hubris* would be endless.

It is natural, then, that one tradition writes his biography as a tragic story. Born around 485 B.C.E. in Abdera along the coast of Thrace, Protagoras matured precisely at the time that Athens was leading Greece toward newfound heights of power. The changes Heraclitus had seen coming were now developing at a rapid pace. The mid-fifth century B.C.E. was thus what John Poulakos describes as a time when "the aristocracy of the nobility was yielding to a democracy of citizens; the aristocracy of the myths was losing its authority to a democracy of public arguments; the aristocracy of the oracles was receding before a democracy of human laws; and the aristocracy of poetry was relinquishing its glory to a democracy of prosaic discourses."[3] Protagoras rode the wave of these changes by helping found a professional class of itinerant teachers, performers, and theorists known as the "Sophists," intellectual practitioners who would bestow their wisdom and expertise to the newly empowered citizens of Greece for a fee. The author of numerous written works, including *On Government, On Wrestling, On Sciences, On Ambition, On Virtues, On the Original State of Things, On the Gods,* and *On Truth,* Protagoras quickly rose to wealth and prominence, eventually becoming friend and counselor to Pericles, the leader of Athens, who assigned him to draft a legal code for the pan-Hellenic colony of Thurii in 444 B.C.E. In 411 B.C.E., however, tragic necessity had apparently caught up with him. With Athens now at the low ebb of its power in its war with Sparta, Protagoras was accused and convicted of impiety and had all of his books burned in the agora. Now fleeing from the mob consisting partly of his former students, the almost ninety-year-old Protagoras hastily climbed aboard a boat heading to Sicily, which the gods in their wisdom tossed on a raging sea and then sank, thereby enacting tragic retribution for his *hubris.*[4]

Yet this dramatic third-century C.E. rendition is contradicted by an equally plausible account in which Protagoras died rich and happy at the ripe old age of seventy around 421 B.C.E., when Athens was still the undisputed power in Greece. This testimony comes from none other than his arch-critic Plato, who had every reason to exaggerate his tragic end. Yet in the *Meno,* Plato has Socrates say, "I believe that he was nearly seventy when he died and had practiced his craft for forty years. During all that time to this very day his reputation has stood high" (91e). And why should he not have a good reputation? Protagoras was not only the oldest and greatest of the Sophists, but he was also as the strongest advocate for the promotion of democratic virtues and institutions, going so far as to initiate in Thurii a policy by which "the sons of all citizens be taught to read and write at the public's expense."[5] According to Guthrie, Protagoras was well known for promoting "invincible respect for the democratic virtues of justice, respect for other men's opinions, the processes of peaceful persuasion as the basis of communal life, and the necessity of communal life to the very survival of the human race."[6] Far from being an arrogant hero eager to take sovereign possession of the world, Protagoras appears as an egalitarian teacher of men who divides the world in equal shares and then bestows these shares upon the citizens of Greece as a gift.

The truth of Protagoras's fate may never be known, but that is only fitting. For the nature of his death represents just another *chrêmata*—meaning a thing, matter, object, or affair—which is up to us to measure. Do the trial and subsequent sea voyage which allegedly killed him exist or not exist? If they existed, what qualities and magnitudes did they possess? Was the trial a momentous occasion in the history of Athens or merely one of a string of show trials put on by the Tyranny of the Four Hundred? And was he drowned in a whirlpool, or did the ship merely spring a leak because of shoddy workmanship? And if all of these things were nonexistent, what reputation did he possess and how widely was he known? Does Protagoras rightly lay claim to the title of the "Father" of the Sophists, or was he just a self-promoting charlatan? Each of these questions is a "thing" upon whose existence, quality, and magnitude we must first pass judgment upon before we then give an account, a *logos*, by which we render our judgment common to all. One can thus imagine that, if there is a Hades, the shade of Protagoras is there smiling when he learns that, even after the passing of two millennia, we are still trying to measure the nature of his personal legacy.

However, one thing is certain about the legacy of his man-measure doctrine —since its first articulation, it has given warrant to individuals to argue what is and is not the case based on his or her experience in the world. For what else does it mean than this to be a "measure" of "things"? It means to take account of, to evaluate, and to make determinate a matter of concern in order to bring an imbalanced situation into proportion. Yet this is no easy task, for what counts as a "thing" to one person may be "no-thing" to another, and even things whose existence is agreed upon can be sized up differently based on dissimilar needs, interests, and perspectives. For Protagoras, as for Heraclitus, the only consistent "thing" that can be posited as permanent in experience is flux itself. At the same time, however, Protagoras no more abandoned us to a relativistic chaos in denying transcendent world orders like the Logos than Heraclitus did by transcending the Homeric gods; he simply replaced the impersonal world order of the Logos, which pervades all things and works from behind and within appearances, with the humanistic and contingent order of the *logos*, which represents the cumulative and continuous human activity of imposing meaning upon appearances through language. This *logos* represents an even more dynamic and relative order that that of Heraclitus, to be sure; but it is an order nonetheless. And it represents the only kind of order which grants to human beings the responsibility and opportunity to collectively craft a structure of power according to their own visions of possibility.

It is Protagoras, in other words, who reveals for the first time what Arendt calls "the promise of politics." For her, this promise amounted to a shared faith in the positive consequences of being able to "assert one's own opinion" and to "show oneself, to be seen and heard by others."[7] Certainly Protagoras would have gained wealth and fame for his persuasion, but his lasting reputation comes from the more meaningful achievement as leader of the sophistical movement. According to Arendt, his "extraordinary skill in argumentation is of secondary importance to the first successful creation by the polis of a political realm. The crucial factor is not that one could now turn arguments around and stand propositions on their heads, but rather that one gained the ability to truly see topics from various sides—that is, politically—with the result that people understood how to assume the many possible perspectives provided by the real world."[8] Protagoras by no means caused generations of Greeks to see issues from multiple perspectives; that was the result of the cumulative effects of history. But what he and the other Sophists accomplished was to articulate a political framework based on a humanistic worldview that gave rational justification for putting these multiple perspectives into meaningful communication with each other in order to collectively measure the affairs of the *polis*.

Seen in this light, Protagoras is not a tragic figure at all. Rather than boldly initiating a forceful challenge to power that convulsed a tormented world, he followed in the wake of a tragic convulsion and measured the order of power that would define and solidify the new boundaries of justice. This new order was democracy, a structure of power grounded less in particular acts of voting than in shared assumptions that human beings were the measure of all things, that the best measurements were produced through the clash and reconciliation of diverse perspectives, and that rhetoric would be foremost among the arts of *logos* by which power would be constituted, critiqued, and transformed. In effect, Protagoras was the first democratic public intellectual who offered citizens a practical metaphysics of political culture which gave them not only rights and responsibilities but also self-understanding rooted in a progressive attitude toward history. After Protagoras, citizens were given a viable alternative to being pious servants of tradition, helpless puppets of divine will, sleepwalkers caught in the currents of Logos, or tragic heroes born to struggle and suffer; they could now be active participants in the making of history through the intervention of rhetoric, the primary medium of power in any truly political culture.

Although Protagoras invented neither rhetoric nor democracy, he warrants an important place in the history of Western thought. It was Protagoras who first articulated a comprehensive humanistic worldview which undergirded democratic practice, and it was Protagoras who spearheaded the sophistical movement tasked with developing and teaching the arts of *logos*—that is, of persuasion, speech, and reason—that would become the specialized discipline we now know as "rhetoric."[9] Thus, although the actual word *rhêtorikê* was likely not coined until the early fourth century B.C.E., in spirit and in tendency Protagoras and the Sophists are justifiably credited with having been the "first to infuse rhetoric with life," demonstrating "to the rest of the world that rhetoric is an integral part of the social life of all civilized people."[10] They accomplished these tasks not by any tricks of persuasion but simply by making clear what John Poulakos calls the "close connection between well-crafted *logoi* and the acquisition of power."[11] In the new Greek democracies, speech was no longer simply a way to maintain convention, give orders to subordinates, or eulogize the reigning tyrant; it became the means by which citizens coordinated voluntary action through persuasion within moments of judgment. The Sophists responded to these changes by revealing the nature of the new medium of power to the Greeks. In their public displays, in their itinerant teaching, and in the political success of their students, they showed in practice what Protagoras articulated in theory—that in Greece in the mid-fifth century B.C.E., *logos* was the medium of power and the democratic citizen was the measure of all things.

Rather than representing the rapacious entrepreneurs and deceptive demagogues, then, Sophists like Protagoras were primarily catalysts for energies already ongoing in Greek culture. When Protagoras established the model for the Sophist as itinerant teacher-for-hire around 460 B.C.E., he did not make a revolutionary political statement but rather served an immediate practical need. For the Greeks were no longer content with Heraclitean-style aphorisms disseminated from afar to stimulate their thinking; the growing population of democratic citizens did not so much want "thinking" as the skills necessary to give them power in both the city (*polis*) and the household (*oikos*).[12] As Roseman explains:

> The appearance of the Sophists filled an urgent need. The ideal of citizenship which the city-state elevated as the highest *arête* required a new kind of education calculated to meet this need. . . . Athenian democracy required the participation of all its citizens. The Greek had to face as part of his daily life fundamental questions of authority and freedom, of leadership and followership. For every citizen the business of education, or the training of the mind to cope with problems of this magnitude, was of utmost significance. . . . This connection between the needs of the city-state and the need of the intellect to meet those needs "was to bring the sophist movement into being."[13]

In short, the driving force behind the sophistical movement was a fundamental shift in how power was distributed and formed. It moved away from a model by which the resourceful few established by proclamation and force the boundaries of justice for the powerless many, and it moved toward a model by which the newly empowered many (to the degree that male citizens represented a "many" as opposed to an "all") determined justice for themselves through collaboration and deliberation in political assemblies and courts of law. The Sophists reacted to this situation by changing the public role of the intellectual. From a counselor to the *aristos* he became teacher of the *demos,* and from oracular prophet he became articulate performer.

Perhaps the most dramatic shift in fifth-century B.C.E. Greek culture which created the opportunity for the birth of the sophistical movement was the transformation of the meaning of the *polis* in the wake of Cleisthenes-style reforms in Athens and elsewhere. Cleisthenes had set the precedent for the democratic "Assembly" in which citizens could, by throwing a black or white stone into a vessel, cast votes of "yes" or "no" on policy proposals advanced by other citizens. But as revolutionary as were the ideas of a citizen assembly and citizen jury, there was a more lasting effect of the changed self-understanding of the *demos* and its relationship to the *polis.* According to Cynthia Farrar, the reforms of Cleisthenes were "designed to undermine the local domination of aristocratic families and to connect every Athenian politically to the wider community."[14] For what Cleisthenes did by redefining the boundaries of the city was to redefine "the *polis* as a political rather than geographical entity."[15] Whereas the Homeric notion of *polis* had differed little from the physical understanding of a village or kingdom, after the fifth century B.C.E. the *polis* suggested a more abstract space which sprung up between people in their creative capacity as citizens. For Arendt, this was perhaps the greatest of Greek discoveries. She writes that this political understanding of the "*polis,* properly speaking, is not the city-state in its physical location; it is the organization of the people as it arises out of acting and speaking together, and its true space lies between people living together for this purpose, no matter where they happen to be."[16] After Cleisthenes, the *polis* was no longer a circle drawn in the sand but an abstract space which represented what Josiah Ober calls "the mediating and integrative power of communication between citizens."[17] Although reliant on physical places like the courts, the assembly, the theater, and the agora to facilitate this communication, should the buildings of Athens be burned to the ground, the *polis* would still exist insofar as its citizens were still capable of gathering together to pass legal judgments, discuss common concerns, create artistic displays, and manage their economic affairs.

As a structural expression of power, then, the *polis* was unique; it could be infinitely expanded without sacrificing depth and continuity for breadth and extension. As long as new members could be integrated into forms of political communication, its power would only continue to grow. This fact was graphically demonstrated after Xerxes marched upon Athens in 480 B.C.E. and burned it to the ground prior to having his own fleet destroyed at Salamis. For even after the physical destruction of the city, the power of the Athenian *polis* not only endured but flourished, quickly surpassing the traditional limits of the city walls. In the aftermath of their victory over the Persians, Athenians took the leadership of the Delian League, which had been organized to push out the remaining Persian forces and to establish a permanent defense against future invasion. But this position of leader (*hēgemōn*), backed by overwhelming naval superiority, had the additional effect between the years 480 and 460 B.C.E. of rapidly changing the landscape of Athens from what George Kerferd calls the "economics of a city state to the economics of empire."[18] Soon Athens had its own network of tribute-paying Greek cities, which provided additional resources to rebuild and then expand the city and make it the cosmopolitan center and cultural crossroads for all of Greece, attracting artisans, entrepreneurs, and intellectuals from all over Hellas. So when Pericles was elected *strategos,* or military archon, in 460 B.C.E., a position he would hold until his death in 429 B.C.E., Athens had begun its "Golden Age," in which it was difficult to know where its *polis* began and ended. This was the age in which Protagoras and the Sophists would prosper, offering not only education and training to citizens but also providing to Greek culture at large a humanistic worldview with the relationship between rhetoric and power at its core.

Unfortunately, the expansive thought of Protagoras has been preserved in history only in the form of fragmentary axioms. Perhaps suggesting the validity of the "tragic" version of his biography, none of his many books has survived, and virtually all of his practical and pedagogical insights into the nature of speech, persuasion, and *logos* have been lost. What we are left with, besides Plato's questionable reconstructions of Protagoras's position in his fourth-century B.C.E. dialogues, is a scattering of reliable quotations that were likely composed and disseminated in writing in order to be memorized and repeated in oral conversation much in the manner of the "books" of Heraclitus. Perhaps, just as with his conflicting biographies, this apparent lack is only fitting because Protagoras's primary audience was not an exclusive class of intellectuals but the *demos.* Consequently, he communicated his most important insights through the same easily transportable aphorisms as Heraclitus had done, only this time meant to empower by enlightening rather than to provoke through paradox. So when he announces that man is the measure of all things, that the gods are unknowable, that there are two sides to every issue, and that it is a virtue to make the weaker argument into the stronger, he gives to the *demos* all they need to know in order to participate in the political affairs of the *polis.*

Perhaps we should expect no more than this today when attempting to reconstruct his perspective.

1. *The human being is the measure of all things, of those things that are, that they are; and of those things that are not, that they are not.* (Gagarin and Woodruff, Protagoras fragment 15)

With the *anthrôpos*-measure doctrine, Protagoras provides the ontological foundation for a politics of appearances. In this form of social organization, power is manipulated and directed through a common and competitive effort to bring forth, transfigure, and give meaning to those appearances which are believed by some to demand the collective judgment of a public. Protagoras, of course, does not actually use the word "appearances" (*phainomena*), but "things" (*chrêmatôn*); the difference, however, is only one of degree. In common Greek usage, according to Nussbaum, appearances referred to "the world *as it appears to,* as it is experienced by, observers who are members of our kind."[19] Appearance thus connoted "a loose and inclusive notion of 'experience,' or the way(s) a human observer sees or 'takes' the world, using his cognitive faculties."[20] A *chrêmata,* being a "thing" that generally has some relevance or usefulness to human beings (i.e., a "good"), is simply a recognizable and definable appearance habitually encountered and given a name. But just because a *chrêmata* represents a recognizable thing does not mean the nature of that thing is simply a given. Protagoras emphasizes the responsibility of anthrôpos to determine what is the case (*ontôn hôs estin*) and is not the case (*ontôn hôs ouk estin*) about all such "things." Things might not be what we thought they were, or they might reveal themselves to exist in unexpected places or to have qualities we did not anticipate. Thus, for Protagoras, human beings are tasked not only with measuring *chrêmata* but with constituting them through the power of the word (*logos*). The politics of appearances therefore represents the persuasive struggle to give the definitive name to appearances which are deemed useful or harmful to human affairs.

This political reading of the fragment resolves two long-standing philosophical debates about its meaning while also illuminating the nature of politics itself. In the first case, the political reading suggests that Protagoras meant *anthrôpos* neither in a purely individualistic nor collective sense but in a communicative one. Plato was thus not confused when he attributed to Protagoras in the *Theaetetus* the seemingly contradictory beliefs that each individual has unique and unrepeatable private perceptions (166c5) and that the basis for ethical judgments is the collective opinion of the city (167c5). This tension is resolved as soon as we understand politics as a means of using *logos* to translate private perceptions into communicable meanings such that a common opinion (*doxa*) can be formed about similar appearances. Whereas perception inhabits the realm of the particular and therefore the individualistic, meanings are inherently general and therefore social. A political opinion is thus a general meaning capable of being applied to a wide enough spectrum of appearances to the degree that it is capable of becoming a norm, habit, rule, or law. In political affairs, we are always simultaneously operating as individuals and collectives, stepping in and out of the proverbial "river" of experience onto the stable bank of meanings as it suits our needs and necessities in the moment.

In the second case, reading the fragment as a political axiom renders irrelevant the question of whether his choice of the word *chrêmatôn* was intended to limit human measurement only to those things relevant to human interests, thus prohibiting by exclusion judgments upon natural events and objects. For one of the central facts about politics is that the only "things" which concern it are *chrêmatôn,* objects which we deem significant within events which affect us in some way. Protagoras is therefore not attempting, as in the tragic reading, to give to human beings the power reserved for the gods; he is simply giving to them the political responsibility of identifying and characterizing the nature of those objects or events which warrant political attention. In other words, within the sphere of politics, what does not concern human affairs for all practical purposes does not really "exist." But this is less a metaphysical statement than a pragmatic one. In the politics of appearances, it is up to citizens to determine for themselves what "thing" shall be brought before the tribunal of the public to determine whether or not it exists, what its properties are, and how it bears upon the question of judgment.

> 1. *Concerning the gods, I am not in a position to know either that they exist or that they do not, nor can I know what they look like, for many things prevent our knowing—the subject is obscure and human life is short.* (Gagarin and Woodruff, Protagoras fragment 20)

Nothing demonstrates Protagoras's commitment to cultivating a humanistic political culture than the "concerning the gods" fragment which formed the centerpiece of his book, *On The Gods.* This book and its famous axiom undeniably articulated a principle that Protagoras believed to be necessary in the coming political order. Although the third century C.E. claim that the work was the cause of his prosecution for impiety, remains doubtful, the conjecture itself shows the fragment's capacity to provoke powerful responses even after the passing of seven centuries.[21] We miss its truly controversial nature, however, if we interpret the statement as simply the opening salvo in what would be a long tradition of theological debate over the existence or nonexistence of God or the gods. As with the *anthrôpos*-measure doctrine, Protagoras is making a political rather than a metaphysical assertion; as he makes clear in the fragment, whether the gods exist or not does not concern him. What does concern him is the cultivation of a political culture emancipated from the constraints of archaic religious dogmas and traditions in order for citizens to determine for themselves what matters to address and how to address them. His public statement concerning the gods was therefore a bold but necessary effort to clear a common deliberative space in which *logos* itself would be the only authority.

When put in conversation with the *anthrôpos*-measure doctrine, the gods fragment clearly demonstrates the guiding norm of democratic deliberation—speak only of appearances which directly and immediately concern human affairs. Although both designate what can or cannot be said to exist, the gods fragment identifies what cannot be measured rather than delimiting everything that can. Apparently, for Protagoras, the gods were not included among the class "things" shown to affect or be useful to human experience. Yet the criteria for this exclusion reveal his normative commitments. Protagoras says he can know nothing of the gods because they can neither be seen nor conceptualized clearly within the short span of human life. When interpreted as a positive statement of political speech, this means that the only accounts (*logoi*) appropriate for the political sphere are those which concern publicly accessible appearances that can be adequately named, evaluated, and acted upon within a timely manner. Protagoras therefore does not criticize or reject personal or even cultural belief in the gods. According to Jaeger, he may have even recommended a serious anthropological study of religion's "meaning and function in human civilization and social structure."[22] What he did restrict, however, was the cluttering of public deliberation with pointless debates about how to honor or what to do about entities which no one had ever seen, whose nature and character were unknowable, and who appeared to have no direct influence in the everyday lives of human beings outside of their usefulness as poetic allegories in myth.

1. *On every subject there are two* logoi *opposed to one another.* (Gagarin and Woodruff, Protagoras fragment 24)

With the two-*logoi* fragment, Protagoras captures the essence of politics. Whereas the anthrôpos-measure doctrine and his statement concerning the gods had established the warrant for engaging in and the criteria for demarcating political speech, the two-*logoi* fragment states the central fact of politics—that because human beings measure appearances differently, the life of politics is disputation. For Greeks living in the new democratic city-states, of course, Protagoras was simply stating the obvious. With the eclipse of the relatively univocal world of Homeric Greece, they had rushed headlong into what John Poulakos calls a "polyvocal world" in which "the status of all things is questionable," which "is why people often find themselves at odds with one another, disagreeing, differing, and seeking to resolve their differences symbolically."[23] For both proponents and detractors of democracy, it was simply a fact to be accepted, for good or ill, that every subject becomes a potential source of disagreement. Notably, Protagoras uses the word *pragmata* rather than *chrêmata* for "thing," a word which encompasses a wider breadth of phenomena and includes any issue, subject, question, deed, event, object, or act whatsoever.[24] In Greece of the fifth century, apparently, it was impossible to make a statement about anything, regardless of its apparent utility, without provoking a counterargument.[25]

Yet Protagoras was clearly making more than a factual observation of his time. For him, it was in the nature of appearances themselves to be open to competing interpretations, just as it was the right and responsibility of engaged citizens to advocate for their own perspectives. The two-*logoi* fragment did not so much state a fact as represent a doctrine, specifically the doctrine of *dissoi logoi*, or "different accounts," which carried with it a political norm. As John Poulakos describes it, *dissoi logoi* is a method based on the premise "that in order to understand an issue, one must be prepared to listen to at least two contrary sides; and in order to decide how to act, one must espouse one of the two sides or come up with a third."[26] That Protagoras intended the two-*logoi* fragment to function as a warrant for argumentative practice is made clear from the titles of two works, *On Contradictions* and *The Downthrowing* [Arguments], which were used as training manuals to teach citizens how to argue both sides of an issue. And by using *pragmata* instead of *chrêmata*, Protagoras simply recognizes that not all issues relevant to human interests show themselves as such in their first appearance. Sometimes we have to argue about appearances before they disclose themselves to be *chrêmatôn*—that is to say, matters which are proper for collective measurement in the political sphere.

1. *Making the weaker* logos *stronger.* (Gagarin and Woodruff, Protagoras fragment 27)

After circling around the question of power in his previous axioms, Protagoras places it front and center with the stronger/weaker fragment. Far from representing a merely professional boast to be able to turn arguments on their heads, this fragment represents the culminating principle of politics—that through mastery of the arts of *logos*, the foundations of any established order can be called into question and any marginal perspective has the possibility of becoming dominant. In contrast to moralistic interpretations that see Protagoras (and the Sophists generally) as making the "worse" argument the "better," the fragment has nothing to do with ethical judgment and everything to do with the relationship between rhetoric and power. As John Poulakos points out, Protagoras intends *hêttô* to refer "to that argument or position which commands less power because the majority shuns it or is not persuaded by it," and *kreittô* to refer "to that argument or position which is dominant because the majority has found it more persuasive than other alternatives."[27] The fact that the stronger tends to be thought by the majority to be better, and the weaker to be worse, does not make it so for all time. Only when these hierarchies are fixed and immutable do strength and morality become synonymous and politics impossible. But when the resources of *logos* can be harnessed by ordinary citizens to challenge, invert, and transform these established hierarchies, genuine politics comes into being.

One may be forgiven for reading Protagoras as a tragic hero, a radical author of the atheistic doctrine of permanent revolution driven by the personal pursuit of power. But if this is the case, it is a wonder they did not execute Protagoras forty years earlier when he was an itinerant Sophist who traveled from town to town earning money by openly teaching eager young men the skills necessary to thrive in this new world order. But Protagoras had at least four decades of high reputation throughout all of Greece, indicating that he was not tragic at all. The same man who made the subject of the gods off limits to political discourse was also famous for creating a variation of the Prometheus myth in order to justify democracy on the basis that Zeus had distributed civic virtue equally amongst all human beings. And the author of the doctrine that the art of *logos* could make the powerful weak and the weak powerful was a longtime friend and counselor to Pericles, the undisputed leader of Athens for two decades. Far from overturning the established order, then, Protagoras was simply providing that order its foundations. By the time he became the first and greatest of the Sophists, the reforms of Cleisthenes had been in place for almost a half a century, and democracy as a political system had spread throughout the Greek world. Protagoras merely recognized and articulated the underlying principles already at work while simultaneously developing and teaching the practical arts necessary to fulfill the promise of politics.

A single anecdote has been preserved through history which gives us a glimpse into how Protagoras put his principles into practice in actual political life. Plutarch, the great historian of the first century A.D., records the following story in his *Life of Pericles:* "When an athlete unintentionally struck Epitimus the Pharsalian with a javelin and killed him, Pericles spent an entire day with Protagoras puzzling over whether one should believe that the javelin or the javelin-thrower or those who arrange the contest were more to blame, according to the most correct *logos*" (Gargarin and Woodruff, Protagoras fragment 30). Here is a *chrêmata* worthy of collaborative measurement—the accidental death of an Olympic athlete—which inspires Protagoras and Pericles to identify and evaluate all of the available appearances in order to make a determinate judgment strong enough to withstand and then overcome opposition. A notable absence from the possible *logoi*, of course, is that the javelin was guided by the hand of Apollo as retribution for the *hubris* of Epitimus, presumably from thinking he could throw a javelin better than the gods. Dismissing this account as irrelevant to human affairs, they instead engage in what appears to be the first documented case of Burkean pentadic analysis in which they compare the validity of agency, agent, and scene as bearing the primary responsibility of the act. And this analysis takes all day. This is the paradigmatic example of democratic politics—to collectively attend to the most pressing appearances at hand through the articulation, exchange, and competition of *logoi* until one *logos* emerges the champion like a Homeric hero emerging victorious from the bloody fray.

Despite Protagoras's similarities to Heraclitus in terms of his embrace of flux, his concern for appearances, his valorization of *logos,* and his irreverence toward the Homeric gods, he shows himself to be a fundamentally political rather than metaphysical thinker. When Heraclitus looks at the flux of experience, no particular appearance strikes him as so important as to render a particular judgment upon it. Appearances are only useful to stimulate the art of thought, the only art which is capable of dwelling on the Logos in its entirety. As Nussbaum observes, for Protagoras the opposite is true: "Protagoras, conservative and humanistic, wants a *technē* which stays close to the ordinary practice of deliberation."[28] For him, an art which stimulates a citizen to think but not to act, to contemplate but not to judge, to reflect but not to overcome, is useless for political affairs. Thinking is certainly important, and he and many of the Sophists were well known for making contributions to the field of knowledge. For instance, Cicero notes that Prodicus, Thrasymachus, and Protagoras all "spoke and wrote a great deal at that time about the nature of the physical world."[29] The Sophist Hippias alone—a reputed polymath—was said to have lectured on "astronomy, mathematics and geometry, genealogy, mythology and history, painting and sculpture, the function of letters, syllables, rhythms and musical scales."[30] But for Protagoras, as for all the Sophists, such thinking and research were primarily valued as preliminary stages of judgment and action in the *polis.* What mattered, in the end, was whether any of this specialized knowledge could ultimately be applied to cases like that of Epitimus. There geometry could inform us about the arc of the throw, psychology might give insight into the psychology of the thrower, and history might reveal whether the organizers of the event had violated the rules of tradition. In other words, in the political order of Protagorean humanism, one cultivated the individual life of the mind primarily to give added force and effectiveness to one's preferred *logos* that, if strong enough, would determine the direction of the social body.

With Protagoras, then, the relationship between rhetoric and power begins to be formalized within a structure of political ethics that undergirds the institutions of democracy. Although Protagoras does not use the word *rhetoric,* his use of the term *logos* clearly conveys the rhetorical notion of a persuasive account put forward within a symbolic environment in order to compete with and overcome opposing *logoi,* each of which is seeking to be the definitive account of and response to problematic appearances. And although none of the definitive fragments refers explicitly to power, the words Plato puts in Protagoras's mouth in the dialogue *Protagoras* is generally taken to be representative of his overall political endeavor. When asked to define his profession, he tells Socrates that he teaches "sound deliberation, both in domestic matters—how best to manage one's household, and in public affairs—how to become powerful [*dunatôtatoi*] in political speech [*legein*] and action" (319a). The word *dunatôtatoi* means "powerful," "influential," or "capable" and is a variant on the word *dynamis,* the Greek word which refers not only to political power but also to any latent potential (learned or innate) that can be actualized in future situations that present optimal stimuli and resources. *Dynamis* is, as Farrell defines it, a "potential for doing" and can apply equally to a tree or the wind as to a human being.[31] When Protagoras promises that his teaching will make an individual *dunatôtatoi* in political affairs, he therefore means that the skills he provides will give that individual the capacity to mobilize the bodies of others through the persuasiveness of one's *logos.* That is to say, he promises that through the mastery of rhetoric one will exercise power in a democracy.

Although many of Protagoras's statements still seem radical when glanced at from a distance, on collective examination they feel uncannily familiar. Indeed, it soon becomes clear that nothing is more conventional in a contemporary democracy then to appeal to these principles in practice. The Jeffersonian maxim concerning the "separation of church and state" which forms the basis of the establishment clause in the U.S. Bill of Rights is Protagoras's "concerning the gods" fragment enshrined in constitutional law. Whenever a citizen advocates for a cause on the basis of individual conscience or experience, rather than an appeal to established authority, he or she acts as an autonomous measure of things, irrespective of the content of the opinion. The casual acceptance of partisan division on even the most trivial of matters confronting the state indicates our acceptance that there will always be two sides to every issue. Political history and popular entertainment alike celebrate the moment when a solitary

individual turns the tables on the powerful through a creative inversion of traditional reasoning, which shows that we love nothing better than the dramatization of the victory of the weaker (but better) argument over the stronger (but
worse) one. Whether we acknowledge it or not, we live in a political culture
characterized by the axioms of Protagoras, a culture in which periods of stability are rare, the structures of hierarchy are always in flux, and rhetoric is the
medium by which men and women seek to measure and define the appearances
of their age within a struggle for power.

CHAPTER 5

Gorgias's *Helen* and the Powers of Action and Fabrication

Logos is a powerful master and achieves the most divine feats with the smallest and least evident body. It can stop fear, relieve pain, create joy, and increase pity.[1]

Logos appears in the Greek world as an ambiguous kind of tyrant. The phrase the Sophist Gorgias of Leontini (480–375 B.C.E.) uses to describe *logos* is *dynastes megas,* also interpreted as "mighty lord" or "great ruler." Yet the power (*dynamis*) it wields over its subjects is an unconventional one. The tyranny of Zeus controlled the bodies of both gods and men by possessing the commanding word (*kratos*) which directed and monopolized the means of violence (*bia*). The tyranny of *logos* eschews these crude methods which require such blunt tools. Its instrument is the word, an invisible medium consisting of the least evident matter yet whose effects are divine in quality and scope. Reminiscent of the effects that the words of Prometheus had upon Io, *logos* primarily controls its subjects by evoking and directing the passions (*pathē*). Pity and fear determine our orientation to things external to ourselves, causing us to draw towards them or flee from them, while pain and joy reflect our attitude toward our present state of experience, and predicts whether we wish to alter or maintain our situation. To control the passions is thus to control the will, and through the will, the body. In the tyranny of the *logos,* the chains of Hephaestus are no longer needed; the domination of the passions by the word creates a basis for power more permanent, forceful, and dedicated than that produced through iron or lightning.

Yet we fundamentally misunderstand the rule of *logos* if we believe that its goal is only to keep saying the same thing. That is the aim of the mortal tyrant, the ambitious human being who wishes to impose his thoughts and will upon a subject population. As pure medium, however, *logos* has no such ambition. The only thing its dynasty requires is that those who seek power must attain it, however temporarily, through the deployment of the *logos*. With *logos* replacing the physical body of the tyrant, power no longer emanates from a single center, enforced through the threat of violence; it is now decentralized, ubiquitous, and fluid. To seek power through the *logos* is to commit oneself to the practice of constant adjustment within a dynamic and competitive environment, in which no position goes uncontested and no hierarchy is sacred. The tyranny of *logos* does not command common assent to a single position; individual arguments will come and go. What matters is that power exists as an extension of *logos* itself, with the remaining influence of violence or convention being subordinate to that of the word.

Cloaked in the *ethos* of both liberator and dynast, *logos* in the fifth century B.C.E. promised to break the chains of inherited convention and emancipate its followers while at the same time boasting that its new regime would be even more dominating than its predecessor. But the nature of this domination would be different. As John Poulakos points out, "in one sense, *logos* deposed the tyranny of the tradition; in another, it imposed the tyranny of innovation."[2] Whereas conventional tyrants survived by restricting to a minimum the sphere of freedom in both action and speech, the tyranny of *logos* forced freedom upon its citizens, drawing them out of their homes to speak and be spoken to within the constant chatter of the assembly, the court, and the agora. For in this sophistical "logocracy," the "command of *logos* is the means par excellence to personal and political power."[3] But this freedom to speak was also a burden, because the new logocracy changed appearances faster than Heraclitus's river. To attain and maintain power thus required more than a single appeal to the masses backed by a bodyguard; it required constant adaptation to a changing environment, which in a logocracy means the invention of novel arguments that make the weaker one appear stronger and vice-versa. Yet whatever particular *logos* was deposed or enthroned, *logos* in general would always remain lord, causing its subjects to quiver, grimace, smile, and weep.

Gorgias's unapologetic valorization of the dynastic character of *logos,* rather than its democratic potential, reveals an attitude very different from that of Protagoras. Despite both being Sophists whose profession it was to theorize and instruct others in the relationship between rhetoric and power, Protagoras investigated this relationship as a political ethicist whereas Gorgias examined it with the technician's eye. Protagoras looked at the *polis* and saw citizens crafting *logoi* as a way to accrue power amongst themselves to effectively manage their affairs. Gorgias looked at the *polis* and saw power being manifested in every specific encounter between *logos* and a receptive mind. In other words, one gets the impression that discussions of democracy rather bored him. More an artist than an ethicist, more a scientist than a sage, Gorgias was fascinated with the way in which a clever turn of phrase could shock the ear, enrapture the mind, and move the body to unexpected and passionate action. Gorgias, more than any other Sophist, made it his life's work to diagnose this process and, by so doing, master it. Consequently, his teaching was based on a paradox. *Logos* was a *dynastes megas,* but through training and practice one could harness its power for oneself. According to Guthrie, Gorgias believed that "'the word' was a despot who could do anything, but like a slave of the lamp it would be at the service of those who took his courses."[4] This metaphor breaks down insofar as democracy makes lamps potentially available to everyone, but it is apt for at least this reason—Gorgias investigated *logos* as an engineer inspects an artifact, looking at it from all sides, taking it apart and putting it back together again, and testing its behavior in different contexts. One did not necessarily solicit the services of Gorgias to become a good citizen; one did so to become a master craftsman.

And a master craftsman he was. Of all the Older Sophists of the mid-fifth century B.C.E., including the likes of Protagoras, Prodicus, Hippias, Thrasymachus, and Antiphon, Gorgias was perhaps the most consummate performer and stylist. Known for his spectacular oratorical displays, in which he challenged the intellect with inventive arguments while seducing the ear with bold figurations, Gorgias possessed unmatched mastery of oratorical display and persuasion. Of course, like all the Older Sophists, Gorgias was unable to translate this skill directly into political influence for himself because his status as a Sicilian, and hence a non-citizen of Athens, excluded him from direct participation in what was the center of power in Greece. Instead, he became "an itinerant, practicing in various cities and giving public exhibitions of his skill at the great pan-Hellenic centres of Olympia and Delphi, and charged fees for his instruction and performances."[5] In fact, Gorgias did not even visit Athens until 427, three years after the start of the Peloponnesian War with Sparta, and was then already over fifty years old; nonetheless, it was said that he "took the city by storm with his novel style of oratory, as well as earning large sums by special performances and classes for the young."[6] His fame came to be so great that, after his death as a wealthy centenarian in 375 B.C.E., a statue was erected in his honor with the following inscription:

No mortal has yet found a nobler profession (*technê*) than Gorgias:
To train the soul for contests of excellence (*arête*)
His statue stands in the vale of Apollo,
A tribute not to wealth, but to the piety of his character.[7]

Despite being excluded from Athenian politics, then, Gorgias nonetheless had a significant impact on its political culture by training souls for the contests of excellence that constituted the activity of the democratic assemblies and courts across Greece. Apparently there was more than one citizen grateful to be given the secret to the lamp of *logos* which allowed him to participate as an active member of the fifth-century B.C.E. logocracy.

The clear reason that Gorgias enjoyed such enduring fame was that he possessed the earliest, most detailed, and most sophisticated understanding of the power (*dynamis*) of *logos* in the Classical Age.[8] Of the fragmentary remains of his work that we possess, one of his two extant texts, *Encomium of Helen,* stands out for its combination of dazzling compositional form and piercing psychological insight. Although not itself a theoretical treatise but rather a fictional speech in defense of the innocence of Helen of Troy, it was clearly written as a pedagogical tool to reveal to students the nature of *logos* and to provide a text suitable for imitation in actual practice. The speech functions as a model for how one might defend oneself in a court of law—namely, by attributing one's actions to forces outside oneself—while at the same time offering a detailed causal account of the effects that persuasive words and striking images have upon the human *psychē*. In the *Helen,* Gorgias focuses less on how *logos* is a medium of power, understood as the human capacity to act in concert, and more on how it is itself a power, understood as that which has a natural capacity to exert directed force. The underlying assumption is that only by understanding and then mastering the power (*dynamis*) of *logos* can one even hope to accrue to oneself and one's allies the political power of the commanding word (*kratos*).

Although likely not in the design of the speech, *Helen* also exemplifies two distinct forms of the *dynamis* of *logos* which find expression in political life: the power of making (*poiesis*) and the power of acting (*praxis*). On the one hand, the *Helen* looks at *logos* from a distance and describes the mechanisms by which rhetoric can fabricate an audience through words, molding and manipulating it into an ideal form envisioned by the speaker. On the other hand, the publication of the *Helen* is a deliberate action on the part of Gorgias, a *logos* composed and disseminated both for his own gratification and as a contribution to the ongoing conversation of Greek culture. In other words, the *Helen* demonstrates the power of *poiesis* insofar as it is a fabricated object (a written text) which in turn articulates the methods by which *logos* can fabricate a product external to itself (the will of Helen); but it also exemplifies the power of *praxis* insofar as the sheer act of creating and expressing a *logos* gives an individual the capacity to satisfy intrinsic standards of excellence while playing some meaningful part in the drama of human history. One of Gorgias's most significant contributions to rhetorical theory is the implicit suggestion that both of these inherent capacities of *logos* must be cultivated and balanced to sustain a healthy rhetorical culture. Rather than set one form of power against another, we must always be both makers and actors. For in the world of Gorgias, human beings acquire and maintain political power only because they are unique amongst the gods' creations in being able to channel the power of *logos* and to act with excellence in a world which is constantly being remade according to our own vision.

That the *Encomium of Helen* is not merely an educational text but a rhetorical one is announced in its opening prelude to the actual defense of Helen. Gorgias uses this written *logos,* or prose account, as an assault upon the Homeric tradition of *mythos,* or the oral recitation and poetic performance of epic tales. Consistent with the overall sophistical endeavor to make *mythos* "an object of analysis—a text that could be analyzed, criticized, and altered," Gorgias makes the mythical Helen the "defendant" in his fictional court speech.[9] Helen, of course, was the most beautiful woman in Greece and the wife of the Greek king Menelaus who abandoned her homeland and husband to marry the handsome Trojan prince Paris, a choice said to be the cause of the Trojan War. Gorgias summarizes her reputation: "Among those who listen to the poets a single-voiced, single-minded conviction has arisen about this woman, the notoriety of whose name is now a reminder of disasters" (DK11.1). But this age of *mythos* has come to an end, for it is the intent of Gorgias to "bring reason (*logos*) to the debate, eliminate the cause of her bad reputation, demonstrate that her detractors are lying, reveal the truth, and put an end to ignorance" (DK11.1). The *Helen* is therefore more than simply a playful defense of a mythic character; it is an attempt to replace the repetitive drone of the chorus of lying and ignorant poets with a lively debate of rational accounts seeking the truth of history.

At the center of this corrective project is to replace the traditional moralistic reasoning of the poets with a contemporary psychological, secular, and naturalistic account of human motivation. For in the Homeric worldview, the painful accidents which befell men and women were almost always seen as divine retribution for some intentional act of *hubris,* in Helen's case for being too beautiful and too proud. What Gorgias does in the *Helen* is to replace this "single-voiced, single-minded conviction" with a many-faceted hypothetical account based on rational inquiry. His defense of Helen is therefore based on her action not perhaps being due to any flaw in her own character, or even her conscious choice, but having been brought about by one of four external causes: necessity (*anankē*), violence (*bia*), love (*eros*), and speech (*logos*). Choose any of those causes, and her acquittal must follow. For "whether she did what she did, invaded by love, persuaded by speech, impelled by force or compelled by divine necessity, she escapes all blame entirely" (DK11.20). But if this is the case, then centuries of Homeric mythic tradition stands convicted of false accusation based on a mindless repetition of lies. So be it, says Gorgias. The time has come for *logos* to "dispel the injustice of blame and ignorance of opinion" (DK11.21).

This assault on the pieties of tradition only continues when Gorgias gives perfunctory attention to the first possible cause. By necessity (*anankē*), Gorgias does not refer to physical necessity but the necessity of fate as dictated by the will of the gods. But if the gods made her do it, then the fault of her action lies with the gods and not with Helen: "for by nature the stronger is not restrained by the weaker but the weaker is ruled and led by the stronger: the stronger leads, and the weaker follows. Now, a god is stronger than a human in strength, in wisdom, and in other respects; and so if blame must be attached to fortune and God, then Helen must be detached from her ill repute" (DK11.6). Employing a clever use of antithesis, Gorgias effectively shows that the poets cannot have it both ways. They cannot blame Helen and praise the gods when it is clear that the gods have manipulated her will like a puppet. Either the poets have to eliminate the gods from their stories in order to affix personal responsibility to her actions, or they must acknowledge that the gods themselves are immoral in forcing human beings to commit acts which violated of the accepted standards of moral behavior.

Gorgias takes slightly longer to dispense with the second causal account of force (*bia*), but only because he wishes to even more definitively condemn violence as an acceptable means to an end, particularly when it comes to the relationships between men and women. Although most readings of the *Helen* pass quickly over his treatment of force, the strong language he uses suggests that Gorgias is actually passing a very specific judgment on the lingering cultural acceptance (still common today) that the victim was responsible and the assaulter blameless for the act of rape. He writes:

> If she was forcibly abducted and unlawfully violated and unjustly assaulted, it is clear that her abductor, her assaulter, engaged in crime; but she who was abducted and assaulted encountered misfortune. Thus, the undertaking undertaken by the barbarian was barbarous in word and law and deed and deserves blame in word, loss of rights in law, and punishment in deed. But she who was violated, from her country separated, from her friends isolated, surely deserves compassion rather than slander. For he did and she suffered terrible things. It is right to pity her but hate him. (DK11.7)

The prosecutorial tone Gorgias takes in this passage is unmistakable. He does not wish simply to acquit Helen of responsibility; he wishes to strip away all of the rights, reputation, and property of the rapist. Yet once again, blame for this barbarous attitude toward women falls to the Homeric poets, who for centuries have raised Greek children on Zeus abduction and rape stories and have endeavored to evoke pity for Achilles when Agamemnon arrogantly decides to steal the hero's Trojan sex slave away from him. The glorification of Odysseus's Penelope and Hector's Andromache notwithstanding, the treatment of women in the Homeric tradition is a veritable show of horrors. With his treatment of *bia,* Gorgias makes a sweeping condemnation of this attitude and all those who have propagated it through the mytho-poetic tradition.[10]

The tone of the speech changes dramatically, however, when Gorgias considers *logos* and *eros* as causes for her actions. *Ananke* and *bia* had been considered largely to embarrass the Homeric poets for their ignorant and barbarous treatment of Helen that made her responsible for being the victim of divine manipulation and barbaric violence. His discussions of *logos* and *eros,* by contrast, represent incredibly detailed investigations of how words and images interact with the faculties of the *psyche* to arouse the emotions, appeal to the intelligence, and move the will. Whereas necessity and violence were dispensed with in a handful of well-crafted sentences, amounting, when combined, to perhaps a tenth of the entire text, the accounts of speech and love combine to over two-thirds, with *logos* having the greater percentage. What we are provided in the second two causes is therefore not an attempt to affix blame but to understand a process.

Why Gorgias pairs *logos* and *eros* in his causal analysis of human motivation is that in most cases they are both equal players in determination of human will and judgment. They represent the influence of the two dominant senses on the *psyche*—the ear and the eye, respectively. Reflecting the materialistic and naturalistic accounts of his age, Gorgias wants to undermine the authority of divine or magical explanations and advance in their place psychological and physical ones. In other words, he wants to make appearances themselves causal factors in human judgment, depending of course on how they impact our sensory apparatus and affect our emotional and cognitive faculties. Consequently, for him, even *logos* is not experienced first as a word, reason, or account; it is encountered first as sound striking the ear or images striking the eye. Similarly, *eros* represents a passion to possess and be possessed by another which is produced through the effect of sight rather than any spontaneous upwelling of the heart. From Gorgias's perspective, Protagoras may therefore be granting human beings too much agency when he declares that man is the measure of all things; a more adequate account might be that human beings are subject to the influence of appearances, either produced by nature (*physis*) or by art (*techne*).

This is why *logos* is a *dynastes megas:* it controls our *psychē* through its power to alter appearances through the word.

To understand the nature of the power of *logos*, Gorgias begins with the individual who had been the foremost conduit of power in Greece for centuries —the rhapsode. Their art of poetry (*poiesis*), which he defines as "*logos* with meter," clearly displays the power of *logos* to anyone who witnesses one of their oral performances of one of the Homeric epics: "to its listeners poetry brings a fearful shuddering, a tearful pity, and a grieving desire, while through its words the soul feels its own feelings for good and bad fortune in the affairs and lives of others" (DK11.9). Here is perhaps one of the most succinct descriptions of the mytho-poetic consciousness, a consciousness characterized by immediate empathetic identification with the characters being embodied and performed by the rhapsode. From this example, Gorgias identifies the first unique power of *logos:* to create a unity of feeling through the poetic dramatization of human struggle, suffering, and triumph. For better or worse, *logos* has the capacity to expand our *psychē* beyond the bounds of our skin and produce a feeling of community by partaking in a common soul.

The second power of *logos* builds on this community of feeling by being able to produce what he calls "illusions of mind and delusions of judgment" which can persuade members of the community to act in this way or that way (DK11.10). Here Gorgias looks beyond the rhapsodes to the "false speech" of traditional practitioners of witchcraft and magic, in which "sacred incantations with words inject pleasure and reject pain, for in associating with the opinion of the mind, the power of an incantation enchants, persuades, and alters it through bewitchment" (DK11.10). What interests Gorgias here is less the generation of shared *pathos* than the capacity for language to call forth images (illusions) in the mind and associate them with feelings of pleasure or pain in order to produce a judgment (delusion). What makes this persuasion (*peitho*) possible is the finite capacities of the human mind: "For if all men on all subjects had memory of the past, <understanding> of the present, and foresight into the future, speech would not be the same in the same way; but as it is, to remember the past, to examine the present, or to prophesy the future is not easy; and so most men on most subjects make opinion an advisor to their minds" (DK11.11). Human incapacities thus make the capacities of *logos* even stronger, for it is through *logos* that we acquire opinions which grant us solace for the past, security for the present, and hope for the future when no other resources are available. *Logos,* that is to say, fills the gaps in our ignorance with attractive illusions that make us see a whole where there is simply a scatter of fragmentary pieces.

These two capacities, to create emotional identification and produce rational persuasion, together represent the power of *logos* as a form of making (*poiesis*). Although often used, as with Gorgias, to narrowly denote the art of poetry, the realm of *poiesis* more generally includes what Arendt describes as "the whole field of the arts and crafts, where men work with instruments and do something not for its own sake but in order to produce something else."[11] In the fabrication process of making, everything "is judged in terms of suitability and usefulness for the desired end, and for nothing else."[12] The fundamental attitude of one who makes is thus reminiscent of the *anthrôpos*-measure doctrine of Protagoras; it is an attitude which sees everything as raw material, as if it "belonged to the class of *chrēmata,* of use objects."[13] A tree is thus potential wood, wood is a potential chair, and a chair is a potential resting place. At each stage, material presents itself as a means to be used for an instrumental end, and every end offers itself as a means in a new situation. So, too, with *logos. Logos* presents itself as a resource for creating useful artifacts, which in turn manipulate the emotions and opinions of people in order to fabricate an audience which can act as an instrument of the speaker's will. Accordingly, Gorgias says that persuasion "has the same power (*dynamis*), but not the same form as necessity (*anankē*)" (DK11.12). *Logos,* in other words, has the same power to manipulate material for an end, but it does so by generating an inner compulsion through persuasion rather than imposing an outer compulsion through force or violence.

What is new with respect to this power of *logos* during the time of Gorgias is *what* is made and *how.* Notably, Gorgias does not leave his students to contemplate only the arts of poetry, witchcraft, and magic to learn the power of *logos.* He begins with these only to show that its power is inherent in all forms of speech, no matter how archaic. But his explicit command to students who wish to learn how *logos* "molds the mind (*psychē*) as it wishes" is to study its more modern manifestations: "One must first study the arguments of astronomers, who replace opinion with opinion: displacing one but implanting another, they make incredible, invisible matters apparent to the eyes of opinion. Second, compulsory debates with words, where a single speech to a large crowd pleases and persuades because written with skill, not spoken with truth. Third, contests of philosophical arguments, where it is shown that speed of thought also makes it easy to change a conviction based on opinion" (DK11.13). The central effect of these types of arguments remains continuous with the arts of witchcraft and magic insofar as their goal is to manipulate opinion through persuasion; however, their scope and methods are different. Witchcraft and magic relied on sacred incantations and other ritualistic symbols to peer into the past, present, and future of particular individuals which brings them to "perilous and uncertain good fortune" (DK11.11); astronomical, legal, and philosophical debates employ complex logical argumentation to persuade large crowds to make binding judgments on vital matters of nature, politics, law, and justice. In other words, *logos* of the fifth century has cast aside its need for "meter" to entrance and delude a particular audience and has embraced prose argumentation to make sweeping claims which potentially might challenge and change deeply held convictions of an entire culture.

In his metaphor which concludes his discussion of *logos,* Gorgias solidifies his materialistic view of persuasion by comparing the effect of *logos* to that of a drug. He says that the "power (*dynamis*) of speech (*logos*) has the same effect on the disposition of the soul (*psychē*) as the disposition of drugs on the nature of bodies. Just as different drugs draw forth different humors from the body—some putting a stop to disease, others to life—so too with words: some cause pain, others joy, some strike fear, some stir an audience to boldness, some benumb and bewitch the soul with evil persuasion" (DK11.14). With the exception of boldness and evil persuasion, this list of effects mirrors almost exactly the one given to prove that *logos* is a *dynastes megas.* For Gorgias, *logos* is a portable pharmacy capable of dispensing an infinite number of potions for those capable of mixing the right ingredients. What makes it a dynast is that, when a powerful drug meets a receptive body, persuasion is compulsory and inevitable. In short, the right words striking the right ear at the right time produce illusions in the mind to which a body reacts with pleasure and pain so as to be deluded into a judgment which makes it fearful, bold, joyous, or numb, sometimes for the sake of its life, but sometimes as a cause of its death. Whatever the outcome, one thing is certain: *logos* is a powerful lord.

Yet *logos* is not *all*-powerful. Gorgias, whose profession as an itinerant teacher of the arts of *logos* gives him every reason to boast as much, concludes *Helen* not with a celebration of the power of speech but with an extended treatment of the effects that striking visual appearances have on the *psychē* quite apart from language or even intentional design. He begins by calling this fourth motivating factor the power of *eros,* but it soon becomes clear he does not mean simply emotional affection. Helen did not leave Troy because she believed she had found her soul mate in Paris and desired their two hearts to be one. What he means by *eros* is an irresistible physical response to beautiful appearances that draws us toward them: "By nature sight grieves for some things and longs for others, and many things make many people desire and long for many deeds and many bodies" (DK11.18). The phrase "by nature" is significant here, for Gorgias asserts that many appearances come directly from nature (*physis*) and affect us without conscious design. Paris, after all, cannot help being handsome. When *eros* overpowered Helen, it snared her mind on its own, "not prepared by thoughts, [but] under the compulsion of love, not the provision of art [*technē*]" (DK11.19). *Eros,* then, is a compulsive response produced when the eye meets a pleasing appearance: "so if Helen's eye, pleased by Alexander's [Paris's] body, transmitted to her soul an eagerness and striving for love, why is that surprising?" (DK11.19).

Most people believe they are in control of their own emotions, thoughts, and behaviors; that is, they believe they are not slaves of appearances. Yet Gorgias severely complicates this assumption. According to Gorgias, appearances force themselves upon us because of their recalcitrant nature. Asserting a kind of metaphysical realism, he asserts that "whatever we see has the nature, not the one we wish, but whatever each happens to have. And by seeing the mind is molded even in its character" (DK11.15). For him, what constitutes an "appearance" is the way in which a thing's nature partially reveals itself to us (or perhaps more accurately *forces* itself upon us) by impacting our sensory apparatus, which triggers certain emotional and cognitive reactions. The process by which we fall in love with appearances is thus identical with the process by which appearances strike fear and terror into our bodies: it happens automatically and immediately: "As soon as men in war arm their bodies against the enemy with armor of bronze and iron—some for defense, some for attack—if the sight sees this, it is shaken and shakes the mind, so that men often flee in panic from danger that lies in the future" (DK11.16). The way Gorgias structures the causal sequence of events in the sentence is telling. The act of donning bronze and iron armor generates a physical appearance which can be seen from a distance by the opposing army, whose minds then interpret it as a recognizable object. This object, being the "invading army," connotes through inference certain consequences in the future, namely a violent clashing of arms and painful, bloody death, that when pictured in the imagination generate an emotional response of panic that causes them to flee as if the enemy were already at hand. In other words, the mind reacts to the senses which are in turn compelled by appearances which emanate from the nature of things. Rather than being the starting point of action, the mind becomes the endpoint of *re*action. Indeed, appearances often so dominate the mind that many "who have seen fearful things, have lost their present purpose in the present moment, so thoroughly does fear extinguish and expel thought; and many have fallen into useless labors, terrible diseases, and incurable madness, so thoroughly does sight engrave on the mind images of things that are seen" (DK11.17). And as love is the counterpart of fear, the same can be said for *eros:* that even a glimpse of a single beautiful face can extinguish thought and condemn a person to incurable madness dwelling upon an image of beauty that he or she can never hope to possess.

But this power of appearances over the human *psychē* is not beyond artistic control, as it first might seem. Although Gorgias seeks to acquit Helen based on the compulsion of *eros* stimulated by the accidental encounter with the beauty of Paris's body, he fully acknowledges that certain appearances are intentionally crafted by human design to produce specific responses: "Whenever painters fashion one perfect bodily form from many colors and bodies, they delight in the sight; the creation (*poiesis*) of statues and the production of works of art provide a sweet sickness for the eyes" (DK11.18). Although the date of *Helen* is impossible to know for certain, one is reminded of the elaborate sculptures of Phidias which adorned the Parthenon, the majestic temple atop the acropolis Pericles commissioned in 447 B.C.E. as a symbol of Athenian power. Although the Parthenon was not itself made of *logos,* its construction was clearly intended as a kind of visual rhetoric, a "visual and spatial text in marble and bronze which Athenians (and non-Athenians) represented themselves and their ideologies."[14] Similarly, both Helen and Paris worked hard to maintain their beautiful physical appearances, carefully adorning themselves in elegant clothes and cosmetics in order to produce desired effects.

An even closer examination reveals yet a more intimate relationship between *logos* and appearances. On the one hand, it is clear that Gorgias separates the world of *phainomena* and *logos,* of sense perception and language. In his more theoretical treatise, *On Not Being,* he says that "someone who speaks does not say <a sound> or a color, but a word, so that a color cannot be thought, nor can a sound, but it is only possible to see a color and hear a sound" (DK3). It is impossible, then, for two people to directly communicate to another, through language, the content of a particular experience, "because things are not words and because no one has the same thing in mind as another" (DK3). On the other hand, Gorgias clearly believes that *logos,* which exists in the cognitive realm of meanings, can classify certain *types* of appearances as certain *types* of things, and that these meanings can be shared. For instance, although the way the glint of bronze armor and the sound of clashing metal might strike the ears of each member of an opposing army differently, all of them understand these appearances to be the same thing—an opposing military force preparing for attack or defense. However, a child inexperienced with war and unfamiliar with Homeric tales of battle would not flee in panic like the grown men around her but stand fascinated at the strange sight. It is the *meaning* of the appearances which causes the fear in the hearts of men, not the appearances themselves, for appearances have no essential meaning. As he says in *On Not Being:* "The nature of true things is not evident [to the senses]" (DK3). But if this is the case, then *logos* must supply the absent meaning for appearances if they are to be more than ephemeral surface irritations of the retina or the eardrum.

This complex relationship between appearances and *logos,* in which both are causal factors in human agency and neither fully dominates the other, is what ultimately provides the foundation for the power of *logos* as a type of *poiesis,* a form of fabrication. As sentient creatures, our senses are constantly buffeted, against our will, by an infinite variety of appearances, most of which escape the realm of meanings. But certain types of appearances we come to recognize as significant, and through the power of *logos* we give them the name and make them into a "thing," a *chrēmata*. Characterizing the attitude of Gorgias, Consigny writes that "we do indeed speak of things in the world, but these 'things' are made possible and thereby fabricated through our routine practices in various rhetorical situations; and the meaning of our words lies in the use to which we put them in everyday life."[15] As with Heraclitus's river, we never encounter the same thing twice in the same way, including the people we love. Through rhetorical practice, however, we are able to speak "as if" that thing or person were the same in order to create a semblance of order on which shared meanings and practices can be established. That is to say, just as an astronomer uses persuasion to make a distant glimmer of light into a divine being, a sign of future events, or a hot stone in the sky, *logos* represents a way of fabricating things out of the flux of past and present appearances through the imposition of cognitive meanings capable of regulating collective practices in the name of a desired good, a good which itself is revealed through future appearances.

Through the consideration of the effects of *eros*, Gorgias thus implicitly adds a third capacity to the power of *logos* as a form of making—the capacity to constitute the objects, events, and people in the world by investing appearances with stable and communicative meanings. In summary, *logos* functions as a vehicle for rhetorical fabrication when it constitutes a situation by meaningfully transforming present appearances in such a way that provokes a combination of fear and desire, when it identifies an audience as possessing shared qualities and emotions which make it a unified group, and when it persuades that audience by manipulating opinion and producing a shared illusion of future outcomes which promises to give pleasure and avoid pain. In the *Helen,* the power that *logos* attains when it pairs with the power of *eros* is exemplified in the opening paragraphs, when Gorgias presents this causal account of how Helen's flight from Greece started the Trojan War: "Many were the erotic passions she aroused in many men, and her one body brought many bodies full of great ambition for great deeds; some had abundant wealth, some the glory of an old noble lineage, some the vigor of personal valor, and some the power of acquired wisdom. All came for love that desires to conquer and from unconquerable desire for honor" (DK11.4).

This description proves first and foremost that appearances matter. Helen's beauty cannot be manufactured by the word. It is something which strikes the human eye and arouses the passions without the need for a description or a name. But a war is something different. The passions her body aroused in the bodies of men did not intrinsically point in the direction of organizing a ten-year campaign against Troy. This was the effect of a *logos* that constituted the appearance of Helen's abandonment of Menelaus to be an affront to the entire Greek culture, that identified the disparate kings of Greece as a unified army, and which persuaded them that victory across the sea would satiate their unconquerable desire for honor. In other words, *logos* needed *eros* to provide the passionate force necessary for effective persuasion, and *eros* needed *logos* to tell it where to go and what to do to satisfy its desire. It was therefore the combined power of *eros* and *logos* which "made" the Trojan War.

Yet the *Helen* offers one last turn which reveals an entirely new power of *logos,* the power of action (*praxis*). In the closing line of the text, Gorgias suddenly reveals his own hand in its production, saying: "I wished to write this speech for Helen's encomium and my amusement [*paignion*]" (DK11.21). The word *paignion* is also translated as "plaything," "toy," "sport," or "game," and in the Greek oratorical tradition tends to be associated with what Consigny calls "those playful encomia of mice or baldness, works that stand as playful doubles of serious encomia."[16] With this statement, Gorgias appears to call into question the truth and validity of everything he has just asserted. Rather than presenting himself as a didactic intellectual concerned with instilling wisdom in his students, he appears as a self-involved artist primarily interested in the pleasure of being able to take a weaker argument and make it the stronger one. As John Poulakos notes, "Gorgias offers a splendid demonstration of the way in which a widely held opinion (*kreitton*) can be shown to be groundless (*hetton*)," thus showing how "no argument or position, no matter how entrenched, can dominate the mental world of an audience once and for all."[17] Far from being interested in constituting any situation, identifying any audience, or persuading people of anything, Gorgias simply wants to turn arguments on their heads because he can, because it puts on a good show for his own gratification and perhaps the gratification of others.

The reason this represents the power of action has nothing to do with Gorgias composing this text with the bodily movements of the hand. For Burke, sheer bodily movement is not action but "motion," a term which refers to the "nonsymbolic operations of nature," such as sleeping, breathing, or eating.[18] In contradistinction, "action" always means *symbolic* action, and is thus "a term for the kind of behavior possible to a typically symbol-using animal (such as man)."[19] Action thus requires motion, just as a dance requires the movements of the body or a speech requires the movements of the vocal cords, but it also requires that motion to be capable of being interpreted by a community as a symbolic gesture whose meaning exceeds the physical effects. Along the same lines, Arendt defines action as those intentional movements which draw from a reservoir of prior communicative understanding and are intended to leave a trace in the collective memory of a plurality of others. Arendt says that genuine action can therefore "manifest itself only in communities, where the many who live together have their intercourse both in word and in deed regulated by a great number of *rapports*—laws, customs, habits, and the like."[20] Without these rapports, no common understanding is possible, and actions intended to convey meaning are stripped of their symbolic significance and become just one more sequence of appearances in the flux of nature.

With respect to *logos,* then, the power to act represents the capacity to appear before others, directly or indirectly, as the author of a new symbolic meaning which has the capacity to contribute in unpredictable ways to the collective conversation of a community. Unlike fabrication, whose goal is to produce an admirable end product whose essential characteristics are reliability and durability, action focuses only on beginnings and the intrinsic satisfaction of performing with excellence before oneself and others. Arendt thus defines the essential characteristic of action as "natality," or that "the new beginning inherent in birth can make itself felt in the world only because the newcomer possesses the capacity of beginning something anew, that is, of acting."[21] Action does not assimilate material together for a determinate end but to gather people together in order to witness a beginning whose end cannot be foreseen. Arendt explains: "In contradistinction to fabrication, where the light by which to judge the finished product is provided by the image or model perceived beforehand by the craftsman's eye, the light that illuminates processes of action, and therefore all historical processes, appears only at their end, frequently when all the participants are dead. Action reveals itself fully only to the storyteller, that is, to the backward glance of the historian, who indeed always knows better what it was all about than the participants."[22]

Within the framework of action, rhetoric is judged less by what it makes than what it initiates and expresses how it is expressed. Rather than just an implement of persuasion, Arendt explains, rhetoric for the Classical Greek mind meant the art of "answering, talking back and measuring up to whatever happened or was done," of "finding the right words at the right moment, quite apart from the information or communication they may convey."[23] In this sense, rhetoric as a practice shared many similarities with other common forms of action, like the staging of the theatrical performance, the spectacle of athletic competition, and the negotiating and selling that went on in the marketplace (*agora*). In each of these spheres, deeds are performed within an ongoing and continuous arc of human interactions in which every action is a reaction and every reaction "strikes out on its own and affects others," never knowing where these actions might lead.[24]

When Gorgias refers to the *Helen* as a *paignion,* he is not belittling the importance of the text; he is rather expressing his sheer joy in actualizing the power to act within the sphere of the new logocracy. For in the end, citizens of a logocracy had to obey only one dictum—that whatever else one desired or felt obliged to do, their essential duty was to speak and to listen to *logos.* For Sophists like Gorgias, there was no contradiction between composing a speech with the desire to fabricate some part of the world according to one's own preferred

vision and performing the speech for the sheer pleasure of beginning something new. One can, in fact, have it both ways. According to John Poulakos,
the Sophists believed that "words are not only instruments of representation
or vehicles of meaning but also actions performed on stages of their own making."[25] Rhetoric was thus a multifaceted practice that enabled citizens not only
to participate in making and remaking their own culture, but to bring people
together to bear witness to *logos* delivered with excellence and performed in the
spirit of play. For while the power to make provides us the capacity to leverage
control over our environment, the power to act reminds us that total control
is an illusion, that political life is partly a game, and that sometimes the most
worthwhile moments in life come upon us when we feel that we have contributed something new to the ongoing drama of history which continues as long
as action is possible in a common world.[26]

For an example of the power of *logos* in action we need go no further than the
other extant text of Gorgias, the *Defense of Palamedes*. In this fictional defense,
Gorgias has clearly chosen to defend the hero with whom he feels the most
kinship. According to Greek myth, Palamedes was one of the most skilled and
intelligent of the Homeric heroes, the Promethean inventor of number, weights,
and measures; draughts; winemaking; military tactics; and most important, the
alphabet, the technology which makes writing and written laws possible. Yet
despite his virtue and talent, the Greeks condemned him as a traitor and stoned
him to death. Here is the Roman poet Virgil describing his fate in the *Aeneid*:

> Report of Palamedes may have reached you,
> Scion of Bels's line, a famous man
> Who gave commands against the war. For this,
> On a trumped-up charge, on perjured testimony,
> The Greeks put him to death—but now they mourn him,
> Now he has lost the light.[27]

The reason for his death was a deception. Palamedes had been sent by King
Agamemnon to retrieve Odysseus to fight in the Trojan War, but instead of
encountering the noble king and warrior of the Odyssey, Palamedes found a
crazed-looking Odysseus plowing his fields with salt. Believing this insane
behavior to be a mere deception to excuse him from fighting in the war, Palamedes puts Odysseus's son, Telemachus, in front of the plow, thereby causing
Odysseus to stop and reveal his sanity. For this act, Odysseus never forgives
him. When Palamedes later advises the Greek to return home from the war
prior to complete victory, Odysseus takes the opportunity to accuse Palamedes

of treason, hiding gold and a forged letter from the Trojan King Priam in his tent. Unable to mount a defense in a proper trial, Palamedes is convicted and executed under the rule of archaic law.

As in the *Helen,* Gorgias uses the *Palamedes* to bring the reason (*logos*) to a traditional debate and to restore the honor of one who has been falsely blamed and ignorantly dishonored; but this time he occupies the voice of the participant, Palamedes, instead of taking the perspective of a critical observer. Consequently, this fictional speech more closely imitates an actual forensic argument in a court of law. Not surprisingly, then, we find the fictional Palamedes making use of the three capacities of *logos* as a form of making. For most of the body of the speech, he constitutes the relevant facts of the situation, calling forth specific appearances already known to his audience and transforming them into "things" which support his innocence. For instance, he refutes the accusation in part because it would have been impossible for any accomplices to have slipped across enemy lines for him to accomplish the deed: "In a camp men live outdoors under arms, and in those circumstances everyone sees everything, and everyone is seen by everyone. It was thus completely impossible for me to do any of these things in any way" (DK11a.12). In this case, of course, he appeals to appearances in order to make other appearances impossible, but the end result of this and many similar types of proofs is the same—the fabrication of the details of a situation in the mind of the audience.

Although the majority of the speech consists of similar types of refutations of fact, the appeal to identification and persuasion appears powerfully at the end. With the critical irony of one who already knows how the story turned out, Gorgias has Palamedes conclude:

> My last words to you are about you, and when I have said them, I shall end my defense. Pity and entreaties and the intercession of friends are useful when judgment takes place before a mob. But among you, who are the foremost of the Greeks in fact and in reputation, I should not persuade you with the aid of friends or entreaties or pity. I must escape this charge by making justice very clear and showing you the truth, not by deceiving you. You must not pay more attention to words than to deeds, or prefer accusations to proofs, or consider a short time to be wiser judge than a long time, or think slander more credible than experience. In all things good men should take great precautions against committing an error, and even more so when matters are irremediable, for these can be controlled by foresight, but are incurable by hindsight. Such things are at issue whenever men judge on a capital charge, as is now the case before you. So if it were possible to make the truth of actions clear and evident to listeners through words, a decision

based on what has been said would now be easy. But since this is not so, safeguard my body, wait for a while longer, and make your decision with truth. (DK11a)

In defense of his innocence, Palamedes makes full use of the remaining two capacities of *logos* as a form of making. First he creates a common identification between himself and his audience by categorizing them all as virtuous Greeks whose task is to pursue the truth in the name of honor. Then, based on this identification, he persuades them that it is in everyone's best interest to examine the evidence of appearances through the resources of foresight and reason rather than to make impulsive emotional judgments based on tribal loyalties. The combined effect of the strategies, he hopes, is to use *logos* to alter their attitude toward appearances so that they can see his innocence revealed through the very nature of the situation.

Of course, all contemporaneous readers of Gorgias's fictional speech know how it turned out. And so we find that the *Palamedes,* like the *Helen,* has its own rhetorical function. For what Gorgias has done is rewrite the tragic history of the Trojan War as if its heroes had carried democratic institutions with them to the foreign shores. When Palamedes speaks, he does not address a vengeful mob led by a hated enemy; he addresses a jury of his peers who have taken on the responsibility for making a judgment on a matter of justice by bringing *logos* to the deliberations rather than pathetic appeals and heroic bluster. And here we see the power of action given its fullest expression as a democratic virtue. For what the Homeric heroes neglected to account for is that their judgment was itself a form of action that began a new story that would continue after their deaths. Unfortunately, for them, the story was not a happy one. Palamedes thus foreshadows their fate in the subsequent narratives of the storyteller:

You run a great risk that by seeming to be unjust you will cast off one reputation and take on another; but good men prefer death to a shameful reputation, for the one is the end of life, the other a disease for life. If you kill me unjustly, it will be evident to many; for I am not unknown, and your wickedness will be known and evident to all Greeks. For this injustice you, not the accuser, will be blamed in everyone's eyes, since the outcome of the trial is in your hands. There could be no greater error than this; for if you judge unjustly, you will not only err against me and my parents, but by doing so you will be in charge of a terrible, ungodly, unjust, unlawful deed: you will kill a comrade in arms, your helper and Greece's benefactor. You will be Greeks killing a Greek, with no proof of evident injustice or credible accusation. (DK11a.35–36)

Considering the tragic fate of Palamedes, this is a damning indictment of archaic forms of justice. In rewriting history, Gorgias speaks to the ghosts of archaic tradition, forcing them to emerge from their caves into the open spaces of the *polis* to be seen and judged for their actions. This space, of course, does not guarantee the truth; it only guarantees that the truth will have a chance to reveal itself before being crushed under a hail of stones or a fury of lightning. For Gorgias, then, one of the most important powers of *logos* is simply to give all citizens the same opportunity that Palamedes should have been given—the power to act in public with honor and with excellence, knowing that whatever they do will be preserved in collective memory.

CHAPTER 6

Thucydides and the
Political History of Power

We did not gain this empire by force. It came to us at a time when you were unwilling to fight on to the end against the Persians. At this time our allies came to us of their own accord and begged us to lead them. It was the actual course of events which first compelled us to increase our power to its present extent: fear of Persia was our chief motive, although afterwards we thought, too, of our own honor and our own interest. Finally there came a time when we were surrounded by enemies, when we had already crushed some revolts, when you had lost the friendly feelings that you used to have for us and had turned against us and begun to arouse our suspicion: at this point it was clearly no longer safe for us to risk letting our empire go, especially as any allies that left us would go over to you. And when tremendous dangers are involved no one can be blamed for looking to his own interest. . . . So it is with us. We have done nothing extraordinary, nothing contrary to human nature in accepting an empire when it was offered to us and then refusing to give it up. Three very powerful motives prevent us from doing so—security, honor, and self-interest. And we're not the first to act in this way. Far from it. It has always been a rule that the weak should be subject to the strong; and besides, we consider that we are worthy of our power. Up till the present moment you, too, used to think that we were; but now, after calculating your own interest, you are beginning to talk in terms of right and wrong. Considerations of this kind have never turned people aside from the opportunities of aggrandizement offered by superior strength.[1]

When the historian Thucydides (460–395 B.C.E.) wrote his inquiry into the causes and consequences of the Peloponnesian War between Athens and Sparta (431–404 B.C.E.), he created the first systematic, empirical study of the relationship between rhetoric and power. For him, political speeches represented neither expressions of personal character nor creative exercises in persuasive artistry; they were first and foremost vehicles by which existing structures of power were recognized in actuality, compared in possibility, justified on principle, and channeled through action. Thus, when the Athenian representatives step before the Spartan assembly in 432 B.C.E. to dissuade them from declaring war on Athens, they do not waste time mouthing platitudes or evading the issue with decorative phrases; they boldly recognize the fact of their own power, compare it with the relative weakness of their opponents, justify their position based on the laws of human nature, and channel their power through military aggression and political intimidation. Everything there is to know about the structural basis for Athenian imperial motivation can thus be read from their rhetoric. Thucydides presents rhetoric as being a necessary and logical reaction to situational conditions which naturally compel human beings to engage in symbolic action for the sake of maintaining and constituting their own power.

Like all the orations presented in his history, the one by the Athenian representatives does not reflect what was actually said, but is a construction of Thucydides's own well-informed imagination. But this does not bother Thucydides. That some type of speech was given is highly likely, and Thucydides made an effort to find out its content and style from what he calls "various informants" (1: 22). But as a historian, he is after something more than mere verisimilitude; he wants to show not the speech that was actually given but the speech that the situation made necessary. As he explains, his method of reconstruction has been, "while keeping as closely as possible to the general sense of the words that were actually used, to make the speaker say what, in my opinion, was called for by each situation" (1: 22). The scientific basis for this method was that human beings, by nature, reacted in consistent and predictable ways to certain types of conflict once their general perspectives and interests were taken into account. As Jaeger explains it, Thucydides's belief in the "objective truth" of his speeches, although they did not mirror what was actually said, was "based on his conviction that every standpoint in such a conflict had its own inevitable logic, and that a man who watched the conflict from above could develop that logic adequately."[2] If the Athenian representatives did not justify Athenian supremacy on the established rule that the weak should be subject to the strong, that merely shows the speaker to be incompetent at recognizing rhetorical necessity. But such speeches are of limited value to the historian concerned with disclosing the truth rather than merely documenting empirical facts.

And the truth is that the desire for power is the only motive capable of moving a group to collective action in the face of resistance. This rule applies even to those who are "weaker"—that is to say, those with only limited capacity to mobilize material resources and unify a mass of population to act in concert.[3] For instance, when the weaker cities in Greece begged Athens to lead the defensive campaign against the Persians, they did so not only out of fear of annihilation but also because they recognized an opportunity to become stronger by backing a winner. But for Thucydides, this was simply to be expected, for they acted in the same way that cities had done all the way back in the day of Agamemnon, when "the weaker, because of the general desire to make profits, were content to put up with being governed by the stronger, and those who won superior power by acquiring capital resources brought the smaller cities under their control" (1: 8). In this situation, it was not only the "strong" who sought power by exploiting the "weak"; it was the weak who sought to become powerful by aligning themselves with the strong in the hopes that they, too, might eventually acquire *dynamis* and *kratos* by accruing capital resources and increasing the mass of their unified population.

What masks the pervasiveness of this motive is simply that the weaker often claim "higher" motivations in order to cloak their impotence with virtue. The Athenians thus pierce this mask of virtue and confront subjective hypocrisy with objective truth when they reproach the Spartans for their infantile retreat to self-righteous talk of "right and wrong." Such appeals, the Athenians point out, never prevented the weak from being parasitic on the strong or the strong from subordinating the weak for its own ends. From their perspective, the Spartans had allowed themselves to be flattered by cities like Corsica who, in asking for Spartan aid against Athens, had invoked an early version of the "just war" doctrine, telling the Spartan assembly that "the likeliest way of securing peace is this: only to use one's power in the cause of justice, but to make it perfectly plain that one is resolved not to tolerate aggression" (1: 71). In contrast to this attempt to persuade through obsequiousness, the Athenian representatives approached the debate without need for such moralistic covering. They simply sought "to make clear how powerful their city was, to remind the elder members of the assembly of facts that were known to them, and to inform the younger ones of matters in which they were ignorant" (1: 72). Applying their objective analysis of the situation, their rhetoric was purely calculative, seeking to demonstrate the facts of their power so that the Spartans would know what sort of city they would have to fight against if they made the wrong decision. For them, judgments based on realistic analyses of comparative power came first, and ideological or moralistic justifications followed in their wake to palliate anxieties and ease a guilty conscience.

From this example, we can see how Thucydides followed Gorgias in under-standing rhetoric through a medical lens, as a symbolic response to a perceived sickness or imbalance in the political body that required *mētis,* or practical skill, to adequately diagnose and properly treat. According to Richard Ned LeBow, Thucydides borrowed the concept of *kairos* from the Greek physician Hippocrates and used it to interpret human motivation and persuasion. For Hippocrates, the role of the physician was to chart "the course of diseases in the human body, noting the symptoms that appeared at their onset and how they built up to a critical moment or crisis stage (*kairos*) that led to death or recovery."[4] Once entire cities or cultures could be interpreted as kinds of living organisms struggling to survive in a threatening environment, it was only a short step to defining *kairos* as what E. C. White calls "a passing instant when an opening appears which must be driven through with force if success is to be achieved."[5] For Thucydides, *kairos* thus meant "an advantage gained by doing the right thing at the right moment," while the *mētis* displayed by some of the greatest generals referred to that "fine sense of timing that, in politics, brings success in part because it catches opponents by surprise."[6] Applied to speech, rhetoric was not a drug slipped on the sly into someone's drink but a form of medical treatment that, when properly applied in a timely moment during a sickness, could bring a diseased organism to health and therefore increase its strength.

Thucydides thus gives us more than a brilliant empirical account of the war grounded in a cyclical conception of history and a universal understanding of the laws of human nature; he also shows how rhetoric functions as the sym-bolic medium by which the material resources of power are channeled through human action within concrete, empirically definable situations. For what dis-tinguishes Thucydides from the Sophists, who clearly influenced him, was his rejection of their humanistic optimism that made either human beings or their *logoi* the measure of all things. For Thucydides, the material conditions of his-tory, and the forms of power those conditions make possible, are the wellspring not only of collective human impulse but also of individual rhetorical expres-sion. In his conception of objective causality, "events which had once seemed to be voluntary actions, subject to moral judgment, appeared to be the result of a long, continuous, inevitable process conditioned by higher necessity."[7] In the Homeric age, this higher necessity was the will of the gods; in Heraclitus, it was the world-order of the Logos; and in Aeschylus, it was the divine spirit of justice; but in Thucydides it is the unavoidable consequence of the pursuit of power under certain material conditions. Allow a population to accumulate capital resources, be organized by capable politicians, and develop strong navies and ground forces, and predictable consequences ensue as if driven by the will of the gods. Consequently, for him, rhetoric that did not directly acknowledge the facts of power and advocate judgments based on those facts might certainly exist and even wield influence for a time, but in the long run it would prove impotent to direct human affairs and could be effectively ignored.

What we gain from Thucydides is thus one of the most sophisticated, historically grounded accounts of how rhetoric actualizes its capacity to persuade only when its *logos* functions as an adequate response to a *kairotic* situation whose limits and possibilities are defined by the changing structures of power. The set speeches that punctuate his history act as demonstrations of what he perceives to be the objective logic of rhetorical invention. For him, the ideal speaker recognizes the recalcitrant facts of the present structures of power, identifies the openings in those structures, and suggests a motive appropriate to these limits and possibilities that would satisfy the self-interest of an audience. At the same time, his choice to often place speeches in competition with one another shows that history is not purely determinate. Consistent with sophistical notions of *dissoi logoi,* Thucydides recognizes that *kairotic* situations are characterized by more than one *logos* being available for speakers to choose from, and more often than not they choose the *logos* which satisfies their short-term yearning for personal gratification and profit rather than the long-term needs of justice for an entire society or culture. In Thucydides, the space in which human agency can act through rhetoric as an autonomous influence in history is narrow, but the consequences which follow from those acts may be vast enough to establish or bring down an empire.

When war between Athens and Sparta broke out in 431 B.C.E., Thucydides did not plan on becoming the historian of the conflict. As an Athenian citizen from a noble family, Thucydides had been born and bred to be a political animal who craved the life of action in the *polis.* What he has Pericles say in his funeral oration is thus an accurate representation of the environment in which Thucydides matured: "Here each individual is interested not only in his own affairs but in the affairs of the state as well: even those who are mostly occupied with their own business are extremely well-informed on general politics—this is a peculiarity of ours: we do not say that a man who takes no interest in politics is a man who minds his own business; we say that he has no business here all" (2: 40). Accordingly, when the war began, Thucydides did not have the option to simply retreat to his estate and compose an epic history by living off the profits of his family's gold mine. The business of the state demanded that he play his part as determined by his station: he would become a general charged with commanding ships in the Athenian Navy.

What he soon recognized was that this war would be no minor skirmish to be finished in a few months: "I myself remember that all the time from the beginning to the end of the war it was being put about by many people that the war would last for thrice nine years" (5: 26). And this intuition turned out to be true. Unlike the Persian War, which was decided "quickly as a result of two naval battles and two battles on land," the Peloponnesian War was fated to drag on for almost three decades (1: 23). This was because Athens and Sparta were almost perfect counterparts to one another. Sparta was an austere oligarchy with a highly conservative social order whose communitarian ethic helped produce a tightly regimented and efficient fighting force on land. Athens was a wealthy, liberal democracy that valued experimentation and used its populist appeal to recruit the poor to provide the necessary manpower for its massive navy. But both had entered the war "in a high state of military preparedness and had gained their military experience in the hard school of danger" (1: 18). So here were two of the dominant powers in the world struggling for supremacy, but each possessing opposite strengths that would make a direct encounter impossible—something Athens made sure of by building enormous city walls extending all the way to the coastal port, the Piraeus, which could provide for the city indefinitely even when Athens was completely surrounded on land. Instead of staging mighty battles, the war would be decided by protracted indirect struggle for the control (or necessary devastation of) allied cities in such a way that inevitably "brought with it unprecedented suffering for Hellas" (1: 23).

Nonetheless, at the beginning of this campaign, Thucydides was as prepared to shed as much blood as the next Athenian who was loyal to his city and its empire. But historical necessity had a different fate in store for him. In the first years of the war, he was commanded to lead a fleet of seven ships to defend Amphipolis from Spartan assault, only to arrive a day too late. The citizens of Amphipolis had already surrendered. This single event, occurring as it did so early in what promised to be a long campaign, was thus responsible for revealing to Thucydides the possibility of writing a history: "I lived through the whole of it, being of an age to understand what was happening, and I put my mind to the subject so as to get an accurate view of it. It happened, too, that I was banished from my country for twenty years after my command at Amphipolis; I saw what was being done on both sides, particularly on the Peloponnesian side, because of my exile, and this leisure gave me rather exceptional facilities for looking into things" (5: 26). Thucydides had become a victim of the Athenian policy of punishing unsuccessful officers in order to motivate them to win at all costs. From that time forward, Thucydides occupied the post of an observer with a great deal of time on his hands and capital resources to support him. As Hamilton puts it, it was then that he decided, "free from bitterness and bias," to "to produce a history as coldly impartial as if it had dealt with a far distant past."[8]

What was truly innovative about this decision was that no such history had ever been written about any subject. Herodotus, it is true, had by that time completed his own history of the Persian War, thus establishing the precedent for a work which "collects and surveys traditional information about the nations inhabiting the known earth, so far as it can be checked by investigation."[9] But Herodotus, despite his critical and rationalist leanings, still remains at heart something of a Homeric poet. At the beginning of inquiry, he states his goal to be that "human achievement may not become forgotten in time, and great and marvelous deeds—some displayed by Greeks, some by barbarians—may not be without their glory; and especially to show why the two peoples fought with each other" (1: 1). Only the last line reflects the motive of contemporary critical history which attempts to diagnose the causes of human events through empirical inquiry. But most of the *Histories* is not concerned with establishing such causation; instead it revels in the rhapsodic love of telling stories about great individuals doing great deeds that preserve for prosperity those practices worthy of remembrance.

Thucydides set for himself a completely different task. His goal is not to survey the entire world and bring together all of its "great and marvelous deeds" for praise and blame; his goal is to write a political history that diagnoses the nature of the state through an unromantic inquiry into the workings of power. What matters for Thucydides is not the unique qualities of a particular act or event, whether it be virtuous or contemptible; what matters is how a series of those acts or events establish a law or principle by which we can understand or predict future acts or events. Thucydides thus writes his history under the explicit pragmatic expectation that his work is actually to serve a political function, an assumption that had begun to become more prominent in Athens as the war progressed. Jaeger writes that, "while concentrated earnestly and exclusively on the present, [Athens] had suddenly reached a crisis in which serious political thinkers were compelled to develop a historical consciousness, although now in a new sense and with a different content. They were forced, in fact, to discover the historical necessity of the crisis which the nation's development had led. This is the real nature of the intellectual revolution reflected in Thucydides' history—historical writing had not become political, but political thinking had become historical."[10] The political history of Thucydides thus met the pragmatic demand of his age to make historically informed judgments in the present in order to somehow break the spiral of suffering that comes from the unbridled pursuit of power.

A third factor crucial to the production of his work, in addition to the accidents of personal biography and a rising historical consciousness, was his ability to apply recent innovations of the Sophists to a new kind of writing. The Sophists had established a new vocabulary of ideas with which to classify psychological processes, explain human motivations, analyze the basis of moral principles, investigate and categorize empirical facts, and advocate for practical judgments. As Havelock explains, Thucydides owes a great debt to men like Protagoras and Gorgias who created this new vocabulary, for

> with the vocabulary of ideas, there was also born a prose of ideas, which finds its most effective and vivid expression in the speeches of Thucydides. Had we more of the Sophistic writings, the historian might not get such exclusive credit. It is plain on the surface how deeply he is in their debt. The very Hippocratic writings of this period demonstrate the same influence. They are essentially essays in the arrangement and the behavior of the human body, and its environment, under categories. They are in the sense all of them Sophistic tracks.[11]

Given the sophistical influence on his writing, it is no wonder that Thucydides would use "set speeches" as a centerpiece to writing a universal history. For him, speeches were not expressions of personal character, style, or opinion; they were rational attempts to interpret reality through a practical vocabulary of ideas in such a way that revealed the facts of a situation, the psychology of the speaker, and the motivation of the audience. It was up to the historian to compose a prose of ideas that would set forth in a written account how speeches of a particular age, logically reconstructed and placed side-by-side, could reveal the objective truth not only about the particulars of a situation but also the universals of human nature.

Lastly, Thucydides was driven to write his work for the sheer love of producing philosophical knowledge that would stand for all time. Following in the tradition of Heraclitus, Thucydides exploits his position as an aristocrat-in-exile to attain the objectivity necessary to pursue an inquiry into the underlying order which exists behind the flux and strife of appearances. He becomes, that is to say, one who "looks into things," not just to see the thing but to discern the eternal laws which determine the nature of those things, which include not only objects but actions, events, cultures, leaders, followers, states, victories, and tragedies. Thucydides is out to produce something more than just a popular narrative to win him wealth and fame: "My work is not a piece of writing designed to meet the taste of an immediate public, but was done to last forever" (1: 22). And what gives his work this eternal quality is that it reveals laws which apply to all human beings. "It will be enough for me," he writes, "if these words of mine are judged useful by those who want to understand clearly the events which happened in the past and which (human nature being what it is) will, at some time or other and in much the same ways, be repeated in the future" (1: 22). Here is the philosopher's ambition to communicate the nature of the universal Logos expressed through the voice of the historian, giving us insight into the laws of the world-order which are common to all, even if we are unaware of them.

In sum, Thucydides took advantage of his exile by putting his sophistically honed skills and natural genius to work compiling material with which to construct a history that would disclose universal laws which could inform political judgments not only in his own age but also in ages to come. This is why his work is not simply a history but a *political* history, written not just *about* politics but *for* it. Despite the pessimistic tenor of his claim that history would repeat itself, he did not believe that we were helpless in the face of necessity. But our limited capacity for self-determination nonetheless required us to account for historical laws. As Jaeger remarks, this attitude "is an essential element in his political outlook; for politicians cannot think ahead and act according to plan unless, in like situations, like causes are always followed by like effects: that kind of sequence makes experience possible, and therefore allows some sort of foresight of things to come, however limited it may be."[12] One of the reasons Thucydides relies on set speeches to tell his history, therefore, is that the speeches show better than any descriptive account how the political judgments of various rhetors led to failure or success based on how well they understood and applied the causal laws established through historical precedent. A reader of his work thus acquires a practical acquaintance with rhetoric which succeeded or failed in practical contexts so that they can learn from the past to craft better rhetoric in the future.

In his history, two such laws stand out most vividly as essential for any political actor to understand if they are to gauge their rhetorical situation adequately—one which determines the nature and magnitude of one's power and the other which predicts how the power dynamics influence human motivation. These two laws can be summed up in the following way. First, the power (*dynamis*) of a political state is the product of technological mastery of available capital resources multiplied by the degree to which a people can collectively act in unity over a sustained period with sufficient passion and ingenuity. Second, the desire to attain or maintain power is the overriding motive of collective human action even when couched in the language of justice. Taken together, these two laws provide a means of analyzing a rhetorical situation marked by a sense of *kairos*, or timely opportunity and urgency brought about through a conflict and transition in the structure of power.[13] In these situations, two or more paths often become available to a group, each offering competing goods both of which appear to serve the interests of that group. It is thus the responsibility of the prudent rhetor to be able to analyze the state of power and its impact on human motivation in order to choose that path most capable of actualizing the power potential of the audience.

The very first set speech by the representatives of Corcyra to the Athenians establishes these rhetorical norms for all the speeches to come. Corcyra was a colony of Corinth which had attempted to separate from its mother city and had come to Athens to appeal for aid after Corinth had responded with military force. However, up until that point Corcyra had also remained a neutral state in the larger Peloponnesian conflict, refusing either to become a tribute-paying satellite of the Athenian alliance or to accept oligarchic rule in exchange for Spartan protection.[14] Their opening remarks recognize their precarious position and state clearly the cause for their distress: "We used to think that our neutrality was a wise thing, since it prevented us from being dragged into danger by other people's policies; now we see it clearly as a lack of foresight and as a source of weakness" (1: 32). Having adequately measured their relative weakness with respect to the larger powers, they clearly see the choice they must face—give up their autonomy for the sake of survival or remain neutral and be destroyed. Prudently, they explain to the Athenians that they have chosen to live as a supplicant: "We must therefore convince you first that by giving us this help you will be acting in your own interests, or certainly not against your interests; and then we must show that our gratitude can be depended upon. If on all these points you find our arguments unconvincing, we must not be surprised if our mission ends in failure" (1: 32). They then summarize their position as follows:

> We have already suggested that such a course would be very much in your own interests. Perhaps the greatest advantage to you is that you can entirely depend on us because your enemies are the same as ours, and strong ones, too, quite capable of doing damage to those who would revolt from them. And then it is quite a different matter for you if you reject alliance with a naval power than if you did the same with a land power. Your aim, no doubt, should be, if it were possible, to prevent anyone else having a navy at all: the next best thing to have on your side the strongest navy that there is. . . .
>
> At the moment your thoughts are on the coming war—a war, in fact, which is almost broken out already. Certainly you will not be showing very much foresight for your own city if, at this time, you are in two different minds whether to have on your side a power like Corcyra, whose friendship can be so valuable and whose hostility so dangerous to you. Apart from all other advantages, Corcyra lies in an excellent position on the coastal road to Italy and Sicily, and is thus able to prevent naval reinforcements coming to the Peloponnese from there, or going from the Peloponnese to those countries.
>
> The whole thing can be put very shortly, and these words will give you the gist of the whole argument why you should not abandon us. There are

three considerable naval powers in Hellas—Athens, Corcyra, and Corinth. If Corinth gets control of us first and you allow our navy to be united with hers, you will have to fight against the combined fleets of Corcyra and the Peloponnese. But if you received us into your alliance, you will enter upon the war with our ships as well as your own. (1: 35–36)

Here we have three of the essential elements of political persuasion as understood by Thucydides: (a) a realistic analysis of one's power with respect to allies and enemies, (b) identification of the audience capable of increasing power either by their voluntary assistance or by their obedient submission, and (c) appeal to that audience based on their own self-interest with respect to their own ambition for power. The only question for Thucydides in the remainder of the history is whether speakers performed these tasks prudently or recklessly.

The case of Corcyra provides an example of both a reckless and a prudent judgment, allowing us to discern by comparison the proper method by which to analyze power. What we find is that there are two factors to consider in any such analysis. First, one must take into account the kind and quantity of capital resources available to an organized political group or state. In Thucydides, the most important of these are independent sources of wealth, a large population of able-bodied citizens, geographic position, naval or land forces, and city walls. For example, prior to direct military conflict with Corinth, Corcyra believed it had the resources to stand on its own. As Thucydides explains in his own objective narrative: "They look down upon their mother city, claiming that their financial power at this time made them equal with the richest states in Hellas and that their military resources were greater than those of Corinth. In particular they boasted of their naval superiority, sometimes even basing this claim on the ground that those famous sailors the Phaeacians had inhabited Corcyra before them" (1: 25). Combined with a city wall and a defensive position on an isthmus near a trade route, Corcyra believed its wealth and skilled navy amounted to a significant base of power with which to resist Corinthian aggression.

Yet this confidence was reckless precisely because it failed to account for the second factor in power, which was the capacity to act in unity not just in the moment but over a sustained period. Although Corcyra won the first naval battle, Corinth quickly set about increasing the strength of its navy for a second assault: "Rowers were collected from the Peloponnese itself, and good terms were offered to bring them also from the rest of Hellas" (1: 31). Corcyra simply had not calculated the degree to which Corinth, as a Spartan ally, had the ability to recruit funds and soldiers from across the Peloponnese and thus act with the backing of the entire Spartan alliance. Soon their own recklessness became apparent: "In Corcyra the news of the preparations provoked alarm.

They had no allies in Hellas, since they had not enrolled themselves either in the Spartan or in the Athenian league" (1: 31). Once they had more prudently assessed their power, they came to the Athenians with a confession: "We recognize that, if we have nothing by our own national resources, it is impossible for us to survive" (1: 32). What they did understand, however, was that they could appeal to the Athenians' own self-interest for protection. For if the Corcyrean capital resources were factored into Athenian unity, Athenian power would be increased to such a degree that they could break the terms of the Thirty Year Peace with Sparta with impunity, for Spartan resistance would no longer pose a real threat to the Athenian goal of attaining complete hegemony in Greece. In short, the representatives of Corcyra had corrected their reckless optimism with a prudent analysis of power which showed how relinquishing their autonomy would serve the greater goal of increasing the power of the entire alliance and their own power within it.

As strong as the Corcyrean *logos* was, however, it still had to overcome the counter-argument from the Corinthians to fully persuade the Athenians. And as the Corinthian reply was quick to point out, Corcyra was still not being completely forthright in its supplication to Athens. In appealing to the Athenian self-interest, it had also engaged in that most persuasive of appeals: flattery. And for Thucydides, the essence of flattery was to assure another party that its ambitious pursuit of power also served a higher cause of justice. For instance, Corcyra had given as one of its reasons that Athens "will not be helping aggressors, but people who are the victims of aggression," an act for which "the world in general will admire you for your generosity" (1: 33). But even this attempt to make the Athenians feel as if they were fighting on the side of the "innocent" required a second act of flattery, this time of the Corcyreans' own motives. By pretending that their choice to remain a neutral state was simply based on the assumption that they preferred to go it alone and stay out of trouble, they portray themselves as making an innocent error in calculation for which the Corinthians are now unjustly punishing them. Flattery in Thucydides thus amounts to the rhetorical appeal by which orators pretend that their motives have nothing to do with the ambition for power but are rather only seeking the honor in representing the highest ideals in action even at the expense of their own self-interest. For the Corinthians, Athenian support of Corcyra would simply show their weakness for flattery and thus their incapacity to make the hard choices necessary to be a leader of Greece.

The *dissoi logoi* exhibited in the dispute over Corcyra demonstrates how effective persuasion in a competitive political culture not only requires one to be an eloquent and passionate advocate for one's position; it also requires one to be an astute rhetorical critic of opposing arguments. In Thucydides, the task of the rhetorical critic is to pierce the mask of flattery and lay bare the base motives at play so that a proper and undistorted measurement is possible. In this situation, the responsibility falls to the Corinthians to give a "clear idea" of what is at stake in the decision, free from such frivolous appeals (1: 37). Typical of speeches in Thucydides, the first things they target are the large virtue-terms which are used as warrants for ethical judgment, showing them to be meaningless:

> "Wisdom" and "moderation" are the words used by Corcyra in describing her old policy of avoiding alliances. In fact the motives were entirely evil, and there was nothing good about them at all. She wanted no allies because her actions were wrong, and she was ashamed of calling in others to witness her own misdoings. The geographical situation of Corcyra gives its inhabitants a certain independence. The ships of other states are forced to put in to their harbors much more often than Corcyraean ships visit the harbors of other states. So in cases where a Corcyraean has been guilty of injuring some other national, the Corcyraeans are themselves their own judges, and there is no question of having the case tried by independent judges appointed by treaty. So this neutrality of theirs, which sounds so innocent, was in fact a disguise adopted not to preserve them from having to share in the wrongdoings of others, but in order to give them a perfectly free hand to do wrong themselves, making away with other people's property by force, when they are strong enough, cheating them, whenever they can manage to do so, and enjoying their gains without any vestige of shame. Yet if they really were the honorable people they pretended to be, this very independence of theirs would have given them the best possible opportunity of showing their good qualities in the relations of common justice. (1: 37)

Of course, the last sentence about "honorable people" is itself a variant of flattery, serving the purpose only to shame the Corcyreans while flattering the Athenians for knowing the difference between virtue and vice. But as the Corinthians make clear through vivid example, no apparent virtue is absent a deeper "evil" motive to accumulate resources and increase one's independent capacity to act in one's own self-interest even if it means wronging others. Consequently, their argument that the Athenians should not help Corcyra is largely grounded on the Athenian self-interest not to break the treaty and therefore initiate a devastating war which they cannot win, for "there is no certainty that war will come" (1: 42). They conclude: "Do not go against us by receiving these Corcyraeans into your alliance. Do not aid and abet them in their crimes. Thus you will be acting as you ought to act and at the same time you will be making the wisest decision in your own interests" (1: 43). Even as the Corinthians attempt to reveal the hypocrisy of their opponents, they cannot help slipping into the same rhetorical strategy of appealing to another's ambition for power while coating it with an attractive veneer of virtue, or what the Corinthians call "acting as you ought to act" (as opposed to how everyone actually does act—for the desire of power).

What Thucydides reveals in rhetorical practice, then, is that rhetorical persuasion in actual practice often incorporates, in addition to a realistic analysis of power and self-interest, two more strategies—the unmasking of the base ideological motives of one's opponent and the construction of "eulogistic coverings" for one's own ideological motives.[15] The term "ideological" (literally, dealing with the "logic of an idea")[16] is used here not because it was a Greek word but because it aptly describes the social psychology that was pervasive in the partisan environment of the mid-fifth century B.C.E. in Greece. Ideologies represent "the system of ideas that constitute a political or social doctrine and inspire the acts of a government or party."[17] For example, Thucydides effectively divides the Greek world into the democratic and oligarchic parties, one based on the idea that by integrating the mass of poor citizens into a popular government one will maximize power by increasing "freedom," the other based on the idea that by vesting authority to a smaller group of wealthy citizens one will maximize power by enforcing "order." And characteristic of these systems of ideas is that they find a way to make the pursuit of one's own self-interest synonymous with the pursuit of virtue. In other words, to use the words of Reinhold Niebuhr, "an ideological taint upon a judgment implies a true and untainted judgment."[18] To act "ideologically" is thus to act on the belief that the parochial interest of one's party is synonymous with the universal interest of the world, and that the ideologies of one's opponents are based on a lie and hence are the product of a "false consciousness" due either to unconscious delusion or conscious hypocrisy.[19] Consequently, the method of the ideological rhetor is to simultaneously validate and unmask, to show how one's own ideology is sanctioned by the means and ends of history and to reveal the ideologies of one's opponents to be bald-faced lies intended simply to hide their shameful acts and evil intentions from both themselves (to reduce cognitive dissonance) and others (to manipulate them).

One of the finest examples of ideological rhetoric appears in the debate of the Syracusans when they first hear news that the Athenians are planning a full-scale invasion of Sicily. In what Thucydides called the "Sicilian expedition," which was initiated in 415 B.C.E., Athens took advantage of a temporary truce to launch an armada to conquer Syracuse and thereby conquer the entire island, expelling the Spartan colonies and gaining considerable access to natural resources. As the young and charismatic general Alcibiades put it, "in going abroad, we shall increase our power at home" (6: 18). However, because Syracuse was itself a democracy which was not directly aligned with either warring power, the Athenians had to mask their true intentions by claiming that their ships were merely supporting the smaller allied city of Segesta in their skirmish with Selinus. Because of this confusion, when word first reached Syracuse of the departing Athenian fleet, a debate arose as to whether they should be making preparations to defend the city. The first speaker, Hermocrates, firmly believed that a full-scale assault was imminent and advised representatives: "the most useful thing for us now is to act as though in the midst of danger and to realize that the safest steps you can take are those taken under the influence of fear" (6: 34). His advice: to send "to Sparta and Corinth urging them to send help to us here quickly and at the same time to go forward with the war in Hellas" (6: 34). In other words, Hermocrates wished the democratic assembly to bestow authority upon the generals to take whatever steps necessary to defend the city, even if it meant aligning themselves with the oligarchic league of Sparta.

Athenagoras, the leader of the democratic party, who "had very great influence with the people," then stepped forward to give what is perhaps an almost perfect ideological response. In his opening remarks, he analyzes the power dynamics in the current political situation, shows how it is not in the self-interest of the Athenians to attack Syracuse, and unmasks the true ideological intentions of his opponents, which have been hidden behind the appeal to self-defense and security. He says:

> Only cowards or people with no sense of patriotism are not anxious for the Athenians to be as mad as they are made out to be, and for them to come here and fall into our power. But as for those who spread such reports and try to scare you with them, I am not surprised at their audacity, but I am surprised at their lack of intelligence, if they imagine that their motives are not perfectly obvious. They have reasons of their own to be frightened, and they want to put the whole city into a state of alarm, so that in the general panic they may disguise their own. So now all the news reports mean is this: they have not arisen in the natural way, but have been made up on purpose by certain people who are always starting these agitations. You, if you are sensible, will not take such reports as a basis for calculating probabilities. . . . It is not likely that [the Athenians] would leave the Peloponnesians behind them and, with the war in Hellas not satisfactorily settled, would go out of their way to take on a new war on just as big a scale. In fact I personally am of the opinion that they are pleased enough to find that it is not a case of us going to attack them, considering the numbers and the strength of our cities. (6: 36)

For Athenagoras, the numbers simply do not add up to an Athenian invasion, not only because Syracuse does not represent an immediate threat, but also because it has a large population; a considerable force of ships, hoplites, and cavalry; access to natural resources; and a functioning democratic government. The real threat comes from the members of the oligarchic party who, through spreading "villainous fabrications," aim to "make you, the mass of the people, frightened, and so gain control of the government themselves" (6: 38). But Athenagoras will not be fooled: "I shall keep my eye on them, and I shall even be a teacher to them; for so, I think, I shall be most likely to turn them from their wicked path" (6: 38). True to his word, Athenagoras then takes the opportunity to instruct his oligarchic opponents in the truth of his own ideology and the falsity of their own:

> There are people who say that democracy is neither an intelligent nor a fair system, and those who have the money are also the best rulers. But I say, first, that what is meant by the demos, or people, is the whole state, whereas an oligarchy is only a section of the state; and I say next that though the rich are the best people for looking after money, the best counselors are the intelligent and that it is the many who are best at listening to the different arguments and judging between them. And all alike, whether taken all together or as separate classes, have equal rights in a democracy. An oligarchy, on the other hand, certainly gives the many their share of dangers, but when it comes to the good things of life not only claims the largest share, but goes off with the whole lot. And this is what the rich men and the young men among you are aiming at; but in a great city these things are beyond your reach. What fools you are! In fact the stupidest of all the Hellenes I know, if you do not realize that your aims are evil, and the biggest criminals if you do realize this and still have to face to proceed with them. But there is still time for you, if not to repent, at any rate to become instructed and to promote the interests of your country that are shared by all your countrymen. (6: 39)

Here we find the core persuasive strategy of ideological rhetoric, which is to align one's own partisan beliefs with the interests of everyone while showing the opposing party to be interested in enriching themselves at the expense of others. Athenagoras thus aptly calls himself a "teacher" when he corrects the false consciousness of his opponents, for that is what all ideological rhetors see themselves as doing—correcting the errors of judgment in others for the sake of producing a universal commitment to a belief in which the desire for power and the commitment to virtue are reconciled through collective action on principle.

But Thucydides shows us examples of ideological rhetoric not to prove that such appeals are necessary but to reveal that all ideological consciousness is false consciousness, and that all types of persuasion that employ ideological appeals are forms of flattery. From his objective stance as a historian, Thucydides unmasks both ideological positions in light of the truth of human nature, which is that no virtue can stand in the way of the pursuit of power when one sees the opportunity to grasp it. He writes:

> Love of power, operating through greed and through personal ambition, was the cause of all these evils. To this must be added the violent fanaticism which came into play once the struggle had broken out. Leaders of parties in the cities had programs which appeared admirable—on one side political equality for the masses, on the other side the safe and sound government of the aristocracy—but in professing to serve the public interest they were seeking to win the prizes for themselves. In their struggles for ascendancy nothing was barred; terrible indeed were the actions to which they committed themselves, in taking revenge they went farther still. Here they were deterred neither by the claims of justice nor by the interests of the state; their one standard was the pleasure of their own party at that particular moment, and so, either by means of condemning their enemies on an illegal vote or by violently usurping power over them, they were always ready to satisfy the hatreds of the hour. Thus neither side had any use for conscientious motives; more interest was shown in those who could produce attractive arguments to justify some disgraceful action. . . . Society had become divided into two ideologically hostile camps, and each side viewed the other with suspicion. (3: 82–83)

For Thucydides, then, nothing in one's ideological commitments had any bearing on the virtue or vice of one's actions. It may very well have been that speakers who espoused these beliefs actually preferred them over others in the abstract, and if liberated from the demands of and desire for power, might have put them into practice. But as it was, human nature showed itself "as something incapable of controlling passion, insubordinate to the idea of justice; [and] the enemy to anything superior to itself" (3: 83). As Hamilton summarizes the fate of all noble-sounding ideologies: "The rule of the one, of the few, of the many, each is destroyed in turn because there is in them all an unvarying evil—the greed for power—and no moral quality is necessarily bound up with any of them."[20] Power breeds corruption and contempt for moral law always and forever.

But since ideological rhetors—or what Thucydides calls *demagogues,* meaning literally "leaders of the people"—need to flatter their audience in order to hide from them their own unabashed love of power, they require a final rhetorical maneuver essential to their success. They must distort the *logos*. For if it is human nature for groups to pursue power through any means necessary, it is equally human nature to desire to feel as if one is acting with truth and with virtue. The solution is quite simple: to use virtuous words to justify immoral actions. Again, Thucydides describes this method with striking precision:

> To fit with the change of events, words, too, had to change their usual meanings. What used to be described as a thoughtless act of aggression was now regarded as the courage one would expect to find in a party member; to think of the future and wait was merely another way of saying one was a coward; any idea of moderation was just an attempt to disguise one's unmanly character; ability to understand a question from all sides meant that one was totally unfitted for action. Fanatical enthusiasm was the mark of a real man, and to plot against the enemy behind his back was perfectly legitimate self-defense. Anyone who held violent opinions could always be trusted, and anyone who objected to them became a suspect. To plot successfully was a sign of intelligence, but it was still cleverer to see that a plot was hatching. . . . [And] most people were more ready to call villainy cleverness than simplemindedness honesty. They were proud of the first quality and ashamed of the second. (3: 82)

For Thucydides, then, courage became aggression, manliness became fanatical enthusiasm, cleverness became villainy, and intelligence became duplicity, with the original meanings of each term translated into a situation in which good and evil were determined by the ability to visibly help one's friends and hurt one's enemies in the immediate present. These terms thus became what Richard Weaver calls "charismatic terms," which "seem to have broken loose somehow and to operate independently of referential connections."[21] In Thucydides, all references to virtue in ideological rhetoric are charismatic terms.

Thucydides's use of set speeches thus reveals what he understood to be a fundamental paradox at the heart of political rhetoric. On the one hand, speakers were ethically and pragmatically charged with realistically evaluating the conditions of power in any rhetorical situation and setting forth a path that would serve the self-interest of the audience, even if that meant willingly submitting to the will of a stronger power. On the other hand, the political and social pressure to conform to partisan ideology forced speakers to distort their language in such a way that flattered one's allies, demonized one's enemies, and favored short-term gratification of a group's ego over long-term prosperity of their bodies and souls. But what this meant was that the only "true" speeches were those delivered by a stronger power to a weaker one, because it is only in those situations when the eulogistic coverings of ideology were totally unnecessary. As is the case with the Athenians speaking to the Spartan assembly, such speakers were free to speak the truth about power because it was in their self-interest to do so and thereby show a weaker power that it is best to submit to the stronger one.

And so we find the Athenians speaking the truth to the representatives of the island of Melos, a formerly neutral city that had become an open enemy of Athens and an ally of Sparta. The Athenians had surrounded the city and had offered to negotiate a surrender, and to accomplish their task they decided to speak the truth without the need for ideological cover:

> Then we on our side will use no fine phrases saying, for example, that we have a right to our empire because we defeated the Persians, or that we have come against you now because of the injuries you have done us—a great mass of words that nobody would believe. And we ask you on your side not to imagine that you will influence us by saying that you, though a colony of Sparta, have not joined Sparta in the war, or that you have never done any harm. Instead we recommend that you try to get what is possible for you to get, taking into consideration what we both really do think; since you know as well as we do that, when these matters are discussed by practical people, the standard of justice depends on the quality of power to compel and that in fact the strong do what they have the power to do and the weak accept what they have to accept. (5: 89)

Here is a rhetoric free of its ideological taint. Indeed, the Athenians go so far as to forbid the Melians from talking about justice at all and to stick purely to an evaluation of comparative power, of profits and losses. For the Athenians, the equation is very simple: "You, by giving in, would save yourselves from disaster; we, by not destroying you, would be able to profit from you" (5: 93). There is no other motive than this, no other calculations to be considered. Prophecies and oracles are useless, the gods are irrelevant, honor is meaningless, and hope is mere fantasy. There is only one safe rule to obey, according to the Athenians: "to stand up to one's equals, to behave with deference toward one's superiors, and to treat one's inferiors with moderation" (5: 111). The only question is to know where one stands and to make the decision accordingly. And when the Melians choose to hope for Spartan aid, the Athenians show them the error of their judgment: they surround the city until they breach the walls, put to death all the men of military age, sell the women and children as slaves, and take the city over for themselves. That is what it means for rhetoric to speak the truth in the world of Thucydides.

On finishing Thucydides's history, one might be excused for thinking that the real world of politics is always red in tooth and claw with no place for the moral rhetor. For it appears that, in Thucydides, truth and justice are incommensurable goals. To speak the truth is to make a calculated judgment of how one can maximize one's own power without concern for justice, while to speak of justice is to either disguise one's true intention or simply to be naively ignorant of the realities of a situation. This is certainly the lesson that Nietzsche takes away from *The History of the Peloponnesian War.* He writes: "Justice (fairness) originates between parties of approximately equal power, as Thucydides correctly grasped (in the terrible colloquy between the Athenian and Melian ambassadors)."[22] And this, for Nietzsche, is always the case. Justice by its nature equals "requital and exchange under the presupposition of an approximately equal power position," thus implying that revenge and gratitude also exist within the domain of justice, but as applied within a relationship between unequal rather than equal powers.[23] The only reason we think otherwise is because we have "forgotten the original purpose of so-called just and fair actions," thus making it "gradually come to appear that a just action is an unegoistic one."[24] We assume, in other words, that the attitude of equal powers to one another should carry over to a situation marked by inequality in power, thus replacing the natural impulse of stronger to enact revenge and the weaker to express gratitude with the unnatural impulse for the stronger and the weaker to treat each other as equals. But the truth, for Thucydides as for Nietzsche, is that justice is a *consequence* of power relationships, not a standard by which they are regulated. The only time one can speak truthfully of "justice" is thus when two equal parties agree not to destroy one another for their own mutual best interests. Otherwise it is a childish hope.

Yet despite all of this apparent cynicism, Thucydides nonetheless seems to hold out a tragic hope that there does exist a rhetoric which can speak the truth, satisfy the will to power, and satisfy the needs of justice. What it requires is not ascetic self-denial or ideological distortion but the Promethean foresight which allows us to endure the suffering of the moment and to make the best out of one's available resources by providing a realistic end-in-view that produces power through knowledge. This is why, despite his disappointments with Athenian governance, he remains at heart a democrat, for democracy represents to him a form of power grounded less on the possession of ships, walls, and wealth than on the capacity for the citizens to act in unity after going through a process of rhetorical deliberation that takes into account every aspect of the situation. As he has Pericles say in his funeral oration, the virtue of the Athenians is that they take "decisions on policy and submit them to proper discussions," knowing that the "worst thing is to rush into action before the consequences have been properly debated" (2: 40). Moreover, this commitment to foresight produces the necessary courage to act in the face of pain, for a "man who can most truly be accounted brave is he who best knows the meaning of what is sweet in life and of what is terrible, and then goes out undeterred to meet what is to come" (2: 40). For Thucydides, then, democracy makes possible a kind of rhetoric that chooses foresight over flattery and allows people to endure short-term suffering to attain what is sweet rather than to succumb to immediate pleasures at the expense of bringing about what is terrible.

There is, then, an ethical ideal of rhetoric latent in Thucydides. To speak virtuously means to acknowledge the truth of human nature, to evaluate the realistic conditions of power, and to advocate judgment that best achieves an increase of power over the longest span of time, even if that means sacrificing short-term pleasure or even the individual reputation of the speaker. Of all the orators in his history, Pericles stands out as the exemplar, for it is only Pericles who possessed the foresight by which the war could be won and the rhetorical skill necessary to produce the unity of action necessary for victory. Thucydides did not question the motives by which Athens sought to expand their empire; this was simply an extension of the human desire for power. But the pursuit of power need not result in reckless violence, intense suffering, and inevitable disaster. What he questioned was not the pursuit of power but the incompetence and selfishness by which it was pursued by the demagogues after the death of Pericles. For what Thucydides respected most about Pericles was that, "because of his position, his intelligence, and his known integrity, [he] could respect the liberty of the people and at the same time hold them in check." (2: 65). Instead of flattering them for his own personal gain, he spoke angrily to them when he believed they were wrong, pointed out imminent dangers when they were overconfident, and bolstered their hope when they were in despair. By contrast, the demagogues, lacking the charisma and foresight of Pericles, advocated policies that provided immediate gratification for their audience, but which profited only the demagogues when successful and which devastated the entire city when a failure. The irony of the term "demagogue," then, is that the method of demagoguery is not to lead the people but to be led by them, which means in effect to validate the immediate impulses of the mob. But for Pericles, power comes from another source: "To face calamity with a mind as unclouded as may be, and quickly to react against it—that, in a city and in an individual, is real strength" (2: 64).

What Thucydides desired was a rhetoric that inspired the courage that comes from foresight and that envisioned a form of power which would also embody the ideals of justice. This did not mean denying the sweetness that comes from the acquisition of power or even the violent conquest of an enemy.

But it did mean affirming that the sweetest power is that which harmonizes the most elements into a whole and creates a sustainable structure of power. Pericles praises precisely this form of power in his funeral oration, clearly representing for Thucydides the highest ideal of Greek culture. As Jaeger observes, the vision of democracy in the oration represents "a sort of Heraclitean harmony of radical and inevitable opposites, maintaining itself through its tension and its equilibrium. He therefore makes Pericles describe it as the interaction of delicately balanced opposites—self-support and enjoyment of the world's products, labor and recreation, business and holiday, spirit and ethos, thought and energy."[25] For Thucydides, then, the ideal of justice lurking behind the Peloponnesian War is that this ideal might be realized throughout all the cities of Greece once the obstacles to its actualization could be removed by force. In this case, justice could be achieved not because the strong would suddenly give up its advantages over the weak, but because there would be no strong and weak; there would only be a single unified Greek culture in which all participated equally in constituting a single power, the ideal of a democratic empire guided by rhetors with courage, creativity, and foresight. This, at least, was the ideological dream of Thucydides.

CHAPTER 7

Aristophanes's *Birds* and the
Corrective of Comedy

INFORMER: Listen, Buster: / my business is the indictment of islands for sub-versive activities. / You see in me a professional informer.

PISTHETAIROS: A splendid calling.

INFORMER: Also an *agent provocateur* of lawsuits and investigations. / That's why I want the wings. They come in handy / for whizzing around the islands delivering my indictments / and handing out subpoenas in person . . .

PISTHETAIROS: Great Zeus Almighty, / Aren't there enough honest means of earning a living / without this dirty little dodge of hatching suits?

INFORMER: Listen, mister: it's wings I want, not words.

PISTHETAIROS: But my words *are* wings.

INFORMER: Your words are wings?

PISTHETAIROS: Wings from words. You know the old men, how they roll around the barbershop / grousing and bitching about the younger gener-ation?— / "Thanks to that damned Dieitrephes and his damned advice," / growls one, "my boy has flown the family nest / to take a flier on the horses." / "Hell," pipes another, "you should see that kid of mine: / he's gone so damn batty over those tragic plays, / he flies into fits of ecstasy and gets goosebumps all over."

INFORMER: And that's how words give wings?

PISTHETAIROS: Right. / Through dialectic the mind of man takes wing and soars; / he is morally and spiritually uplifted. And so I hoped / with words of good advice to win you on your way / toward some honest trade.

INFORMER: It just won't work.

PISTHETAIROS: But why won't it?

INFORMER: I cannot disgrace my family name. / We have been informers now for several generations, you see . . .

PISTHETAIROS: Right, I've got it. . . . And guess what I have got here for you: / a lovely little set of Korkyrean wings.

INFORMER: Hey, that's a whip!

PISTHETAIROS: Not a whip, it's wings / to make your little top go round. Got it?

INFORMER: Ouch! Owwoooooo![1]

In 414 B.C.E., just a few months after the massive Athenian armada had departed the port of Piraeus for its anticipated conquest of Sicily, the comic poet Aristophanes (446–386 B.C.E.) lifted the imaginations of the Athenians even higher by carrying them aloft on the winged words of the *Birds*. The play narrates the adventures of the ambitious Pisthetairos and his sidekick Euelpides, two self-exiled Athenians seeking escape from the restlessness, disorder, and contentiousness of the city to "some land of soft and lovely leisure / where a man may loaf and play and settle down / for good" (14–15). Their destination: the land of the birds, that natural symbol for all escapist fantasies. Yet when they arrive, they meet with something less than open arms; the birds have learned to distrust the humans who hunt and kill them. Forced to justify their presence, Pisthetairos proposes to the birds an ambitious plan that purports to serve their mutual interests—that the birds, under Pisthetairos's leadership, should pursue their right and inheritance to build their own empire, Cloudcuckooland, capable of defeating the gods, subduing the humans, and making the birds the foremost power in the world. By the end of the comedy, all goes according to plan. The humans no longer hunt birds but desire to be part of their city, Poseidon and Herakles negotiate a truce between the birds and the gods, and Pisthetairos marries "Miss Universe" (*Basileia*, literally "Sovereignty," "Dominion," or "Kingdom"), the mistress of Zeus, as he accepts the position of tyrant of Cloudcuckooland: "Reach me your hand, dear bride. / Now take me by my wings, / O my lovely, / my sweet, / and let me lift you up, / and soar beside you / through the buoyant air!" (107). With slowly beating wings, the two characters rise toward the heavens with the help of stage machinery, and with them are carried the lofty hopes of the Athenians who see mirrored in the *Birds* their own desire to conquer all of Hellas in their dream of absolute control.

What makes this dream possible is the motivational power of words that act like wings, by which Aristophanes clearly means *logos* buoyed by the spirit of *eros*. This connection between *logos* and *eros* is established at the very beginning of the play, when Pisthetairos persuades Hoopoe, the aging and soon-to-be-usurped leader of the birds, to gather his avian subjects together to announce the grand plan of domination. Hoopoe says of the two Athenians: "Their motive is Love (*eros*). / Love is the burden of all their words. / Love of your life / and Love of you, / to live with you / in Love always" (35). *Eros,* that emotional striving to attain the object of one's desire, is thus the motivating force behind their *logos*. In this case, it is a desire for what Hoopoe calls "a vision of glory, / a dream so fantastic / it staggers the sensible mind" (35). As William Arrowsmith explains, "this Eros is not only metaphysical and sexual and material; it is also profoundly political," encompassing "the love of glory, envy, lust for power, partisan zeal, greed for money or conquest."[2] One of the dominant themes in the *Birds* is thus how words can evoke this desire by stimulating fantastic images in the mind, which mobilizes the will to make the images a reality. Just as words cause ambitious sons to crave the glories of chariot racing or the euphoria of tragic catharsis, so too can words bring about a desire for an empire once the mind of human or bird takes wing and soars.

Yet all is not perfect in Cloudcuckooland. First, its rise to power has attracted all manner of common parasites familiar to Athenian life—longwinded priests, hackneyed poets, arrogant prophets, indecipherable geometers, meddlesome inspectors, overbearing legislators, bombastic tragedians, impudent delinquents, and, worst of all, rapacious informers whose job it is to instigate and deliver indictments in order to confiscate other people's property. All arrive uninvited to Cloudcuckooland to peddle their wares in the new center of power, and one by one Pisthetairos must expel them from the city by mercilessly lashing them. Second, the play ends with the smell of cooking poultry in the air, a celebratory feast made possible by roasting "jailbirds sentenced to death on the charge of High Treason against the Sovereign Birds" (98). Not only have outsiders invaded the city, seeking power for themselves, but a seditious movement of rebellious birds has already sprung up to resist the current power structure. As the eyes of the audience follow Pisthetairos and his new bride skyward, they also are distracted from the dangerous undercurrents brewing beneath the illusion of perfect order.

Clearly one reason for this lack of unity is that *logos,* despite its power to give one wings, is not the *dynastes megas* that Gorgias made it out to be. As Pisthetairos's failure to reform the Informant demonstrates, *logos* reaches its limit when it cannot provide an attractive alternative to a competing calculation of power. The Informant rejects winged words in favor of actual wings because his desire already has its object—to maintain his "family name" by increasing the speed with which he can "dart out to islands with stacks of subpoenas and summons, / whiz back home to defend the case in court, / then zip right back to the island again" so that when the defendants arrive, they will have been condemned *in absentia* for being too late (89). All he needs are actual, material wings fast and light enough to make such travel virtually instantaneous. For the Informant, the ideal of making an honest living in the empire of Cloudcuckooland has no attraction for him, and hence he desires only to get his wings and fly off to another court trial. And the same goes for all the other human interlopers. They remain unpersuaded either to leave or to abandon their private ambitions by words alone, and their recalcitrance means that an act of violence is required on the part of Pisthetairos—usually a whipping—to purge them from the city to maintain its purity of purpose.

Worse still, the final meal of "jailbirds" being prepared by Pisthetairos is a symptom of the inability of *logos* to sustain a unity of passionate desire over time. For it is not the sheer act of cannibalism which is threatening, but the fact that the cannibalism is justified as a necessary act of violence to purge a treasonous element within the birds themselves. After all, the whole basis of power in the bird empire was the ability of the birds—each relatively helpless on its own—to act as a collective to challenge the power of gods and humans. The plotting of certain birds against the new tyranny of Pisthetairos is thus far more threatening to the power of the regime than the appearance of priests, prophets, and delinquents. Whereas humans are parasites to power, birds represent its constituent parts. For a contingent of birds to begin forming a new body of power thus weakens the entire organism from the inside. Moreover, it shows that *logos,* once again, has begun to splinter into *dissoi logoi,* as the *eros* generated by the initial persuasive word has been channeled in different directions by a competing *logos* which seeks to attach *eros* to a different object of desire.

However, Pisthetairos is neither a clear hero nor a villain. As Arrowsmith argues, Pisthetairos is better understood as simply the personification of the dominant characteristic of all Athenians—*polupragmosunē,* which can loosely be translated as being "hyperactive." On the one hand, *polupragmosunē* positively "connotes energy, enterprise, daring, ingenuity, originality, and curiosity," and, on the other hand, negatively "means restless instability, discontent with one's lot, persistent and pointless busyness, meddling interference, and mischievous love of novelty."[3] For Athenians to watch Pisthetairos rousing the birds' revolutionary energies at the same time that he throws their historically peaceful community into turmoil is to witness their most salient national characteristic brought to life, showing itself to be simultaneously glorious and embarrassing, clever and shortsighted, loving and cruel. The irony, of course, is that the two Athenians had left Athens in search of the opposite of *polupragmosunē,* called *apragmosunē,* a characteristic typically associated with the more conservative Sparta. Yet Aristophanes shows that Athenians anywhere will still act like Athenians and will reproduce the Athenian spirit even in an environment completely hostile to it.

What marks all of these competing elements of the play as distinctively comic, rather than partisan, is that all of the characters, no matter how repulsive in appearance or speech, are written with some sense of affection. Indeed, one of the reasons it is so difficult to determine a clear ideological position in Aristophanes, or any true comedy for that matter, is that all of the major characters retain elements of virtue and thereby humanity. Pisthetairos may end up a tyrant who has rhetorically manipulated the birds into a position where they are now not only his subjects but also his dinner, but the audience cannot help but like him just the same, because he *is* the audience, both in virtue and in vice. As Arrowsmith explains: "Energy, lustiness, enterprise, chicanery, rascality, ingenuity, and restless, inquisitive, innovative intelligence—these are his nature. No less a part of his nature is the other side of the same coin—that mischievous meddlesomeness, that insatiability . . . that metaphysical discontent that makes Athenian man and the imperial city the new giants of a contemporary Gigantomachy."[4] For Athenians to see Pisthetairos strutting about on stage is to gain a perspective on themselves by seeing a personification of their own city reflected in a different light, using distorted mirrors. Rather than being offended at seeing their most glorified ideals represented as a bulging phallus and their most eloquent speech delivered with a protruding tongue, they are able to laugh at their own limitations and thus provide themselves the ability to do what Achilles could not—yield, forgive, smile, pity, and ultimately change course.

When comedy is understood this way—that is, as an expression of a general attitude rather than a vehicle for a specific idea—whatever ideological tendency a particular play or playwright might express becomes less important than how it cultivates in the members of an audience an ability to take oneself lightly and to bestow grace upon another. For the comic attitude is simply to be aware that all of one's most heroic actions, noblest beliefs, and idealistic goals often appear ridiculous and partial in the objective light of the whole, and that our conflicts more often than not are the result of our mistakenness about ourselves, about others, and about our situation brought about by a combination of ignorance, *eros,* and *hubris.* But if this is true, then comedy has a crucial part to play in the maintenance of power in a rhetorical culture. For if authentic political power represents not simply the capacity to act in concert in the moment but over time, then true power requires an audience capable of voluntary self-correction in order to avoid the tragic suffering that comes from the one-way movement of necessity. So just as the Informant must choose between wings and words, so too are political actors constantly challenged to either transcend their animal origins and seek a higher purpose over the horizon, or rest content with the satiation of their bodily pleasures in the moment. The question for rhetoric is whether, through the power of words, audiences are manipulated into forgetting the difference, thereby allowing them to give divine sanction to their most libidinal impulses. But comedy always stands ready to remind us that sometimes we are eager to achieve great goals is because, deep down, we just really desire to take a shit whenever we want or to lay our lovers in peace.

A funny thing happens when Pisthetairos returns to the stage after having persuaded the birds to support his ambitious plan to storm Mount Olympus—he sprouts wings. Tiny wings, to be sure, with just a few feathers, but wings nonetheless, the result of eating a "wonderful magic root" given to him by Hoopoe (47). Therefore, despite his later argument that words are even more powerful than wings, he nonetheless desires wings. Wings, after all, can still do what words cannot. During the *parabasis,* or the break in the middle of the play when the chorus speaks directly to the audience on behalf of the playwright, the birds attempt to convince the humans in attendance that an avian hegemony would be beneficial to them as well. In addition to providing the gift of prophecy, the end of corruption, a hideout from the law, health, wealth, happiness, youth, long life, laughter, peace, dancing, and lots to eat, they also can literally give humans wings, which provide innumerable benefits:

> Think, spectators.
> Imagine yourself with a pair of wings!
> The sheer joy of it! Not having to sit those tragedies out!
> No getting bored. You merely flap your little wings and fly off home.
> You have a snack, then you make it back to catch the COMIC play.
> Or again, suppose you're overtaken by sudden need to crap.
> Do you do it in your pants?
> Not a bit.
> You just zoom off,
> fart and shit to your heart's content and whizz right back.
> Or perhaps you're having an affair—I won't name any names.
> You spot the lady's husband attending some meeting or other.
> Up you soar, flap your wings, through the window and into bed!
> You make it a quickie, of course, then flutter back to your seat.
> So what do you say?
> Aren't wings just the most *wonderful* things? (55)

Anticipating the logic of the Informant, the chorus praises wings for their purely instrumental function as a form of transportation, only in this case giving people a greater ability to escape, defecate, and fornicate rather than deliver subpoenas. And Pisthetairos, too, despite his praise of words over wings, still acknowledges wings' instrumental value. Although it is unclear what instrumental use Pisthetairos will make of his wings, one thing is at least clear: he sees the power of words somehow being an extension of the power of flight rather than its competitor or replacement. His attempt to persuade the Informant to choose words rather than wings was therefore not to denigrate wings, but to encourage the Informant to put his wings (if he acquired any) to use pursuing a more virtuous and civilized goal than profiting off of others' misery. At the very least, he could simply rest content with the pleasures of farting and screwing at his leisure.

The parallel between words and wings established in *Birds* represents more than just a particularly creative trope; it also exemplifies one of the central motifs of comedy, which is the continuity between our highest ideals and our most primitive impulses. Indeed, if there is a consistent theory of power in the plays of Aristophanes, is that all forms of "civilized" power, including the power of politics, religion, culture, and war, is in one way or another simply an extension of the natural erotic impulses that we share with all living creatures. Among the most enduring images of Aristophanic comedy are actors dressed as animals, donning padded rumps and bellies, and strutting with erect phalluses. Three of his plays, *The Wasps, The Frogs,* and *Birds,* literally describe human beings as if they were animals, and almost all others have some graphic display of sexuality, defecation, and physical violence reminiscent of a pack of dogs.

However, these costumes and behaviors were not intended as some shocking disclosure of suppressed human bestiality lurking beneath the veneer of human civilization. As Kenneth Rothwell Jr. has argued, the animal imagery in Aristophanes had a far more positive and natural symbolism. In his reading of the Greek rituals from which comedy emerged, "animals represent the forces of fertility and procreation in the world around us, and for that reason were associated with gods such as Dionysius, Artemis, and Poseidon."[5] Rather than representing an antithesis and threat to the virtues of civilization, animals were thought to be able to "contribute to human civilization"—at least provided that their native impulses and powers were either superseded or transformed.[6] From this perspective, when Pisthetairos grows wings it does not symbolize a dissent into savagery, but rather an ability to use words to channel the power of nature toward even higher aims and purposes.

Yet the persistent lesson of comedy is that these higher aims and purposes, however noble and inspiring they may be, are never fully detached from their biological origins and accompanying corruptions and absurdities. As high as Pisthetairos flies with word-powered wings, he will always exhibit those base instincts and raw erotic desires that he shares with his animal brethren. For instance, immediately after having pronounced the glories of the new empire to the chorus of birds, exhibiting his *eros* for them and their noblest aspirations, Pisthetairos is reduced to shouting cat calls at Prokne, the beautiful Nightingale wife of Hoopoe who has emerged to escort him and Euelpides into her home: "Almighty Zeus! Gosh, what a baby of a Birdie! / What curves! What grace! What a looker!" (49). Euelpides is even more overcome with erotic desire, slobbering: "Gee! By god, / I'd like to bounce between her thighs right now!" (49). Contemporary political morality might consider this juxtaposition of idealistic vision and sexual craving to be something of a scandal, but on the comic stage in Athens it is simply a reflection of the human condition. The same impulse which drives Pisthetairos to persuade the birds to become like gods is the same impulse which makes him wants to seduce the Nightingale and bounce between her thighs, a fact which is less a sign of depravity than of mortality.

Indeed, if one characteristic stands out among all others in the "Old Comedy" of the fifth century B.C.E., of which Aristophanes is the highest example, it is the relentless juxtaposition of grandiose ideas and inflated personalities with the most elementary bodily functions that make us indistinguishable from all other natural organisms. In contrast with the "New Comedy" of the fourth and third centuries B.C.E., which established the model for contemporary dramas largely focused on a realistic representation of the humorous trials and tribulations of ordinary people, most often in romance, "Old Comedy" used fantastic sets, nonlinear plots, grotesque imagery, and spectacular caricature to shine the most ridiculous light upon contemporary affairs and the people at the center of power.[7] Still, as Hamilton notes, there is nothing essentially cruel about comic irony. In Old Comedy, "life looks a coarse and vulgar thing, lived at the level of nature's primitive needs, but it never looks a foul and rotten thing. Degeneracy plays no part. It is the way of a virile world, of robust men who can roar with laughter at any kind of slapstick, decent or indecent, but chiefly the last."[8] That "robust" women were also at the heart of many of Aristophanes's comedies, notably *Lysistrata* and *The Congresswomen,* also bears mention, for few other stimuli make virile men act like idiots than the appearance of a woman with strong character and beautiful countenance. The laughter was not from feeling superior to a particular person who possessed a particular vice, but rather from showing how even the most powerful leaders had to crap after dinner, how even the most cultured democratic public wanted to gorge themselves on free sausage, how even the most ascetic philosopher had uncontrollable erections, and how even the stateliest old matrons still wanted to get laid.

In order to understand the potential rhetorical significance of this dramatic form, it is crucial to first recognize that the form of Old Comedy grew out of much older traditions whose function was largely social and ritual. Following the argument first articulated by Francis Macdonald Cornford, the spirit of Old Comedy is not an original product of fifth-century politics invented to advance the ideologies of the playwrights or critique the ideologies of the powerful, but a creative modification of seasonal festivals common to many ancient cultures and which continue in some form in the present day. According to Cornford, the structure of Old Comedy was based on the dramatic form of the primitive seasonal pantomime in which there was a ritual combat (*agōn*) between two antagonists (usually representing one of the dialectical pairs of the Old Year and New Year, Summer and Winter, Rainfall and Drought, Life and Death, Age and Youth, etc.), the death and resurrection of one of the warring parties, usually accompanied by a feast, and a sacred marriage whereby the victor chooses a bride (often a kind of "May queen") as a means of promoting fertility and regeneration in the new season, year, or age. Finally, these festivals usually ended in a *komos,* or "revel," which was a bawdy, drunken procession often accompanied by people carrying giant mock phalluses and singing "phallic songs." Cornford concludes that "the protagonist in comedy must originally have been the spirit of fertility himself, Phales or Dionysus," which would account for where comedy got its name, *komoidia,* the song (*ode*) of the *komos.*[9]

The list of possible resources upon which Old Comedy drew for inspiration has since expanded since Cornford proposed his thesis in 1914, with Rothwell also demonstrating continuities with symposiums, ritual masquerades, formal choruses, and pre-comic choruses which often featured "padded dancers, phallic dancers, satyrs, men wearing animal ears, and foreigners."[10] Thus, although Cornford's effort to fit every single one of Aristophanes's comedies into the form of seasonal pantomime now seems forced, his basic point remains well-supported—that comedy was a dramatic continuation and adaptation of the carnival character of more ancient festivals. Rothwell notes that "role-reversals and carnivalesque inversions, in which we find that authority figures are deposed or humiliated and that representatives of marginalized members of society triumph, have always been among the most powerful engines driving the genre of comedy," and that "festivals are fitting models for comedy in that both operate by temporarily violating proper decorum in overturning the conventions of everyday life."[11] In ancient Greece, Dionysian festivals offered temporary release from social norms and sanctions, and it was not unusual during these festivals to find prisoners released, legal proceedings and state business banned, leaders held up to public ridicule, revelers dressed in fantastic costumes shouting obscenities, and slaves and foreigners given free rein to enjoy lavish banquets. For Greeks to see the same things occurring on stage would simply signify for them that their spontaneous celebrations had inspired a form of conscious art whose primary function was to evoke the uninhibited laughter of collective revelry.

And for the Greeks, this laughter itself represented a form of power. But comic laughter was a curious kind of power, because it was not grounded in any explicit "content" or "truth" which could be embodied in a Logos and validated by reason or verified by appearances. Rather, it represented the pure form of what Arendt calls *natality*, or "the capacity of beginning something anew."[12] In comedy, it is often unclear just *what* has begun because the birth has just occurred and the rest of the story remains to be told. But comedy, unlike tragedy, is not concerned with endings, but beginnings. The power it represents is simply the power to start over. This facet of comedy is perhaps expressed most fully by Mikhail Bakhtin in his discussion of the history of laughter. Laughter, he says, "liberates not only from external censorship but first of all from the great internal censor; it liberates from the fear that developed in man during thousands of years: fear of the sacred, of prohibitions, of the past, of power."[13] Unlike the seriousness which lurked behind tragedy, then, "laughter created no dogmas and could not become authoritarian; it did not convey fear but a feeling of strength. It was linked with the procreating act, with birth, renewal, fertility, abundance. Laughter was also related to food and drink and the people's earthly immortality, and finally it was related to the future of things to come and was to clear the way for them."[14] Just as bawdy, rollicking celebrations still accompany modern celebrations of Halloween, Mardi Gras, New Year's festivals, bachelor and bachelorette parties, graduations, and birthdays, so too did ancient festivals evoke comic laughter whenever the transition between the old and the new gave people the opportunity to abandon themselves completely to the consciousness of freedom out of which sprung the eternal power of renewal.

What was striking about the Greek experience of the fifth century B.C.E. was not, therefore, the mere existence of the comic spirit, which had been cultivated for centuries not only in Greek festivals but in those throughout the ancient world; what was striking was that it appeared as an officially sanctioned art that often took as its subject matter explicit political and cultural controversies of the day. Hamilton remarks that "nobody and nothing escaped the ridicule of Old Comedy. The gods came in for their share; so did the institutions dearest to the Athenians; so did the most popular and powerful individuals, often by name. The freedom of speech is staggering to our ideas."[15] By "our ideas," Hamilton clearly means the prevalent notions that freedom of speech, while important to a democracy, reaches its limits when it threatens security, offends sacred beliefs, or undermines the legitimacy of power. Yet for the Athenians of the fifth century B.C.E., who lived in a pure democracy in which power ultimately rested with the people, nothing was considered off limits. They flocked to the theater to see a play like *The Knights*, Aristophanes's brutal parody of the demagogue Cleon, who is shown competing with a sausage-seller for control of the *demos* (personified as Demos, an old man), only to be continually outwitted and ultimately "condemned to peddle the sausages made of dog-meat and donkey-dung which his victorious successor used to sell."[16] One can only imagine the fate of an artist today who would publicly ridicule and lampoon a nation's leader at an analogous time of crisis and war. At the very least, this artist would be subject to public condemnation and at worst convicted of treason; he or she most certainly would not win first prize at a popular competition, as *The Knights* did at the Lenaia festival in 424 B.C.E.

Aristophanes could get away with this kind of thing because even his clear references to Cleon did not always carry explicit ideological commitments that were akin to rhetorical arguments. In other words, the plays of Aristophanes did not resort to the kind of explicitly partisan humor which Burke refers to as "burlesque" rather than comic, in which burlesque represents a kind of "pamphleteering " that uses as its primary method a "reduction to absurdity" which is intended to belittle and mock one's opponents.[17] Whereas comedy tends to hold all aspects of society up to equal scrutiny, burlesque has a narrower vision which is strategically partial in its representation. Burke explains: "The method of burlesque (polemic, caricature) is partial not only in the sense of *partisan,* but also in the sense of *incompleteness.* As such, it does not contain a well-rounded frame within itself."[18] In other words, burlesque selectively chooses only the negative characteristics of undesirable others in order to exaggerate them into a kind of imbalanced monstrosity to be held up to ridicule, much as old-time minstrel shows in the United States employing the crassest of racial stereotypes to flatter the superiority of the white audience. By contrast, comedic satire often draws a more sympathetic and complete portrait of the other, even as it exaggerates his or her idiosyncrasies and flaws. This is because, as Burke points out, "the satirist attacks *in others* the weaknesses and temptations that are really *within himself.*"[19] Satire is thus consistent with the comic intention not to take sides but to implicate all of humanity in the crime of stupidity; only it does so by showing the weaknesses of humanity at work in the portrayal of the few or the one.

This more humanistic, more inclusive characteristic gave comedy a central place in the *polis* quite apart from any party's ideological commitments. Attic comedy flourished precisely because it served a crucial function in the maintenance of power within a democratic state. The Athenians realized that the greatest threat to their own power was an excess of the very thing which produced that power, which was liberty itself—specifically the liberty to say, and thereby potentially to do, whatever one wished. As Jaeger puts it, "comedy was produced by democracy as an antidote to its own overdose of liberty, thereby outdoing its own excesses, and extending *parrhesia,* its vaunted freedom of speech, to subjects which are usually tabu even in a free political system."[20] From its origins in festive rituals that welcomed the new in a celebration of uninhibited freedom, Attic comedy evolved into an art by which a political culture could use laughter to continually liberate itself from its own ideological dogmas, habitual blindnesses, and outworn conventions. Thus, "when it chose, it censured not only individuals, not only separate political acts, but the entire governmental system, the character and the weaknesses of the whole nation. It controlled the spirit of the people, and kept a constant watch on education, philosophy, poetry, and music . . . [which] were brought to judgment in the theater before the whole Athenian people."[21] Through comedy, the *demos* was able to laugh at itself and thus ensure that the collective will and enthusiasm which constituted its power did not allow the people to develop uncritical belief in their own superiority, infallibility, and virtue.

An excellent example of how comedy keeps a watchful and critical eye on the spirit of the whole people occurs when a messenger arrives to immediately prostrate himself in front of Pisthetairos after the announcement of the birds' victory over the gods. The messenger had been sent to earth to solicit the allegiance of human beings, and now he returns with a crown of gold "proffered in honor of your glorious wisdom and chicane by an adoring world" (81). Pisthetairos is deeply honored but asks why the humans selected him to be their lord. The messenger's answer indicates how Aristophanes had been keeping careful notes on the latest fashions:

> O fabulous founder of great Cloudcuckooland,
> how can you ask such a question? Have you not heard
> that Pisthetairos has become the darling of the mortal world,
> a name to conjure with, that all mankind
> has gone Clouccuckoolandophile,
> madly, utterly?
> And yet, only yesterday,
> before your dispensation in the sky became a fact,
> and Spartan craze had swept the faddish world.
> Why, men went mad with mimicry of Sokrates,
> affected long hair, indifferent mood,
> rustic walking sticks, total bathlessness,
> and led to, in short, what I can only call
> a Spartan existence.
> But then suddenly, overnight,
> the birds became the vogue, the *dernier cri*
> of human fashion. And men immediately began
> to feather their own nests; to cluck and brood;
> play ducks and drakes; grub for chickenfeed;

hatch deals, and being rooked or gulled,
to have their little gooses cooked. But if they grouse,
they still are game.
In sum, the same old life,
but feathered over with the faddish thrills of being
chic. (81–82)

Although this example points out only one non-bird fashion trend in Athenian culture, that of the Spartan chic of Socrates and his followers, one can imagine that there was likely an infinite number of examples Aristophanes could choose from. For one of the essential attitudes of the comedian is a watchful and critical eye toward any novelty in culture that could be presented before the public in exaggerated form to be laughed at and thereby judged. Just as it is human nature to chase after novelties for the sake of being chic, it is in the nature of comedy to stand just far enough away to ridicule fashion with a knowing wink.

As with tragedy, then, comedy has a complicated relationship with rhetoric insofar as a work diminishes in comic effect to the degree that it is interpreted as advancing an explicit partisan intent. Just as tragedy becomes didactic under ideological pressure and thereby loses its capacity to evoke transcendence, comedy becomes burlesque and therefore severely constricts the experience of freedom that accompanies laughter. In comedy, this constraint occurs regardless of the ideological interpretation. For instance, Konstan points out that, in the nineteenth century, the *Birds* was interpreted allegorically to be both a celebration and a condemnation of Athenian imperialism. On the one hand, J. W. Suevern argued that the *Birds* "is a kind of allegory to dissuade the Athenians from the Sicilian expedition by exposing its folly."[22] On the other hand, H. A. T. Kőchly argued the reverse, that Cloudcuckooland is actually is an affectionate exaggeration of an ideal city: "it is to be a democracy, but yet to have a head: a Periclean democracy. And the head recommended or hinted at . . . is Alcibiades."[23] These two interpretations point to different aspects of the play for support, but the effect of each is the same—to reduce the comic play to a rhetorical vehicle for an idea, with laughter as its lubricant. But if this is the case, then comedy, no less than tragedy, is in reality a variant of rhetoric—a trope—and cannot stand alone as a poetic category.

This is not to deny that comedy often has a very close relationship to ideology; it is simply to insist that this relationship is not one of vehicle to content. Rather, comedy uses ideology as a resource from which to build dramatic tensions and disclose humorous incongruities which are immediately recognizable to an audience. Burke, in fact, offers a definition of ideology in his early writings which makes explicit this relationship insofar as he calls ideology "the nodus of beliefs and judgments which an artist can exploit for his effects."[24] For Burke, any dominant ideology of a culture is often not as "harmonious" as it is made out to be: "some of its beliefs militate against others, and some of its standards militate against our nature. An ideology is an aggregate of beliefs sufficiently at odds with one another to justify opposite kinds of conduct."[25] Whereas the function of the partisan is to downplay these tensions in order to justify a particular action based on a coherent rationalization, the function of the artist is to inhabit these points of opposition and conflict and magnify their intensity and complexity for the sake of achieving aesthetic form. Tragedy, for example, often places its characters in the middle of an event which represents the central ethical, spiritual, or political upheaval of an era to reveal the depth of a moral crisis, while comedy follows its characters through a multitude of lesser conflicts in order to show the breadth of absurdity within a heterogeneous culture. And it is for the latter reason, Burke concludes that "humorous writers are better equipped today than the tragic ones, since humor results of a discrepancy between ideological assumptions, and the great conflict of standards in contemporary society gives the artist a considerable range of such discrepancies to select from."[26] And it is for the same reason that Old Comedy flourished in the middle of the fifth century B.C.E., when Athens represented the crossroads of the Western world.

Because of the nature of the "content" of comedy—the tensions, disjunctions, and incongruities within and between ideologies—most comic works of art, by sheer acts of selection and emphasis, tend to favor certain ideological tendencies over others. In his reading of Old Comedy, for instance, Konstan concludes that, although there is no explicit political message or unambiguous authorial voice in any of Aristophanes's remaining plays, "there is, however, a complex of ideologically valorized elements that are not wholly reconcilable with each other, but which in combination yield determinate ideological effects: not a political line, necessarily, but an angle of vision, from which some social possibilities are occluded and others are rendered especially visible."[27] Although comedy convicts all of humanity for the crime of stupidity, not all acts of stupidity are created equal. Konstan reads the *Birds* neither as an explicit criticism nor as a valorization of the Sicilian expedition and its leaders, but rather as a work of art which uses the expedition as an opportunity to dramatize the conflicts in Athenian culture, in which some sides come off looking better than others. In his reading, "*Birds* portrays a utopian regime that is complexly imagined as both passive and restlessly aggressive, united in a primitive communalism yet driven by libidinous impulses to domination and riven by hierarchical tensions. In the midst of Athens' bid in 414 B.C. for domination over the entire Mediterranean, *Birds* projects a fantasy of limitless power that simultaneously reasserts the conservative ideal of a bygone age of social harmony."[28] In this way, Konstan follows Arrowsmith in finding the central theme of *Birds* to be exaggerating the virtues and vices of Athenian *polupragmosunē*, but concludes, on balance, that Aristophanes finds more to ridicule in contemporary democratic ideologies than in the more conservative traditions of the past.

Comedy thus inevitably takes on a rhetorical character insofar as an audience interprets certain habits, situations, beliefs, attitudes, ideologies, people, or institutions as being held up to "special" mockery in order to undermine authority through a combination of familiarity (which demystifies) and laughter (which levels). For instance, the character of the insubordinate son who wishes to beat his father is a frequent target of ridicule in Aristophanes's plays, and appears again in the *Birds* as a "delinquent" who comes to the new city because he has heard of a "splendid custom you got / that permits a little Bird to choke his daddy dead" (84). Representing the upstart power of the rising generation, Aristophanes uses this character to place a special critical judgment on lack of piety for tradition and respect for elders. Yet because the play is a comedy and not a burlesque, the intended effect is not necessarily to condemn these characters and literally purge them from the city, as occurs in the play. Rather, this hyperbole is to be interpreted more generously because an audience understands that it is the function of comedy, in Burke's words, to use "ridicule to deter men from temptations that would threaten the social order."[29] That is why the parade of unwanted visitors to Cloudcuckooland is so necessary for the comic function of the play, even though it does not advance any kind of plot. More important to Old Comedy than telling a good story is the ability to wheel on stage every absurdity of Greek culture for proper ridicule—and Aristophanes found more absurdities in the extreme tendencies of democracy than in anything else.

If there is a general "purpose" to the *Birds,* it has little to do with whether we should celebrate or condemn the character of prophets, delinquents, informants, birds, the gods, the demos, or Pisthetairos. As Arrowsmith points out, Aristophanes ironically ridicules almost every aspect of Greek culture, but his "irony is, I think, loving."[30] And this essentially "loving" character is the central mark of comedy. According to Burke, the primary attitude of comedy is not one of rejection but of acceptance, specifically the acceptance that we should picture "people not as *vicious,* but as *mistaken,*" that "all people are exposed to situations in which they must act as fools, [and] that *every* insight contains its own special kind of blindness."[31] From this perspective, Aristophanes uses the language of praise and blame not in an explicitly rhetorical sense to criticize the Sicilian expedition, to undermine Athenian imperialist ambitions, or to create sympathy for the suffering allies; he uses it in a poetic sense to show artistically how all people, put in certain circumstances, will pursue the most sublime ambitions while revealing themselves to be utterly ridiculous—and that the Athenians are the most ridiculous of all Greeks because they are also the most powerful.

Yet if pure comedy is not rhetorical in the sense of advocating a particular *logos* in competition with others, it does nonetheless have rhetorical significance insofar as it uses dramatic irony to illuminate human relationship to power. As Burke explains it, dramatic irony allows the audience to see "the operations of errors that the characters of the play cannot see; thus seeing from two angles at once, it is chastened by dramatic irony."[32] Specifically, by showing how the grand ambitions often create spectacular failures and are based on gross misunderstandings, the audience is "is admonished to remember that when intelligence means wisdom (in contrast with the modern tendency to look upon intelligence as merely a *coefficient of power* for heightening our ability to get things, be they good or bad), it requires fear, resignation, the sense of limits, as an important ingredient."[33] By doing so, comedy thus returns "again to the lesson of humility that underlies great tragedy," but it does so without cloaking its heroes in nobility that accompanies the capacity to suffer greatly for a virtuous cause.[34] Instead, comedy tells us that more often than not our cause is mistaken, our facts are in error, our illusions are too grandiose, our judgments are too harsh, and our image of ourselves is too distorted. Rather than validating our suffering by attributing it to fateful necessity, it tells us that most of our suffering is unnecessary because it was produced by foolishness and that such suffering can be remedied through mutual understanding made possible by critical self-awareness, forgiveness of others, and an acceptance of contingency.

One of the ethical themes of comedy is that sometimes, by dropping our dogged resistance and yielding to the requests of others, we can achieve not only greater happiness but greater power. In the *Birds,* a series of such comic reconciliations occurs, beginning with the collaboration between Hoopoe and the two Athenians and then between the Athenians and the rest of the birds. The second of these confrontations is the most dramatic. When Hoopoe attempts to introduce Pisthetairos and Euelpides to the rest of the birds, their leader, Koryphaios, immediately declares Hoopoe to be a traitor and orders an assault on the two interlopers. Showing their resourcefulness, the Athenians defend themselves with platters (for shields), skewers (for spears), and jugs (for helmets), and hold off the assault until a momentary truce is called. At this point comic reconciliation occurs as the two parties agree to consider each other's perspectives:

KORYPHAIOS: Why spare these men any more than wolves? What worst enemy than men do we Birds have?

HOOPOE: Enemies by nature, I admit. / But these men are exceptions to the rule. They come to you as / friends. Moreover, they bring a scheme from which we birds stand to / profit.

KORYPHAIOS: Are you suggesting that Birds should take advice from men? / What can *we* learn from men?

HOOPOE: If wise men learn from their enemies, / then why not you? / Remember the advantage of keeping an open mind. / Preparedness, after all, is not a lesson taught us by our friends / but by our enemies. It is our enemies, not our friends, who teach / us how to survive. / I might cite the case of cities: was it from their friends or their foes / that mankind learned first to build walls and ships in self-defense? / But that one lesson still preserves us all in all we have.

KORYPHAIOS: There is something in what you say. / Perhaps we'd better hear them. (33)

This kind of reconciliation between sworn enemies is a consistent trope of comedy. As Aristotle explains, in comedy "the bitterest enemies in the piece . . . walk off good friends at the end, with no slaying of any one by any one" (*Poetics*, 1453a35). But even more important than the "happy ending" is the reason it comes about. In comedy, reconciliation is made possible only after a series of absurd, usually agonistic actions that expose each party to be mistaken both about themselves and the other. It is the dramatization of these actions, like the madcap battle between Pisthetairos and Koryphaios, which form the centerpiece of comedy; for without first seeing ourselves as ridiculous, it is impossible to ever transcend our own biases and limitations that inhibit our ability to act in concert with others with understanding and charity.

Fortunately for comedy, this state of perfect understanding and humility is never actually attained; the human capacity for manipulation and self-delusion is infinite. For instance, no sooner has Pisthetairos reconciled with Koryphaios and the birds than he attempts to exploit this newfound trust in order to make the birds do his bidding. In a masterful satire of the demagogic style, Aristophanes shows Pisthetairos methodically working the birds into a jingoistic frenzy that establishes them as the superior race above both gods and humans. His method: to give the birds a feast, a "dinner of words, a fat and succulent haunch of speech, a meal to shiver the soul" (38). His goal: to "envisage a vision of glory, / a dream so fantastic / it staggers the sensible mind" (35). Aristophanes then presents what is, in effect, a succinct breakdown of the steps of this method, at each point exaggerating its tactics while subtly revealing its essential shallowness and absurdity.

For Aristophanes, then, the content of Pisthetairos's speech is less important than its form. "Cloudcuckooland" is simply a stand-in for any fantasy of absolute power; what matters is not the particularity of the fantasy but the manner in which rhetoric generates erotic desire for that fantasy in the minds and bodies of an audience capable of translating that desire into collective action. At the same time, however, Pisthetairos is a genuine advocate for the birds for whom we cannot help but feel some sort of affection and loyalty. It is this feeling of duality—of being drawn to a person or argument at the same time that one recognizes its inherent flaws—that is the most productive consequence of comic discourse, for it habituates an audience to feelings of doubt and ambiguity that are the enemies of dogmatism and ideology and enablers of reflection and deliberation. In short, one of the most important political contributions of the *Birds* is its ability to unmask and critique the rhetorical methods of the demagogue that came to play such a central role in the constitution of Athenian power after the death of Pericles.

It is through Pisthetairos's speech, then, that we get the clearest rhetorical critique of the methods of the demagogue, even as those methods are portrayed with the greatest degree of ridiculousness. Demonstrating the function of comedy as a form of social censor, Aristophanes uses the speech to hold up for public judgment the way that demagogues use proofs of *ethos, pathos,* and *logos* to whip his audience into the frenzy that makes them the willing instruments for someone else's political aims. For instance, Aristophanes realistically begins the speech by having Pisthetairos accomplish the first aim of the imperialist demagogue, which is to flatter an audience into believing in the superiority and virtue of its *ethos* by grounding it in *mythos.* He does this, however, by making the most grandiose claim possible—that the birds were the original rulers of the universe. Yet this assertion is strategically dropped only as a hint that piques the curiosity of the audience, thus showing Pisthetairos's sophistication as a rhetor: "Unhappy Birds, I grieve for you, / you who were once kings—" he says, at which point he is immediately interrupted by the skeptical Koryphaios: "Kings? Of what?" (38). Having planted the seed of the audience's own greatness, Pisthetairos starts cultivating their *hubris* by weaving a mythic history of origins that establishes their nobility of birth and their fall from power: "Kings of everything. / Kings of creation. My Kings. This man's kings. Kings of king Zeus. / More ancient than Kronos. Older than Titans. Older than Earth" (38). But if this is true (proven by the fact that "the Lark is the oldest thing in the world"), then there are political consequences (38). For "if the birds are older than Earth, / and therefore older than gods, then the birds are the heirs of the world. / For the oldest always inherits" (38). Yet this has not happened, Pisthetairos argues, because the gods, "mere upstarts and usurpers of a very recent date," have attempted to erase this hidden history and thereby keep the birds in a state of miserable subservience (39). But now that Pisthetairos has revealed the truth, it is time for the birds to seek their rightful place in power.

Having established the principle, Pisthetairos must then accomplish the second task, which is to provide a veneer of empirical validation for this *mythos* which is capable of persuading a skeptical audience. He does so by pointing to specific phenomena that function as signs of the birds' former glory, thus demonstrating the capacity of language to alter the nature of appearances and thereby evoke powerful emotional responses to images in the imagination. Again, this is a common strategy in political rhetoric, but the comic treatment makes it explicit by having Pisthetairos draw the most radical inferences from the most mundane observations. For instance, he argues that the rooster is called the Persian Red because, eons ago, "the kingdom of Persia lay prostrate beneath the sway of the Rooster" (39). The reason that "mankind goes meekly off to work" when the cock crows is because memory has enshrined the ancient power of a birds' command in habit (39). For similar reasons are the scepters of Homeric Kings like Agamemnon tipped with bird feathers, and why Zeus "wears an Eagle upon his helmet as the symbol of royal power," just as "Athena uses the Owl, and Apollo, as an aide to Zeus, a Hawk" (40). And finally, "that's why when men sacrifice to the gods, the Birds swoop down / and snatch the food, / thereby beating out the gods, and so asserting their old priority" (40). These, he says, are the remnants of "the honors you held in the days of your greatness," days that he suggests may return if the birds are able to act in concert to assert their power (41). When it comes to flattering an audience, apparently, any evidence will suffice.

Now Pisthetairos begins the third task of rousing the *pathos* that shatters the complacency of an audience and prepares them for passionate action. He does this not only by concentrating attention on an immediate exigency to rouse feelings of fear, anger, and urgency, but by doing so in lyrical verse in order to use music to create a whole body response. Pisthetairos laments: "whereas now you've been downgraded. / You're the slaves, not lords, of men. / They call you brainless or crazy. / They kill you whenever they can." (41). But this fact alone is not enough to make them sigh, weep, and beat their breasts with their wings. Further graphic display is required. Satirizing the tendency for speakers of all types to bewail their sorry state brought about by no fault of their own, Aristophanes presents the ideal audience for the demagogue as a group who feels as if they are analogous to a cooked chicken:

> And when you're taken, they sell you
> as tiny *hors d'oeuvres* for lunch
> and you're not even sold alone,
> but lumped and bought by the bunch.

And buyers come crowding round
and pinch your breast and your rump
to see if your fleshes are firm
and your little bodies are plump.

Then, as if this weren't enough,
they refuse to roast you whole,
but dump you down in the dish
and call you a casserole.

They grind up cheese and spices
with some oil and other goo,
they take the slimy gravy
and they pour it over you!

Yes, they pour it over you! (41)

The power of this grotesque imagery is overwhelming. After the song concludes, the birds in chorus break into a heartrending lament over their own failure to emancipate themselves: "stranger, forgive us if we cry, / reliving in your words / those years of cowardice that brought / disaster to the Birds:— / that tragic blunder / and our fathers' crime. / Complacency whose cost / was greatness and our name, / as dignity went under / in a chicken-hearted time, / and all was lost" (42). Never mind that such a history did not exist; for the birds, the rhetoric of Pisthetairos has made real to their imaginations a tragic history to which they must urgently respond by pledging themselves, their nests, and their chicks, to Pisthetairos, "Savior of the Birds, / Redeemer of our Race!" (42). For an audience that feels as if it is about to be put into an oven and served with gravy and vegetables, what other choice is there?

Even at this point, the goal of the demagogue has not been accomplished. A fourth and final task remains, which is to direct the combined forces of *ethos*, *mythos*, and *pathos* through a critical *logos* that sets forth a clear path of action capable of mobilizing the energies of the collective in the immediate present. Thus, when the birds give the floor back to Pisthetairos, he immediately puts them to work: "my plan, in gist, is this—a city of the Birds, / whose walls and ramparts shall include the atmosphere of the world / within their circuit. But make the walls of brick, like Babylon" (42). To accomplish this revolution, the birds must follow his plan to the letter. After building the city walls, they must then: first, proclaim a Holy War against the gods, "then slap embargoes on their lust, forbidding any gods / in a manifest state of erection to travel through your sky / on amatory errands down to earth to lay their women— / their Semeles,

Alkmenes, and so forth. Then, if they attempt to ignore / your warning, place their offending peckers under bond / as contraband and seal them shut" (43); second, inform human beings that "the Birds demand priority / in all their sacrifices," and if they refuse to worship the Birds, "then swarms of starving sparrows / shall descend on their fields in millions and gobble up their seats. / They'll damn well go hungry" (43); third, actively recruit human allies by promising them rewards for proper obedience, including using owls to wipe out locusts, "troops of Thrushes to annihilate the bugs," the proper interpretation of oracles which will promise them riches, the promise to locate shipwrecks for buried treasure, and the promise of longevity (44–45). The plan works perfectly. Hoopoe, the former and soon-to-be-deposed leader of the Birds, expresses succinctly the intended effect of Pisthetairos's rhetoric: "Action, dammit, action! That's what we need. / Strike while the iron's hot. No dawdling around / like slowpoke Nikias" (46).[35] His persuasive goals complete, Pisthetairos exits the stage with Hoopoe to gorge himself on a feast while gaping at the curves of the beautiful nightingale, Prokne.

That Aristophanes has clearly intended his portrayal of Pisthetairos as a critical unmasking of demagogic persuasion, and its accompanying *hubris,* is made evident at the very end of the play when the chorus of birds gives its final evaluation of the new tyrant. Reminding the audience that Gorgias had used his own persuasive skills to appeal to Athenians for military support of his Sicilian hometown of Leontini, the chorus associates the rhetoric of Pisthetairos with that of the Sophists and then suggests to the audience what to do with those who peddle their wares:

> Beneath the clock in a courtroom,
> down in the Land of Gab,
> We saw a weird race of people,
> earning their bread by blab.
>
> Their name is the Claptraptummies.
> Their only tool is talk.
> They sow and reap and shake the figs
> by dexterous yakkity-yak.
>
> Their tongues and twaddle mark them off,
> barbarians every one;
> but the worst of all are in the firm
> of GORGIAS & SON.
>
> But from this bellyblabbing tribe,
> one customs here to stay:

in Athens, when men sacrifice,
they cut the tongue away. (104)

In this rollicking song, Aristophanes punctures the inflated fantasies of the powerful and shows them to be expressions of their own self-serving ambitions and erotic desires. According to Arrowsmith, this final ode is a comic effort to bring people back to the earth from flights into possibility made possible by words. He writes: "a politics rooted in reality, in things-as-they-are, in true *physis,* is the only alternative to fantasy politics; just as reality, the experience of failed fantasy, of crashing to earth, is the only ultimate consequence and conclusion of fantasy politics."[36] For Aristophanes, only when we are able to correct our own fantasies through laughter grounded in reality can we avoid an inevitable fall not only from grace but from power.

Rhetoric adopts a comic attitude whenever it acknowledges that the unchecked pursuit of power culminates in stupidity. From the comic perspective, lasting power does not come from the uninhibited pursuit of grandiose ambitions made possible by rhetorical aggrandizement and manipulation; rather, it is produced when rhetoric creates mutual understanding between antagonistic parties which allows them to act in concert, despite their differences, toward the attainment of proximate goals. In this way, the comic sensibility in rhetoric acts as the perfect corrective to its tragic tendencies. The tragic sentiment in rhetoric gives to audiences the courage to make impossible choices and thereby suffer nobly for a dimly defined cause that shakes a tormented world; the comic sentiment in rhetoric produces the laughter which deflates false pretensions, generates self-knowledge, acknowledges different perspectives, and ultimately facilitates collaborative judgment. Because of these characteristics, Farrell has written that "comedy is the most characteristic deliberative orientation of rhetoric."[37] As the *Birds* demonstrates, comedy is the only orientation that produces the humility and understanding by which antagonistic parties might actually listen to one another, and by doing so create a form of power more flexible, forgiving, and ultimately more intelligent.

To argue comically does not mean continually undercutting oneself, being timid about advancing claims, or making light of a crisis. It means to see oneself as one actor among many in a complex situation that exceeds the capacity of any one perspective to account for in its totality. Not surprisingly, then, do we find the greatest humor in ridiculing those with the pretense of omnipotence and omniscience (like Cleon and Socrates in the eyes of Aristophanes), for they expose themselves to comic embarrassment to the degree that they purport to embody perfection. Ralph Waldo Emerson thus gets it right when he observes that "the essence of all jokes, of all comedy, seems to be an honest or well-intended halfness; a non-performance of what is pretended to be per-formed, at the same time that one is giving loud pledges a performance. The balking of the intellect, the frustrated expectation, the break of continuity in the intellect, is comedy; and it announces itself physically in the pleasant spasms we call laughter."[38] No one becomes an easy target for comic ridicule who does not, at some level, think themselves superior in some way, or who lacks the power and pride to act as if they possessed some aspect of truth, beauty, and goodness that is to be their gift to the world. Yet this does not mean that the aim of com-edy is to condemn such actions; in fact, comedy demands a constant flood of them to keep the comic spirit alive. What matters is not the fact that our most "perfect" beliefs and behaviors always exhibit the character of halfness, but that we are able to recognize and laugh at our own incompleteness after the fact. Emerson concludes that "comedy is a tie of sympathy with other men, a pledge of sanity, and a protection from those perverse tendencies and gloomy insani-ties in which fine intellects sometimes lose themselves."[39] As flawed beings in a world of flux, we must act if we are not simply to be acted upon. The comic attitude simply reminds us that our actions are always partial and incomplete, and that we attain enduring power only by maintaining affectionate sympathy with other men and women.

In the conclusion of the *Birds*, the avian chorus sings a hymn to Pisthetairos and his new bride as the chorus members are slowly lifted up on wings to soar through the buoyant air toward heaven. They sing: "Now let the Golden Age of Birds begin / by lovely marriage ushered in, *Hymen Hymenaios O!*" (105). Reminiscent of the archaic festivals, the old king has been replaced by a young one, celebrated with a marriage that signals the dawn of a new age marked by freedom and the capacity to start anew. Of course nothing promises that what is new will be better than what is old, only that it will be different. What was on top will be on bottom, and what thrived on the margins will take its place in the center. Inevitably a new crisis will ensue, and a new *agôn* will begin. What matters is not that a utopia has descended upon earth from heaven, but simply that human life will go on, with each new generation having to relearn the les-sons of the old as it makes the same mistakes, suffers the same sins of pride, seeks perfection despite inescapable flaws, and pursues fantasies that exceed the limits of human accomplishment.

And it is precisely this striving which makes human beings something more than the beasts. We are comic creatures precisely because we are always striv-ing to be something greater than what we are. This striving is the core both of tragedy and of comedy, but comedy holds out the hope that, while our grandi-ose projects almost always end in failure, our proximal goals may be achieved if we can take ourselves and others more lightly. Rhetoric channels this comic attitude when it acknowledges the necessity to act yet at the same time accepts the possibility of error, not only about the world but about ourselves. Comedy is the only art explicitly dedicated to producing this capacity for humility. Thus, although any comic work of art may not be explicitly rhetorical, rhetoric can integrate the comic attitude insofar as it tempers its assertions with fallibility, sees opponents not as evil but as mistaken, and holds out the promise of compromise in a contingent world.

CHAPTER 8

Plato's *Protagoras* and the
Art of Tragicomedy

After Alcibiades it was Critias, I think, who spoke next: "Well, Prodicus and Hippias, it seems to be that Callias is very much on Protagoras's side, while Alcibiades as usual wants to be on the winning side of a good fight. But there's no need for any of us to lend partisan support to either Socrates or Protagoras. We should instead join in requesting them both not to break up our meeting prematurely."

Prodicus spoke up next: "That's well said, Critias. Those who attend discussions such as this ought to listen impartially, but not equally, to both interlocutors. There is a distinction here. We ought to listen impartially but not divide our attention equally: More should go to the wiser speaker and less to the more unlearned. For my part, I think that the two of you ought to debate the issues, but dispense with eristics. Friends debate each other on good terms; eristics are for enemies at odds. In this way our meeting would take a most attractive turn, for you, speakers, would then most surely earn the respect, rather than the praise, of those of us listening to you. For respect is guilelessly inherent in the souls of the listeners, but praise is all too often merely a deceitful verbal expression. And then, too, we, your audience, would be most cheered, but not pleased, for to be cheered is to learn something, to participate in some intellectual activity, and is a mental state; but to be pleased has to do with eating or experiencing some other pleasure in one's body."

Prodicus' remarks were enthusiastically received by the majority of us, and then the wise Hippias spoke: "Gentlemen, I regard all of you here present as kinsmen, intimates, and fellow citizens by nature, not by convention. For like is akin to like by nature, but convention, which tyrannizes the human race, often constrains us contrary to nature. Therefore it would be disgraceful for us to understand the nature of things and not—being as we are the wisest of the Greeks and gathered here together in the veritable hall of wisdom, in this greatest and most august house of the city itself—not, I say, produce anything worthy of all this dignity, but bicker with each other as if we were the dregs of society. I therefore implore and counsel you, Protagoras and Socrates, be reconciled and to compromise, under our arbitration, as it were, on some middle course. You, Socrates, must not insist on that precise, excessively brief form of discussion if it does not suit Protagoras, but rather allow free rein to the speeches, so they might communicate to us more impressively and elegantly. And you, Protagoras, must not let out full sail in the wind and leave the land behind to disappear into the Sea of Rhetoric. Both of you must steer a middle course. So that's what you shall do, and take my advice and choose a referee or moderator or supervisor who will monitor for you the length of your speeches."[1]

Despite the beautiful setting in the house of Callias, contention has broken out amongst the guests. Just after dawn, Socrates had appeared uninvited at the front door, alongside his young friend Hippocrates, to seek an audience with Protagoras, who had just arrived in Athens. The house had been packed. Sophists like Protagoras, Prodicus, and Hippias were freely pontificating on all manners of topics while dozens of young Athenian nobles and foreigners crowded around them, eager to absorb their wisdom. As Socrates remembers it, Protagoras was a sight to behold: "When he turned around with his flanking groups, the audience to the rear would split into two in a very orderly way and then circle around either side and form up again behind him. It was quite lovely" (315b). Yet this highly choreographed dance had come to a stop when Socrates, on behalf of his own eager student, began questioning Protagoras about the nature and value of his teaching. Soon the eyes of the entire house had fallen upon these two men, and the normally confident Protagoras had become frustrated as his desire to make lengthy speeches had been thwarted by the austere dialectic of his counterpart. With each party refusing to alter their communication style to suit the other, the discussion had broken down, its complete dissolution prevented only by the firm grip of Callias around Socrates's wrist. Yet this act of physical force had only heightened the tension, as members of the audience had felt compelled to become partisans, with Alcibiades backing Socrates and Callias coming to the defense of Protagoras. The speeches by Prodicus and Hippias were thus meant as virtuous interventions in an increasingly political dispute, a way to showcase how the best intellects of Greece were capable of managing crises not only in the state but in the household, proving that sophistical wisdom was the one true vehicle for making actual the promise of *paideia*.

As a purely self-contained dramatic episode, the dispute between Socrates and Protagoras has a distinctively comic tenor. Here is the traditional *agôn* of the comic stage, with the magnificent and aging Protagoras and his Sea of Rhetoric set against the younger (but still ugly and barefoot) gadfly of Socrates who interrupts his counterpart's impressive and eloquent speech with sharp, stinging questions. And surrounding them is a panoply of equally ridiculous figures. Alcibiades, the brash young aristocrat and soon-to-be demagogue who is just sprouting a beard, intervenes with typical competitive fervor for the sake of victory. Prodicus, the Sophist well known for his precise definitions of words as well as his susceptibility to the pleasures, is introduced in the dialogue as still in bed and covered with furs, yet who leaves the comforts of his bed only to make a lot of trivial distinctions that do not lead anywhere. And then there is the bombastic polymath Hippias, one of Plato's favorite comic characters, who never misses an opportunity to display his encyclopedic knowledge of trivia. In this case, Hippias uses this breakdown in dialogue as an opportunity to pontificate on the abstract difference between nature (*physis*) and convention (*nomos*), until finally making a mealy mouthed suggestion that we should resolve the dispute by choosing a "middle course" that will be judged by the subjective opinion of an audience member who may know nothing at all about what is being discussed. Taken together, these characters represent a comic chorus surrounding the two competitors in the *agôn* whose victor will determine the character of the coming age, at which point we might imagine revelry to ensue.

But revelry does not, in fact, ensue. For the dramatic date of the dialogue is around 433 B.C.E., the year leading up to the start of the Peloponnesian War. Protagoras has visited at a time of high optimism and power, when total supremacy seemed within the reach of Athens and its cultural and intellectual superiority was unquestioned. Yet Plato is actually writing the dialogue around the end of the first decade of the fourth century B.C.E., when Socrates was long dead, executed by the democracy that had been restored to Athens a year after its crushing surrender to Sparta in 404 B.C.E. So when Plato's contemporary audience read this comic scene, it carried a tragic sentiment, for they knew the trauma which was soon to come. Martha Nussbaum explains: "Plato chooses to set this dialogue right on the 'razor's edge.' It is a time of pride and prosperity—about two years before the outbreak of the Peloponnesian War, three years before the great plague that devastated Athens, both physically and morally. Diseases of the body, diseases of character, the disease of war—all, we know, will shortly strike, unforeseen, this intelligent city that prides itself so much on artfulness and foresight."[2] Because of this dramatic irony, the comedy has an almost grotesque feel. That happy past we see imagined in the house of Callias, with all of its characters content in the permanent value of their habits and traditions, was long gone: "The setting, with its allusions to the plague, its metaphors of disease, works to make this jolly conservatism seem anachronistic, inappropriate to the seriousness of impending contemporary problems."[3] Consequently, Nussbaum concludes, it "is not a surprise that the dialogue compares Socrates' interview with these sophists to a living hero's visit to the shades of the dead heroes in the underworld. It is a dead generation, lacking understanding of the moral crisis of its own time."[4]

Plato's purpose, however, is not to walk on the graves of the dead but to guide the affairs of the living. Although often caricatured today as what John Dewey calls the "original university professor," unconcerned with the contingencies of the world and interested only with abstract definitions of transcendental "Forms," Plato was in fact a committed political reformer who used the new literary genre of the philosophical dialogue to bridge the gap between reason and action in order to create a more intelligent practice.[5] As Dewey explains, "the purpose of the dialogues . . . is not just to ridicule Plato's rivals in philosophy. It is also to bring out the nature of certain problems and define them in such a way as to prepare for constructive treatment."[6] According to the pragmatic and democratically minded Dewey, then, "nothing could be more helpful to present philosophizing than a 'Back to Plato' movement; but it would have to be back to the dramatic, restless, cooperatively inquiring Plato of the *Dialogues,* trying one mode of attack after another to see what it might yield; back to the Plato whose highest flight of metaphysics always terminated with a social and practical turn."[7] Understood in this way, the *agôn* between Socrates and Protagoras does not hold our interest because we want to see which character gets the best of the other; it matters because at the center of the drama is a question that remains vital for political cultures of all ages, which is: "how do we teach civic virtue?"

Here is no irrelevant detour into the metaphysics of Forms.[8] Rather, one finds in the *Protagoras* a clash between two opposing answers, that of sophistical rhetorical training and philosophical dialectical inquiry. According to Jaeger, it depicts Socrates's "contest with the sophists' paideia as one of the decisive battles of his age, as the struggle between two opposing worlds for the primacy in education."[9] For Plato, however, history had already condemned the failure of the Sophists to anticipate how their teaching would create the demagoguery that would bring Athens to its knees and death to its citizens. The ironic tone of the *Protagoras* thus carries an underlying rhetorical motive. Nussbaum explains that "since the reader, by hindsight, is aware that a vulnerable moral consensus is soon to be unhinged by external pressures, by the pull of conflicting obligations, by the strength of the appetitive desires, since he knows that among this dialogue's characters some will soon be dead and others will soon be killing, he will feel impatience with the lack of foresight that says that things in Athens are all right as they are. He will look for signs of disease beneath the optimism; he will look for a pessimistic and radical doctor."[10] What this pessimistic and radical doctor will provide, implies Plato, is a brutally honest critique of the failure of sophistical treatments to heal the *demos* followed by a rigorous diagnosis of its true maladies and its possible cures. In other words, he will lay the basis for a genuine political art, a *politike* technê, capable of correcting the limitations of the sophistical knack for persuasion which had confidently and blindly guided Athens toward an abyss.

But this is simply another way to say that, with Plato, philosophy had finally become rhetorical. Ever since its origins in the aphoristic puzzles of Heraclitus that attempted to shake the Greeks from their Homeric trance and stimulate thinking about the Logos, philosophy had been associated with a transcendent and rationalistic state of mind contemptuous of the affairs of practice and the judgments of the *demos*. Guthrie, in fact, describes Sophists like Protagoras as exemplars of "the humanistic reaction against the natural philosophers, whose contradictory speculations were bringing them into disrepute among practical men."[11] With Plato, however, one finds a concerted effort to demonstrate that philosophy, and not sophistical rhetoric, represents the genuine political art, and that it is Socrates, not Protagoras, who is the genuine rhetorician. As Socrates says in the *Gorgias:* "I believe that I'm one of a few Athenians . . . to take up the true political craft and practice the true politics. This is because the speeches I make on each occasion do not aim at gratification but at what's best. They don't aim at what's most pleasant" (521e). The whole of Plato's confrontation with the Sophists revolves around this basic task—not so much to destroy rhetoric but to reform it by limiting its scope and making it subservient to those higher virtues defined by philosophy.

And just as Heraclitus deployed a new the form of expression to stimulate thinking in the few, Plato sought to master the literary genre of the philosophical dialogue to create habits of inquiry in the many. For unlike Heraclitus, Plato was not content simply to create logical puzzles that would poetically disclose glimmers of the world-order behind appearances. Plato wished to speak to an increasingly literate populace in order to train a greater portion of the *demos* in the arts of critical dialectic he believed were necessary for the creation of a beautiful state. To accomplish that task, he needed to draw from every available poetic resource much in the way that tragedy had done at its origin in the sixth century B.C.E. Nietzsche explains that, "if tragedy had absorbed all previous artistic genres, the same can be said, in an eccentric sense, of the Platonic dialogue, which was created by mixing all available styles and forms together so that it hovers somewhere midway between narrative, lyric, and drama, between prose and poetry, thus breaking the strict older law about the unity of linguistic form."[12] The result was what Nietzsche believed to be the forerunner of the modern novel, a new kind of prose style which broke all of the conventional poetic rules precisely because its primary goal was neither poetic nor philosophical but political and ethical; Plato wanted to use this new genre of literature to dramatize how careful philosophical inquiry into the Logos, into the rational structure of the world, was central to the prosperity of a republic in which true power was not in competition with virtue but was its apotheosis. In this vision, rhetoric would no longer be a means for the demagogue to flatter the ignorant for short-term pleasure, but would be an instrument of the philosopher to reveal the true nature of the Good to those divided souls yearning to become whole again.

Plato thus established the model for a rhetoric of the public intellectual that would be imitated for ages to come. For regardless of how one evaluated the content of his message, one could not easily dismiss the power of its form. With Plato the capacities for reflective thought, poetic dramatization, and rhetorical advocacy are channeled and take form through the medium of the written word, capable of influencing a mass audience over time about enduring matters of public concern.[13] Thus, it is ultimately Plato, and not Socrates, who establishes the precedent for this kind of rhetoric. Although Socrates remains a model for oral dialectic in face-to-face settings of inquiry, whether in the sober seminar or drunken symposium, it is Plato who reveals the unique power of the written word to produce the kind of far-reaching perspectives in individual members of the public that are necessary if they are to cooperatively meet the complex challenges of a civilized state. Thus, even those who challenge the premises of Plato's philosophical position nonetheless have to contend with his philosophical style, which meets us on our terms only to show those terms to be partial, but which through careful inquiry promises the pleasure of reconstituting those parts into a whole which is good, true, and ultimately beautiful.[14]

When Plato (429–347 B.C.E.) wrote *Protagoras,* the tragic age of the Greeks had come to an end. The sixth and fifth centuries B.C.E. had represented the spirit of the tragic age, but not simply because it produced suffering; it was tragic precisely because that suffering was seen as a necessary means of inaugurating a new order of justice that produced radically new forms of power. The twin arts of tragedy and comedy had flourished in Athens in particular because the audience could identify with the heroes on stage. Only citizens who could conceivably see themselves as liberating kings could experience the pity and fear of seeing the fall of Oedipus, and only a public confident in its ultimate virtue and success could find humor in seeing its vices mirrored in the actions of wasps, frogs, and birds. But after ten years of war, death, and decline following the collapse of the Sicilian expedition, culminating in the humiliating surrender to the Spartan general Lysander in 404 B.C.E., Athenians came to consider the possibility that much of their apparently tragic striving and suffering was in fact in vain, that what before seemed comic errors of judgment were actually disastrous mistakes, and that the progress of civilization might simply be an illusion masking the true reality of inevitable catastrophe.

For Plato, who never lived a year of his youth free of the specter of war, this lesson was brought home most powerfully by the prosecution, conviction, and execution of his beloved teacher, Socrates, on the charge of impiety. Whereas Sophists like Gorgias and Protagoras had acquired great wealth and fame by training ambitious young men to acquire power through speech in the new political order, Socrates was forced to drink poison hemlock as a reward for a life dedicated to the pursuit of wisdom at the expense of worldly pleasures. This, for Plato, was the representative act of democratic power—to reward those who lead you to destruction and to punish those who would question the wisdom of the mob. But a people seeking true power would have pursued another course. They would have so valued Socrates that they would have given him free maintenance at state expense. In Plato's eyes, the only "tragic" wisdom gained by his death was that the *demos* would always do evil unwillingly when guided by rhetoric rather than philosophy, precisely because it was the nature of democratic/demagogic rhetoric to acquire self-destructive power through flattery rather than sustainable power through wisdom. Of course, if Socrates had been killed by the puppet regime of the "Thirty Tyrants" set up by the Spartans after the defeat of Athens, perhaps Plato might have thought differently; but this regime lasted only a year before it was thrown off by the Athenians and an even more radical democracy restored. Socrates was therefore not executed by an occupying force. He was executed by Athenian citizens, many of whom were students of the Sophists and who had learned to cloak the most heinous acts of atrocity with the ideological trappings of virtue.

The death of Socrates marked the end of the tragic age of Greece for two reasons. First, his death was not a divine retribution for any violation by *hubris* of some transcendent notion of justice but rather a wholly mortal act of vengeance by an ignorant mob. In classical tragedy, heroic actions were grandiose precisely because they were vehicles for disclosing the sublime moral order of the universe. Jaeger remarks that "the spirit of Greek poetry is *tragic* because it sees in our mortal destiny an indissoluble link between every event, even the noblest of human endeavors, and the rule of heaven."[15] One of the essential components of tragedy is that it reveals the relationship between the mortal and the divine and shows that, despite the nobility and greatness that a human being is capable of achieving, there is always some *moira,* some deserved or undeserved misery fated by the gods, that we bring down upon ourselves as we struggle against the old order of justice. But in the case of Socrates, his crime was not *hubris* and his punishment was not produced by the gods. Socrates's crime was simply the act of seeking wisdom based on knowledge of his own ignorance, and his punishment was produced by the rhetorical manipulation of sophistically trained demagogues who had absolutely nothing to do with the gods. As Plato records him as saying in his courtroom defense, the *Apology*: "I was convicted because I lacked not words but boldness and shamelessness and the willingness to say to you what you would most have gladly have heard for me, lamentations and tears and my saying and doing things that I say are unworthy of me that you are accustomed to hear from others" (38d). His death reveals the fault to be purely our own, and the emotional consummation it produces is not catharsis but simply regret combined with shame.

Second, Socrates does not bewail his fate but accepts it willingly, even carelessly. For Socrates, the aim of living is not simply to keep one's body alive and satiated with physical pleasures for as long as possible, but to cultivate one's soul in the expectation that one will be rewarded by the "true judges" in the afterlife, wherever and whatever that might be. As he explains in the *Apology,* rather than try to avoid death, "I am willing to die many times if that is true. It would be a wonderful way for me to spend my time whenever I met Palamedes and Ajax, the son of Telamon, and any other of the men of old who died through an unjust conviction, to compare my experience with theirs. I think it would be pleasant. Most important, I could spend my time testing and examining people there, as I do here, as to who among them is wise, and who thinks he is, but is not" (41b–c). For Socrates, his conviction does not represent a tragic end but merely a transition to another kind of existence. In this world to come, the capacity to reason is rewarded far more than the possession of force, resulting in an inversion of the conventional hierarchy of power. When Socrates dies, he will join two others who have suffered injustice at the hands of the mob, Palamedes and Ajax, and together they will sit at the right hand of the gods.

In what Nietzsche refers to as the "dying Socrates," Plato thus found a symbol that he believed could help usher in a new, non-tragic age. The classical tragic hero was one who shook a tormented world to usher in a new order of justice, but who neither understood the nature of this order nor could predict the suffering that its arrival would produce. By contrast, the dying Socrates is "a man liberated from fear of death by reasons and knowledge," and who represents "the heraldic shield over the portals of science, reminding everyone of its purpose, which is to make existence appear comprehensible and thus justified."[16] For Nietzsche, Socrates challenged the entire metaphysical foundation

that supported the tragic sensibility of the prior age. Against the tragic assumption that the true meaning of the world would always be hidden from human
beings and that the fate even of the most virtuous soul ultimately was in the
hands of often fickle gods, Socrates posited a proto-scientific view that suffering was primarily the result of ignorance and that true power would issue neither from violence nor manipulation but through knowledge. Thus, "in the face
of this practical pessimism, Socrates is the archetype of the theoretical optimist
whose belief that the nature of things can be discovered leads him to attribute
to knowledge and understanding the power of a panacea, and who understands
error to be inherently evil."[17] Through Socrates we thus catch a glimpse of the
possibility that perhaps suffering might be avoided altogether if we only commit ourselves to the pursuit of a kind of knowledge that could finally order our
souls and our state according to the laws of nature, morality, and beauty.

But this "Socrates" that accomplishes these tasks is not the real man but a
literary creation of Plato. Plato's new prose genre of the philosophical dialogue
turns Socrates turns from historical figure to literary trope and then offers him
as a replacement for both the tragic and the comic hero, a hero capable of rhetorically harnessing the power of poetics for the purposes of rational enlightenment. According to Bakhtin, the underlying temporal and spatial structure
(or "chronotope") of this new kind of dramatic narrative can be summarized
as "the life course of one seeking true knowledge."[18] Here, "the life of such a
seeker is broken down into precise and well-marked epochs or steps. His course
passes from self-confident ignorance, through self-critical skepticism, to self-
knowledge and ultimately to authentic knowing (mathematics and music)."[19]
In Plato's Socratic dialogues, both tragic and comic elements are present, but
transformed. Like the tragic hero, Socrates suffers because he struggles against
a dying order for the sake of justice; and like a comic hero, each confrontation
takes the form of a rhetorical *agôn* with all manners of bunglers and buffoons.
These tragic and comic tensions are in fact necessary to make the journey of
the seeker an actual drama and not simply a didactic exercise. However, unlike
tragic heroes, Socrates lacks *hubris,* cares nothing for political power, and is
unconcerned with his physical fate; and unlike comic heroes, his own absurdities are apparent rather than real, for behind his ironic mask lies the soul of a
philosopher. In short, Socrates-as-hero represents the wise man amongst fools,
the humble inquirer who would cheerfully suffer for the sake of knowledge,
courageously challenge the so-called "powerful" and "wise" in order to reveal
their impotence and ignorance, and generously encourage all those lovers of
wisdom even at the price of his own death.

The dramatic core of the Platonic dialogue is thus always the tension
between Socrates and his surroundings. Socrates represents the "theoretical
man" who wishes only to pursue the truth in unfettered dialectic, but he is a

man whose thought and action are constantly interrupted and obstructed by those in power who think him both a lunatic and a heretic. These antagonists, very often portrayed as Sophists or their students, are so focused on gaining immediate pleasure from what is close at hand that they simply cannot fathom that greater meanings lie behind the veil of appearances. It is to overcome their resistance and disclose the hidden truth through the power of rational speech that motivates Socrates-the-hero, and it is the expectation of his ultimate success, despite the sufferings and absurdities along the way, that transforms the tragic and comic elements into the synthetic genre of tragicomedy. For although we sense the tragedy of Socrates's imminent death and laugh at the comic spectacle of Sophists making fools of themselves, the ultimate payoff is our own edification. In the dialogue, Socrates is not an object of empathy but an object of imitation, a person who embodies a model of critical inquiry through which we can acquire the knowledge that will provide the basis for genuine power.

And this edifying effect is more than just a product of the "content" of the dialogue; it is an outgrowth of the prose form itself. Whereas traditional poetry used verse and music to evoke intense aesthetic experience, prose tends toward the expository and generates in the imagination of the reader a particular point of view on the world. Dewey remarks that the prosaic "realizes the power of words to express what is in heaven and earth and under the seas by means of extension; the other by intension. The prosaic is an affair of description and narration, of detail accumulated and relations elaborated. It spreads as it goes like a legal document or catalogue. The poetic reverses the process. It condenses and abbreviates, thus giving words an energy of expansion that is almost explosive."[20] Dewey's description aptly accounts for Plato's preference of prose over poetry because it turns our attention away from the explosive energy of our inner emotions and pleasures and toward the larger world in which we live and seek to understand. But it also explains why his dialogues tended to take issue with the Sophists rather than the poets, for it was the Sophists who had made the first significant steps toward prose development in their attention to the *logos* of argumentation.[21] In the *Republic*, Plato had banned the poets from the ideal *polis* for reasons not so different from what we find in Gorgias's *Helen*— that they were promoters of irrational and often immoral tradition. But what to do with the Sophists, who claimed to be the vehicle for Greek enlightenment, was another story.

The *Protagoras* was Plato's response to this challenge. It represents Plato's most concerted attempt to distinguish the *paideia* of Socrates from that of the Sophists through the medium of dramatic prose. In the earlier *Gorgias*, of course, he had already set rhetoric and philosophy in opposition by narrating a kind of street brawl that pitted Socrates against the aging Gorgias and his more ambitious young followers, Polus and Callicles. His aim was to show that rhetoric was not an art but a mere knack for flattery that could do nothing but lead to injustice and impotence. Yet the focus of the *Gorgias* was specifically on defining (and then condemning) rhetoric (*rhêtorikê*) as a specific commodity sold by the Sophists, not on analyzing the general project of sophistical education in civic virtue. The *Protagoras* takes up this much more daunting task. The change in setting is indicative of the magnitude of the challenge. Instead of pushing Socrates in a gang fight, he invites him into an elegant intellectual environment and surrounds him with the greatest teachers of his age. Jaeger remarks that "the conversation takes place before a large audience in a wealthy house; the great sophists are impressive, even majestic figures, followed by swarms of pupils and admirers; all these details enhance the importance of the occasion."[22] Thus, unlike the doddering portrayal of Gorgias in the earlier dialogue, Protagoras is presented as a respected and respectful gentleman who clearly possesses an intellectual capacity which far surpasses any other Sophist of his day. Here is an antagonist clearly worthy of Socrates the seeker of knowledge.

The dramatic conflict of the dialogue will be the clash between Socratic and sophistical *paideia*. This point is brought home by the presence of Hippocrates, a representative of the younger generation who is seeking what Protagoras later claims to offer: "sound deliberation, both in domestic matters—how best to manage one's household, and in public affairs—how to realize one's maximum potential for success in political debate and action" (319a). Like most young men of his age, Hippocrates desires a combination of wisdom and power, and he believes that sophistical training will be the correct means to attain these goods. In contradistinction to the *Gorgias*, in which Socrates himself initiates the confrontation with Gorgias, in the *Protagoras* he speaks on someone else's behalf. The entire function of their dialogue is to impress upon Hippocrates that one or the other man has the pedagogical goods to lead the next generation into the future. And clearly the stakes are high, for the manner by which Hippocrates enters the story indicates that all is not well in the state of *paideia*—that is, the state by which citizens are educated in the highest ideals of Greek culture. This is because Hippocrates is something of a mess. As Socrates recounts the whole episode to a friend, before dawn that very morning, Hippocrates had urgently banged on his door, seeking his counsel. Already stressed from his slave Satyrus having run away from him—a frustration only compounded by his neglecting to tell Socrates the moment it happened— Hippocrates then discovers (only from a passing remark by his brother) that Protagoras has just arrived in Athens. Knowing almost nothing about Protagoras except his celebrity and his reputation for being a clever speaker, Hippocrates nonetheless is full of "fighting spirit" and "excitement" at the prospect of becoming his student, and he solicits the aid of Socrates to make an introduction (310d). His state of anxiety and urgency at the beginning of the dialogue thus raises the expectations for the reader that a major clash of intellects is about to ensue.

For Plato, of course, it is a foregone conclusion as to who will reveal himself to be incompetent. The very character of Hippocrates already condemns sophistical education before he has even been exposed to their teaching. Here is an eager, intelligent, and ambitious young man full of promise, yet who also is incapable of running his household, lacks the capacity to keep his thoughts together, does not possess any sort of stable educational environment, and must rely on hearsay for news and look to public opinion for advice. And the final humiliation is that his only apparent prospect for growth is to pay for the services of an itinerant Sophist who promises everything under the sun and yet seems to lack a clear and comprehensive program of education. Moreover, the chaotic nature of sophistical education is implied by the very atmosphere inside Callias's home. When Socrates and Hippocrates enter, they find activity everywhere. In fact, they are initially mistaken for Sophists themselves and denied entry because of "all of the traffic of Sophists in and out of the house" (413d). Once inside, they realize why the porter wished to prevent anyone else from entering. Here is Protagoras walking back and forth in the portico with crowds following him. There is Hippias sitting on a high seat in the colonnade answering questions on astronomy and physics. And buried on the bed under a pile of sheepskin fleeces and blankets is Prodicus, speaking in a booming voice that makes it impossible to hear what he is saying. From Plato's perspective, it is no wonder that young men like Hippocrates cannot think straight in the midst of such disarray.

The ironic character of what initially appears to be a magnificent setting is finally revealed when Plato draws an analogy between Socrates's visit to the house of Callias and Odysseus's journey to Hades.[23] Like the shades of Achilles and Ajax in Hades, the Sophists speak and move about, sometimes beautifully, but they lack both the coherence and substance of something reliable and real. One can thus almost hear the question asked of Odysseus by his royal audience when the hero began retelling his tale: "How did you find your way down to the dark / where these dimwitted dead are camped forever, / the after images of used-up men?" (*The Odyssey*, 11: 560). At the same time, Plato is no more interested in scorning the dead than was Odysseus. True, Odysseus ended up fleeing Hades in fear, for his presence had attracted "shades in thousands, rustling / in a pandemonium of whispers" which had evoked a horror darker than "some saurian death's head" (11:751). However, Odysseus had descended into the underworld to seek counsel from the blind prophet Teirêsias about how to return to Ithaca, and the knowledge he acquired there was absolutely necessary for overcoming the obstacles ahead. Although he departs in fear, he leaves wiser than when he entered, confident that he could finish the journey. Similarly, Plato presents Socrates as himself having gained wisdom from the encounter with Protagoras. This is the reason Plato begins the dialogue a day after the actual encounter between Socrates and Protagoras, and why he makes Socrates recount the preceding day's event to a friend. Like the *Odyssey*, which narrates the gathering of shades through the voice of Odysseus retelling his journey over dinner, Socrates retells his descent into the underworld of the Sophists as an experience which left him shaken but also enlightened from having learned lessons from the dead in order to benefit the world of the living.

And what Socrates learns from Protagoras is perhaps the most essential principle of any modern, civilized culture: *that civic virtue can and must be taught*. Establishing this principle in Greek culture was the singular accomplishment of the sophistical movement, and Plato gives to Protagoras generous space in the dialogue to further advance this principle. In no way does the dialogue present any kind of serious counterpoint to this perspective, notwithstanding the initial challenge by Socrates that he does not think it could be taught. One simply has to look at the evidence invoked by Socrates to see that his initial opinion is based not on any philosophical principle but on the barrenness of the available educational opportunities in Athens of the fifth century. For example, he points to the sons of Pericles who happened to be in attendance: "Look at Pericles, the father of these young men here. He gave them a superb education in everything that teachers can teach, but as for what he himself is really wise in, he neither teaches them that himself nor has anyone else teach them either, and his sons have to browse like sacred cattle and pick up virtue on their own wherever they might find it" (320a). Reminiscent of the example of Hippocrates, Pericles's sons prove nothing about the inherent virtue or ignominy of their birth but rather reveal the lack of any proven benefit that the disorganized forms of Greek education have provided them. So when Protagoras defines the goal of his own teaching in terms of cultivating the "art of citizenship," Socrates becomes intrigued: "When I hear what you have to say, I waver; I think there must be something in what you are talking about" (320b). The initial skepticism of Socrates thus functions as a narrative excuse for Protagoras to define the virtuous aims of education, aims that establish the common ground between the two men which links sophistical and Socratic *paideia*.

Being a Sophist, of course, Protagoras uses two lengthy and eloquent rhetorical speeches to answer Socrates's questions. His first speech takes the form of *mythos* in which Protagoras deftly shows how the Sophists were able to master and co-opt the poetic forms of the Homeric tradition for their own purposes. For what Protagoras does in his *mythos*, later referred to as his "Great Speech," is transform the pessimistic origin story of Hesiod, in which Prometheus brings suffering to human beings via the arts of toil, into a story of the ascent of civilization. Reminiscent of *Prometheus Bound,* Protagoras's Great Speech narrates how, after the initial failure of the god Epimetheus ("afterthought") to properly outfit human beings with the natural tools of survival, Prometheus ("forethought") was forced to steal knowledge of the practical arts, along with fire, and distribute them to human beings in order to survive. Yet even then, human beings constantly fought and wronged each other because they lacked the political wisdom necessary "to band together and survive by founding cities" (322b). Lacking the power to act in concert, they continued to be slaughtered by animals despite their possession of fire and the practical arts. It is at this point, Protagoras says, that Zeus "sent Hermes to bring justice and a sense of shame to humans, so that there would be order within cities and bonds of friendship to unite them" (322c). This is the crucial modification that Protagoras makes to the origin story. Whereas the earlier aristocratic tradition had distributed the capacity for civic virtue as unequally as Prometheus had done with the practical arts, Protagoras follows the spirit of democracy by declaring the capacity for civic virtue not only universal but necessary if people are to live together at all.

The argument (*logos*) which follows this narrative (*mythos*) then bolsters its claims by providing empirical evidence for assertion that the capacity for civic virtue is universal and that its actualization requires careful development and teaching by professional educators. Once again challenging the Homeric tradition of informal poetic education, Protagoras argues for a more sustained sophistical training throughout the entire youth of a citizen in justice, temperance, and piety, instructing them through organized lessons and punishing them when necessary in order to straighten them like a bent piece of wood bows to pressure (or, when faced with the unreformable delinquent, condemning them to death or exile as due punishment for being a "pestilence to the city") (322d). Showing the increasing prevalence of literacy at the time, Protagoras gives the example of "the practice of writing teachers, who sketch the letters faintly with a pen in workbooks for their beginning students and have them write with letters over the patterns they have drawn." (326). This example shows how Protagoras sees education as primarily an imitative affair in which students are taught to model their thoughts and behaviors on the best examples of the past. Not only do students learn to play the lyre and thereby learn moral decency and restraint by reciting the works of great poets, but they also understand writing and spoken language as well: "they are given the works of good poets to read at their desks and have to learn them by heart, works that contain numerous exhortations, many passages describing in glowing terms good men of old, so that the child is inspired to imitate them and become like them" (326b). In this way, Protagoras balances a respect for tradition with a progressive attitude toward democratic civic education in which each virtue is carefully inculcated through a particular method and subject matter. For a sense of justice and piety, the tales of the good men of old; for temperance, a training in the harmony and rhythm of music and poetry; for courage, the intense discipline of the athletic trainer (326a–c). By effectively transforming the resources of Greek tradition into a kind of classroom textbook, the Sophists maintain continuity with the past while imposing new, more rigorous and disciplined techniques of teaching reading, writing, and ethics necessary to produce a more uniformly competent democratic citizenry.

When Socrates assents to these two fundamental principles of Protagoras— that everyone has an equal capacity for virtue and that its actualization requires careful teaching and development—he is not being facetious. Like Odysseus visiting the underworld, Socrates has gained wisdom from his interaction with the shades of the Great Sophists. In fact, the visit by Protagoras to Athens shakes Socrates from his pedagogical slumber. It is no accident that Hippocrates asks, "Socrates, are you awake or asleep?" while banging on his door in the early morning (310b). For Socrates is simply lying quietly in the dark, waiting for the sun to rise, seemingly unconcerned with the goings-on of the city around him. But in the world outside, Hippocrates and the other youth of Athens are scrambling to find teachers who can make them into good citizens who wield power in the city and household. So when Socrates follows Hippocrates to the house of Callias to meet the Sophists, he does not go to do battle as he does in the *Gorgias;* he enters the house to discover his true calling as a pedagogue. The lengthy speech by Protagoras demonstrates to Socrates the necessity for intellectuals to come out into the open and proudly announce that they are teachers of men rather than hiding behind the guise of being a poet, prophet, or musician (316d–317a). In the new civilized age, announces Protagoras, a new kind of formal education in the arts and virtues of civilization is necessary. In effect, Protagoras throws down the gauntlet to Socrates: either have the courage to declare oneself a teacher of men or go back to bed and allow the Sophists to educate the waking world.

The challenge Socrates accepts when he picks up the gauntlet is not to defend the claim that virtue cannot be taught; that it can be taught has already been decided. His challenge is to offer an alternative to sophistical pedagogy as a means to the teaching of civic virtue, a means which ideally should include three things: an adequate definition of virtue, a rigorous method of intellectual inquiry, and a reliable art of practical and ethical judgment. But this is a challenge that Socrates is eager to meet. Despite the reputation of Protagoras, Socrates quickly recognizes that none of these issues had been properly explored in the two speeches by the Sophist. As Socrates complains that this absence of analytical patience and precision is common to sophistical rhetoric, making speakers sound like "bronze bowls that keep ringing for a long time after they have been struck and prolong the sound indefinitely unless you dampen them. That's how these orators are: ask them one little question and they're off on another long-distance speech" (329b). And this is the primary problem with rhetoric as an explanatory or pedagogical instrument, according to Plato. If rhetoric is portrayed in the *Gorgias* as a weapon of war used for the cause of injustice, rhetoric in the *Protagoras* is a vehicle for pleasurable obscurity whereby one can acquire great fame for simply sounding smart. The problem in this dialogue is therefore not that Sophists like Protagoras, Hippias, or Prodicus are themselves disreputable men cut in the mold of the more rapacious Callicles; the problem is that they do not seem to know how to teach what they claim to teach because everything is mixed up together in their cacophonous orations.

Unfortunately, discerning the precise nature of rhetoric in the *Protagoras* is difficult because it is not explicitly a topic of discussion as in the *Gorgias*. Yet if we take the character of Protagoras to be the very performative embodiment of the spirit of rhetoric, a very clear understanding emerges—that rhetoric in the *Protagoras* is presented as a means of consolidating, channeling, and glorifying the power of the *demos* through competitive display. This is the reason that Plato describes Protagoras in such magnificent terms, for his greatness is a product of being a rhetorical conduit for the public opinion of the most powerful city in the civilized world. Not only does Protagoras frequently align his own opinion with the "majority position" within the dialogue (333c), but he also provides a clear account of his relationship to the *demos* when he gives the reason for refusing Socrates's request to abbreviate his answers: "I have had verbal contests with many people, and if I were to accede to your request and do as my opponent demanded, I would not be thought superior to anyone, nor would Protagoras be a name to be reckoned with among the Greeks" (335a). Everything one needs to know about the rhetorical method of inquiry is encompassed in this passage. Rhetoric acts as a method of inquiry when it moves a question out of a private or specialized sphere of discourse into public view, with the answer being decided by which side of a *dissoi logoi* wins over the *demos*. That "Protagoras" is a name to be reckoned with among the Greeks is thus a sign less of wisdom than of power, defined here in terms of the capacity of one's language to consolidate multiple beliefs, attitudes, and passions into a unified whole capable of action in the present. In short, the rhetorical method of inquiry is to define truth in terms of power, and to trust that the power of public opinion always equals the truth.

The task of Socrates—and of all subsequent public intellectualism after him—is to invert that relationship, and to show that genuine power requires a different method of inquiry which presumes that there are truths which are prior to and have authority over merely public opinion. That this dialogue presents itself as a clash of methods is revealed as soon as Protagoras finishes his lengthy speech and Socrates takes up the gauntlet. At this very moment Socrates radically alters the register of discourse from eloquent rhetoric to critical dialectic. Although acknowledging the ability of Protagoras to deliver a "beautifully long speech," Socrates now requests that Protagoras demonstrate how he "is also able to reply briefly when questioned, and to put a question and then wait for and accept the answer—rare accomplishments these" (329c). Protagoras's ready agreement to these conditions belies his overconfidence; it soon becomes apparent that he cannot keep up with Socrates, an imbalance leading to the breakdown in communication and the threat of partisan division. Nor does the eventual decision to change the role of questioner do Protagoras any good, as his debater's attempt to catch Socrates in a contradiction ends up exposing Protagoras's own ineptness. At each turn, Socrates gets the better of his counterpart, revealing the rhetorical method of inquiry to be, for Plato, a method of disguising intellectual shallowness with cleverness and verbosity.

In one way, of course, what Socrates requests seems rather benign. Dialectic in its basic form is simply a commitment by two or more speakers to begin with a statement of accepted, common belief and then interrogate it through brief questions and answers in order to analyze its parts and create a new and richer synthesis. But Socratic dialectic takes on a much more disruptive form when set against the more traditional form of eloquence whereby audience members were invited to immerse themselves in the beautiful, poetic speech of an orator. The interruption of the latter by the former, as Havelock explains, could be seen almost as an act of impudence and aggression, and most certainly did not produce pleasure:

The original function of the dialectical question was simply to force the speaker to repeat a statement already made, with the underlying assumption that there was something unsatisfactory about the statement, and that it had better be rephrased. Now the statement in question, if it concerned important matters of cultural tradition and morals, would be a poeticized one, using imagery and often the rhythms of poetry. It was one which invited you to identify with some emotively effective example, and to repeat it over again. But to say, "What do you mean? Say that again," abruptly disturbed the pleasurable complacency felt in the poetic formula or the image. It meant using different words and these equivalent words would fail to be poetic; they would be prosaic. As the question was asked, and the alternative prosaic formula was attempted, the imaginations of speaker and teacher were offended, and the dream so to speak was disrupted, and some unpleasant effort of calculative reflection was substituted.[24]

For Havelock, the radical and even violent nature of dialectic can only be fully understood when a dialectician is placed within a poetic environment, such as the one presented in the *Protagoras*. Although the Sophists are not poets in the Homeric sense, they clearly see themselves as inheritors of the poetic tradition, a tradition channeled through their own version of rhetorical eloquence. The fluidity of speech and movement Plato describes in the house of Callias indicates the kind of nebulous dream state he associates with Homeric poetry, and the sudden freezing of motion with the introduction of Socratic dialectic is not a merely superfluous narrative detail. The presence of Socrates in the company of Sophists represents a shock to their entire movement, an interruption of their confident sleepwalking, and a sign of the coming wakefulness that Plato believes will be a consequence of an education in philosophy.

And what Socrates shows through his methodical annihilation of Protagoras is that dialectic alone is capable of deriving the axioms upon which an education in virtue can be based. For it soon becomes clear that Protagoras has little to say about the nature of virtue beyond the maxims concerning its universality and teachability. Even in his lengthy defense, he fails to maintain a consistent account of the nature and origin of virtue. Initially he credits Zeus with bestowing upon human beings the virtues of justice and shame, but then later says that the collective virtue of humankind consisted of justice, temperance, and piety, only later adding courage as a virtue taught by athletic trainers. Finally, when pressed by Socrates, he adds wisdom to his growing list of virtues. But even with his list apparently complete, Protagoras is unable to show how the individual virtues are related to one another except through the analogy of parts of a face, with senses like the eyes, ears, mouth, and nose each having its own function but somehow working together to constitute a single organism. But just what each "part" is supposed to do, and how it relates to the other parts, Protagoras does not seem to know. Courage, for instance, does not seem the same to him as wisdom, and yet he considers both to be virtues even though one apparently is taught in the gymnasium and the other through poetry. But this would be akin to saying that each sense organ of the face operates independently and sometimes in competition with the others, thus allowing for the possibility that the parts of the face might end up at war amongst themselves about which should be the dominant sense. Protagoras, however, seems unconcerned with such fineries. Rather than expend energy on philosophically defining the nature of virtue and its parts, he chooses to simply teach them by relying upon traditional methods of imitation, with his choice of model being determined not by his own intellectual analysis but by the conservative judgment of *endoxa*, or the accepted opinion of most respectable people concerning what is true and good.

Although easily lost in the abstract nature of the dialectic, at the heart of the question concerning the unity of virtue is whether we shall embrace a tragic vision of human action. From Plato's perspective, Protagoras is the most tragic of all the Sophists not only because his own greatness contributed to the ruin of Athens, but also, and more significantly, his humanistic philosophy valorized a radical pluralism that denied the existence of any common measurement of existence beyond the flux of individual or communal experience. And what goes for existence also goes for virtue. For Protagoras, the virtues are as potentially incommensurable as the diverse forms of subjectivity. But this fact, according to him, is not something to be lamented and avoided but respected and managed. After all, the clash of competing goods only magnifies the nobility of human struggle. Just as we see the clash between justice and piety in Sophocles's *Antigone,* so too do we find in all great tragedies a conflict between competing virtues that pull great heroes in opposite directions until they must make a tragic choice and embrace the suffering that follows from necessity. Politically, of course, Protagoras does not wish democracy to end tragically, which is why he puts his faith in the collective measurements of *dissoi logoi* to resolve tragic disputes through rhetorical competition rather than violence. But, as Nussbaum points out, by denying the "unity of the virtues, maintaining against Socrates that they are irreducibly heterogeneous in quality, he keeps alive the possibility of tragedy," not just on stage but in political life.[25]

Seen in this light, the dramatic motive of Socrates becomes clear—to overcome the tragic spirit of rhetoric with the philosophical ideal of unity. For Plato had lived through three decades of "tragic" choices thrust upon his city by the rhetoric of its leaders, choices which had resulted not in a beautiful new era of justice but the pathetic facts of death, defeat, and desolation. Today, from the safe distance of over two millennia, we might find this long debate about whether virtue is one or many to belabor a trivial point of definition, but for the Athenians of the fourth century, it was the most central of all questions. After all, the war had been fought and administered by "courageous" souls ready to sacrifice their bodies for a cause, confident that they were pursuing the good. But what kind of disastrous fate is in store for a city that splits courage off from wisdom, temperance, piety, and justice and then hands the "courageous" the reins of power and the instruments of war? And what resources are available to those who would aspire to a judgment which satisfies all the virtues if the virtues are, by nature, incommensurable? Without a unified conception of virtue, the tragic conflict between virtues is inevitable, and the rhetorical battle between them can only lead inexorably toward a confident but blind rush into the abyss.

To avoid a second tragic fate, Plato dramatizes Socrates's encounter with the shades of dead Sophists. The goal of the narrative is to propose a new, unified ideal of virtue for the present and future. In place of Protagoras's analogy of the parts of a face to describe the relationship amongst the virtues, Plato has Socrates propose an analogy to different objects which differ in size and shape but are made of the same substance, gold (329e). And for Socrates, that substance is *knowledge*. Piety means knowing what to honor, temperance means knowing the proper balance between extremes, justice means knowing how to put things in their correct place, courage means knowing what to fear and what to fight for, and wisdom simply means the possession of knowledge itself. In each of these particular acts of virtue, the same "gold" shines through. From this perspective, what appears to be a "tragic choice" at first glance turns out to be a case of mismeasurement based on ignorance, defined by Socrates as having "a false belief and to be deceived about matters of importance" (358c). The existence of a common substance thus makes it impossible for the virtues ever to be in conflict or contradiction except to those lacking in knowledge and unconcerned with truth.

We can get a clear conception of Plato's reinterpretation of tragedy-as-ignorance by looking at the example of Sophocles's *Antigone*. When Creon forbids the proper burial of Polynices for having raised an army against his brother Eteocles, he believes he acts in the name of justice as the rightful punishment of a traitor. He thus feels completely justified in rejecting the pious appeal by Antigone that Creon obey the traditional rights of burial as dictated by the gods. For Plato, it is Creon's narrow-minded insistence that justice and piety cannot be reconciled, and not any inherent necessity of the situation, that brings about a tragic choice. Even Sophocles implies this, for at the end of the play Creon relents after glimpsing the common "gold" that bridges the division between himself and Antigone. However, it comes too late; by that time, Antigone has already hanged herself in the tomb in which her brother's body decays. Similarly, Athens only realized too late that rhetorically pitting the virtues against each other for the sake of power only caused its own tragic destruction. But for Plato this was an avoidable fate. Had the intellectuals of the fifth century understood the unity of virtue and developed a systematic form of civic education with the dialectical pursuit of knowledge at its core, the war might have ended differently or been avoided altogether. Having failed in their endeavor, however, they were condemned to the same tragic end as Creon. In Plato's eyes, it was time to leave such tragic endings behind; it was time for a new generation to reconstitute Greek power on a more solid basis than tragedy and its political counterpart, sophistical rhetoric.

This new basis of power Socrates calls an "art of measurement" (356e). Clearly proposed as a rival to Protagoras's *anthrôpos*-measure doctrine, the art of measurement rejects the pluralism of its sophistical competitor and assumes that there exists a common scale by which all appearances can be weighed,

compared, and judged. Whereas Protagoras had advanced a rhetorical humanism by which appearances are what they appear to us to be (but which are
also capable of being subsequently altered through the power of *logos* for the
"betterment" of experience), Socrates suggests that appearances are *never* what
they appear to be and that it is our responsibility to measure them accurately if
we are to not to succumb to their deceptions. In contrast to mere acquaintance
with appearances, which represents the material for both rhetoric and opinion,
true knowledge represents a grasp of the nature of things themselves gained
through the process of reasoning through dialectic. In this new ideal, virtue
becomes identified with the ability to translate knowledge into good practice
while judgment ceases to be a product of rhetorical disputation and becomes
instead the capacity to make choices based on a mathematical measurement
of alternatives. Here, in its totality, is the new model of *paideia* that the fully
awake Socrates proposes to Plato's generation.

Yet as the dialogue makes perfectly clear, the need for rhetorical argumentation and persuasion has not disappeared altogether. As long as the perfect
circle has not been completed, and the beautiful state remains a work in progress, the tools of rhetoric will be necessary to bring recalcitrant audiences into
willing compliance. Explicitly defining the function of this noble form of rhetoric occurs more explicitly in the *Gorgias* and the *Phaedrus* than it does in the
Protagoras, however. In the *Phaedrus,* Socrates had proposed that the rhetorical
art represents "a way of directing the soul by means of speech," meaning that
rhetoric serves the end of virtue when it directs the soul toward that goal which
dialectic has shown to be good, beautiful, and true (261b). For Plato, rhetoric
in effect becomes a pedagogical instrument for teaching the uninitiated and
inspiring the reluctant. Here the orator is more a teacher than an advocate,
more a source of wisdom than of flattery. For instance, in the *Gorgias,* Socrates
tells Callicles that the "skilled and good orator" will "always give his attention
to how justice may come into the souls of his fellow citizens and injustice to be
gotten rid of, how self-control may come to exist there and lack of discipline
be gotten rid of, and how the rest of excellence may come into being there and
badness may depart" (*Gorgias,* 504d). In Plato's new ethical republic, rhetoric
ceases to be a medium for advancing one's own position against opposing *logoi*
in a competitive public sphere and becomes instead a tool for the wise to cultivate the souls of citizens by moving them collectively to embrace the universal
good. As the personified voice of rhetoric says in the *Phaedrus*: "Even someone
who knows the truth could not produce conviction on the basis of a systematic
art without me" (260e). Put another way, what makes rhetoric necessary is that
people need a sweetener to make the truth go down.

What the *Protagoras* adds to the *Phaedrus* and the *Gorgias* is a display
of such rhetoric in action. For in the other two dialogues, noble rhetoric was

discussed but never enacted, precisely because the *demos* itself was never present as an audience. Remarkable about the *Protagoras* is that Plato finally has
Socrates direct his speech toward the people in order to demonstrate what a
"noble" rhetoric might be. Reminiscent of the comic *parabasis* when the playwright makes a direct appeal to the audience, Socrates at the end of the dialogue begins addressing his arguments to the "many" (the *demos*) who hold
opinions that function as roadblocks to developing an art of measurement. This
shift is made possible, of course, only because of Plato's characterization of Protagoras as a man of the *demos* who becomes uncomfortable when he is forced
into a position to challenge public opinion. Plato's ingenious solution is to have
Socrates suggest that, instead of wrestling with Protagoras, he should hold a
mock dialogue with "most people" in order to reconstruct their logic and win
them over to a new belief. Not surprisingly, then, the often barren dialectic of
Socrates begins to soften as he speaks to a public audience, until eventually this
manner of speaking disappears altogether and is replaced by a passionate rhetorical appeal for their salvation. In other words, the dialogue concludes with
Socrates demonstrating the manner by which the skilled and virtuous orator
uses rhetoric to move the souls of the public in the direction of the good.

Notably, the opinion which he seeks to challenge represents more than simply a historical reflection of Greek public opinion in the fifth century B.C.E. It
also reflects a pervasive belief, then as well as today, that the public relies upon
to rationalize the sorry state of its own political culture: that the demands of
reason and temptations of pleasure are always in conflict, and that the force
of reason usually proves the weaker. Reminiscent of the position of Gorgias's
Helen, in which *logos* acquires most of its dynastic power from a combination
of erotic desire, fear, and imagination, the "many" think well of reason but
do not believe it to be a primary motivating force for action. How could it
be otherwise, given the notorious susceptibility of public opinion to quacks,
demagogues, rumor, jingoism, and the latest shiny bauble in the marketplace?
Speaking for the "many," Socrates puts the position this way to his dialectical
partner for the sake of argument:

> Come now, Protagoras, and reveal this about your mind: what do you
> think about knowledge? Do you go along with the majority or not? Most
> people think this way about it, that it is not a powerful thing, neither a
> leader nor ruler. They do not think of it in that way at all; but rather in
> this way: while knowledge is often present in man, what rules him is not
> knowledge but rather anything else—sometimes desire, sometimes pleasure,
> sometimes pain, at other times love, often fear; they think of his knowledge
> as being utterly dragged around by these things other as if it were a slave.
> (352b–c)

Despite their hope for a rational society, then, the public usually maintains a more pessimistic view that "most people are unwilling to do what is best, even though they know what it is and are able to do it" (352a).[26] But this is simply another way to say that, although people might possess wisdom, they lack the courage of their principles. According to the public, it is courage alone which is capable of overcoming our bodily addiction to pleasure and to do what is right despite the threat of pain, torture, or death. That is why courage, for Protagoras, is taught by a physical trainer and not a philosopher—because only by strengthening the body can one resist the desire for pleasure which originates in that same body. The mind has nothing to do with it.

The rhetorical consequences of this attitude are significant. On the one hand, the belief that pleasure almost always trumps reason provides ethical sanction for the demagogue to persuade an audience through the promise of immediate pleasures even if he or she might know better, precisely because that it is the only "realistic" route available for collective action. Reminiscent of the analogy of "pastry baking" in the Gorgias, rhetoric here is seen as a necessary means of moving an audience in the right direction by tempting it with sweets, much as a child is convinced to go to the doctor for the reward of a candy. On the other hand, the desire for an audience to feel "superior" to its desires provides a way for ideologues to point to the intense pain and misery produced by their policies as evidence for their inherent rationality. As demonstrated by Thucydides, this rhetorical position becomes necessary once the promise of pleasure is thwarted and an audience must now justify its own suffering while making atrocities against others into a virtue. Of course, these two strategies are opposite sides of the same coin. In both cases, the origin of base rhetoric is the same: the supposed division between pleasure and reason is exploited in order to disable the possibility of thinking, the effect of which is to bring about suffering that poets can then glorify through the lens of the "tragic." Thus, despite their apparent opposition, these rhetorical strategies are actually counterparts of one another; as exemplified in the first and second speeches of Pericles before and after the start of the war, the first establishes the conditions for tragic suffering which must then be brutally endured and celebrated in the second.

The rhetorical exigence for Socrates is to break this tragic cycle and provide a more secure ground for public opinion formation. He must persuade the "many" that this dualism between reason and pleasure should be discarded and replaced with a unitary faith in the power of knowledge to move people toward a collective good that promises the reward of pleasure in the long term. To accomplish this task, however, Socrates accepts for the sake of argument a very un-Socratic position: the hedonistic premise of the Sophists. Socrates is thus presented in a rare light in the Protagoras insofar as he appears to defend the position of the "many" that "to live pleasantly is good, and unpleasantly, bad" (351c). For the man who willingly suffered execution rather than compromise his principles in the *Phaedo,* and who in the *Gorgias* argued that to suffer the physical effects of injustice is better than to inflict them, this starting point might seem intentionally ironic. Perhaps Socrates is toying with his audience in order to draw them into a trap. But in this case it is not a trap. It is simply a starting point Socrates uses to make a genuine effort to persuade the *demos* that he has developed a philosophy which reconciles the tension between pleasure and reason, and thus he naturally begins with the position of hedonism to establish identification with the people and to show that his aims are continuous with theirs. For if rhetoric has taught him anything, it is that he cannot bring about the ideal Republic on this earth if he cannot rally the people to his side.

The way he slowly pulls the "many" toward his ultimate position is a masterful demonstration of dialectical subtlety and rhetorical persuasion. To establish identification with his audience, he appeals to that most basic of human motivations—the desire for long and healthy lives for oneself and one's children. Drawing from common-sense examples, he argues that most apparent conflicts between pleasure and reason are really between two different kinds of pleasures and pains, those that are near and those that are far. When people say they have been "overcome by pleasure," for instance, they often mean they have overindulged in "pleasant things like food or drink or sex" despite their awareness that later they "bring about diseases and poverty and many other things of that sort" down the road (353d). These types of pleasures the people term "bad pleasures." Inversely, some say that there are some pains which are "good," including "athletics and military training and treatment by doctors such as cautery, surgery, medicines, and starvation diet" (354a). Thus, whereas a bad pleasure brings about gratification in the present but pain in the future, a good pain makes one suffer now for the sake of benefits later. But both of these statements really amount to the same thing—that actions we call "good" are those which produce more pleasures than pains over a span of time, and those which we call "bad" do not. There is thus no such thing as a good or a bad pleasure, but only the sum total of pleasures and pains in comparison. Socrates elaborates: "Weighing is a good analogy; you put the pleasures together and the pains together, both the near and the remote, on the balance scale, and then say which of the two is more" (356b). It is this act of weighing multiple things according to a common scale that embodies the art of measurement, an art which is exemplified in the medical profession and the character of the doctor who speaks the truth for the sake of the good despite the immediate pain one must endure to acquire health.

But Socrates is a peculiar sort of doctor. Sometimes, after all, his prescribed treatment is to suffer injustice and to embrace death without complaint. But if the good life is one that is lived pleasantly, what possible art of measurement would tell me that painful death is preferable to pleasurable life? No wonder even intellectuals like Protagoras think courage to be separate from wisdom, for no amount of hedonistic reasoning seems capable of validating a willing embrace of death unless one faces, like Prometheus, a future of unbearable physical torture. That is why soldiers are sent into battle not with the fear of death but with the promise of victory and all the accolades that come from heroism. But Socrates insists that courage is the opposite of ignorance and consists of "wisdom about what is and is not to be feared" (360d). How can this be? Do not soldiers have every right to fear the enemy and the bloody slaughter that comes from battle? Socrates says that the coward who runs from battle is fleeing the wrong thing, and those who fight and risk death actually pursue that which is not to be feared but desired. As Socrates explains to Protagoras, although physical injury and death may be painful, this pain is nothing compared to the rewards of honor, meaning the courageous man always goes "toward the more honorable, the better, and the more pleasant" (360a). Likewise, when Socrates later chooses to drink hemlock rather than forsake his teaching, his courage does not consist of facing that which is fearsome but possessing the wisdom to choose the path that is pleasurable.

The solution to this paradox turns on what type of thing we are measuring and what measure we are using. The problem with conventional hedonism is that it only attends to the health of the mortal body and measures physical pleasures and pains, when in fact a philosophical hedonism attends equally to the health of the immortal soul and its triumphs and sufferings. For Plato, then, a glutton who speaks of being "overcome by pleasure" actually confesses to knowing nothing about the value or meaning of health just as a coward who speaks of being "overcome by fear" knows nothing of the meaning of honor. It is this difference between apparent and true knowledge which allows Plato to make the assertion that nobody willingly does evil but always pursues that which they believe to be good.[27] Having lived through three decades of brutal war, Plato is hardly blind to the weaknesses of human beings and the frequency by which they say one thing and then do the opposite. But he accounted for this not by the inherent evil of human beings but by their pervasive ignorance about the nature of the good. Once this knowledge was revealed to a person in its fullest and most beautiful disclosure, the soul could not help but fall in love with it and sacrifice everything for its beloved.

Thus it is only at the very end of the dialogue that Socrates reveals the aura of transcendence that surrounds the art of measurement. Far from representing an enlightened hedonistic calculus grounded in a scientific and technological materialism, the art of measurement turns out to be a highly spiritual rationalism whereby the eternal rewards of a virtuous soul far outweigh the ephemeral sufferings of the physical body. The art of measurement thus weighs not only the pleasures and pains that our judgments produce in our mortal body but also those which our immortal souls endure once we pass into the next world, whatever that world might be. In the *Gorgias,* Socrates describes the disciplinary consequences of this art of measurement through the language of myth:

> It is appropriate for everyone who is subject to punishment rightly inflicted by another either to become better or profit from it, or else to be made an example for others, so that when they see him suffering whatever it is he suffers, they may be afraid and become better. Those who are benefited, who are made to pay their dues by gods and men, are the ones whose errors are curable; even so, their benefit comes to them, both here and in Hades, by way of pain and suffering, for there is no other possible way to get rid of injustice. (*Gorgias,* 525b)[28]

Anticipating the language of Christian morality, a true art of measurement has us put temporal and eternal pains and pleasures on the same scale so that even the pain of death appears as only a small price to pay for living with the gods on the Isle of the Blessed.

Having started with the hedonistic axiom of public opinion, Socrates thus works his way toward rhetorical transcendence, whereby a beautiful and higher unity is glimpsed through an apparent contradiction.[29] The "many" had assumed that pleasure and reason were always in conflict, and that what is closer at hand always has more motivational force than what is far away. Having now set in place the idea that there is a single "gold" of knowledge that provides the universal substance of the different virtues, Socrates embraces the role of the skilled and noble orator to persuade his audience to willingly embrace a new standard of judgment:

> Answer me this: Do things of the same size appear to you larger when seen near at hand and smaller when seen from a distance, or not? . . . And similarly for thicknesses and pluralities? And equal sounds seem louder when near at hand, softer when far away? . . . If then our well-being depended upon this, doing and choosing large things, avoiding and not doing the small ones, what would we see as our salvation in life? Would it be the art of measurement or the power of appearance? While the power of appearance often makes us wander all over the place in confusion, often changing our minds about the same things and regretting our actions and choices with respect to things large and small, the art of measurement in contrast, would make the appearances lose their power by showing us the truth, would give us peace of mind firmly rooted in the truth and would save our life. . . .

Well, then, my good people: Since it has turned out that our salvation in life depends on the right choice of pleasures and pains, be they more or fewer, greater or lesser, farther or nearer, doesn't our salvation seem, first of all, to be measurement, which is the study of relative excess and deficiency and equality? (356c–e)

Few orators today would consciously choose the language of mathematics as a medium of rhetorical transcendence and ethical/political reform, yet this is precisely what Plato puts in the mouth of Socrates.[30] Not yet the "duty" of the Stoic nor the "morality" of the Christian, Plato's concept of transcendent ethics is rooted in a rational measurement of pleasures and pains both in this life and in the next. His rhetoric is thus neither materialistic nor idealistic but holistic, believing that true persuasion consists of showing how every part of the universe hangs together in a totality while demonstrating that it is our responsibility to act according to both the physical and moral laws of the cosmos.

Plato introduced a new relationship between rhetoric and power. In the old relationship, rhetoric was seen as a medium by which people could act in concert to achieve collective ends. Socrates, in fact, appeals to this sense of power in his discussion with Protagoras when he introduces the hedonistic hypothesis. Concerning things like medical treatment or athletic training, he asks of the "many" the following question: "Would you call these things good for the reason that they bring about intense pain and suffering, or because they ultimately bring about health and good conditions of bodies and preservation of cities and power over others and wealth?" (354a). Protagoras and Socrates agree that they would assent, for all of these things represent the traditional ends toward which rhetoric had been used. Yet in his discussion of courage and honor, Socrates implies a new conception of power which appears more explicitly in the *Gorgias*: the power to achieve not only earthly goods through the practical arts but also to attain ultimate happiness by cultivating a virtuous soul through knowledge of the good. Here is the rhetoric not of the political demagogue but of the martyr, the prophet, the revolutionary, and the poet; it is the rhetoric of anyone who would rally people to sacrifice themselves for a virtuous ideal, though their cause be impossible and their fate be one of torture, suffering, and even death. In Platonic rhetoric, the art of true measurement brings all apparent pains into perspective and makes them seem trivial in light of the glorious whole that can be glimpsed over the horizon, the Promised Land in which all virtuous souls are to enjoy pleasurable communion in virtue unto eternity.

In the closing scene of the *Protagoras,* the drama seems to come to a comic end. After having wrestled with each other for hours in tense but controlled combat, suddenly the spirit lightens. Socrates mocks both of them for having apparently switched positions. "How ridiculous you are, both of you!" he laughs from the newly imported perspective of the Logos, which has now taken on a voice of its own. Speaking through the Logos, Socrates finds it amusing that he now seems to be saying that virtue can be taught (because virtue is knowledge) while Protagoras seems to be saying that it cannot (because for him it is something other than knowledge). Yet these are matters to be settled another day. At this point the spirit of Old Comedy reappears, and Protagoras—the representative of the "old king"—bestows his blessing on the "new king," Socrates. He pronounces: "Socrates, I commend your enthusiasm and the way you find your way through an argument. I really don't think I am a bad man, certainly the last man to harbor ill will. Indeed, I have told many people that I admire you more than anyone I have met, certainly more than anyone in your generation. And I say that I would not be surprised if you gain among men high repute for wisdom" (361e). Here is the final blessing on Socrates to carry on the tradition of Greek *paideia* which the Sophists had done their best to cultivate, despite their limitations. If Socrates had wings, he would fly off stage, but Plato's prose is more subtle: Socrates has another appointment, and must be off. *Exeunt.*

Plato, however, is not writing a comedy any more than he is writing a tragedy. Rather, what Plato provides us in the *Protagoras* is the new hybrid literary, intellectual, and rhetorical genre of tragicomedy that dramatizes the journey toward enlightenment. That Plato saw himself as writing in this hybrid genre is made explicit in the closing lines of the *Symposium,* when he has Socrates try to persuade the tragic poet Agathon and the comic poet Aristophanes that "authors should be able to write both comedy and tragedy: the skillful tragic dramatist should also be a comic poet" (223d). In that dialogue, the two poets are too drunk to understand, and quickly nod off as the evening grows old. But we have the luxury of encountering his words fully awake. And what we learn is that, like tragedy, Plato's dialogue presents apparently incommensurable choices that lead to heroic suffering. Like comedy, it reveals the great to be small as they bluster and blunder through circumstances. Yet the journey of Socrates concludes neither with the fear and pity of tragedy nor the farcical celebration of comedy. Instead, his tragicomic drama goes through tragedy and comedy toward transcendent enlightenment that shows suffering and laughter alike to be necessary trials we must pass through in order to learn the nature of the good which will heal out bodies and save our souls. And this is what makes tragicomedy rhetorical: "Tragicomic rhetoric destroys the familiar and banal to display the strange and extraordinary, creating within its audience feelings of fear and yearning, shock and security, which culminate in the productive transformation of experience within the lived world."[31] So even if we suffer, our suffering is welcome because it is our ironic reward for a virtuous soul; and even if we stumble, our stumbling is a gift because only by failure can we correct ourselves. Tragicomic rhetoric takes us on a journey of learning through the taken-for-granteds of culture, including the things we consider fearful or desirable, in order to transcend these conventions and open up the sphere of the possible in which virtue and power are reconciled.

In Plato's prosaic tragicomedy we thus see the model for the rhetoric of all those who wish to reconcile poetry and philosophy, action and intellect, persuasion and truth, and politics and power. For only in the literate form of the narrative drama can we trace the detailed journey of the seeker of wisdom who methodically inquires into the nature of appearances to find the gold hidden behind the veil. In contemporary culture, this rhetoric often takes the form of the novel, the movie, or the literary essay, each dramatizing the experiences of a sojourner who has been compelled to bring his or her revelations to the people in poetic form. But it appears most powerfully in prophetic social movements that combine tragic judgment with comic hope in order to mobilize a people to suffer for an ideal that perhaps only their children or their children's children may see actualized on earth.[32] Tragicomic rhetoric may not always end with the happy life of the protagonist, either in this life or the next; the only thing it guarantees is that justice will eventually come with power when an enlightened rhetoric moves the collective souls of humankind with knowledge and courage toward a future that brings the promise of the good, the true, and the beautiful.

CHAPTER 9

Isocrates's "Nicocles" and
the Hymn to Hegemony

There are people who frown upon eloquence and censure men who study philosophy, asserting that those who engage in such occupations do so, not for the sake of virtue, but for their own advantage. Now, I should be glad if those who take this position would tell me why they blame men who are ambitious to speak well, but applaud men who desire to act rightly; for if it is the pursuit of one's own advantage which gives them offence, we shall find that more and greater advantages are gained from actions than from speech. Moreover, it is passing strange if the fact has escaped them that we reverence the gods and practice justice, and cultivate the other virtues, not they we may be worse off than our fellows, but that we may pass our days in the enjoyment of as many good things as possible. They should not, therefore, condemn these means by which one may gain advantage without sacrifice of virtue, but rather those men who do wrong in their actions or who deceive by their speech and put their eloquence to unjust uses. . . .

But the fact is that since they have not taken the trouble to make distinctions after this manner in each instance, they are ill disposed to all eloquence; and they have gone so far astray as not to perceive that they are hostile to that power which of all the faculties that belong to the nature of man is the source of most of our blessings. For in the other powers which we possess we are in no respect superior to other living creatures; nay, we are inferior to many in swiftness and in strength and in other resources;

but because there has been implanted in us the power to persuade each other and to make clear to each other whatever we desire, not only have we escaped the life of wild beasts, but we have come together and founded cities and made laws and invented arts; and, generally speaking, there is no institution devised by man which the power of speech (logos) has not helped us to establish. For it is this which has laid down laws concerning things just and unjust, and things honorable and base; and if it were not for these ordinances we should not be able to live with one another. It is by logos also that we confute the bad and extol the good. Through logos we educate the ignorant and appraise the wise; for the power to speak well is taken as the surest index of a sound understanding, and discourse which is true and lawful and just is the outward image of a good and faithful soul. With the faculty we both contend against others on matters which are open to dispute and seek light for ourselves on things which are unknown; for the same arguments which we use in persuading others when we speak in public, we employ also when we deliberate in our own thoughts; and, while we call eloquent those who are able to speak before a crowd, we regard as sage those who most skillfully debate their problems in their own minds. And, if there is need to speak in brief summary of this power, we shall find that none of the things which are done with intelligence take place without the help of speech, but that in all our actions as well as in all our thoughts speech is our guide (hēgemōn), and is most employed by those who have the most wisdom. Therefore, those who dare to speak with disrespect of educators and teachers of philosophy deserve our opprobrium no less than those who profane the sanctuaries of the gods.[1]

Sometime around 370 B.C.E., on the island of Cyprus, a political pamphlet appeared in the hands of its citizens. As with Plato's latest dialogue, multiple copies transcribed onto papyrus scrolls made their way among both the ruling class and the ruled, sometimes to be read in private but more often to be performed aloud in a public or private gathering. But unlike the works of Plato, this pamphlet was not meant to be read allegorically in order to discern some hidden philosophical meaning through dramatic irony; it spoke in a clear voice about pressing matters of state and the role of the citizen in governance. Addressed directly to the people of Cyprus by their ruler Nicocles, the young king who had taken power in 374 B.C.E. after the death of his father Evagoras, the pamphlet urged the Cyprians to voluntarily accept the wise and temperate rule of monarchy as the best medium for their own acquisition of power. Employing the language of contract, Nicocles lays out the terms in the conclusion: "If I continue to treat you as in time past, and you continue to give me your service and support, you will soon see your own life advanced, my empire increased, and the state made happy and prosperous" (*Nicocles*, 62). Here is a public bargain that few would be wise to refuse—empire, happiness, and prosperity in return for service to and support of the monarchy. And best of all, because the contract is inscribed on papyrus and spread far and wide to the populace, Nicocles would find it hard to go back on his word. His written logos binds him to his promise just as strongly as it binds the people together in virtue, law, and culture. For the logos is not the ephemeral expression of the voice into the air; it is a collective and enduring *hēgemōn,* a leader, ruler, and guide.

Given the clear relationship between logos and the power, it is no wonder that Nicocles bristles at those who would censure the arts of eloquence as if men of words were somehow more deceitful than men of action. Certainly, such critics fail to distinguish the nature of a tool from the character of its use and its user. After all, a temple robber has more to gain through action than a funeral orator does through speech, but that does not make us condemn the use of hammers. The haters of eloquence grossly underestimate the power of the tool itself. For while it is true that men of action may act virtuously like Ajax at the ramparts, the nature of the bodily medium localizes the consequences in space and time; only men of words like Homer have the power to memorialize and preserve those actions for all people across history. Whereas action can produce this or that particular event or object, only logos can fabricate those shared possessions so essential for civilization—laws, arts, cities, virtues, and understanding. In short, to condemn eloquence is to condemn the only means by which virtuous governance is possible, a position that is anathema to all leaders who would establish justice on any basis other than the sword.

And Nicocles is no tyrant. In addition to being the legitimate heir of his father's rule and of the bloodline of Teucer, Nicocles also boasts of his ability to run the affairs of state through the virtues of temperance and justice for the benefit of the entire city. For instance, despite being offered the same pleasures that corrupted many a weaker man, Nicocles boasts: "I did not fall a victim to any of these temptations; nay, I attended so devotedly and honourably to my duties that I left nothing undone which could contribute to the greatness of the state and advance its prosperity: and toward the citizens of the state I behaved with such mildness that no one has suffered exile or death or confiscation of property or any such misfortune during my reign" (32). For what Nicocles understood was that the leadership of a city is not simply a reward to be savored by the powerful for their own self-gratification; leadership is a responsibility bestowed upon one with self-discipline and virtue for the good of all. As he explains, his duty as a leader of people is to act as a model for the people: "I desired both to put myself as far above such suspicions as possible and at the same time to set up my conduct as a pattern to my people, knowing that the multitude are likely to spend their lives in practices in which they see their rulers occupied" (37). His was not to be a rule by force but a rule by the character of the word.

The publicity of Logos makes this new kind of political order possible. For unlike the tyrannies or monarchies of old, in which power accrued to a privileged elite with a monopoly on material resources, the power of this new autocracy derived from the capacity for the governed to evaluate the Logos of its leader and then to judge it as worthy of their support insofar as it reflects their own values and aims. The goal of "Nicocles" is thus not to prove himself to be a god and thereby command obedience from lesser mortals. As Takis Poulakos explains, "according to the logic of the oration, his rule will be made secure and his leadership will remain uncontested so long as he learns to speak like a citizen."[2] This is why Nicocles praises, above all the other powers of the Logos, its capacity to make things clear. Clarity, in fact, turns out to be the source of most of our blessings, for it is only through clarity that we acquire shared understanding of what to expect from one another. Clarity not only enables citizens to act together based on shared beliefs, but it also makes true leadership possible. As Nicocles explains: "if I did not make clear what I desire you to do, I could not reasonably be angry with you if you were to mistake my purpose; but if, after I have announced my policy beforehand, none of my desires are carried out, then I should justly blame those who fail to obey me" (11). But this goal of universal clarity is only possible through the publicity of writing. Nicocles "speaks" not with his voice but with a pamphlet—it is the only medium whereby he can make his desires clear to an entire citizenry in such a way that will produce their consent to be governed according to that logos.

But for all that, "Nicocles" appears to be playing an ironic joke on the demos. As it turns out, the "true and lawful" logos that he disseminates far and wide is not even his own, and that "good and faithful soul" of which this logos is an "outward image" is not even the Cyprian King Nicocles; it is the Athenian Sophist and pamphleteer Isocrates (436–338 B.C.E.). In actual fact, then, the pamphlet "Nicocles" functions as a companion piece to a previous pamphlet, *To Nicocles*, the latter composed as a kind of "open letter" to the monarch in which Isocrates gives him wise counsel. This relationship between the two pamphlets is made explicit in the text of *Nicocles*: "On the former topic, how a ruler should act, you have heard Isocrates speak; on the following topic, what his subjects must do, I shall attempt to discourse, not with any thought of excelling him, but because this is the most fitting subject for me to discuss with you" (*Nicocles*, 11). Of course, this explanation only compounds the irony. Neither did the public "hear" Isocrates "speak" on the former topic (but instead looked at his writing), nor are they currently hearing Nicocles speak humbly of his own talents now. They are instead bearing witness to Isocrates trying to outdo himself in writing by composing another pamphlet.

Whether the Cyprians actually appreciated the irony of these pamphlets is hard to discern; but one thing is at least apparent—the Athenians did not. When they found out that, by Isocrates's own admission, Nicocles had bestowed "many great presents" upon him, the Athenians condemned them as payment for services rendered by a faithful servant of a foreign tyrant hostile to democratic ideals (*Antidosis*, 40). Yet Isocrates believed that his critics were both factually in error and missing the larger point. In defense of his reputation in his later pamphlet *Antidosis*, he asks, "can any of you be persuaded that Nicocles made me these presents in order that he might learn how to plead cases in court—he who dispensed justice, like a master, to others in their disputes?" (40). From the perspective of Isocrates, his pamphlets were not written as if by some lackey for the purposes of flattering a tyrant and manipulating his subjects; they were written to provide a model for speaking for all aspiring orators. According to Takis Poulakos, "Nicocles is not merely an oration but also a textbook, a requirement in the education of students interested in learning how to speak, according to Isocrates, like leaders in the polis."[3] Whether the speaker was democratically elected was a secondary concern for Isocrates; what mattered was that his Logos was the outward image of a virtuous soul and was therefore worthy of being granted hegemony by the citizens as a means of actualizing the promise of *paidea*.

At the core of Isocrates's lifelong ambivalence about the great fifth-century debates over the respective merits of democracy, oligarchy, and monarchy is his superior confidence in a new form of power that he saw emerging in the fourth century facilitated by the rhetoric of the written word. Although Isocrates never denied the innate power of oral rhetoric to move an audience to passionate action about pressing affairs in the moment, he found more impressive the rapidly growing power of written rhetoric to address a wider, literate audience of Greek citizens about weighty and complex issues that transcended the parochial interests of any one city-state. That is why we find in Isocrates a new fourth-century hegemonic vision of logocracy to replace the dynastic image put forward in the fifth century B.C.E. by Gorgias. Whereas Gorgias had portrayed Logos as a dynast, focusing on what John Poulakos calls "the power of language to impose, to undermine, to violate, to deceive, and to distort," Isocrates characterizes Logos as a leader, thus underscoring "logos' capacity to collect, to unify, to lead, to shape, and to facilitate."[4] But this contrast simply maps onto what Isocrates saw as the difference between the spoken and written word. For him, the future of Greek power would not be determined by this or that demagogue who could incite the passions of the mob in the assembly; it would be determined by the mechanisms of publicity, whereby the Logos of aspiring leaders could be disseminated to the citizens and then judged by them to reflect their own shared interests and virtues. Consequently, in this new hegemonic logocracy, the particular institutions of government were less important than the ability for eloquent and virtuous leaders to gain citizens' voluntary assent to act as *hēgemōn* for the good of the whole, which for Isocrates meant not Athens, Sparta, or Cyprus, but all of Hellas unified by a common culture made possible by possessing a common Logos.

Perhaps without fully recognizing it, Isocrates acted as an expression and catalyst of the tendencies of his era, a man who stood at the nexus of forces awaiting a new form of expression. His writing was the vehicle for power like pollen on the wind; it did not create anything new or impose ideas through force, but facilitated the emergence of a then still inchoate notion of a Panhellenic empire unified by a common Logos. As he writes in the *Antidosis*, he desires a new kind of rhetoric crafted "not for private disputes, but which deal with the world of Hellas, with affairs of state, and are appropriate to be delivered at the Pan-Hellenic assemblies" (46). The rhetoric of Isocrates, both in medium and in content, thus anticipated a kind of political order that would burst the limits of the city-state and establish a new form of power for a new age. In this new form, according to Yun Lee Too, "writing is now a powerful mode of civic communication, a new form of political activity which, so he claims, and endows its practitioner—in this case, Isocrates—with the status of 'leader of words' in all Greece."[5] His Logos thus represented something different from the transcendent world order of Heraclitus or the dynastic force of persuasion of Gorgias; it became identified with a discourse of power which held society together in such a way that constituted a collective personality called *paidea*.

Isocrates was an accidental prophet of the coming age of power. Indeed, no one would have seen the young Isocrates, maturing during the early years of the Peloponnesian War, as a person destined for leadership of any kind. In his *Panathenaicus*, written when he was ninety-four years old, he recounts that he was born without "the two things which have the greatest power in Athens—a strong voice and ready assurance," handicaps which made him not only incapable of being heard in a public setting but also unable to muster the confidence to speak in the first place (10). Yet Isocrates is proud that his limitations inspired him to a greater goal: "I did not permit these disabilities to dishearten me nor did I allow myself to sink into obscurity or utter oblivion, but since I was barred from public life I took refuge in study and work and writing down my thoughts, choosing as my field, not petty matters nor private contracts, nor the things about which the other orators prate, but the affairs of Hellas and of kings and of states" (*Panathenaicus,* 11). Everything there is to know about the character of Isocrates is embodied in these passages. Neither a politician nor a philosopher, Isocrates is first and foremost a writer, a man who looks out upon the sweeping panorama of the known world from the perspective of his study and seeks to fabricate out of that material a unity called "Hellas." Little else about Isocrates is spectacular except this point of view; but it is one that we can recognize, with the benefit of hindsight, turned out to be more prophetic than any other idea put forth by Greek intellectuals or artists of his age.

In his own time, however, Isocrates was not known as a prophet but as a schoolteacher. Like his counterpart and competitor Plato, Isocrates perceived a need for a new kind of higher education to train the future leaders of Greece. His solution: to open his own school in 392 B.C.E. This school would be located in Athens and would charge high tuition for three to four years of concentrated education to no more than nine students at a time. But unlike Plato, Isocrates did not believe that true leadership was contingent on possessing some abstract "art of measurement." On the contrary, he believed that "the world must banish utterly from their interests all vain speculations and all activities which have no bearing on our lives" (*Antidosis,* 269). What leaders needed was not some Platonic "gymnastic of the mind" (265), but the disciplined experience, natural talent, habitual virtue, and practical wisdom to size up situations and determine the right course of action based on an evaluation of probabilities and a realistic appraisal of what is possible. Hamilton describes the resulting educational method this way: "The training he offered, although not on Plato's austere heights, was excellent. The lads were required to compose speeches on great and noble subjects which, he said, would elevate and liberate their minds, turning their attention to lofty causes and making them acquainted with lives of high endeavor. Such a discipline, Isocrates believed, formed their taste and freed them from the bondage of the commonplace."[6] The impact of his school was equally impressive. Unmatched in success and popularity, for over five decades it served as a reliable source for professional orators, historians, philosophers, statesmen, and generals, all the while making Isocrates a highly wealthy and very influential man.

Unlike the high-minded Plato and the flamboyant Gorgias, then, Isocrates wears the *ethos* of respectable administrator of a professional school tasked with producing leaders of the Greek community, each an "able speaker or an able man of affairs" (*Antidosis,* 191). His method is wholly pragmatic, disciplined, and individualized, combining the civic and rhetorical emphasis of the Sophists with the institutional and far-sighted character of the academy to produce supremely competent civic professionals. As summarized by Takis Poulakos, Isocrates's pedagogy "encourages nonformalistic approaches to learning, values knowledge on the basis of its potential uses rather than for its own sake, and assesses professional educators on the basis of their contribution to the quality of democratic life in the polis rather than on the basis of their technical expertise."[7] When he calls his teaching "philosophy," then, he does not mean that he teaches something antithetical to rhetoric. He simply means that he teaches "true rhetoric" as opposed to the kind of eristic and demagoguery frequently taught by less reputable Sophists. According to Jaeger, Isocrates believed that "true rhetoric, which is true philosophy and culture, leads to a higher kind of self-enrichment than that achieved by greed, theft, and violence—namely, to the culture of the personality, which is its implicit aim."[8] In short, Isocrates wanted his school to produce those noble personalities who would speak a *logos* which would inspire the ideals of personality in all Greek citizens and city-states, thus finally making the highest ideals of Greek culture, politics, and education—that is to say, of *paideia*—a reality.

Of course, what made Isocrates a successful cultivator of "personality" was also what made him rather mundane. In Isocrates's writing, one frequently hears extended passages, such as this one in *To Nicocles*, in which he takes on an avuncular tone reminiscent today of the voice of Shakespeare's Polonius or Benjamin Franklin's *Poor Richard's Almanac*, but which at the time was probably recognizable as the voice of wise old Nestor in the *Iliad*. Addressing the necessity for temperance in all affairs, Isocrates writes:

> Do not consider that the great souls are those who undertake more than they can achieve, but those who, having noble aims, are also able to accomplish whatever they attempt. Emulate, not those who have most widely extended their dominion, but those who have made best of the power they already possess: and believe that you will enjoy the utmost happiness, not if you rule over the whole world at the price of fears and dangers and baseness, but rather if, being the man you should be, and continuing to act as at the present moment, you set your heart on moderate achievements and fail in none of them. (*To Nicocles*, 25–26)

A more un-tragic vision of leadership could hardly be expressed; but it is nonetheless consistent with what Jaeger calls the essentially "practical bourgeois character" of Isocrates.[9] Like all bourgeois, observes Robert Hariman, Isocrates "reveres professional authority and organization, attempts to restructure society according to linked conceptions of expertise and character, and uses educational institutions as the primary means for social validation and individual success."[10] Isocrates did not want to cultivate tragic heroes willing to kill or die for an impossible and dimly glimpsed ideal; he wanted to create personalities who were respectable even at the risk of being somewhat dull, people from whom one would not expect oracular wisdom or blinding eloquence but decorous speech which displays reliable proficiency, middle-class respectability, and a certain prudent ambition.

Yet Isocrates merits our continued interest less because of the bourgeois virtues he instilled in his students and more because of the prophetic vision of a new relationship between rhetoric and power that was expressed in his capacity as a pamphleteer. For the genius of Isocrates was his decision to commit himself to the mastery of the new medium of written rhetoric that was best adapted to managing this new political environment. Ekaterina Haskins observes that, "unlike the Older Sophists, whose oral practices are inextricably connected with democratic institutions, Isocrates is a literary rhetorician, seemingly removed from daily concerns of the assembly. He distances himself from the public places of democracy and instead creates a new, literary forum for the discussion of cultural and political issues."[11] For Isocrates, the oral rhetoric of the assembly, while still a force to be reckoned with in the fourth century B.C.E., had not only descended into mob oratory but was losing its capacity to direct the course of Greek civilization.[12] Isocrates freely acknowledges that oral rhetoric is uniquely fit for generating localized and intense passions that can produce moments of power, particularly when "delivered on subjects which are important and urgent" (*To Philip*, 26). The problem was that it moved people to passionate action in the moment at the expense of long-term success. Such orators "pretend to have knowledge of the future but are incapable either of saying anything pertinent or of giving any counsel regarding the present" (*Sophists*, 8). But this is the natural constraint of oral rhetoric when it is so tightly bound to the emotional needs of an audience in the moment.

In contrast, written rhetoric transcends the constraints of the oral performance in search of style which encompasses a broader vision. Haskins characterizes this rhetoric at its best as "culturally sensitive, pragmatically oriented, and aesthetically influential."[13] For Isocrates, written rhetoric produces a calmness of mind that allows one to give "attention to the facts alone" to take up these facts "one by one in your thought and scrutinize them" with "close reasoning and love of knowledge" (*To Philip*, 29). In addition, free from the constraints of time and situation, literary authors can "set forth facts in a style more imaginative and more ornate; they employ thoughts which are more lofty and more original, and, besides, they use throughout figures of speech in greater number and of more striking character" (*Antidosis*, 47). Although Isocrates admits that a written speech, lacking the presence of its author, is unable to correct any "misconception" when it arises, he nonetheless attributes to writing a great capacity to influence those with power, to reach a broader audience, to present facts more clearly and with greater eloquence, and to address weighty themes with greater scope and complexity (*To Dionysius*, 3). His apparent "retreat" into a literary public sphere was thus not a retreat at all, but a means of detaching himself from one medium of rhetorical power in order to attach himself to the medium he believed more appropriate to managing the collective affairs of Hellas.[14]

That medium was the written word, and the form of power it sought to bring about was a Panhellenic political order produced not through military imperialism but through voluntary submission to hegemony. George Norlin accurately identifies the relationship between medium and aspiration when he describes Isocrates as a "political pamphleteer" and the "first great publicist of all time" whose lifelong campaign was to use this new medium to agitate for "a great confederacy of free states voluntarily united under a single leadership (*hēgemōn*), in the cause of a final and decisive war against their common enemy, the Persian Empire."[15] Isocrates thus used the written word to accomplish what the spoken word had not done and could never do—unify the Greeks under the banner of a common Logos. Specifically, Isocrates advocated his entire life for a Panhellenic confederacy under some form of leadership (*hēgemonia*), irrespective of whether it took the form of a single city (like Athens) or a single leader (like Nicocles). Who specifically took the leadership did not so much matter to Isocrates; what mattered was that some form of leader was voluntarily appointed for the sake of unity, justice, and power. According to Jaeger, Isocrates's model of hegemony was the very opposite of "domination founded on force"; it would rest instead on honor, with leadership given to that city or individual who was selected and then appointed by the entire Greek citizenry based on demonstrated virtue both in action and in Logos.[16]

As with most ideas expressed by Isocrates, the notion that the future of Greece would be determined by its ability to achieve Panhellenic unity was hardly his own creation. In fact, the first advocate for the ideal was Isocrates's own teacher, Gorgias. It was Gorgias who popularized a notion of pan-Hellenism that would bring all the Greek city-states into harmony, largely by uniting them in common cause against the "barbarians" (*bárbaros*), a general term that encompassed all non-Greek "foreigners" and usually referred specifically to the Persians. In one of the fragments from his *Funeral Oration*, Gorgias says, "Triumphs over the foreigners demand festive songs; but those over Greeks, laments."[17] This Panhellenic attitude would have been natural for such cosmopolitan figures as the Sophists, not only because of their worldly experience with diverse cultures, but also because harmony was good for the business of an itinerant teacher in wisdom. The more that the Sophists were free to travel from city to city and town to town across Greece, preaching the doctrine that all Greeks were worthy of instruction by the Sophists, the more their own fame was assured and profits guaranteed.

The problem was that the chosen medium of Gorgias and the Older Sophists actually served to undercut the goal of Panhellenic unity that they preached. Proving once again Marshall McLuhan's maxim that "the medium is the message," it was their continued reliance on the medium of the spoken word which actually constituted the general scale, pace, and pattern of Greek culture quite apart from any particular "content" delivered by this or that Sophist.[18] According to John Poulakos, two qualities of oral rhetoric had the effect of creating divisions quite irrespective of the content of the speeches. First, spoken eloquence naturally generates feelings of emotional attachment and identification amongst the specific audience members in attendance, with the effect that it tends to "perpetuate provincial values, thereby maintaining differences and hostilities between one city-state and another."[19] Second, oral rhetoric is ephemeral: "Lacking materiality, the spoken word was fated to vanish as soon as it was uttered," meaning that what "was said one day could not be trusted to hold the next."[20] With the Older Sophists, then, Panhellenism existed only as a rhetorical trope that livened up a speech for a particular audience, but could not be relied upon as a political ideal capable of transcending parochial differences in culture or policy. Quite the opposite, as the Sicilian expedition demonstrated and Aristophanes made great fun pointing out, its actual effect was to validate the imperialistic dreams of the Athenians who took it upon themselves to simply make Greek unity a fact by military force.

Yet in the wake of the Peloponnesian War, a more realistic goal began to take shape of a regime capable of transcending the limits of agonistic provincialism and bringing harmony to all of Hellas. According to Jaeger, with the dream of military imperialism fully discredited after the defeat of Athens, followed by years of instability in which Sparta, Athens, and Thebes all fought amongst each other for a supremacy that would never take shape, the notion began to spread that the "only harmony which could be of any use now was one which embraced all the Hellenes."[21] This notion was then backed by the growing feeling "that all its people spoke the same language (although in different dialects), that they were all members of an invisible political community, and that they owed one another mutual respect and mutual assistance."[22] This change in atmosphere is reflected in Isocrates's attempt to surpass Gorgias's *Helen* with his own masterpiece, one which no longer simply revels in turning arguments on their heads for the author's own amusement. Instead, Isocrates praises Helen for having united the Greeks against a common enemy, the Trojans, much as he wishes to unify them now in battle against the Persians. In Isocrates's hands, Helen is no longer an innocent victim of persuasion but a proud and noble symbol of Panhellenic unity.

And there is something beautiful about this vision. Within the rhetoric of Isocrates one finds a glimpse of a unified culture free from the strife of war and emancipated from blood loyalties of race. This political vision, writes Jaeger, "grows from a deep insight into the true character of the Greek mind and of Greek *paideia*," and from "his words we can feel the living breath of Hellenism."[23] What Isocrates accomplished, according to Jaeger, was to articulate the notion that "Greek *paideia* was something universally valuable," not just for individual states but for all states and, indeed, all the world.[24] How Isocrates accomplished this feat was simply to define *paideia* culture in terms of a common Logos (and all the virtues, habits, and personality that accompanied it) rather than a common racial heritage. In Isocrates's words: "the name 'Hellenes' suggests no longer a race but an intelligence, and that the title 'Hellenes' is applied rather to those who share our culture (*paideia*) than to those who share a common blood" (*Panegyricus* 51). Isocrates thus articulates more than the traditional sense of cultural superiority that largely functioned as a way for Greeks to distinguish themselves from so-called "barbarian" races; what we find is a universalist notion of culture that, once uncoupled from blood concepts of race, bound to Logos, and disseminated through rhetoric, becomes the primary vehicle for a potentially unlimited expansion of political power that eschews violence in favor of a peaceful but inexorable integration of parts into a virtuous whole.[25]

Of all of the pamphlets he penned, *Nicocles* acts as the vehicle through which we catch a glimpse of Isocrates's prophetic vision of the rhetorical power that would be inaugurated with the Hellenic age. This is because it is the only pamphlet which functions as a mechanism for power maintenance by speaking directly to the *demos* through the voice of their existing political leader. Other pamphlets are either written as "open letters" to specific individuals, like *To Philip*, as pseudo-orations (i.e., a piece of writing written "as if" it was a speech) to Athenians or to the Greeks in general about matters of shared concern, like *On the Peace*, or as literary creations meant to showcase his skill as a writer and to function as models for imitation for students in his school, like his own version of *Helen*. *Nicocles*, by contrast, combines elements from each of these three types of pamphlets to produce a radically new rhetorical genre of representative publicity, a genre made possible by the ascendency of the written word as medium of power not just for the ruling class but also for the ruled. In this genre, professional speechwriters (logographers) compose and disseminate written pseudo-orations in the name of actual political leaders in order to help those leaders accrue and maintain hegemonic political power amongst a literate public through greater reliance on the language of contract.[26]

The reason the contractual language of "clarity" and "promise" suddenly becomes so central to the new literate era of hegemonic power can be best understood in comparison to the passing era of oral dynastic power. In the age of the Older Sophists, rhetoric was still practiced "before small gatherings of interested spectators or larger audiences in public functions."[27] When Gorgias calls Logos a tyrant, he really means the tyrant's *voice* has become more powerful than any force of arms he might acquire. According to Jacques Derrida, when the Older Sophists equate rhetoric with power, they hardly mean to include writing, which in its "breathless impotence" repeats "itself and remains identical in the type, cannot flex itself in all senses, [and] cannot bend with all the differences" among those present.[28] For the Sophists, it is clear that the one who speaks "is not controlled by any preestablished pattern; he is better able to conduct his signs; he is there to accentuate them, inflect them, retain them, or set them loose according to the demands of the moment, the nature of the desired effects, the hold he has on the listener."[29] The one who writes thus does so from impotence; writing "is considered a consolation, a compensation, a remedy for sickly speech."[30] The fact that Isocrates initially embraces writing as itself a compensation for his own "sickly" voice indicates the secondary place that writing held in a culture still influenced by the oral traditions or heroic eloquence in which all negotiations and promises were made between kings through face-to-face exchange of winged words.

By the fourth century B.C.E., however, the rise in literacy rates, the availability of papyrus, the spread of democratic norms and institutions, and the increased wealth and mobility of Greek citizens had dramatically changed the relationship between rhetoric and power since the time of the Persian invasion a century earlier. Governing, writes John Poulakos, was no longer a "one man proposition" dominated by aristocratic rulers, but had evolved into a complex political culture which had to balance the vested interests of numerous parties: "In many states, propertied elites, merchants, workers, intellectuals, and aliens represented political interests to be reckoned with."[31] Moreover, the polyglot of isolated city-states that had come together to resist the Persians had slowly grown into a far more interconnected entity. Alongside the proliferation of different interest groups developed a growing sense that there existed a unitary ideal of Greek culture toward which everyone should be striving; thus, this vision of *paideia,* "once gathered primarily in Athens, was now being spread throughout Hellas by traveling Sophists, artists, and book merchants."[32] With the increase in the speed and ease of communication, both physically and through the written medium, Greece of the fourth century was more and more becoming a political entity rather than a merely geographical one, and its increased scope and complexity required a medium of power, the written word, as well as a pattern of rhetorical address which could coordinate the affairs of multiple parties over a distance with detail and reliability.

One therefore overlooks the revolutionary character of *Nicocles* if one pays attention only to its explicit "content" and not the medium of its dissemination and its form. For as with most things Isocrates, the content includes moments of creative brilliance which decorate a bed of unremarkable platitudes under which lie certain autocratic sympathies. After beginning with the eloquent hymn to Logos, the pamphlet follows a fairly predictable structure. First, Nicocles presents comparative arguments that show monarchy to be superior to democracy insofar as monarchs do what is best for everyone while democratic leaders seek glory and rewards for themselves. For example, democratic leaders "honour those who are skillful in haranguing the crowd, while [monarchs] honour those who understand how to deal with affairs" (*Nicocles*, 20). Second, Nicocles defends his title as monarch not only by proving his goodwill and practical wisdom ("I have never wronged any man, that, on the contrary, I have been of service to many more of my citizens and of the Hellenes at large" [35]) but also by showing himself to possess the virtue of character ("no one can charge me with having approached any woman but my own wife" [36]). Lastly, having defended his role as leader, he proceeds to make clear what he requires from the *demos* if he is to increase the power and prestige of the city, a list which appears to be a handbook for obedience. Citizens must embrace their appointed positions and do the tasks assigned to them with pride; they must not be jealous of others but know that their jobs, however menial, serve to enrich the whole of which they are a part; they must conceal nothing from the monarch and denounce those who conspire against him; they must train their children to be respectful of authority and instill in them the virtues of temperance and justice necessary to sustain the rule of law; and they must treat the word of the monarch as the source of that law in the knowledge that collective obedience to his authority is the only way to improve their lives, increase the dominion of the state, and produce harmony which benefits all. This is the choice before them. As he concludes: "it lies in your power, without suffering any hardship, but merely by being loyal and true, to bring all of these things to pass" (63).

Of all the specific claims that Isocrates makes in the pamphlet, only the last one captures the radical nature of this new structure of power and the uniqueness of the form of address. One "hears" the voice of a new kind of *rhetor* who speaks in the language of the marketplace, meaning a negotiated exchange of goods and services in a public space. Rather than evoke *pathos* through style, offer virtuous transcendence through wisdom, or rally a mass to collective action in pursuit of imperial domination, Nicocles requests his audience to make a pragmatic evaluation of the costs and benefits of establishing a contractual relationship with a leader in order to serve the enlightened self-interest of both parties. And just as any contact is only enforceable when its terms are inscribed on paper or in stone and open to examination by third parties, the political language of contract only becomes viable when it, too, has durability, portability, and clarity. Consequently, this new genre of representative publicity only comes into its own when it can be fully detached from the oral performance of its author (even as it mimics its style), thus making its persuasive power dependent on the capacity for a mass of individuals to examine its claims in relative isolation and come to a reflective judgment as to whether the terms set forth meet their needs in both the short and long term.

Indicating its contractual nature, the most dominant stylistic quality of this genre of rhetoric is therefore the reliance on the conditional. Embodied in the pairing of "if/then" as it concerns the responsibilities of two parties bound by a contract, the emphasis on the conditional is a subtle but significant shift in rhetorical style. Rhetoric in the past had certainly employed conditional logic as well, but it had usually been used to demonstrate how—as in Prodicus's *Choice of Heracles*—one path of action would produce goods (truth, virtue, power, pleasure, justice, and the like) that another would not. With Isocrates, however, the conditional becomes intimately tied to the logic of the "deal." In this deal, a contract outlines a set of mutual responsibilities and commitments which act as the necessary means by which both parties pursue their respective (and very often dissimilar) goods. For instance, "Nicocles" includes some of the following conditionals: "Consider that in my safety lies your own security; for while my fortunes are on a firm foundation, your own will be likewise" (56). And: "if [your children] learn to submit to authority they will be able to exercise authority over many; and if they are faithful and just they will be given a share in my privileges; but if they turn out to be bad they will be in danger of losing all the privileges which they possess" (57). And: "Once these claims have been established, who would not condemn himself to the severest punishments if he failed to heed my councils and commands?" (13). Taken together, these represent neither the language of the Homeric hero, nor the tragic poet, nor the sophistical performer, nor the philosophical sage; they represent the language of the businessman whose business is good government.

The fact that his "Nicocles" speaks as a monarch and not as a democrat matters little to Isocrates for one simple, prophetic reason: he perceived that both forms of power would eventually go obsolete in the new age of representative publicity. As a result, what matters for Isocrates is less mandating the particular institutional structure through which power is exercised than in ensuring the freedom of speech by which leaders disseminate their *logoi* to a judging *demos*. It is through this contractual logic that Isocrates can make the assertion, with a straight face, that "it is easy to exercise the supreme power and at the same time to enjoy as good relations as those who live as citizens on terms of perfect equality" ("Helen," 214). He can make this seemingly paradoxical claim precisely because representative publicity allows for ruler and ruled to be bound by the terms of a common Logos that is shared by all, equally, yet which concentrates executive power for the sake of administrative efficiency for the good of the whole.

Accordingly, Isocrates's ideal leader is not Solon or Cleisthenes, the idols of democratic reforms, but Theseus, the founder-king of the "common fatherland" of Athens. It was Theseus, after all, who first demonstrated the superiority of a hegemonic monarchy over a pluralistic democracy. Theseus, writes Isocrates, "was so far from doing anything contrary to the will of the citizens that he made the people masters of the government, and they on their part thought it best that he should rule alone, believing that his sole rule was more to be trusted and more equitable than their own democracy" (*Helen*, 36). The point of this story, which reappears time and again in Isocrates, is that authentic power derives neither from governing system nor military force but the "goodwill of the people" (37).

In Isocrates, then, words like "democracy," "monarchy," and "oligarchy" cease to have any meaningful reference. For him, there are only two forms of governance, *rule* and *domination*: "it is the duty of those who *rule* to make their subjects happier through the care for their welfare, whereas it is a habit of those who *dominate* to provide pleasures for themselves through the labors and hardships of others" ("On the Peace," 91). Like any good business relationship that might take many different concrete forms (i.e., a farm, a small business, or a corporation), the relationship between ruler and ruled should not be judged by the nature of the institution they create but by the pragmatic consequences they produce. Just as a business contract produces mutual wealth by limiting and guiding cooperative actions through mutual agreement on responsibilities and obligations, so too does a political contract bring about mutual well-being and power by instituting just "rule" rather than manipulating people into a state of "domination." But this is another way of saying that "rule" occurs only in a context in which everyone possesses a clear and universal knowledge, disseminated through the written word, of the means and ends of good governance, whereas "domination" is a natural outcome of being constantly inundated with the false promises, half-truths, emotional appeals, and the rest of the familiar tactics of the oral performances of the demagogue.

This type of rule by representative publicity, in which different *logoi* vie for hegemony by offering attractive terms to the public in the language of contract, requires for its actualization one last but crucial element—that of mutual assurance. For a "contract" means nothing if the actions and motives of each party are hidden from each other. After all, even tyrants like Pisistratus likely attempted to gain the voluntary support of the people by grand displays of his *ethos* (primarily through the arts) backed by promises to direct material and political resources toward the goal of growing the power of the city and bringing wealth to its citizens. However, the people under Pisistratus had no access to or influence over the tyrant's mind, behavior, or policies, and Pisistratus had only a superficial knowledge of the people's true needs and desires. This left the people completely in the dark about how the tyrant was to fulfill his promises and the tyrant always suspicious of the loyalties of the people. As a result, the people became largely passive recipients of his cruelty or largess, keeping the tyrant in check only through the constant threat of organized violent revolt, which in turn increased the paranoia of the ruler. The predictable result, played out in the short-lived ruled of his son Hippias, was attempted assassination followed by a brutal campaign of repression until his eventual deposition. In short, the lack of mutual assurance creates a spiral of suspicion leading to violent conflict and a complete breakdown of contractual relationships grounded in the rule of law.

What breaks this spiral in Isocrates's "hegemonic" monarchy is the logic of writing. Power based on the written word emancipates a society from tribal loyalties and suspicions by instituting a regime based on transparency, discipline, and surveillance. We have already seen transparency at work, defined here as the responsibility of the ruler not only to describe in detail the operations of his administration but to disclose the innermost secrets of his character. Only through such transparency can he be judged worthy of respect and trust and thereby of authority. In the passage below, Isocrates establishes the model for transparency that continues virtually unchanged in contemporary republican politics. In this model, candidates display their virtue by the way they offer the public an insight into the workings of government:

As to my sense of justice, you can best observe it from these facts: when I was established in power I found the royal treasury empty, all the revenue squandered, the affairs of the state in utter disorder and calling for great care, watchfulness, and outlay of money; and, although I knew that rulers of the other sort in similar straits resort to every shift in order to write their own affairs, and that they feel constrained to do many things which are against their nature, nevertheless I did not fall a victim to any of these

temptations; nay, I attended so devotedly and honorably to my duties that
I left nothing undone which could contribute to the greatness of the state
and advance its prosperity; and toward the citizens of the state I behaved
with such mildness that no one has suffered exile or death or confiscation of
property or any such misfortune during my reign. (*Nicocles*, 31)

Notable about this passage is the attention to empirical "facts" capable of con-
firmation by anyone who would investigate these claims. For representative
publicity to be effective, transparency is necessary in order for the governed
to be able to verify claims that in a tyranny may simply be pretty words. As
Nicocles later explains, unlike others who must rely on his "words alone," the
people are actual "witnesses that all I have said is true" (46). The act of transforming the public from a "target" to a "witness" is perhaps one of the most
revolutionary shifts that arrives with the regime of representative publicity and
its ethics of transparency.

If transparency allows the people an insight into the workings of governance, the institution of surveillance allows the ruler to keep a close eye on
the people. Made possible by the creation of written case files on a multitude
of citizens and groups, surveillance gives assurance to the leader that nothing
is being hidden from view that would threaten the security and stability of the
regime. Nicocles, for instance, warns people against forming "political societies
or unions without my sanction; for such associations may be an advantage in
the other forms of government, but in monarchies they are a danger," inevitably
leading to revolutions which "destroy states and lay waste the homes of the
people" (55). Of course, the warning itself is nothing new, representing as it
does a universal anxiety of all leaders, autocratic and democratic alike, about
the menace of potentially hidden insurgencies. What *is* new is the manner in
which Nicocles responds to such dangers. Rather than making grave threats
of punishment and torture, he simply indicates the presence of a kind of surveillance that makes treasonous ideas impossible. He warns: "Let none of you
imagine that even what he secretly thinks in his own heart will be hidden from
me; nay, let him believe that, though I be absent in body, yet my thoughts are
present at what goes on; for, being of this opinion, you will be more restrained
in your deliberations on all matters" (51–52). As indicated by the phrase "let him
believe that," this surveillance still has something of the aura of a hypothetical.
Whether it actually exists is secondary to the fact that the people *think* it does
and act accordingly. Still, as Isocrates makes clear in *Evagoras* (the third pamphlet to Nicocles that is a eulogy to his father), the goal remains the establishment of a system of perfect surveillance. Isocrates says that Nicocles's father
maintained order because he left "nothing unexamined," possessed a thorough

"knowledge of each of the citizens," and made sure that no "citizen remained unknown" (*Evagoras*, 42). Clearly Nicocles would have inherited this proto-police system of which the people would have been all too familiar, making his suggestion that his thoughts (and eyes) would be present in their deliberations quite literal.

Once again, however, one should not consider this system of police surveillance purely an oppressive mechanism on the model of the old tyrants. In the contractual logic of hegemony, the citizens' assent to being monitored was acquired voluntarily by the promise of compensation. Nicocles praises monarchies not only for their superiority in "planning and carrying out any course of action required of them" (*Nicocles*, 17), but also for keeping very careful written records on each citizen in order to properly reward them for loyalty and excellence. Whereas democracy "works in the interest of the worthless" by treating everyone equally and allowing the best to pass unnoticed "in the hurly-burly of the mob," monarchies, by keeping "an appraising eye upon the characters and actions of men," are capable of making "the highest award to the best man, the next highest to the next best, and in the same proportion to the third and the fourth and so on" (15–16). Thus, surveillance does not merely identify and root out treasonous thoughts and actions; it also promotes those individuals whose habits and accomplishments can act as exemplars for the rest of the people and therefore raise the bar of excellence for the entire city.

The combined effect of both transparency and surveillance is to enhance and to alter the value of self-discipline in maintaining and developing power. In itself, the emphasis on self-discipline is nothing new. Isocrates is merely carrying on a long Greek tradition of empathizing discipline going all the way back to Homer. Moreover, in the fifth century B.C.E., the Older Sophists frequently emphasized the importance of self-discipline insofar as the formation of a strong character capable of resisting temptation and focusing one's energies on the task at hand was necessary in achieving one's desired ends. Isocrates carries on this tradition particularly when he speaks specifically to individual leaders who must take responsibility for the rule of the nation. In *To Nicocles*, Isocrates tells the young monarch to "govern yourself no less than your subjects, and consider that you are in the highest sense a king when you are a slave to no pleasure but rule over your desires more firmly than over your people" (29). But this is no different from the advice given by his predecessors Protagoras, Prodicus, and Hippias when they were attempting to sculpt young Greeks into masters of assembly and household.

But something new appears when Isocrates speaks to the people. Instead of emphasizing the need for discipline to satisfy one's individual desire for power, it becomes a means of collective regulation in order to form a stable society in harmony with the hegemonic Logos. In *Nicocles,* the *demos* is thus given the following counsel from their monarch: "Scrutinize your actions and believe that they are evil when you wish to hide from me what you do, and good when my knowledge of them will be likely to make me think better of you. Do not keep silent if you see any who are disloyal to my rule, but expose them; and believe that those who aid in concealing crime deserve the same punishment of those who commit it" (52–53). Here the notion of discipline becomes synonymous with surveillance, understood as a methodical process whereby one monitors, with the help of writing, the thoughts of oneself and others so that they can be carefully transcribed and reflected upon.

Once again, however, citizens should not do this out of fear but for their own prosperity. Nicocles writes: "Consider fortunate, not those who escape detection when they do evil, but those who are innocent of all wrongdoing; for it is probable that the former will suffer such ills as they themselves inflict, while the latter will receive the reward which they deserve" (53). Although we hear echoes of Plato and Socrates in this message, the spirit of the passage is completely different. In the contractual order of the Logos, the common art of measurement is not some transcendent virtue but a set of written agreements that provide a clear (and fully secular) basis for punishments and rewards. It is on this contractual basis, and not on any idealistic faith or ideological distortion, that the hegemonic order is based.

With respect to rhetoric, the redefinition of *logos* from a tyrannical to a hegemonic medium completely alters the scope and function of the art. In the old sophistical logocracy, individuals sought power for themselves by overcoming opposition in the competitive sphere of *dissoi logoi* in which rhetoric still could evoke the same overpowering and passionate response as oral poetry. In the new hegemonic logocracy, collective bodies of citizens carefully consider the *logoi* disseminated by their leaders through representative publicity and choose the most reasonable contract that will produce the greatest gain in power for the whole while demanding the least amount of suffering from its parts. As Jaeger interprets Isocrates, rhetoric is no longer to be considered "a series of devices to influence the mob, but the simple and fundamental intellectual act which everyone daily performs in his own soul as he discusses his own welfare with himself."[33] The resulting rhetorical culture could hardly be more different in tenor. In the logocracy of the Older Sophists, any Logos, upon gaining tyrannical power, could be immediately challenged by an even more spectacular one, thus setting in motion a constant cycle of dynasties in which the new deposed the old and was then, in turn, deposed again. In the literary logocracy of Isocrates, once a Logos became accepted by the citizens, it had the character of contract and thereby of law, binding both ruler and ruled to a set of responsibilities that were universally known and thereby universally enforced.

With Isocrates, rhetoric thus shifts its attention away from passionate oral advocacy of this or that policy in the assembly and toward responsible administrative maintenance of the state through written pamphlets which promote its leaders and cultivate its citizens. This is the rhetoric of Isocrates. From the security of his study, he sends forth letters and pamphlets as if they are pollen on the wind, carrying the seeds of *paideia* on the wings of Logos, landing on the heads of tyrants and citizens, cities and empires, binding them together in a glorious, disciplinary whole. Isocrates possesses the key to the new regime of power—the rhetoric of the written word, which not even the soon-to-be leader of the coming empire can ignore.

Here, for instance, is how Isocrates counsels the young Alexander, son of Philip of Macedon, to value rhetoric in the coming hegemonic order: "Rhetoric . . . is of use in the practical affairs of everyday life and aids us when we deliberate concerning public affairs. By means of this study you will come to know how at the present time to form reasonably sound opinions about the future, *how not ineptly to instruct your subject people what each should do,* how to form correct judgments about the right and the just and their opposites and, besides, *to reward and chastise each class as it deserves*" (*To Alexander,* 4, emphasis added). As indicated by his attention to making sound opinions through deliberation about public affairs, rhetoric retains its traditional emphasis on kairotic judgment; but these judgments are no longer made within an assembly of citizens but behind closed doors with one's counselors. In public, rhetoric has clearly become an art of the ruling class, designed both to persuade the people to accept the legitimacy of one's rule, to provide them an administrative system in which duties are fairly distributed, and to offer a written contractual basis that gives a clear summary of rewards and punishments that gives them incentive to voluntarily accept a regime based on surveillance and self-discipline.

For Isocrates, here was a rhetoric that could finally function as a medium by which the warring city-states could agree upon a common political order under a common leadership that was organized not by force but by a common Logos. Yet one cannot help judging Isocrates more harshly in the light of history. Isocrates, after all, had given up on his dream of Athenian hegemony and instead had put his hopes in Philip of Macedon to be the unifier of all of Greece, the leader who would bring together all of the Greek cities and its homeless citizens in a battle against the barbarians. On the one hand, this Panhellenic vision of a unified Greece under a hegemonic order is inspiring, causing Jaeger to observe that, without Isocrates, "there would have been no Macedonian Greek world-empire, and the universal culture which we call Hellenistic would never have existed."[34] On the other hand, Jaeger acknowledges that the pamphlets of Isocrates also have the characteristics of "cultural propaganda" reminiscent of "the modern machinery of press publicity which grinds into action before

economic and military conquest begins."[35] Especially given that much of what
he prophesized actually came to pass, it would have been hard to imagine a
more effective propagandist for the Macedonian conquest of Greece than
Isocrates, the ideological father of the empire of Hellas.

What matters in the relationship between rhetoric and power, however, is
less how Isocrates influenced the particular outcome of Greek history and more
how he conceptualized the role of Logos in a hegemonic political order. For
easily missed in the eloquent passages that make up the "Hymn to *Logos*" is the
dramatic reconceptualization of this relationship. When Isocrates declares that
"in all our actions as well as in all our thoughts speech is our *hēgemōn*," he is
not simply rehearsing old clichés (*Nicocles*, 9); he is announcing that Logos has
evolved from a practical tool into a total environment. Rather than function as
a competitive instrument of the orator to direct power in the *kairotic* moment,
Logos becomes the substance of thought itself and thereby the ground on which
all power is constituted. Moreover, this Logos is different from that of Homer or
Heraclitus. In Heraclitus, the Logos existed as a mysterious world order hidden
from us through a veil of appearances; in Isocrates, the Logos is ubiquitous and
manifest, confronting us in both public and private through the omnipresent
medium of writing. And whereas Homeric heroes were thoroughly embedded
in the atmosphere of their oral culture, the literate Isocratean citizen is able to
separate mind from body and thereby establish a uniquely cognitive relationship to Logos that makes him capable of individual reflection and thereby of
"thinking." What makes Logos a *hēgemōn* is not simply that it commands power
but that it does so explicitly and rationally; that is what makes Logos a "guide"
and not a god, a tyrant, a world-order, or a winged word.

In Isocrates, then, the art of rhetoric, primarily through representative publicity, turns its attention to constructing and disseminating a discourse of power
that can form the basis of collective action on a pace, scale, and complexity never
before seen in the Western world. In this hegemonic order, oratory still reigns
supreme when particular audiences must confront immediate challenges with a
combination of prudence and passion, thus leaving room for the traditional arts
of eloquence. However, the new art of rhetoric (or what Isocrates calls "philosophy") also recognized the need to develop an art commensurate with the ascent
of writing into a truly "mass" medium of power, meaning a medium capable of
addressing a mass audience across space in relatively simultaneous time. As
Isocrates acknowledges to Philip, this philosophical rhetoric is not designed to
compete with the "ravings of platform orators," but is rather designed for that
leader who "is high-minded, who is a lover of Hellas, who has a broader vision
than the rest of the world" (*To Philip*, 129, 122). This "philosophical" rhetoric
would thus be concerned less with advocating specific actions than with establishing, in the thoughts and languages of a "people," a shared and explicit body

of premises, maxims, values, habits, and aims capable of constituting a common culture (*paideia*) that overrides parochial differences between cities, regions, and races. And when successful, this Logos will replace thoughtless conventions with a rational guide, a *hēgemōn,* capable of transforming the cacophony of petty voices into the universal language of a consolidated power, the material embodiment of the dream of Hellas made real through the rhetoric of the written word.

In Plato's *Phaedrus* we encounter one of the most curious figures in Greek literature, the so-called "non-lover" of the Sophist Lysias. During a pleasant walk outside the city walls, the non-lover intrudes on the conversation between Socrates and the Phaedrus by appearing in the form of a manuscript tucked into the younger man's cloak. Phaedrus had just heard Lysias deliver a feast of eloquence in the city and was eager to recount its highlights for Socrates, impressed as he was with the cleverness of the argument that "it is better to give your favors to someone who does not love you than to someone who does" (227c). However, not wanting to confess to Socrates that he had failed to commit the speech to memory, he had surreptitiously hidden the scroll away until his ruse is revealed. But Socrates is not angry, only curious. As a man devoted to learning, he says, he is intrigued by the idea that wisdom can be carried around on a piece of parchment. Indeed, "just as people lead hungry animals forward by shaking branches of fruit before them, you can leave me all over Attica or anywhere else you like simply by waiving in front of me the leaves of a book containing a speech" (230e). Encouraged by Socrates, Phaedrus finds a place to sit and read out loud the entire script verbatim.

Surrounded by a beautiful, wooded resting place near a stream, the non-lover makes his abrupt appearance and begs his case. According to Lysias's manuscript, when a beloved—that is, a younger man seeking a pederastic relationship with an older man capable of rewarding him with resources and counsel—must decide on whom to give his "favors" to, he should choose one who is not, in fact, in love with him. After all, a lover will be possessive and judgmental, will desire the beloved's body rather than his character, and will be jealous of others and seek to isolate the beloved in order to maximize the lover's own pleasure. In contradistinction, non-lovers are more plentiful than lovers, they possess the self-control that comes with detachment, they provide clearly defined material benefits, and, being men of public virtue, they are well respected, open, and will remain friends even if the beloved finds another lover. As Richard Weaver sums up the argument of Lysias, the non-lover represents "a disinterested kind of relationship which avoids all accesses and irrationalities, all the dementia of love. It is a circumspect kind of relationship, which is preferred by all men who wish to do well in the world and avoid tempestuous courses."[36] It is through this logic that Lysias proves his case that those wishing to prosper in the world should seek not those rare individuals who see in the beloved an object of their passion, but rather the most available non-lover capable of satisfying utilitarian needs with the least risk, the most reliability, and the greatest freedom.

As with most things sophistical in Plato, this speech by Lysias is immediately held up to ridicule by Socrates for being a stylistic monstrosity full of logical fallacies and ethical failings. Yet as the dialogue continues, it soon becomes apparent that both the content and the medium of the speech are carefully selected for a greater purpose—to criticize the entire genre of literary rhetoric arising in the fourth century B.C.E. Socrates thus argues, through his version of an Egyptian myth, that writing does not increase wisdom but introduces forgetfulness. Once words are written down, they represent the external signs of others rather than the internal meanings of the soul (275a); they roam about indiscriminately, speaking to "those with understanding no less than those who have no business with it" (275e); and, being fixed on a page, they cannot defend themselves when attacked or answer questions when asked (265e).[37] Worse still, writing promotes professions in speechwriting and the authorship of laws, thus producing a new breed of man who "has nothing more valuable than what he has composed or written, spending long hours twisting it around, pasting parts together and taking them apart" (278d). No wonder that Lysias, himself a writer of pamphlets, would praise the character of the non-lover, for such an individual, surrounded as he is by nothing more than his own writings on scraps of parchment piled on his shelves, knows nothing of love beyond how to spell it.

But Lysias is a red herring. The real non-lover, as it turns out, is Isocrates. In the closing passages of the dialogue, Phaedrus asks Socrates to inform his "friend," the "young" and "beautiful" Isocrates, about the dangers of becoming wrapped up in one's own writing (279a). Socrates promises that he will, for he foresees a great future in store for Isocrates if he follows the right path:

> It seems to me that by his nature he can outdo anything that Lysias has accomplished in his speeches; and he also has a nobler character. So I wouldn't be at all surprised if, as he gets older and continues writing speeches of the sort he is composing now, he makes everyone who has ever attempted to compose a speech seem like a child in comparison. Even more so if such work no longer satisfied him and a higher, divine impulse leads him to more important things. For nature, my friend, has placed the love of wisdom in his mind. (279a)

This praise drips with irony. For when Plato wrote the dialogue around 367 B.C.E., Isocrates was almost seventy years old and was busy spending long hours pasting speeches together and taking them apart. According to Jaspeer Neel, this reveals the *Phaedrus* "not as an attack on Lysias but as an attack on Isocrates, Plato's principal rival as an educator in mid-fourth-century Athens. . . . Thus Plato's manipulation of his reader is finally revealed: in order to attack a rival, who is both a rhetorician and a writer, Plato creates a fictional dialogue, sets it forty-three years in the past, when both he and his rival were young, puts his argument in the mouth of the martyred Socrates, and excoriates rhetoric, writing, and sophistry."[38] Plato calls forth the image of the young and beautiful Isocrates in order to show how old and decrepit he had become, and how all the promise of wisdom had been wasted because of his infatuation with writing pamphlets.

Not that Plato wishes to ban the act of writing; after all, the *Phaedrus* itself is a written document. What Plato condemns is the thoughtless embrace of writing as a transparent medium that somehow can act as a receptacle and disseminator of wisdom. Alexander Nehamas and Paul Woodruff suggest that "Plato is not here attacking all writing, but only a certain attitude toward it, an attitude which induces us to take for granted anything written, to refuse to question it, to consider it true, simply on the grounds that it has been written."[39] For instance, Socrates explicitly says that "writing speeches is not in itself a shameful thing," but that "what's really shameful is to engage in either of them shamefully or badly" (258d). Writing speeches is shameful when it lacks that sense of "playful amusement" embodied in Plato's dialogues, that sense of ironic detachment that encourages us to take a second look at writing and to use it as a prompt for further dialectical inquiry in an oral context (278b). Writing can serve higher purposes when it satisfies these criteria: if it is written in "with a knowledge of the truth," if the author can "defend your writing when you are challenged," and if the author can "yourself make the argument that your writing is of little worth" (278b). For Plato, any piece of writing is shameful when composed and read in isolation with the assumption that the frozen words on the page are sufficient for the production and absorption of wisdom. What makes writing virtuous is when it acts as a playful and ironic stimulus for two or more "lovers" to pursue wisdom together through the give-and-take of intimate dialogue.

Whether Plato's solution to the challenge of writing is valid need not concern us here; what matters is how clearly he perceived Isocrates's pamphlets to disclose the character of the non-lover. For unlike the demagogic style of platform orators like Alcibiades, who spoke in the passionate language of the base lover who flatters his immediate audience and then exploits them for his own gain, the contractual style that Isocrates gives to leaders like Nicocles proves the means to rally the support of a wider population through the language of enlightened self-interest. Nicocles does not fall in love with the people and become passionate about inspiring their bodies and souls and spirit; he looks at the people as possible clients with whom he can do business. Plato opens the speech by Lysias with this passage: "You understand my situation: I've told you how good it would be for us, in my opinion, if this worked out" (231). Now listen to the voice of the non-lover in the closing paragraph of *Nicocles*: "And if you do this, why need I speak at length of what the results will be? For if I continue to treat you as in time past, and you continue to give me your service and support, you will soon see your own life advanced, my empire increased, and the state made happy and prosperous" (64). In the hegemonic regime of representative publicity, every politician becomes a non-lover, every citizen becomes a client, and every sophist becomes a speechwriter for hire.

We are still wrestling with the consequences of this regime, even as the mass medium of writing has been supplemented first with that of print, then with the electronic media of radio, photography, and television, and now with the rise of digital media. At each stage, the same fears and the same hopes arise anew. On the one hand, the increase in pace and scale introduced by any new medium brings about fears of totalizing propaganda capable of recruiting a bewildered and stunned mass population to violent action, which is precisely why Victor Vitanza sees in Isocrates's Panhellenic ideal a darker undercurrent which makes it "a forerunner of 'manifest destiny' and the Third Reich."[40] On the other hand, the same medium put in the hands of citizens brings forth hopes for increased freedom and opportunity, giving them a new medium of power whereby they can challenge the old order and bring reason to irrational convention. That is why Takis Poulakos finds in the writings of Isocrates a far more noble aim, "the task of making individuals into citizens by guiding their self-understanding in the direction of citizenship."[41] Whatever one's judgment on Isocrates the man, however, the fact remains that the hegemonic understanding of rhetoric he introduced is capable of producing both effects, sometimes simultaneously. But more often than not it produces something in between. We vacillate today between apocalyptic fears of totalitarianism and utopian hopes for democracy, yet most of our lives are spent as non-lovers in the faith that our contracts will be honored. Plato might lament that fact, but as Isocrates would be quick to point out, the rhetoric of the non-lover possesses this one virtue above all—it is the only thing that allows us to live together in a republic here on earth and not just in fantasy.

Rhetoric in Isocrates thus facilitates power by spreading the ideals of *paideia* through great works of Greek literature, by creating a new network of laws and political relationships through written correspondence, and by inculcating a population in the new dictates both through political pamphlets and disciplinary technologies. Plato was correct to associate Isocrates with the non-lover, for in Isocrates we have the arrival of a moderate, contractual rule by the written word, a power which can be carried within the cloak of each citizen and used to regulate their associations with a multitude of citizens and strangers. Certainly, this is cause for concern for those, like Plato and the Older Sophists, who had matured in a world in which virtue was the combination of words and deeds performed before intimate others in a sphere of common appearance. With Isocrates, the author becomes a rhetorical fiction, an ironic persona created on the page in order to act as the vehicle for disseminating a universal discourse. But with this eclipse of the heroic orator letting forth winged words with the full force of body and soul also comes a gain—the capacity to bring together this dispersed mass into an even greater power than had ever appeared in the world, the power of the empire of Logos.

CHAPTER 10

Aristotle on Rhetoric and Civilization

Rhetoric is useful because (1) things that are true and things that are just have a natural tendency to prevail over their opposites, so that if the decisions of judges are not what they ought to be, the defeat must be due to the speakers themselves, and they must be blamed accordingly. Moreover, (2) before some audiences not even the possession of the exactest knowledge will make it easy for what we say to produce conviction. For argument based on knowledge implies instruction, and there are people whom one cannot instruct. Here, then, we must use, as our modes of persuasion and argument, the notions possessed by everyone, as we observed in the *Topics* when dealing with the way to handle a popular audience. Further, (3) we must be able to employ persuasion, just as strict reasoning can be employed, on opposite sides of the question not in order that we may in practice employ it in both ways (for we must not make people believe what is wrong), but in order that we may see clearly what the facts are, and that, if another man argues unfairly, we on our part may be able to confute him. No other of the arts draws opposite conclusions: dialectic and rhetoric alone do this. Both these arts draw opposite conclusions impartially. Nevertheless, the underlying facts do not lend themselves equally well to the contrary views. No; things that are true and things that are better are, by their nature, practically always easier to prove and easier to believe in. Again, (4) it is absurd to hold that a man ought to be ashamed of being unable to defend himself with his limbs, but not of being unable to defend himself with *logos*, when the use of rational speech is more distinctive of a human being than the use of his limbs. And if it be objected that one who uses such power of speech unjustly might do great harm, that is a charge which may be made in common against all good things except virtue, and above all against the things that are most useful, as strength, health, wealth, generalship. A man can confer the greatest benefits by a right use of these, and inflict the greatest of injuries by using them wrongly.[1]

Between the years 335 and 323 B.C.E., many of the brightest young minds of Athens gathered in the buildings of the Lyceum to absorb the collected wisdom of the Western world as taught by the master, Aristotle (384–322 B.C.E.). In one way, Aristotle was carrying on a noble tradition. Greek youth had come to the same spot on the gymnasium grounds for over a century to hear the greatest intellectuals of their age disseminate wisdom, including figures like Prodicus, Protagoras, Socrates, Plato, and Isocrates. Located outside the city walls, the Lyceum had long been an ideal place for intellectual inquiry with its campus of multi-use buildings, its large open spaces, and its shady groves of trees in which people could assemble, talk, and exercise. Yet in another way, Aristotle's arrival transformed this place from a public gymnasium into the *Lyceum,* or something we might recognize as a modern university, managed as it was by a junior faculty of exceptional students who maintained and contributed to a growing research library. Hamilton writes that "the Lyceum was new in every sense. Its object was not to arouse the love of the good and develop the search for it, but to train and inform the mind."[2] The intimate, quasi-erotic dialectic of Plato was thus replaced with lecture halls and dissection laboratories in which students were taught subjects "comprising such degrees of difference as the principles of dramatic criticism and the reproduction of the eel."[3] Nothing was off limits in Aristotle's school, for its goal was nothing less than an encyclopedic knowledge of nature (*physis*) itself.

That Aristotle would include rhetoric as part of this curriculum was hardly controversial; even Plato included rhetoric as part of the training of the Academy and, according to George Kennedy, Aristotle wrote the first two books of the *Rhetoric* while tenured there.[4] But in the Lyceum it was taught under very different assumptions. The Academy saw rhetoric as a necessary evil to be disciplined and tamed by a higher ideal. But at the Lyceum, rhetoric was understood as a natural extension of the *physis* of the human being expressed in speech (*logos*). Aristotle articulated the basis for this understanding in the *Politics,* where he states that "man is by nature a political animal (*zōon politikon*)" and "the state (*polis*) is a creation of nature" (*Politics,* 1253a1). Other creatures, too, have the capacity to manipulate nature through the direct application of force. Our ability to construct a house by use of the hand and the hammer is different only in degree from the ability of a bird or a beaver to construct the home from sticks and wood. But "man is the only animal whom she [*physis*] has endowed with the gift of speech (*zōon* logon *ekhon*)" (*Politics* 1253a10). Sounding themes similar to Isocrates, Aristotle remarks that "the power of speech is intended to set forth the expedient and inexpedient, and therefore likewise the just and the unjust. And it is a characteristic of man that he alone has any sense of good and evil, of just and unjust, and the like, and the association of living beings who have this sense makes a family and a state" (*Politics,* 1253a12–19). To study rhetoric in Aristotle's school, then, is not simply to learn tactics for manipulating others; it is to study the *physis* of the *zōon politikon* by careful inquiry into the practice of rhetoric which provides the material for writing a natural history of power.

Aristotle's famous definition of rhetoric reflects this attitude of the researcher and critic who is more interested in acquiring knowledge than achieving argumentative victory in the law court or the assembly. Unlike those who would equate rhetoric with persuasion, Aristotle asserts that "rhetoric may be defined as the faculty (*dynamis*) of observing (*theōrēsai*) in any given case the available means of persuasion" (*Rhetoric,* 1355b10). His use of the term *theōrēsai* indicates that rhetoric has shifted its perspective from participant to observer; *theōrēsai* means "to see," or more specifically, "to be an observer of and to grasp the meaning or utility of."[5] For instance, things that one "sees" in a rhetorical situation might include the difference between what is necessary and what is contingent, the complex motives of the audience, the available proofs of character (*ethos*), emotion (*pathos*), and reasoning (*logos*), the range of possibilities that determine a realistic goal, and all the surrounding resources of potentiality that can be harnessed for the sake of power. Aristotle does not deny rhetoric its status as a *technê,* and one can certainly see how observing the available means of persuasion is a necessary precondition to actual persuasion. However, as a philosopher dedicated to the pursuit of knowledge, he also wants to emphasize that rhetoric represents subject matter for the historian, the logician, the psychologist, the metaphysician, and the political scientist. Sometimes, after all, one investigates the available means of persuasion in any given case simply to understand better what it means to be a political animal.

If this view of rhetoric might seem too academic for a citizen defending his life and property in a court of law, it represented emancipation for young Athenian intellectuals tired of rehashing the Platonic debates between philosophy and rhetoric. For Aristotle, it was time to put these partisan battles aside and to see rhetoric for what it was: a natural extension of the capacity for rational speech with which human beings were endowed in order to control the flux of appearances and advance the cause of civilization. For students in Aristotle's Lyceum, this redefinition transformed rhetoric from a hodgepodge of strategies used to leverage personal influence in the *polis* into a rich history of the struggle of truth to manifest itself in the sphere of political and forensic

discourse. Here was a subject matter worthy to be included as part of a theoretical life, which for Aristotle meant not "the life of quiet 'contemplation,'
serene and unemotional, but the life of *nous,* of *theōria,* of intelligence, burning, immoderate, without bounds or limits."[6] Earlier, Plato's Academy had
attempted to stoke this passion for the theoretical life of his students, but it had
always kept rhetoric at a distance, concerned more with taming it than with
understanding it. But Aristotle had something Plato did not, which is faith in
the world. Indeed, as Jonathan Lear explains, "his philosophy is an attempt to
give the world back to creatures who desire to understand it."[7] And as rhetoric
was part of that world, he saw it as his task to give rhetoric back to the culture
that created it so that the Greeks might better understand themselves through
a study of their own *logoi.*

And what Aristotle still gives back to us is an understanding of rhetoric
as a civilizing power. Rhetoric, for him, becomes identified with process by
which truth (*aletheia*) becomes revealed over time to the minds of the popular audience and then embodied in shared practices which contribute to the
growth of civilization. To be sure, Aristotle recognizes that rhetoric can be used
more narrowly as a means of self-defense or even as a tool of manipulation; but
rhetoric as understood as a form of collective inquiry into appearances cannot
be so easily dismissed. For Aristotle has faith in rhetoric. But his faith is not
that any particular rhetorical act will always be just or true; it is a faith in the
innate power of human beings to recognize the truth over a longer course of
rhetorical deliberation. As he explains, "the true and the approximately true
are apprehended by the same faculties; it may also be noted that men have a
sufficient natural instinct for what is true, and usually do arrive at the truth"
(*Rhetoric,* 1355a15). For Aristotle, this or that person or this or that city may have
their judgment warped by *logoi* which exploit the worst characteristics of habit,
blindness, fear, and desire; but human beings in general will eventually cast off
these shackles of ignorance and embrace that logos which discloses the truth
in all its fullness. For it is in the nature of falsity to come out in the wash of
history.

In Aristotle's comprehensive vision, then, rhetoric becomes the means by
which political power purifies itself through trial and error. It is an imperfect
means, to be sure; but in a world fraught with chance, contingency, and prob-
ability, an imperfect means is better than a useless ideal. For in situations in
which we can plausibly imagine things to be otherwise, in which events might
turn out this way or that way, rhetoric is the only means by which human
beings can hope to act intelligently and to disclose a latent truth through the
interaction among rhetoric, judgment, and appearances. Rhetoric alone takes
upon itself to advocate a judgment even when all the facts are not in, knowing
that sometimes we have no choice but to act when crisis and uncertainty press

in upon us. As Aristotle writes: "the duty of rhetoric is to deal with such matters as we deliberate upon without arts or systems to guide us, in the hearing
of persons who cannot take in at a glance a complicated argument, or follow
a long chain of reasoning. The subjects of our deliberation are such as seem to
present us with alternative possibilities: about things that could not have been,
and cannot now or in the future be, other than they are, nobody who takes
them to be of this nature wastes his time in deliberation" (*Rhetoric*, 1357a1–5).[8]
For Aristotle, a rhetorical situation is one in which contingency is an actual fact
of existence, in which we lack more specialized arts or systems to guide us, in
which our audience consists of members of the public, and in which that audience feels tasked with the burden of judgment that will determine the outcome
of the future for themselves and others.[9] In any other situation, speech might
happen, but it will not function as rhetoric—that is, as a medium for power that
mobilizes an audience for passionate action toward an end that is capable of
actualization.

Undoubtedly, many of these judgments will prove themselves to be impru-
dent or even disastrous for the participants; but for the observer, these judgments amount to tests of hypotheses. Regardless of whether any situated
rhetorical act proves to be just or unjust, expedient or inexpedient, it proves
something to be the case. As demonstrated by the work of Thucydides, critical
reflection can wring truths even from the ranting of a demagogue, revealing
the paths of judgment not taken, the motivations of the audience at the time,
the complex causal factors which led to the speech's success and failure, and the
universal characteristics of human nature which make demagogues possible.
These truths then become preserved in the specialized arts and sciences and
taught in schools like the Lyceum in the hope that the lessons learned from
rhetorical criticism will enlighten the public rhetoric of future generations. For
Aristotle's students, here was a way in which the demands of truth and power
could be reconciled without the intellectuals becoming philosopher kings. They
could instead be rhetorical critics, helping purify public discourse from a
distance in the faith that, as Robert Wardy pithily puts it, "mighty is the truth
and it shall prevail."[10] For Aristotle, rhetoric finds its place as practice, theory, and
criticism within the arts of civilization whose ultimate goal is the creation and
maintenance of the good life.

Put another way, Aristotelian rhetoric represented the art by which fal-
lible creatures attempt to bring appearances under the control of reason, and a
rhetorical culture represented one that embraces its fallibility at the same time
that it strives for perfection. But Aristotle did not simply rest this vision on an
airy idealism that believed truth to be self-justifying. His faith was grounded in
a thoroughgoing naturalism in which truth disclosed itself to be true through

our interaction with appearances. According to Christopher Long, Aristotle believed that "truth is a matter of the assiduous attempt to say it like it is, to articulate things according to the ways they show themselves, and to live in accordance with such articulations."[11] Truth, in short, means a way of talking about "real" things, people, and events that holds up to our experience with them over time and supports pleasurable habits in accordance with the good. But this is simply another way of affirming the naturalistic premise that truth proves itself true by actualizing power, specifically those powers which bring us in harmony with our environment. Rhetoric by no means is the only art by which this harmony might be produced, and one can reasonably argue that it is even the least desirable one; but it is also the art most necessary as long as chance and contingency are real characteristics of a world still in the making.

Perhaps of all the Greek intellectuals, Aristotle's life reflects qualities that we might recognize as modern. Born in 384 B.C.E. in the sleepy Macedonian village of Stageira to the son of the court physician to King Phillip, Aristotle was given a thorough education to prepare him for a successful public life. Unlike Plato's generation, Aristotle's upbringing was not disrupted by the ambitions of empire, the tyranny of the demagogue, the ravages of war, and the shame of defeat. When he left his home to attend Plato's Academy at age eighteen in the year 366 B.C.E., where he would spend the next twenty years of his life, he encountered an Athens which had put the war behind it in its ambition to become, yet again, a leader in the Greek world. Forming a Second Naval Confederacy with Thebes and its former enemy Corinth against Sparta in 379 B.C.E., Athens was "astute enough to bind her allies closely to her by avoiding the domineering policy that had broken up her first league," thus ensuring its hegemony for over two decades until its dissolution in the Social War between its allies in 354 B.C.E.[12] That meant, for at least the first ten years of Aristotle's stay at Athens, he experienced life in the relative peace and prosperity of the leading city of Greece. Jaeger writes that these decades were something of an "Indian summer of Athens," a time of extended prosperity in which the "young men of Athens, absorbed in philosophical study or vainly dissipating their time on adventure and sports, were swept into the great current of history which seemed to be carrying Athens forward once again to play a leading part in the political life of Greece."[13]

This secure, middling confidence of the Athens of Aristotle's youth was reflected in the changes in tragedy. For the Sophists, Plato, and Isocrates alike, the experiences of the fifth century had demonstrated, in part, that anything is possible, that conflict is inevitable, that fortune is fickle, and that there is no natural limit to power. This is why the great sin of fifth-century tragic heroes is *hubris*, the overarching ambition to live like a god that brought forth the retribution of divine justice. Yet by the fourth century, individuals had begun to retreat into their private lives and busy themselves with trying to live prosperously rather than finding a way to die with honor. Reflecting this trend, tragedy had largely become formalized as a recognizable human drama, a tendency already present in the late-fifth-century plays of Euripides. Nietzsche complains, for instance, that "thanks to him people from everyday life pushed their way out of the audience and on to the stage; the mirror which once revealed only great and bold features now became painfully true to life, reproducing conscientiously even the lines which nature had badly drawn."[14] In the place of the sublime, poetic stature of a figure like Aeschylus's Prometheus were inserted representatives of "bourgeois mediocrity" whose only outstanding feature was to be able to "observe, to negotiate, and to draw conclusions artfully and with the most cunning sophistication."[15] It is no wonder, then, that Aristotle would not be troubled by the tragic spirit. No historical horrors haunted his memory, and, being a foreigner and non-citizen, he was not as closely bound to the glory and misery of Athens. He accepted the relative stability of his age as the natural way of things and set about, with a combination of passionate curiosity and systematic discipline, compiling and adding to the comprehensive knowledge of the world as it was and would continue to be.

Aristotle's attitude was thus fundamentally "conservative," but understood here less as a political conservatism than an ecological one.[16] In sharp contrast to the reactionary attitude of Aristophanes or the reformist stance of Plato, the watchword of Aristotle's attitude was what Arendt calls "conservation," whose "task is always to cherish and protect something."[17] Aristotle was thankful to the world because he saw himself as a part of it. That is why, as Dewey remarks, "Aristotle was above all a naturalist."[18] By this, Dewey means Aristotle interpreted every event, object, action, or species as a part of a larger natural whole that gave an individual existence in purpose, function, and meaning.[19] Moreover, it meant that humans were not somehow alien beings forced to endure our time on earth. Even Aristotle's conception of the soul (*psychē*), writes John Herman Randall Jr., does not stand above and outside the natural world; it represents "the behavior of the organism as a whole in its environment" in which the life of that organism is understood as "the power of living and knowing, the power of selective response of the organism to the world."[20] His model of inquiry was thus based on this naturalistic premise that neither art nor nature makes anything in vain or apart from the whole; everything that exists is meant to serve a function in a given context. It is therefore the duty of the philosopher and scientist to interrogate the appearances of the world in order to determine how things come to be, in what capacity they function to the best of their potential, and why they pass away.

Pursuing this type of inquiry is a great luxury of the leisured mind, to be sure, but it is also more than that for Aristotle; it is the means by which we gain the power to achieve that most important of all things—happiness. For despite his consistent valorization of the life of the reflective mind over that of the laboring body, Aristotle nonetheless held consistently to a single principle of ethics: that "life is an activity" (*Nichomachean Ethics,* 1175a11), and that the only true "end" of life is happiness (*eudaimonia*), defined in terms of "an activity of soul in accordance with perfect virtue" (1102a5). Significantly, the word translated as "activity" is *energeia,* which is a term Aristotle invented to function as the dialectical partner to "power" (*dynamis*). Also translated as "actuality," *energeia* represents the activity by which a thing actualizes its potential. Arendt interprets *energeia* to designate "all activities that do not pursue an end . . . and leave no work behind . . . , but exhaust their full meaning in the performance itself."[21] Aristotle explains that *energeia* stands in relationship to *dynamis* as "building to that which is capable of building," as "waking to the sleeping," as "seeing to that which has its eyes shut tight" (*Metaphysics,* 1048a30). With respect to power, *energeia* refers to the perfected action of which *dynamis* is the potential. *Energeia* is thus the actualization of *dynamis* when the proper conditions are in place, and happiness is a life that strives for *energeia* in body, soul, and mind.

For Aristotle, happiness is power. To say that life is activity means that life consists of being able to do, every day, the thing one has the power to do to the best of one's capacity, so long as that activity is in harmony with both one's nature and a concept of the good. But this is not to say that everyone has the same powers. Our power potentials are not innate, uniform, and unchangeable like those of an acorn or a mollusk. As Hans-Georg Gadamer explains, Aristotle suggested that "human civilization differs essentially from nature in that it is not simply a place in which capacities and power work themselves out, but man becomes what he is through what he does and how he behaves."[22] For instance, Aristotle says that each man is "active about those things and with those faculties that he loves most; e.g. the musician is active with his hearing in reference to tunes, the student with his mind in reference to theoretical questions, and so on in each case" (*Nichomachean Ethics,* 1175a12). As indicated by the examples, *energeia* represents a different kind of actuality than "form" (*eidos*), which stands more for the perfected image of its completed product within the process of fabrication, much as the completed musical composition is the *eidos* present in the imagination of the songwriter. *Energeia* represents not the end result but the manner in which one pursues the end—in this case, the act of songwriting or performing. Essential to the good life is understanding that activities are innately pleasurable when done well. We pursue the good not just out of a sense of duty but also for the sake of pleasure; and "pleasure completes the activities, and therefore life, which they desire" (1175a15). Happiness thus represents the power to cultivate and actualize one's capacities for the sake of both virtue and pleasure in this world.[23]

Unique to Aristotle's understanding of power, therefore, is its distinctly polar nature that gives it natural limiting conditions. Power is not an unlimited resource to achieve unlimited aims, like the *dynastes megas* of Gorgias's logos; power in practice represents the dynamic between potentiality and actuality which is both enabled and restricted by environmental conditions. What allows Aristotle to take this position is his thoroughgoing naturalism. As Randall explains: "There is nothing that can become anything else whatsoever. A thing can become only what it has the specific power to become, only what it already is, in a sense, potentially. And a thing can be understood only as that kind of thing that has that specific power; while the process can be understood only as the operation, the actualization, the functioning of the powers of its subject or bearer."[24] In other words, just as no amount of alchemy can turn lead into gold, no amount of persuasion will move the members of an audience to action if they do not have the potential already latent within themselves. To fear that rhetoric unleashed will somehow tyrannize over man and nature alike is thus not to be a "realist" about power; it is to exist in a fantasy world of Homeric word magic in which the gods can make heroes evaporate in thin air on command and seduce young maidens by turning themselves into bulls.

In actual fact, the power of rhetoric to influence belief and action is highly circumscribed. Most of the time, after all, human beings leave most of their judgments to habit and largely ignore argumentative appeals to change their behavior. But there are some moments in which we might actively seek out rhetoric to guide us. These are moments in which we are torn between two or more competing paths which force us to activate that uniquely human faculty Aristotle calls *proairesis*. Literally translated as "forechoice" (*pro* = before, *hairesis* = choice), *proairesis* refers to what Arendt calls a "deliberate planning ahead," a "choice in the sense of preference between alternatives—one rather than another."[25] It is forechoice which combines desire and reason to mobilize the will according to a logos.[26] Gadamer calls *proairesis* "a yearning in which there is thought" or a "thinking in which there is yearning."[27] *Proairesis* refers to a miniature dramatic event that begins with an object of desire, proceeds through a stage of deliberation over means, and consummates when the imagination perceives a clear path forward. None of this drama is present in the merely irrational encounter between two physical entities; it plays out only within souls of rational beings capable of weighing alternatives. And it is only in situations that *proairesis* is activated that rhetoric becomes a medium of power.[28]

In Aristotle, then, one finds a defense of rhetoric grounded not in the ethical standing of the rhetor but in the nature of the situation itself. Whereas the practice of scientific knowledge (*epistēmē*) and the faculty of intuitive reason (*nous*) deal with the affairs that are eternal and necessary, the art of rhetoric and the faculty of forechoice address those situations marked by contingency that concerns "what is future and capable of being otherwise" (*Nichomachean Ethics,* 1139a724). Of course, the situated character of any persuasive act had been recognized as far back as Homer, and the Older Sophists had continually emphasized the importance of a speaker having a sense of *kairos,* that intuitive grasp of the "right moment," in order to translate *logos* into power. With Aristotle, however, *kairos* is given a naturalistic basis; it therefore ceases to be a mysterious quality that occasionally appears within phenomena and instead becomes à more determinate characteristic of specific types of contingent situations that call out for rhetorical response. A rhetorical situation, in short, is one in which appearances confront our senses against our will and demand an accounting, forcing us into speech that would disclose the possible truths within those appearances, bring order to chaos, and thereby produce power in the place of anxiety, fragmentation, confusion, and fear.

In contradistinction to the haughty attitude of Plato's noble rhetorician, then, the Aristotelian rhetor *engages* and goes *through* appearances to find their truth rather than going around them, above them, or behind them. Consistent with what Nussbaum calls his overall project to "save appearances and their truth," Aristotle views rhetoric as a means by which even contingent appearances might ultimately have something to show us.[29] For Plato, of course, this was an attitude not of the philosopher but of the slave. For the dedicated Platonist, the appearances which come to us through subjective sense-perception (*aesthesis*) are something transient and illusory, mere shadows of the ideal. To take such appearances seriously is thus to condemn oneself to studying trifles instead of "struggling for an unconditional vantage point outside of appearances" and developing a philosophy that would take "us away from the 'cave' and up into the sunlight."[30] Although dedicated to the pursuit of truth, the Platonist conceived of truth as something transcendent rather than immanent. Aristotle rejected this attitude as unscientific. For him, appearances are neither illusions nor mere resources but the very gateways to truth. Here we find in Aristotle what Arendt calls the "fundamental insight that whatever appears is there to be seen, that the very concept of appearance demands a spectator, and that therefore to see and to behold are activities of the highest rank."[31] Consequently, only when we are willing to approach appearances without aversion, contempt, or prior judgment are we able to welcome the disclosure of the truth they contain, both in the realm of the sciences and in rhetoric.

In summary, the responsibility of the rhetor in Aristotle is to reconfig-
ure appearances in such a way that the moral and practical character of their
truth is brought to bear in moments of contingency and judgment. According to Farrell, Aristotle believed that by means of rhetoric "appearances shared
by assembled human beings are *re*-presented in the guise of a practical consciousness which guides and legitimates collective human conduct."[32] What was
new about this attitude in Aristotle's time was that it challenged the logocratic
assumptions of both Plato and the Sophists, both of whom often spoke as if
logos itself—whether in the form of philosophical reason or rhetorical persuasion—was sufficient for constituting the power of the city and guiding collective human judgment in times of crisis. For Aristotle, by contrast, logos could
not act alone. In Farrell's words: "While language continues to value *logos,* the
very grounds of disputation are found in the particularities of appearances."[33]
And this fact applies to rhetoric and science alike. Although the *telos* of each
discipline differs, one seeking to disclose the truth in appearances for its own
sake and the other for the sake of revealing an ethical possibility, both share the
same commitment to and respect for appearances, however ugly or distasteful
they might appear at first glance. What matters, in both rhetoric and science,
is less how appearances strike the senses at first glance and more what they
reveal and where they might lead us after being transformed through interaction with a logos.

This naturalistic commitment to investigating appearances made rhetoric and science such close (if antagonistic) partners in Aristotle's philosophy.
Indeed, we find one of perhaps the finest examples of the collaboration between
rhetoric and science in his defense of biological inquiry in *On the Parts of Animals.* There, Aristotle reaches back to Heraclitus for an anecdote to defend his
laboratory practice of dissecting "less valued" animals to find what truths lie
revealed in their inner appearances. He writes: "And just as Heraclitus is said
to have spoken to the visitors, who were wanting to meet him but stopped as
they were approaching when they saw him warming himself at the oven—he
kept telling them to come in and not worry, 'for there are gods here too'—so
we should approach the inquiry about each animal without aversion, knowing
that in all of them there is something natural and beautiful" (*On the Parts of Animals,* 645a23). Unmistakable in this passage is Aristotle's use of metaphor and
enthymeme to overcome our aversion to certain appearances by reconfiguring
them through logos, the result of which is a practical and ethical judgment—to
enter and not be afraid, knowing that behind even the most quotidian and distasteful appearances there is something divine. We thus see how Aristotle actually rhetorically transforms common appearances as a precondition to making
scientific inquiry into those same appearances possible.

The fable Aristotle tells of Heraclitus thus not only sings the praises of biological study but also proves the necessity for rhetoric from an empirical standpoint. For it is rhetoric which reveals the possibilities inherent in appearances and facilitates those actions necessary for the disclosure of truth. Aristotle knew, from long study of human nature, that human animals often stand anxious and uncertain before the doorways to possibilities that require activity. Neither content with sitting still nor confident in continuing forward, they simply wander off to something else, validating their inaction on the assumption that thinking or speaking the logos is sufficient for achieving our aims. The visitors to Heraclitus, for example, have sought out the obscure philosopher ambitious for wisdom and expecting transcendence, and yet on arrival they pause. Before them is not a scene of majesty but one of banality—Heraclitus the Obscure rubbing his hands before a fire like a common servant. The moment of judgment arises in which they must decide whether this is the true gateway to wisdom. Sensing their reticence, Heraclitus responds with an enthymeme structured in the language of metaphor: "Come in and do not worry, for there are gods here too." The aphoristic appeal functions as a challenge. Only those able to bring before the eyes the missing premise (that the search for the divine necessitates an inquiry into the natural and the common) are prepared to cross the threshold. Likewise, Aristotle challenges his audience to cast off their aversion to biology, for only by seeing oneself as part of the world and then acting within it with discipline, virtue, curiosity, and intelligence can one disclose the beauty and wonder of the truth embedded in its multiform appearances.[34]

Aristotle demonstrates through the Heraclitus anecdote that the necessary precondition for the actualization of truth in *epistēmē* is the rhetorical consideration of possibility in the imagination through *energeia*. Rhetoric therefore stands as a necessary counterpart to science just as possibility does to actuality, imagination to fact, and learning to verification. That Aristotle considered rhetoric a form of "teaching" is clear both in his discussion of enthymeme and metaphor. He writes that the most persuasive enthymemes are those in which "some kind of learning takes place," and the best-crafted metaphors are those that make it clear to the listener "that he learned something different from what he believed, and his mind seems to say, 'how true, and I was wrong'" (*Rhetoric*, 1410b25, 1412a20). Rhetoric produces this effect by using logos to call forth and give form to appearances in the imagination in order for their possible truth to be brought from a state of potentiality (*dynamis*) to actuality (*energeia*). Learning is thus a temporal, dramatic process that moves a person from a state of conflict and doubt to one of harmony and belief and is accompanied by the feeling of pleasure. As he says in the *Rhetoric:* "to learn and to admire are usually pleasurable; for in admiration there is desire, so the admirable is desirable,

and in learning there is the achievement of what is in accordance with nature"
(1371a.21). Rhetoric thus brings pleasure when its logos introduces us to possibilities that we feel bring us closer in accordance with the truth of nature.

The enthymeme and the metaphor share the same capacity for bringing
about learning, but do so through slightly different forms. The function of metaphor is to evoke emotions, instill attitudes, and convey ideas by using creative
and unconventional comparisons which bring "before-the-eyes" (*pro omma-
ton poiein*) dramatic images that "signify things engaged in activity" (*Rhetoric*,
1411b).[35] In metaphor, impressions of sense-perception (*aesthesis*) preserved in
imagination (*phantasia*) are thus transformed through logos so that "something
seems living through being actualized" (1412a). When done with artistry, persuasion achieves the status of an "urbanity," which is directly connected with
learning: "Urbanities in most cases come through metaphor and from an added
surprise; for it becomes clearer [to the listener] that he learned something different from what he believed, and his mind seems to say, 'How true, and I
was wrong.' The urbanity of epigrams derives from their not meaning what is
[literally] said; for example, that of Stesichorus that 'the cicadas will sing to
themselves from the ground.' Good riddles are pleasing for the same reason; for
there is learning" (1412a6). The urbanity Aristotle chooses is by Stesichorus, the
lyric poet who sang of the Trojan War, who uses the image of ground-dwelling
cicadas to imply that after the battle the land will be devastated, leaving the
singed bodies of cicadas without any trees to sing to. To imagine how this
might produce "learning," one need only put this statement in the mouth of an
oracle consulting Priam on the political future of his city upon the arrival of
Greeks to the shores of Troy.

The enthymeme, in contrast, produces learning by carefully crafting a logical argument that leaves open a space for audience participation, much as one
might craft a riddle that brings a feeling of accomplishment on discovering
the answer. Jeffrey Walker, for instance, argues that enthymematic reasoning generates a passionate "adherence to a particular stand" that strikes them
with "an abrupt and decisive flash of insight."[36] In this reading, the enthymeme
accomplishes persuasion through *energeia* and putting "before-the-eyes" no
less than metaphor. Aristotle claims, for instance, that the enthymemes "most
applauded" are the ones they "foresee from the beginning" yet which nonetheless present an audience with some degree of challenge to figure out (*Rhetoric*
1401b). This means that people, being natural organisms accustomed to action,
crave the journey more than the destination and learn more from the experience than they do the statement of fact. For instance, when Empedocles wished
to defend the principle that killing any living thing is against the law of nature,
he used this argument that Aristotle identifies as an example of enthymematic
reasoning: "'Tis not just for some and unjust for others, / But the law is for all

and it extends without a break / Through the wide-ruling ether and the bound-less light" (1373b2). In a purely mechanical fashion, one might simplify the syl-logism by saying that since killing is unjust for all living beings (and since I am a living being) then killing is also unjust for me. But this enthymeme does more. It brings before the imagination of an audience a sublime image of the infinite universe of which we are but a small and meager part. To violate its law is thus not simply to go against its Logos; it is to reveal a *hubris* of such magnitude that one feels superior to the wide-ruling ether and the boundless light. In other words, Empedocles uses the enthymeme to invite consideration that, despite the inequities of power and wealth and virtue, we are all bound by the same law and thus equal in the eyes of the cosmos.

None of these arguments, of course, is proven true simply because the audi-ence has considered their possibility in the imagination and experienced the pleasure of learning; the verification of truth, for Aristotle, comes only through careful scientific investigation of appearances in actual experience followed by their analysis and careful documentation. But rhetoric is a necessary precon-dition for the production and dissemination of truth for three reasons. First, rhetoric overcomes the recalcitrance of an audience toward certain distasteful appearances that often block the road to inquiry. Without rhetoric, the inertia of convention, with all its blindness and biases, would prevent us from identi-fying the hidden potential of things that only logos can reveal to the rational imagination. Second, rhetoric actually creates new appearances by facilitating those actions necessary for the disclosure of truth. This is the logic also behind "dissection"—to perform an action, through the intervention of physical tech-nique, which reveals heretofore unseen appearances and their latent potentiali-ties. Third, rhetoric uses the technical sphere as a resource for argument in the public sphere, taking from it the leading principles or warrants that can be used to construct enthymemes or metaphors about a given case that calls for judg-ment, just as Aristotle does when he uses the "true" principle that "in all natural things there is something wonderful" to encourage students to overcome their resistance to studying the parts of less valued animals. Rhetoric therefore not only creates the possibilities and actions which enable scientific inquiry, but also helps spread the truths of science by using them as premises for rhetorical arguments in the public sphere.

Given the reality of contingency, of course, nothing guarantees that any particular warrant, no matter how valid or necessary, was applied correctly in any given case. Deciding what premises to use to judge any particular case is the function of forechoice (*proairesis*), which in turn represents a faculty which can never hope to achieve absolute certainty as long as chance is a real causal factor in the universe. But only a fool, a demagogue, or a madman would prefer to build arguments out of inferior material, knowing that the whole edifice will collapse because of the weakness of its axiomatic foundations (its *archai*). It is from this perspective that we can make sense of Aristotle's assertion that rhetoric is not necessarily the power to persuade but the power to see the available means of persuasion in any given case. For what he realized is that chance might always conspire against even the most persuasive and virtuous orator in the short term. What matters is that rhetors take the long view and try to see those forms of persuasion which, over time, might reveal the latent potentialities and their accompanying truths to the eyes of public opinion. Because for every one hundred students that Aristotle fails to entice into his biological research laboratory, there is one or two who might be able to see the wonder within those distasteful appearances splayed out on the dissection table. But soon two becomes four, and four becomes ten, and ten becomes a school dedicated to research into truth and the gradual enlightenment of the public sphere.

When Aristotle defends rhetoric because truth has a tendency to win out over its opposite, he is not offering a pious hope. He is offering a realistic judgment based on two centuries of recorded history that show a progressive development toward truth in Greek culture, a progression made possible by the spread of literacy, facilitated by the creation of organized schools and libraries, and finally culminating in the development of research laboratories like those in the Lyceum. As he indicates in his defense of rhetoric, Aristotle was not so naive as to believe that truth would win the day in any particular encounter, especially knowing the weaknesses of human nature and the often uncertain state of opinion. However, he also believed that poor judgment would reveal itself over time, and its lessons would become preserved in *endoxa,* meaning that body of reputable opinions which "are accepted by everyone or by the majority or by the wise, i.e., by all, or by the majority, or by the most notable and reputable of them" (*Topics,* 100b). *Endoxa* thus represents opinions that have stood the test of time and experience to represent the collected wisdom of history, which is something worthy of our respect. As he remarks in *On the Soul,* "it is necessary, while formulating the problems of which in our further advance we are to find the solutions, to call into council the views of those of our predecessors who have declared any opinion on this subject, in order that we may profit by whatever is sound in their suggestions and avoid the errors" (403b23). As he stands to the words of past philosophers, so too does he approach the collected wisdom of poets, politicians, scientists, and citizens. In each group, certain truths have been revealed and preserved in their respective *logoi* which represent the progress of civilization.

In Aristotle, then, a rhetorical democracy finds a new justification as the best means for the cumulative development of truth through the dialectical interplay between the public and technical spheres. In Aristotle's political culture, specialized arts and systems would be given authority over the management of recurrent problems that could be guided by reliable truths and techniques, while the public would be responsible for rhetorically deliberating over judgments made in contingent circumstances. To use the language of G. Thomas Goodnight, a "sphere" denotes "branches of activity—the grounds upon which arguments are built and the authorities to which arguers appeal."[37] Thus, we speak of a "public" sphere when we deem it appropriate to appeal to shared traditions, values, maxims, and other social knowledge to construct arguments about matters of public choice, and we refer to a "technical" sphere when we deem it appropriate to appeal to the more specialized forms of reasoning in the sciences in order to resolve particular cases through established methods that carry with them the aura of certainty.[38] In Aristotle, an oblique reference to the technical sphere appears when he remarks that rhetoric emerges only when we deliberate upon matters "without arts or systems to guide us" (*Rhetoric,* 1357a1). But this statement actually makes a very assertive claim about its priority. For Aristotle, rhetoric comes into play only after the more specialized arts and sciences have failed to give a determinate solution to a problem, a failure which opens up the field of judgment to the public out of the acknowledgment both of contingency and the necessity for political judgment.

Even here, public deliberation was performed not just for the sake of expediency in the moment, although that was certainly it proximate aim; it also was performed with an eye to the cumulative development of a richer truth made possible through the exchange of perspectives about some shared experience. For Aristotle, any particular perspective was probably necessarily limited, false, and distorted; yet the exchange of perspectives inevitably produced a shared truth which not only illuminated the mind but was the vehicle for the establishment of collaborative practices that bring us closer to a state of *eudemonia.* In the *Politics,* for instance, Aristotle gives us a striking metaphor of a "feast" to show his new relationship between truth, power, and democracy that makes each serve the good of the other:

> For the many, of whom each individual is but an ordinary person, when they meet together may very likely be better than the few good, if regarded not individually but collectively, just as a feast to which many contribute is better than a dinner provided out of a single purse. For each individual among the many has a share of virtue and prudence, and when they meet together, they become in a matter one man, who has many feet, and hands, and senses; that is a figure of their mind and disposition. Hence the many are better judges than a single man of music and poetry; for some understand one part, and some another, and among them they understand the whole. (*Politics,* 1281a1–10)

In this example, Aristotle rejects the individualistic reading of his faith in the capacity for human beings to recognize the true and the just. This recognition does not happen all of a piece, revealing itself to an individual mind in a solitary moment. Each individual is able to perceive and evaluate some specific aspect of a thing or event and then, though communication and shared experience in collective activity, to unite these parts into a whole. Thus, Aristotle goes on, objections that people are base, ignorant, and fickle "are to a great extent met by our old answer, that if the people are not utterly degraded, although individually they may be worse judges than those who have special knowledge—as a body they are as good or better" (1282a15–17). Democracy represents a clearing whereby multiple perspectives can interact in the public sphere not just for the sake of power but also for the sake of truth, which is the recognition of a principle which organizes past experience into a unity which can be preserved in the technical sphere from which it can serve as a reliable standard of public judgment in the future. One should not thus draw back from democracy out of a childish distaste for rhetoric, for in all logos there is something natural and beautiful that might lead us toward the good.

In short, rhetoric for Aristotle represents the means by which the competing ends of power and of truth are reconciled through the progressive constitution of the good life of *eudemonia*. Rhetoric serves the end of power by representing both the capacity (*dynamis*) of seeing the political and ethical possibilities inherent in appearances and the art of crafting symbols to bring to actuality (*energeia*) those possibilities in the imagination, reason, and action of others. But rhetoric serves the end of truth when what is brought before-the-eyes produces learning, stimulates inquiry, and calls attention to those appearances which allow the *demos* to dwell upon the truth (*aletheia*) in a way that produces conviction. Of course, no one rhetorical act will ever meet all of our needs; to assume it could is to invite the tyranny of a god. The construction of our happiness is a piecemeal affair, a long-term process of trial and error in which a civilization preserves its truest arguments in its memory, habits, and laws. The task of rhetoric is to thus articulate and fight for the truth, to actualize those truths through power, and to invite the many to participate in that feast of eloquence we call democracy.

For Aristotle, a rhetorical culture meant a culture of the *polis,* an autonomous city-state bounded by walls, regulated by law, and maintained by the active cooperative of its citizens. The *polis* thus represented a kind of Golden Mean between extremes, between the life of the beasts and the life of the gods, both of which exist beyond the realm of civic virtue. That a beast lacks virtue is obvious, for it merely follows its instincts and appetites according to necessity, not forechoice. But just "as a brute has no vice or virtue, so neither has a god;

his state is higher than virtue" (*Nichomachean Ethics*, 1145a25). Aristotle gives the frightening consequences of this attitude in the *Politics:* "Man is by nature a political animal. Anyone who by his nature, and not simply by ill luck, has no state is either too bad or too good, either subhuman or superhuman—he is like the war-mad man condemned in Homer's words as 'having no family, no law, no home'; for he is such by nature mad on war: he is a non-cooperator like an isolated piece in a game of draughts" (*Politics*, 1253a1–4). Like a lion isolated from the pride and surrounded by prey is how a god stands among humans. However, whereas beasts lack virtue because they are incapable of any form of association foreign to their biological instincts, gods lacks virtue because they transcend virtue's constraints. Like Homer's heroes, they are worlds unto themselves who have neither need nor desire to take into account the perspectives of others. They simply march confidently onto a field of battle until they are inevitably confronted with an immovable object that extinguishes their fire and brings darkness to their solipsistic universe.

The specific passage in the *Iliad* to which Aristotle refers when making this point is revealing. The quote comes from a speech by Nestor, the wise, aged advisor to the Achaean kings, when he confronts Diomedes, the boastful hero that Homer identifies as "lord of the war cry" and one of the youngest of the Greek warriors (*Iliad* 9: 33). The encounter occurs midway through the *Iliad*, after the tide had turned against the Achaeans, causing King Agamemnon to suggest that the Greeks "cut and run" to "sail home to the fatherland we love!" (9: 30). On hearing these orders, "stallion-breaking" Diomedes rises to condemn Agamemnon for lack of courage and rally the remaining soldiers to "fight our way to the fixed doom of Troy," come what may (9: 56). For Nestor, however, Diomedes (being too young) has failed to consider the matter fully: "You don't press on and reach a useful end" (9: 66). Moreover, Diomedes has failed to see his own recommendation in their true light: "Lost to the clan, lost to the hearth, lost to the old ways, that one who lusts for all the horrors of war with his own people" (9: 74). Having had his heroic pride offended by Agamemnon's cowardice, Diomedes is prepared to sacrifice the clan, the hearth, and the old ways to gratify his own superhuman urges. But the most prudent way forward has not yet been determined, suggests Nestor. He concludes: "Come, gather us all and we will heed that man who gives the best advice. That's what they need, I tell you—all the Achaeans—good sound advice" (9: 87). Hence begins the council that concludes with an embassy to Achilles (himself a war-mad man) to swallow his hurt pride and rejoin the campaign.

In Aristotle's reading of this episode, Diomedes acts with superhuman contempt for merely mortal concerns (like suffering and survival) and brushes aside the need for further deliberation and judgment. In his mind, "we all sailed here with god" (9: 57). Thus, with his fate already determined by divine decree, he merely needs the courage to see it through to the end. His speech is thus not really meant to persuade others or contribute to a deliberative process; it simply calls out Agamemnon for cowardice and appeals to a higher will. Only Nestor's insistence that "I must speak up and drive the matter home" spares the Achaeans from certain destruction (9: 71). By calming Diomedes's passions and bringing him into deliberative counsel with others, Nestor extracts the truth from the hero's assertion that they should stay and fight, but mixes that truth with his own counsel that they should first send an embassy to Achilles. In this assembly, speech takes the form of rhetoric, that category of Aristotelian discourse which facilitates deliberation by allowing multiple perspectives to be gathered together and considered under the common light of an assembly. No longer simply the emotive expression or irresistible command of a superhuman demigod, rhetoric becomes a medium of communication among equals charged with the formation of judgment.

For Aristotle, then, the greatest threat to the *polis* did not come from bad rhetoric. Unlike Plato, for whom rhetoric was a symptom of human frailty and a sign of an imperfect state, Aristotle believed that a lively rhetorical culture was the sign of a healthy *polis*. What mattered to Aristotle was less the quality of individual speeches than the integrity of the forum in which they were performed and the virtue of the audience that judged them. From this perspective, the threats to the *polis* were not rhetorical at all. They came from the corruption of civic virtue and the institutions of state by the influx of beasts and gods. The threat from "beasts" arises when the harmony of the city corrodes to the point at which brute force becomes the only mechanism of accomplishing one's will or resolving disputes. The threat from "gods," however, is more subtle; it comes from self-styled heroes with the charisma and resources to simply dominate the *demos* and wipe away the institutions of state as meager and unnecessary. Like Diomedes speaking before the Achaeans, such "gods" do not persuade but simply command, accruing a following that eagerly does their bidding and is prepared to sacrifice their bodies in the name of an order higher than mere civic virtue. But the result of either influence is the same: the rhetoric of the *polis* is silenced and its rhetorical forums destroyed.

But these dystopian nightmares seemed far away from Aristotle's world—and for good reason. Aristotle was hardly blind to the horrors of Greek history, but he was secure in that what happened in any particular case could not disrupt the natural course of the development of the *polis*. For human beings, despite their capacity to act as "the most unholy and the most savage of animals," were not placed on this earth to destroy one another (*Politics* 1253a35). The social instinct and a sense of justice was implanted in all men by nature, and the development of these faculties required the *polis*. Only a "madman" would say otherwise, one for whom perceptions do not correspond to realities.

To be a human being was to live in the *polis,* and to live in a *polis* meant to use rhetoric to facilitate deliberative judgment about affairs through the thoughtful desire which is forechoice. The violence of the beasts and the commands of the gods might threaten this order, disrupt this stability, and even overwhelm a particular state for a time; but history in accord with nature would bring things back into a balance. With science as its technician and rhetoric as its guide, the *polis* would progressively arrange appearances into a unified truth on which would be built the perfect state of contemplation in leisure. In Aristotle one thus hears the satisfied voice of all moderate progressive states that are confident in their virtues, tolerant of difference, willing to admit gradual change, committed to the pursuit of knowledge, proud of their accomplishments, and secure because, despite the occasional turmoil of history, they truly are fortunate to live in the best of all possible worlds.

Conclusion

The first governments were kingships, probably for this reason, because of old, when cities were small, men of eminent virtue were few. Further, they were made kings because they were benefactors, and benefits can only be bestowed by good men. But when many persons equal in merit arose, no longer enduring the preeminence of one, they desired to have a common-wealth, and set up a constitution. The ruling class soon deteriorated and enriched themselves out of the public treasury; riches became the path to honor, and so oligarchies naturally grew up. These passed into tyrannies and tyrannies into democracies; for love of gain in the ruling classes was always tending to diminish their number, and so to strengthen the masses, who in the end set upon their masters and established democracies. Since cities have increased in size, no other form of government appears to be any longer even easy to establish.[1]

When Aristotle died in 322 B.C.E., the *polis* died with him. Of course, the exis-tence of the autonomous Greek city-state had been in question for some time. In 338 B.C.E., the combined forces of Athens and Thebes were destroyed by Philip of Macedon. Under the name of the League of Corinth, the Greek World was forced to submit to Macedonian hegemony—this point being made very clear when the entire city of Thebes was razed to the ground and turned into a Macedonian garrison after attempting to revolt after Philip's death in 336 B.C.E. In Athens, however, the dream of the *polis* still lived. Because both Philip and Alexander wanted to form an empire based partly on voluntary participation by subject states, they largely left existing constitutions intact so long as they accepted Macedonian rule and paid tribute, much in the way that Athens had once ruled its own empire. There was thus good reason to believe that nothing fundamentally had changed. Indeed, much of Aristotle's writing on the politics of the *polis* was composed during the period of Alexander's rule after Aristotle had returned to Athens in 335 B.C.E. to open the Lyceum. Hardly blind to the politics of empire, Aristotle clearly believed that it would be a passing phase in the history of the *polis*. Like most Athenians, he believed that the natural political order would be restored, and so he busied himself preparing blueprints for the harmonious state that could be revived after the Macedonian aberration.

When Alexander died in 323 B.C.E., Athens led a revolt against Macedonian rule. Aristotle, now under suspicion as a Macedonian, decided to flee Athens to his dead mother's estate in Euboea, reportedly saying that he would not allow Athenians to sin against philosophy a second time (the first sin being the execution of Socrates). Aristotle, however, could not live outside a *polis*. He died within a year. Meanwhile, Athenians discovered that they could not live inside a *polis*. Their forces were crushed a second time by the Macedonians, who now had the full resources of the former Persian Empire at their command. This defeat finally signaled the end of the *polis* as an independent state. The democratic constitution of Athens was abolished, replaced by an oligarchy which in turn was subservient to rule by Macedonian kings. Athens itself survived, of course, and its cultural and political institutions lived on in a recognizable form even into the Roman *municipia*. In fact, even under imperial rule, Athens "continued to be looked to as an economic heavyweight and a centre of high culture."[2] But, as Donald Kagan remarks, these characteristics did not change the central fact that an age had passed: Post-classical cities "represent a mere shadow of the vital reality which had been the true *polis*. Deprived of control of foreign affairs, their really important internal arrangements determined by a foreign monarch, the post-classical cities had lost the kind of political freedom which was basic. They were cities but they were not city-states; the passage of time marks their steady decline from sovereign states to municipal towns, merged in military empires."[3] Aristotle did not live to see the final demise of his naturalistic order. Yet he could hardly have missed the irony that the one man most eager to transcend the boundaries of the *polis* was the same young man he had once tutored. In the final tragic irony, the philosopher of the *polis* had been complicit in the killing of the thing he most loved.

What replaced the *polis*, however, was not a tyrannical wasteland but simply a new form of power. This form was the empire, of what McLuhan describes as a "universal state" made possible by the speed up and "extension of human senses in wheel, road, and alphabet."[4] In this form of power, the hierarchical logic of delegation reigned supreme, allowing for the creation of a centralization of authority that could rule through action at a distance. Innovations in transportation and media thus combined with prevailing political and economic conditions to explode the boundaries of the *polis* that Aristotle had taken for granted as an internal limiting condition to the size of the state. The result was less a violent suppression of city-states—although that did and had to occur for the sake of example—than simply the absorption of the *polis* into a new power structure. The new Hellenistic politics of empire was therefore far more federalist than the old tyrannical model of fifth-century B.C.E. Athens. Although control over foreign policy and military matters was removed from individual cities, much of the politics within *poleis* continued much as before. Indeed, in many ways, life improved under Macedonian rule. With the constant threat of war between city-states removed, the countryside became more populated with villages, and long-distance trade flourished. With increased travel came a greater cosmopolitanism that replaced the rigid boundaries between citizens and noncitizens and made it possible to form associations "united by commercial, cultic, or ethnic interests."[5] Women, too, found greater freedom in Hellenistic culture as the patriarchal *oikos* lost its central place in the diverse economy of empire. Thus, while the "third- and second-century *polis* in general was a dependent polis, less able than before to formulate independent military or diplomatic goals," it was also "less exclusive in its membership, more cosmopolitan, more pluralist in its religions and ethnic make-up, and perhaps slightly less restrictively masculine."[6]

In many ways, then, the conquests of Philip and Alexander fulfilled the goals of unity that Isocrates had struggled for all of his life. At the same time, had he lived to witness it, Isocrates would have been fundamentally dissatisfied with the form of political organization which supplanted the *polis*. Although no lover of the parochialism of *polis* politics, Isocrates had nonetheless envisioned a new hegemony based upon the shared culture of Hellas that had developed in the context of the city-state. Although Philip had succeeded in uniting (albeit through force) the Greek *poleis* and Alexander had turned their combined force against Persia, what resulted was not the complete triumph of Greek *paideia* over the barbarian hordes. Rather, on gaining control over a polyglot empire, Alexander immediately proceeded to put on Persian clothing, support intermarriage with Persian women, appoint Persians as local administrators, replace his Macedonian military with a multi-ethnic force, and even tried briefly to legitimate his rule by adopting the trappings of a divinely appointed king. All of these strategies represented Alexander's effort to bridge the divide between cultures by creating a more inclusive, cosmopolitan identity necessary to provide stability in an empire made up of diverse ethnic groups. His hope was to transcend the parochialism of the *polis* and create a more universal form of power in which logos became the logic of delegation legitimated through cosmopolitan virtue, universal knowledge, organizational proficiency, and superior military force.

For rhetoricians of the age of the *polis,* the ascendancy of empire clearly meant the decline of sophistical rhetoric as a medium of power. For the Sophists of the fifth and fourth centuries B.C.E., to be trained as a citizen meant to be trained as an athlete in words. For instance, Ober observes that Demosthenes "undertook vigorous physical training of various sorts, including declaiming while exercising and with his mouth full of pebbles," which he says "catches the spirit of the level of dedication necessary to become an effective political speaker in the competitive political atmosphere of fourth-century Athens."[7] In a sphere of politics which was the democratic logocracy, power accrued to those disciplined orators who could master the word. Yet in the new politics of empire, the range of rhetorical action was more circumscribed. As Zeller explains, "there was less scope for creative ingenuity than for resolute self-devotion; less for outward actions than for inward feeling; less opportunity for public achievements, more for private reforms."[8] Thus, according to Zeller, "Stoic apathy, Epicurean self-contentment, and Sceptic imperturbability, were the doctrines which suited the political helplessness of the age."[9] In the place of a rhetor training to propose and defend policies in the assembly of a city he loved, one had a responsible citizen of a polyglot world empire trying to make the best out of a situation in which he had limited control, less understanding, and very little rhetorical opportunity.

The difference between rhetoric in the age of the *polis* and rhetoric in the age of the empire is perhaps best explained in terms of the difference between the sophistical and Stoic views on logos. Even though both Sophistry and Stoicism had Logos at the center of its theory of power, their understanding of the nature of logos differed radically. On the one hand, the Sophists inhabited what John Poulakos calls a "polyvocal world" in which "the status of all things is questionable; and this is why people often find themselves at odds with one another, disagreeing, differing, and seeking to resolve their differences symbolically."[10] Power resided in the logos and constituted both human beings and the world, but it did so without a pre-ordained plan, instead generating the capacity to act in concert through a playful and unpredictable process of *dissoi logoi,* the clashing of differing perspectives out of which genuine novelty emerges. The Stoics, by contrast, lived in cosmopolitan cities which were part of a unified and relatively stable empire. For them, all differences were but partial manifestations of the logos of reason which held the parts together into a coherent whole. They thus perceived themselves to live in a "univocal world," in which "every single utterance would have its place unquestionably, and there would be no need for debate or persuasion—everyone would be listening to and speaking the same logos."[11] The Stoic logos was not the argument invented by political figures competing in the *polis* for influence; it was the logos of reason itself which was binding on all rational human beings who were members of the world state.

But if this vision of logos appears monotonous and sterile to the sophistical mentality, it represents a realm of new possibilities to the Hellenistic mind. For within this Stoic ideal is embedded a utopian vision of power that in many ways transcends the bureaucratic logic of empire in which it first appeared. For the Stoic world state, although guided by reason, was also egalitarian to its core in such a way that would later inspire Emmanuel Kant and many Enlightenment thinkers. Long describes their political utopia this way:

> In the ideal world the state withers away because each Stoic sage is self-sufficient and his own authority. But he is united with his fellows by the bond of friendship, for all wise men are friends to each other and it is only between them that friendship in its true sense can exist. A communal way of life which dispenses with all distinctions based upon sex, birth, nationality, and property—this is the pattern of social behavior. . . . Stoic political theory is not a blue-print for reform but a paradigm of the world as it might be if men could be united not by artificial ties but by the recognition in each other of common values and common purposes.[12]

Paradoxically, then, the same tradition that matured in the context of the imperial bureaucratic state also gave rise to that of the egalitarian global community which at its perfection becomes synonymous with a kind of utopian anarchism. In this form of power, rhetoric thus ceases to be seen as a means of athletic competition and instead becomes a transparent vehicle by which a communion of souls organizes itself in universal love and reason.

Whether such a vision of power is feasible or even desirable is an open question; what matters is simply that, even in such a state, some form of rhetoric will remain a medium of power insofar as human beings organize themselves through logos. For as Aristotle recognized in his narrative of the development of the *polis,* different forms of power come into existence as material, technological, and social conditions change, but what remains constant in any human community is the reliance upon speech to constitute and regulate itself. Of course, Aristotle did not anticipate the appearance of the empire any more than he anticipated the development of a republic or a nation state; despite his genius, his own conservatism inhibited his ability to imagine a future other than what he knew or had known. However, by analyzing the world in which he lived, he gave to posterity a wealth of "truths" that remain a resource for our rational imaginations as we confront the same challenges of flux in our own time. For the basic qualities of the "world order" have not significantly changed since the days of Heraclitus. We still cannot step twice into the same river, and for the most part we remain sleepwalkers quite unaware of the underlying world order that presses in upon us and discloses itself through appearances. Yet the faith of both Heraclitus and Aristotle remains our own whenever we act and speak on the assumption that through the agency of logos we might gain wakefulness and catch a glimpse of a better world through the turmoil of appearances surrounding us.

Within this faith, rhetoric functions as a medium of power whenever logos awakens us to new possibilities in contingent appearances in such a way that actualizes our potential for collective action toward an imagined good. Rhetoric will thus always remain a necessity in human civilization as long as the structure of power remains imperfect, incapable of covering over its gaps and eliminating the need to imagine and reason, sacrifice and strive, and hate and love within a common world. For what makes human beings human is precisely that we are born into the world wishing to exercise our power in whatever way we can, and if we find that we cannot do it through speech, we will do it through violence. But as long as power remains in flux and speech remains open to us, rhetoric will thrive. For the fact is that the rhetorical impulse (if not always the art) is a native capacity of the political animal. Rhetoric therefore springs up naturally between people whenever appearances are in dispute and the burden of judgment presses upon them. As much as we like to flatter ourselves by looking at other human beings as passive herds who want nothing more than to be relieved of the burden of thought and agency, it is not in human nature to willingly submit to power simply because it is power. What we perceive as passivity in the other is more often than not simply the expression of a form of power that we ourselves do not understand because it is not our own. This misunderstanding between two forms of power is itself one of the primary causes of rhetorical contention, both past and present.

The drama of classical Greece reveals to us universal forms and patterns of rhetoric that remain as vibrant today as when they originated in the fifth and fourth centuries B.C.E. Heroic bursts of winged words and epic retellings of great events still retain their capacity to bind people together in a poetic experience that constitutes our public memory. The flux of appearances that flood our senses continues to hint at a deeper order of the universe that only thought can reveal and the aphorism can convey. The spirit of humanism constantly springs anew whenever human beings encounter each other within a plurality, while the dynastic power of persuasion almost inevitably follows on its heels. Tragic rhetoric remains a necessity when we are faced with an impossible decision that will bring suffering upon us, and the comic corrective will forever follow the tragic spirit because of our yearning to hear words of reconciliation that help us forgive both others and ourselves for acts of stupidity and absurdity. But the imperatives of collective action will constantly overcome our comic weaknesses and give us that pride and confidence that only ideology can bring to a mass. And through all of these changes, the yearning for order will remain a constant. Faced with constant temptation from different appearances and the cacophony of different views, we will demand a single discourse which brings everything into proper proportion and measurement; we will ask for leaders who can promise to deliver us security, prosperity, and power and hold them to account; and we will desire a view of history which can reconcile our need for rhetorical deliberation and debate with our yearning to seek the truth. All of these rhetorical impulses were present in classical Greece and remain part of the drama of political culture today.

However, we cannot understand the contemporary dynamics of power simply by using models from the past. Although these rhetorical forms are universal, as circumstances change, these forms take different concrete manifestations and channel power in different ways. Classical Greece saw a rapid transition from the oral culture of parochial kingdoms to a literate culture of cosmopolitan city-states, ending in the establishment of a new form of empire grounded in roads, legions, and law. At each point, new technologies, knowledge, habits, and arts change the pace and scale of human association which inevitably alter how rhetoric is theorized and practiced. And these changes continue, now at even a greater rate. Thus, just as Plato realized that the introduction of writing would radically alter Greek society and its structure of power, we need to fully comprehend how the development of print, radio, photography, the telegraph, the press, the telephone, the movie, the computer, and the revolution in global communication technologies alter how earlier rhetorical forms are manifested and develop new rhetorical forms unimaginable in the ancient world.

But these changes do not make the insights of the agents irrelevant or obsolcte. Quite the opposite. They give us insight into universal characteristics of rhetoric which, at their most basic level, remain relatively unchanged, while also providing a model of inquiry that we might follow when confronting our own unique challenges and problems that arise within the relationship between rhetoric and power. For what makes thinkers like Heraclitus, Gorgias, Thucydides, Plato, and Aristotle so remarkable is that they attempted to step out of the flux of appearances in which they were immersed in order to gain perspective on the nature of power so that they might better control their fate through a more insightful rhetoric. Each of these intellectuals and artists, in his own way, tried to accomplish that end reserved for all great art—to open a sphere of freedom capable of resisting the inexorable movement of necessity through the stimulation of reflective thought and the evocation of deep feeling (and, if we had more of the thoughts of women like Aspasia or Sappho preserved in Greek history, this "his" would also be a "her"). Each of them recognized the danger that accompanies the rush of both elites and masses to exploit the available media of power without fully understanding their origins and consequences, and each knew that rhetoric was almost always the most powerful of those media. That is why, even when *rhêtorikê* may not have been a word, the spirit of rhetoric thoroughly penetrated their work. And what they all called for was not an end to rhetoric but a kind of logos which might "know itself" before it ran roughshod over the Greek landscape.

To what degree their artistic, philosophical, and rhetorical interventions created that sphere of freedom in their own time, it is hard to tell; but what is perhaps clear from their example is that we do not have the luxury to simply sail effortlessly on the currents of power without understanding the nature of its structure and its relevance to the way we think, speak, act, and persuade. Not only do we possess the means of violence that were once reserved for the gods, but we possess the means of communication whose scope and power can only be compared to Heraclitus's Logos. In Aeschylus's play, it was the Titan Prometheus who was bound to a crag by Zeus for bestowing the arts to hapless humans; in our time, it is we who have become gods capable of subduing all of nature to our will. Yet we remain just as anxious as Zeus had been to know what the future has in store, to possess that forethought to see what is to come so that we might avoid bringing ruin upon ourselves because of our own blindness and pride. So there is still a lesson to be learned from Aeschylus. Like him, we, too, have the choice to resist necessity by putting power on stage so that we might, through the medium of speech, direct the course of power toward our own salvation and thereby actualize our potential for freedom.

Rhetoric as a conscious art of constituting, transforming, challenging, and channeling power came into being within the drama of Classical Greece during the height of its tragic age, and it is only within a dramatic retelling that we can capture its spirit. Today, it is tempting to speak of the decline of rhetoric in a technological age, when organized campaigns of propaganda attempt to strike our senses and pummel our consciousness at every waking moment, and when the great oral performances of the rhapsode and the Sophist are replaced by the manipulations of public relations specialists and the tyranny of the sound bite. Yet we must take heart in the fact that the same dystopian visions that arise with every rapid transformation of power never come to full fruition, notwithstanding the recurrent disruptions of the subhuman and superhuman which constantly threaten the virtues of civilization. The tragic spirit which pervaded classical Greece is not dead, and the human drama is not over. We have within our own power the freedom to direct our own fate, however limited that freedom might be at any time. But the only way to become free is to act as if freedom is possible.

The faith that grounds the theory, practice, and ethics of rhetoric does not come easy. Cynicism arises effortlessly in this and any age, and we are all too willing to retreat into specialism, nihilism, or fancy rather than accept our own rhetorical responsibility within the drama of history. But the human spirit is resilient and always born anew. For every passing generation that sees the end of humanity over the horizon, there is a new generation that perceives tragic possibilities and accrues to itself the resources of rhetoric to overcome suffering and inaugurate a new form of justice. Cynics will shake their heads and mutter maxims about the stupidity of the herd, the irresistible force of propaganda, and the helplessness of the individual in an interconnected world. But meanwhile, all around them, people gather together to develop and deploy new and surprising forms of power grounded in that most basic pleasure of the political animal: to use the medium of logos to appear before one another for the sake of collective action. The faith of rhetoric is that through the power of speech we can recognize our interdependence in a contingent world and seek, together, to constitute a form of power supported by the truth, directed toward the good, and exhibiting the qualities of the beautiful. To many this sounds like a fanciful dream, and perhaps it is. But it is the only dream worth struggling for in a tragic world.

NOTES

Introduction

1. Aeschylus, *Prometheus Bound* (1–8).
2. Podlecki, *The Political Background of Aeschylean Tragedy*, 105.
3. Herington, "Introduction," 12.
4. Matthews, "Translator's Preface," 154.
5. Hesiod, *Theogony*, 20.
6. Atwill, *Rhetoric Reclaimed*, 60.
7. Ibid.
8. Arendt, *On Violence*, 46.
9. Clearly, speech is often a precondition for mastery of violence, as in the discourses of apprenticeship. An army doctor can only perform a tracheotomy on the battlefield because he or she has gone to school to learn the art. However, violence refers not to preconditions or capacities but the direct act of using material for instrumental ends. Thus, even an illiterate child, acting alone, can blow herself and others to pieces in a crowded marketplace without knowing what she is doing.
10. Havelock, *The Liberal Temper in Greek Politics*, 57.
11. The Greek gender of the word *Bia* indicates that Violence is female.
12. Arendt, *On Violence*, 44.
13. Foucault, "The Subject and Power," 135.
14. King, *Power and Communication*, 4.
15. In their basic form, rhetoric handbooks were specifically designed for modeling a proper judicial speech "with a prooemion to secure the interest and good will of the judges, followed by a narrative of the facts, confirmed by probabilities," and ending with an epilogue. See Aristotle, *On Rhetoric*, trans. Kennedy, 302.
16. Havelock, *The Liberal Temper in Greek Politics*, 64.
17. Ibid., 156.
18. Ibid., 20.
19. For instance, Prometheus was complicit in Zeus's overthrow of his father, Kronos. A master of forethought, Prometheus knew that "not by brute strength nor violence could the cause be won, but by guile only" (142–43). The Titans ignored this advice; but Prometheus, knowing the outcome, struck a deal with Zeus to secure his position. As D. J. Conacher writes, "Doing good to one's (political) friends and evil, extreme evil, to one's (political) enemies is quite consistent with the climate of the preceding divine power struggles, in which Prometheus himself has played his part on the same terms."

Also, despite his brief praise of writing, none of the arts given to the human race was explicitly identified as a *civic* art, and at no time does Prometheus treat humans as being capable of self-rule. Conacher thus rejects the interpretation of Prometheus as the "*daimon* of civilization"; he notes instead that not only "the fine arts but also the political arts are omitted from the god's claims in these two speeches." In short, a Titan complicit in the overthrow of his own kin, who subsequently betrays the loyalty of the new tyrant in sympathy for humans, only to withhold from them the very arts necessary for sustaining democratic political and social life, is thus an odd choice for a democratic hero. See Conacher, *Aeschylus' Prometheus Bound*, 132, 561.

20. Lattimore, "Introduction," 11.

21. Gagarin, *Aeschylean Drama*, 135.

22. Lattimore, "Introduction," 11. See also this account: "The rule of Peisistratus was mild, wise, and popular. . . . Peisistratus encouraged commerce, enlarged and beautified Athens, built aqueducts and roads, and drew to his court a brilliant circle of poets, painters, architects, and sculptors, from all Hellas. The first complete edition of the Homeric poems is said to have been put together at his command and expense. . . . The tyrant gave new splendor to the public worship, and instituted rural festivals in various parts of Attica, to make country life more attractive. He divided the confiscated estates of banished nobles among landless freemen, and thus increased the number of peasant landholders. Attica was no longer plundered by invasion or torn by dissension. Since the Athenians could not yet govern themselves, it was well they had a Peisistratus." See West, *The Ancient World from the Earliest Times to 800 A.D.*, 118–19.

23. Burke, *Language as Symbolic Action*, 318. Specifically, after Heracles arrives to slay the bird which gnaws at Prometheus, a deal seems to have been worked out whereby Zeus liberates his prisoner in exchange for his assistance and piety, with the final play hinting at a ritual celebration of Prometheus as the "Firebearer" in which he is "restored to honours perhaps higher than he had enjoyed before." See Conacher, *Aeschylus' Prometheus Bound*, 113.

24. See West, *Studies in Aeschylus*.

Chapter 1: Homer's *Iliad* and the Epic Tradition of Heroic Eloquence

1. Homer, *Iliad* (18: 110–50).

2. Havelock, *Preface to Plato*, 91.

3. Cole, *The Origins of Rhetoric in Ancient Greece*, 40.

4. Jaeger, *Paideia* 1: 21.

5. MacIntyre, *After Virtue*, 122.

6. Ibid.

7. Cole, *The Origins of Rhetoric in Ancient Greece*, 4–12.

8. Ibid., 15.

9. MacIntyre, *After Virtue*, 126.

10. Jaeger, *Paideia* 1: 3.

11. Ibid., 26.

12. MacIntyre, *After Virtue*, 128–29.

13. Havelock, *Preface to Plato*, 145.

14. Ibid., 92.

15. Ibid., 157.
16. See chapter 3 in Ong, *Orality and Literacy.*
17. Jaeger, *Paideia* 1: 54.
18. Ibid., 5.
19. Havelock, *Preface to Plato,* 39.
20. Ibid., 157.

Chapter 2: Heraclitus and the Revelation of *Logos*

1. Heraclitus, as cited in Waterfield, *The First Philosophers,* F34.
2. The aphorism is thus very different from the maxim, although both often take the form of a short, poetic observation. The difference is that the function of an aphorism is to disclose a complex intellectual truth through the language of striking paradox whereas the function of a maxim is to embody a moral truism through eloquent principle. A maxim simply condenses the already known into an easily accessible package that can be delivered and unwrapped at a moment's notice. It does not bring something close which was far away but rather discloses the practical relevance of that which is already familiar. The aphorism thus speaks to a much narrower audience than does the maxim. Friedrich Nietzsche, one of its great masters, says that an aphorism is a form of "eternity" and that the ambition of the writer of the aphorism is to "say in ten sentences what everyone else says in the book—what everyone else does *not* say in a book." In other words, the aphorism is not merely a condensed summary of what you get in a normal book; its unique capacity is to actually reveal more than what a book could even say. The reason is that a book rarely "shocks" one into that state of wonder which is the true stimulus of thinking. The goal of the aphorism is not to teach but to provoke, not to direct one's attention but to interrupt our habits, not to attend to practical problems but to contemplate eternal questions. See Nietzsche, *Twilight of the Idols,* 51.
3. Waterfield, *The First Philosophers,* F61.
4. Ibid., F17, F18, F19.
5. Kirk et al., *The Presocratic Philosophers,* 196.
6. Kierkegaard, *The Essential Kierkegaard,* 28.
7. Jaeger, *The Theology of the Early Greek Philosophers,* 116.
8. Guthrie, *The Sophists,* 210.
9. Jaeger, *Paideia* 1: 154–55.
10. Kirk et al., *The Presocratic Philosophers,* 217.
11. Ibid., 195.
12. Arendt, *Life of the Mind* 1: 144.
13. Reminiscent of Prometheus, Cleisthenes himself was an aspiring tyrant with no particular love for the *demos.* What made him unique amongst his political competitors was his realization that the political landscape of Greece was no longer fit for conventional tyrannical domination. "The power of the ruling elite, based largely on the deferential habits and lack of political consciousness of the masses, had been shattered by the tyrants and the revolution," writes Josiah Ober. "No organized group within the state could hope to exert authority by coercion or impose order by force." To solidify lasting power within a situation rife with division and discontent with the old order, he had to give up the dream of uncontested sovereignty. "Lacking authority, then, Cleisthenes

resorted to a politics of consensus." His radical experiment began by breaking up the structures of the traditional order and then making broader appeals for rival parties to find common identification as "citizens," each having a share in running the state through the institutions of the assembly and the court. See Ober, *Mass and Elite,* 69.

14. See Martin, *Ancient Greece.*

15. The Persians effectively left each city under the management of *satrap,* or a local administrator, whose primary concern was collecting revenues to pay tribute to the "Great King" Darius. Despite being under the rule of an empire, the intellectual and artistic culture in Ionia was surprisingly liberal. For Heraclitus, it was in this atmosphere of cosmopolitan Ionia, rather than the more suffocating environment of mainland Greece, that radical intellectuals like himself could thrive. Jaeger remarks: "There they were left in peace; elsewhere their independence offended others and brought them into trouble." So Heraclitus was not exactly pleased to learn that this protection was coming to an end. See Jaeger, *Paideia* 1: 154.

16. One of these changes was indicated by the Persians not responding with the institution of repressive tyrannies. Quite the opposite happened. Herodotus writes that Persian General Otanes "suppressed the tyrants in all the Ionian states and set up democratic institutions in their place." The purpose was clear—instituting democracy would remove the irritation of tyrannical rule and provide the stability and prosperity that would make for reliable tribute-paying satellites. The Persians themselves thus recognized how the structure of power was already changing. See Herodotus, *The Histories* 6: 43.

17. Herodotus, *The Histories* 5: 97.

18. Innis, *Empire and Communications,* 87.

19. Of course, this "break" occurred gradually over the course of several centuries. Despite their use of books to publish the results of their thinking, the choice of Heraclitus (and of Presocratic philosophers generally) to still compress their major insights into aphorisms reflects the fact that the spoken word remained the primary means of communicating even the most complex ideas. Nonetheless, the Presocratic philosophers represented a movement "away from the closed traditional society (which in its archetypal form is an oral society in which the telling of tales is an important instrument of stability and analysis) and toward an open society in which the values of the past become relatively unimportant and radically fresh opinions can be formed both of the community itself and of its expanding environment." See Kirk et al., *The Presocratic Philosophers,* 73–74.

20. McLuhan, *Understanding Media,* 84.

21. Havelock, *Preface to Plato,* 208.

22. Kirk et al., *The Presocratic Philosophers,* 246.

23. Jaeger, *Paideia* 1: 179.

24. Ibid.

25. Thinking thus has a relationship to sense perception much different from willing or judging. The purpose of thinking is to, as it were, make "sense" of the appearances through contemplative reflection. Arendt writes: "in other words, what we generally call 'thinking,' though unable to move the will or provide judgment with general rules, must prepare the particulars given to the senses in such a way that the mind is able to handle

them in their absence; it must, in brief, de-sense them." See Arendt, *The Life of the Mind* 1: 76–77.

26. Arendt, *The Life of the Mind* 1: 77.

27. Ibid., 185.

28. Kirk et al., *The Presocratic Philosophers*, 232.

29. *Understanding Media,* 31. As McLuhan was fond of pointing out, Francis Bacon believed that aphorisms were often more effective in encouraging the growth of mind than what he called "methods," which represented more conventional strategies of logical articulation and rhetorical persuasion: "Aphorisms, representing a knowledge broken, do invite men to inquire farther; whereas Methods, carrying the show of a total, do secure men, as if they were at farthest." For Bacon, methods are comprehensively articulated arguments which give an audience a sense that they have been shown the "total" and thereby secure them that they are "at farthest," meaning the place at which one clearly perceives the answer. By contrast, aphorisms provoke audiences by their incompleteness and create a curiosity and motivation for people to inquire of their own accord into the nature of its truth. It is evoking this sense of *more,* and thereby stimulating the activity of thinking in pursuit of this more, that represents the essential function and character of the aphorism (cited in McLuhan, *The Gutenberg Galaxy,* 102–3).

30. Nietzsche, *Human, All-too-Human* 1: 178.

31. Kirk et al., *The Presocratic Philosophers*, 207, 208.

32. Arendt, *The Life of the Mind* 1: 19.

33. Ibid., 143.

34. Kirk et al., *The Presocratic Philosophers*, 227.

35. Ibid., 209.

36. Ibid., 198.

37. Ibid., 211, 212.

38. Nietzsche, *Philosophy in the Tragic Age of the Greeks,* 62.

39. Ibid., 62.

40. Kirk et al., *The Presocratic Philosophers,* 250.

41. Ibid., 211.

42. Dewey, "Logic," 3.

43. Zeller, *Outlines of the History of Greek Philosophy,* 19.

44. Cole, *The Origins of Rhetoric in Ancient Greece,* 143.

45. Ibid.

46. Arendt, *The Life of the Mind* 1: 192.

47. Ibid.

48. Jaeger, *Paideia* 1: 152.

49. Niebuhr, *The Essential Reinhold Niebuhr,* 7.

50. Ibid., 7.

51. Niebuhr, *Moral Man and Immoral Society,* 34.

Chapter 3: Aeschylus's *Persians* and the Birth of Tragedy

1. Aeschylus, *The Persians* (250–94, 515–20). I have selected the Alan H. Sommerstein translation because of the simplicity and directness of the prose, which makes it easier to follow the narrative and to translate the speech into rhetoric. For a better

representation of the poetic beauty of the play, see the translation by Janet Lembke and C. J. Herington.

2. Hamilton, *The Greek Way*, 173.

3. Herington, *Aeschylus*, 19.

4. Hamilton, *The Greek Way*, 188.

5. Ibid., 171–72.

6. Nietzsche, *The Birth of Tragedy*, 105.

7. Hamilton, *The Greek Way*, 181.

8. Burke, *A Grammar of Motives*, 39.

9. Nietzsche, *The Birth of Tragedy*, 106–7.

10. Nussbaum, *The Fragility of Goodness*, 389.

11. Benjamin, "Fate and Character," 203.

12. Ibid.

13. Ibid.

14. Ibid.

15. Kierkegaard, *The Essential Kierkegaard*, 28.

16. Hamilton, *The Greek Way*, 177.

17. Benjamin, "Fate and Character," 203.

18. Jaeger, *Paideia*, 1: 103.

19. Farrell, *Norms of Rhetorical Culture*, 133–34.

20. For Nussbaum, tragedy occurs in the "presence of circumstances that prevent the adequate fulfillment of two valid ethical claims" (*The Fragility of Goodness*, 25).

21. West, *The American Evasion of Philosophy*, 120.

22. Farrell, *Norms of Rhetorical Culture*, 136.

23. Nussbaum, *The Fragility of Goodness*, 388.

24. Hamilton, *The Greek Way*, 194.

25. Ibid., 182.

26. Gagarin, *Aeschylean Drama*, 43.

27. Other minor illuminations include the following lessons that can be learned from the Persian defeat. First, we learn that wealth (*ploutos*) may ultimately be opposed to prosperity (*ploutos*). The Queen, anxious for news about the battle, recites a traditional maxim that "great wealth may make the dust rise from the ground by tripping up the prosperity that Darius, not without the aid of some God, had built up" (163). And Darius, too, commands "let no one despise the fortune he possesses and, through lust for more, let his prosperity go to waste" (825). Second, overconfidence in technological prowess can lead to one's destruction, as evidenced by the effort to create a bridge across the Hellespont (746). Third, Xerxes made many poor military decisions, most notably splitting his forces between sea and land (728) and then being deceived by the ruse (that the Greeks were fleeing) which sent his ships into a trap (355). Lastly, the army needlessly offended the gods when they set fire to temples, destroyed alters, and uprooted the abodes of deities from their foundations (810). For those looking to gain a practical "clarity" on the world following the cathartic purging of contamination, these lessons provide reassurance that there were good reasons for their defeat, and that such defeat is avoidable to those who act with prudence, foresight, and piety.

28. And of course the Queen quickly changes her description from "bold Xerxes" to "rash Xerxes" (753).

29. Weaver, *The Ethics of Rhetoric*, 23n.

30. Hamilton, *The Greek Way*, 194 (modified). This was the passage that Robert Kennedy quoted on learning of the assassination of Martin Luther King Jr. Kennedy, of course, gets the quote wrong, replacing "despite" with "despair." But this captures the essence of tragedy better.

Chapter 4: Protagoras and the Promise of Politics

1. Protagoras, *On Truth* (15). Citations from Protagoras will follow the numbering given by Gagarin and Woodruff in *Early Greek Political Thought*.

2. See Schiappa, *Protagoras and Logos*, 119.

3. Poulakos, *Sophistical Rhetoric in Classical Greece*, 14.

4. See Kerferd, *The Sophistic Movement*, 43.

5. Schiappa, *Protagoras and Logos*, 160.

6. Guthrie, *The Sophists*, 268.

7. Arendt, *The Promise of Politics*, 14.

8. Ibid., 167.

9. We cannot formally say that the Sophists invented rhetoric because, at the time of the Sophists, the term *rhêtorikê* had likely not yet been coined. This is not to say that the art of using symbols to persuade others to action did not exist. *Peithō* was already an ancient god for the Greeks, and the motivational capacity she represented undoubtedly was recognized by human beings as soon as they began using language. But rhetoric does not refer simply to the persuasive capacities of *logos*. Rhetoric is *rhêtorikê*, a term that appeared only after the death of Socrates and is used most notably by Plato to refer to the art (the ending -*ikê* meaning "art of") of the *rhêtôr*, the latter which Edward Schiappa explains is "a technical term designating politicians who put forth motions in the courts or the assembly" (*Protagoras and Logos*, 41). Rhetoric, in other words, refers not simply to an isolated act of persuasion or object which persuades; rhetoric refers specifically to what Schiappa characterizes as a "discipline," which suggests both a "sense of control, as in the disciplining of a child, as well as a sense of productive rigor, as in the discipline of an athlete or musician" (*Beginnings of Rhetoric*, 23). To create rhetoric is not just to speak; it is to be a kind of artist of words designed to move citizens to action in the *polis* for a political end. But this discipline was still in its formative stages during the time of the Sophists, and its methods were bound up with those of what would come to disciplines like politics, ethics, aesthetics, and logic.

10. Poulakos, "Toward a Sophistic Definition of Rhetoric," 35.

11. Poulakos, "Rhetoric and Civic Education," 78.

12. Although it is not often emphasized, the Sophists did more than teach the arts of persuasion. They also taught the fundamental arts of economic self-rule connected with the *oikos*. According to Foucault, the "*oikos* compromises more than just the house proper; it also includes the fields and possessions, wherever they may be located (even outside the boundaries of the city)" (153). It thus defines a whole sphere of activities for masters of households "connected to a lifestyle and an ethical order" whose end is to

"maintain and increase the family wealth and bequeath it to those who bear their name" (152–3). With regard to this private sphere, Sophists provided the not the art of persuasion but the "art of ruling." (152). In this case, instruction in *logos* did not refer to persuasion but to the art of rationally ordering one's household through reason and command. A large part of what the Sophists offered Greek citizens, in short, was an *askesis*, or what Foucault defines as a "practical training that was indispensable in order for an individual for form himself as a moral subject" (77). The Sophists not only gave skills to the citizen but also taught people how to be a certain type of person capable of ruling one's own household and family. See Foucault, *The Uses of Pleasure*, 153

13. Roseman, "Protagoras and the Foundations of His Educational Thought," 76.

14. Farrar, *The Origins of Democratic Thinking*, 21.

15. Ibid.

16. Arendt, *The Human Condition*, 198.

17. Ober, *Mass and Elite in Democratic Athens*, 25.

18. Kerferd, *The Sophistic Movement*, 15.

19. Nussbaum, *The Fragility of Goodness*, 245.

20. Ibid., 244.

21. As Schiappa notes, "it is unlikely that Protagoras would have been unmolested for 40 years if 'On The Gods' had been considered dangerously heretical" (*Protagoras and Logos*, 145).

22. Jaeger, *The Theology of the Early Greek Philosophers*, 176.

23. Poulakos, *Sophistical Rhetoric in Classical Greece*, 58.

24. Schiappa, *Protagoras and Logos*, 91.

25. For instance, one probable quotation demonstrates how Protagoras believed that one could dispute the fact of whether he is sitting: "It is manifest to you who are present that I am sitting; but to a person who is absent is not manifest that I am sitting; whether or not I am sitting is obscure" (21). Here is a *pragmata* capable of producing *dissoi logoi*.

26. Poulakos, *Sophistical Rhetoric in Classical Greece*, 58.

27. Ibid., 53, 65, 64.

28. Nussbaum, *The Fragility of Goodness*, 99.

29. Sprague, *The Older Sophists*, 85A.9.

30. Kerferd, *The Sophistic Movement*, 47.

31. Farrell, *Norms of Rhetorical Culture*, 63.

Chapter 5: Gorgias's *Helen* and the Powers of Action and Fabrication

1. Gorgias, *Encomium of Helen* (DK11.8). Citations from Gorgias will follow the Deils-Kranz notation followed by the paragraph numbers included in Gagarin and Woodruff.

2. Poulakos, "Rhetoric and Civic Education," 72.

3. Ibid., 75.

4. Guthrie, *The Sophists*, 25.

5. Ibid., 270.

6. Ibid.

7. Gagarin and Woodruff, *Early Greek Political Thought*, DKA8b.

8. "In the case of Gorgias, one of the most important theoretical contributions of the *Helen* is that it engaged in relatively systematic, secular, physical explanation and description. Gorgias provides a serious account of the workings of *logos* and the psyche. With respect to *logos*, Gorgias enumerates its qualities, describes its effects, and explains how it works. The *Helen* is the earliest surviving extended discussion of *logos* and certain the most sophisticated of his time" (Schiappa, *The Beginnings of Rhetorical Theory in Classical Greece*, 126–27).

9. Schiappa, *Protagoras and Logos*, 161.

10. In this respect, the possibility that Gorgias may have instructed Aspasia, the controversial and eloquent consort of Pericles who is said to have helped him write his speeches, takes on a new significance.

11. Arendt, *The Human Condition*, 156–57.

12. Ibid., 153.

13. Ibid., 158.

14. Hurwit, *The Athenian Acropolis*, 280.

15. Consigny, *Gorgias*, 79.

16. Ibid., 66.

17. Poulakos, *Sophistical Rhetoric in Classical Greece*, 66–67.

18. Burke, *On Symbols and Society*, 53.

19. Ibid.

20. Arendt, *The Life of the Mind*, 200.

21. Arendt, *The Human Condition*, 9.

22. Ibid., 192.

23. Ibid., 26.

24. Ibid., 190.

25. Poulakos, *Sophistical Rhetoric in Classical Greece*, 39.

26. According to Arendt, the possession of a common world is what makes human action possible. For her, the "common world is what we enter when we are born and what we leave behind when we die. It transcends our lifespan into past and future alike; it was there before we came and will outlast our brief sojourn in it. It is what we have in common not only with those who live with us, but also with those who were here before and with those who will come after us." In other words, animals do not have a common world because they do not have a perception of sharing in the same historical time. What makes the common world possible is therefore the capacity to share meanings through *logos* and create a realm of meaningful history that transcends our finite existences as individuals (*The Human Condition*, 55).

27. Virgil, *The Aeneid* 2.81–89.

Chapter 6: Thucydides and the Political History of Power

1. Thucydides, *History of the Peloponnesian War* 1: 75–76.

2. Jaeger, *Paideia* 1: 392.

3. Andrew King defines the equation of power: "power has two components: mass and unity. Power results from the unification of mass as achieved through the mobilization of resources. The power of a particular group is the product of the size of its

resources and its potential for unity. A small highly organized group may dominate a much larger, unorganized mass because the smaller group has been mobilized for decisive, unified action. Similarly, a huge mass of people—despite infinitely greater resources (numbers, wealth, skills, and knowledge)—may be easy prey for a small, elite group because the larger group's members lack a unifying consciousness, singleness of purpose, and intensity of organization necessary to bring their aggregate bulk to bear" (*Power and Communication*, 39).

4. LeBow, *The Tragic Vision of Politics*, 143.
5. White, *Kaironomia*, 13.
6. LeBow, *The Tragic Vision of Politics*, 198.
7. Jaeger, *Paideia* 1: 393.
8. Hamilton, *The Greek Way*, 141.
9. Jaeger, *Paideia* 1: 382.
10. Ibid., 384.
11. Havelock, *Preface to Plato*, 304–5.
12. Jaeger, *Paideia* 1: 389.

13. I have elsewhere defined the rhetorical situation as "a shared experience of crisis and conflict in public moral judgment that lends force and effectiveness to rhetorical discourse." The term "moral" here is not intended to mean that one must always be pursuing the "Good" as opposed to an evil. Rather, it occurs when conflict arises between two competing value systems or aims that posit two incommensurable goods, both of which can be attained only through the exertion of power. See Crick, *Democracy and Rhetoric*, 43.

14. Thucydides observes that the two alliances had much differently organized structures of power: "The Spartans did not make their allies pay tribute, but saw to it that they were governed by oligarchies who would work in the Spartan interest. Athens, on the other hand, had in the course of time taken over the fleets of her allies . . . and had made them pay contributions of money instead. Thus the forces available to Athens alone for this war were greater than the combined forces had ever been when the alliance was still intact" (1: 19).

15. Burke, *On Symbols and Society*, 304.
16. Arendt, *The Origins of Totalitarianism*, 468.
17. Burke, *On Symbols and Society*, 303.
18. Niebuhr, *The Essential Reinhold Niebuhr*, 206.
19. Ibid., 207.
20. Hamilton, *The Greek Way*, 142.
21. Weaver, *The Ethics of Rhetoric*, 227.
22. Nietzsche, *Human, All-too-Human*, #92.
23. Ibid.
24. Ibid.
25. Jaeger, *Paideia* 1: 410.

Chapter 7: Aristophanes's *Birds* and the Corrective of Comedy

1. Aristophanes, *Birds*, 88–89.
2. Arrowsmith, "Aristophanes' Birds," 131, 133.

3. Arrowsmith, Introduction to *Birds,* 3.

4. Arrowsmith, "Aristophanes' Birds," 129.

5. Rothwell, *Nature, Culture, and the Origins of Greek Comedy,* 2.

6. Ibid., 3.

7. David Konstan describes the difference this way: "bold actions; earthly humor; immediate social or political relevance; personal attacks on contemporary figures that break the dramatic illusion; choruses in the guise of animals such as wasps, birds, and frogs, or dressed as clouds—all mark Old Comedy as an exuberant and satirical genre, rich in fantasy and spunk. New Comedy, by contrast, tends to naturalism. . . . [A]ll of Menander's comedies dealt with the theme of erotic passion. He favors the representation of young, middle class lovers who must contend with strict parents and a lack of resources in order to achieve the object of their desire. His heroes are more hapless than bold, and they depend to a great extent on luck, which manifests itself to the brilliantly contrived coincidences that are characteristic of the genre" (*Greek Comedy and Ideology,* 4).

8. Hamilton, *The Greek Way,* 121.

9. Cornford, *The Origin of Attic Comedy,* 66.

10. Rothwell, *Nature, Culture, and the Origins of Greek Comedy,* 6.

11. Ibid., 20.

12. Arendt, *The Human Condition,* 9.

13. Bakhtin, *Rabelais and His World,* 94.

14. Ibid., 95.

15. Hamilton, *The Greek Way,* 96.

16. Jaeger, *Paideia* 1: 368.

17. Burke, *Attitudes Toward History,* 54–55.

18. Ibid., 55.

19. Ibid., 49.

20. Jaeger, *Paideia* 1: 364.

21. Ibid.

22. Quoted in Konstan, *Greek Comedy and Ideology,* 31.

23. Ibid., 31.

24. Burke, *Counter-Statement,* 161.

25. Ibid., 163.

26. Ibid., 162.

27. Konstan, *Greek Comedy and Ideology,* 6.

28. Ibid., 7.

29. Burke, *Essays Toward a Symbolic of Motives,* 11.

30. Arrowsmith, Introduction to *Birds,* 3.

31. Burke, *Attitudes Toward History,* 41.

32. Ibid., 42.

33. Ibid.

34. Ibid., 41.

35. Nikias, of course, is the other general alongside Alcibiades in charge of the Sicilian expedition who initially spoke against the expedition as a needless and risky endeavor. Eventually, he was put in charge of the invasion and became the sole leader

after Alcibiades switched sides to Sparta to save himself from prosecution for impiety. According to Thucydides, he suffered nobly alongside his men and was eventually executed by the Syracusans.

36. Arrowsmith, "Aristophanes' Birds," 145.

37. Farrell, *Norms of Rhetorical Culture,* 118.

38. Emerson, "The Comic," 206.

39. Ibid., 207–8.

Chapter 8: Plato's *Protagoras* and the Art of Tragicomedy

1. Plato, *Protagoras,* 336e–337e.

2. Nussbaum, *The Fragility of Goodness,* 91.

3. Ibid., 105.

4. Ibid., 105–6.

5. Dewey, "From Absolutism to Experimentalism," 155.

6. Dewey, "The 'Socratic Dialogues' of Plato," 125.

7. Dewey, "From Absolutism to Experimentalism," 155.

8. This tired notion that Plato was only interested in somehow using the dialogues as a delivery vehicle for transcendent Forms is exploded by Gerald Press. For him, "what the dialogues create in us in the *experience* of this as philosophy, and of Plato's vision: of human life as lived in a reality through which we catch enrapturing glimpses of the ideal; but frustratingly, the ideal remains beyond our grasp just because we live in time and space. Precisely because of their disconcerting combinations of the eternal and the ephemeral, the ideal and the real, the dialogues actually *embody* (what some of them try to articulate) how the eternal and ideal is glimpsed but never really grasped in the ephemeral real world in which alone we philosophize" ("Plato's Dialogues as Enactment," 148).

9. Jaeger, *Paideia* 2: 107–8.

10. Nussbaum, *The Fragility of Goodness,* 91.

11. Guthrie, *The Sophists,* 186.

12. Nietzsche, *The Birth of Tragedy,* 69.

13. In another work, I have defined public intellectuals as "those who respond to their philosophical situation by producing a work that conceptualizes and provides direction for solving long-standing and pervasive problems and are then successful in helping change the habits and practices of a public." A public intellectual is not simply a person with a university position who happens to get published in a mass medium but one whose work stimulates meaningful thinking by the public and significantly alters their habits about significant affairs as a result. See Crick, "Rhetoric, Philosophy, and the Public Intellectual," 139.

14. This motivational aspect is emphasized by Francisco Gonzalez, who characterizes the dialogues "as 'inspiring' us, as providing us with a 'vision' of the world, as 'exhorting' us to action, as expanding our imaginations, as 'orienting' us in our own inquiry, as communicating a form of reflexive, practical, and nonpropositional knowledge, or as inviting us to a conversation in which we must actively participate in order to arrive at the truth." See Gonzalez, "Introduction," 2.

15. Jaeger, *Paideia* 2: 218.

16. Nietzsche, *The Birth of Tragedy*, 73.

17. Ibid., 74.

18. Bakhtin, *The Dialogic Imagination*, 130. Bakhtin explicitly defines the chronotope as "the intrinsic connectedness of temporal and spatial relationships that are artistically expressed in literature. . . . In the literary artistic chronotope, spatial and temporal indicators are fused into one carefully thought-out, concrete whole. Time, as it were, thickens, takes on flesh, becomes artistically visible; likewise, space becomes charged and responsive to the movements of time, plot and history. This intersection of axes and fusion of indicators characterizes the artistic chronotope" (84).

19. Ibid., 130.

20. Dewey, *Art as Experience*, 250.

21. Again, Bakhtin observes that rhetoric "for centuries has included artistic prose in its purview." This was natural given the fact that rhetoric had its origin in courts of law in which both prosecution and defense had to create a narrative account of an action that was plausible and coherent (*The Dialogic Imagination*, 267).

22. Jaeger, *Paideia* 2: 108.

23. Plato writes "and *then I perceived* (as Homer says) Hippias of Elis . . . " (315c). This is a reference to Odysseus encountering Heracles. "Next *I saw manifest* the power of Heraklês / a phantom, this, for he himself has gone / feasting amidst the gods, reclining soft / with Hêbê of the ravishing pale ankles, / daughter of Zeus and Hêra, shod in gold." Of all the references in this chapter of the *Odyssey*, this one portrays the shade as being adorned in great riches much like the Sophists. The other explicit reference is to Prodicus as Tantalus, the shade who is tortured by being ever thirsty and hungry but never being able to drink or eat (*The Odyssey*, 11: 715).

24. Havelock, *Preface to Plato*, 209.

25. Nussbaum, *The Fragility of Goodness*, 105.

26. From Romans 7:15: "I do not understand what I do. For what I want to do I do not do, but what I hate to do."

27. John Dewey, despite his vigorous rejection of Plato's aristocratic politics, nonetheless offers a "defense" of Plato to critics who accuse him of being idealistic: "Plato's answer to the critics would be, I take it, that knowledge which does not pass into action according to what is known is not knowledge; it is opinion, hearsay, a second-hand acceptance of ideas advanced by others. The measure of knowledge, we can imagine him saying, is precisely the action is does arouse and direct. To the charge that he exaggerated the importance of intelligence and underrated that of practice, skill, habit and the emotions, he might reply by point out that he made a prolonged and severe exercise in deeds, and a systematic training of the affections, of likes and dislikes, a precondition of the manifestation of that intelligence which is capable of realizing the good" ("Philosophy and Education," 291).

28. It is hardly accidental that Socrates goes on to mention the sufferings of Tantalus and Sisyphus in the *Gorgias*, both figures whose eternal punishment are depicted as warnings for those still living. In the *Protagoras*, Prodicus is explicitly described as Tantalus and Protagoras appears as Sisyphus.

29. Burke says that transcendence always begins with two opposites, followed by "the adoption of another point of view from which they ceased to be opposites." For

instance, a true believer who burns a heretic at the stake for the sake of love might seem to be acting on a contradiction, but this contradiction can be resolved through a transcendent move "for the greater glory of God" (*On Symbols and Society,* 275–76).

30. Again, Dewey describes Plato's vision in eloquent terms: "In Plato the resultant analysis of the mutual implications of the individual, the social and the natural, converged in the ideas that morals and philosophy are one: namely, a love of that wisdom which is the source of secure and social good; that mathematics and the natural sciences focused upon the problem of the perception of the good furnish the materials of moral science; that logic is the method of the pregnant organization of social conditions with respect to good; that politics and psychology are sciences of one and the same human nature, taken first in the large and then in the little. So far that large and expansive vision of Plato" ("Intelligence and Morals," 47).

31. Crick and Poulakos, "Go Tell Alcibiades," 14.

32. Plato's art of measurement need not rest only on the presumption of a life after death. Martin Luther King Jr. famously wrote that "the arm of the moral universe is long but it bends toward justice." For King that arm of the universe might include its extension into God's arms in heaven, but for people suffering the effects of segregation in this world, that arm extended into historical time and included all the generations to come (*I Have a Dream,* 124).

Chapter 9: Isocrates's "Nicocles" and the Hymn to Hegemony

1. Isocrates, *Nicocles,* 1–9.
2. Poulakos, *Speaking for the Polis,* 27.
3. Ibid.
4. Poulakos, "Rhetoric and Civic Education," 70.
5. Too, *The Rhetoric of Identity in Isocrates,* 149.
6. Hamilton, *The Echo of Greece,* 59.
7. Poulakos, *Speaking for the Polis,* 8.
8. Jaeger, *Paideia* 3: 151.
9. Ibid., 142.
10. Hariman, "Civic Education, Classical Imitation, and Democratic Polity," 221.
11. Haskins, *Logos and Power in Isocrates and Aristotle,* 121–22.
12. Isocrates's rather contemptuous attitude toward the assembly is given fullest expression in his letter to Philip of Macedon. Explaining his choice to address Philip by "open letter," he writes: "I have determined by addressing my discourse to you at the same time to set an example to my disciples and make it evident to them that to burden our national assemblies with oratory and to address all the people who there throng together is, in reality, to address no one at all; that such speeches are quite as ineffectual as the legal codes and constitutions drawn up by the sophists; and, finally, that those who desire, not to chatter empty nonsense, but to further some practical purpose, and those who think they have hit upon some plan for the common good, must leave it to others to harangue at the public festivals, but must themselves win over someone to champion their cause from among men who are capable not only of speech but of action and who occupy a high position in the world—if, that is to say, they are to command any attention" ("To Philip," 12–13). For Isocrates, oral rhetoric still had its capacity to move

individuals to passionate commitment, but that is *all* that it could do. In an age that necessitated a political discourse capable of reaching everyone, oral persuasion to a few dozen or a few hundred people amounted to speaking to no one.

13. Haskins, *Logos and Power in Isocrates and Aristotle*, 102.

14. This lengthy passage in his letter to Philip of Macedon shows the level of sophistication Isocrates had achieved as a critic of media by the end of his life. Of particular interest is how Isocrates justifies his use of writing by its ability to help its reader attend to the facts and pursue inquiry in the name of a sounder judgment. He writes: "I do not fail to realize what a great difference there is in persuasiveness between discourses which are spoken and those which are to be read, and that all men have assumed that the former are delivered on subjects which are important and urgent, while the latter are composed for display and personal gain. And this is a natural conclusion; for when a discourse is robbed of the prestige of the speaker, the tones of his voice, the variations which are made in the delivery, and, besides, of the advantages of timeliness and keen interest in the subject matter; when it has not a single accessory to support its contentions and enforce its plea, but is deserted and stripped of all the aides which I have mentioned; and when someone reads it aloud without persuasiveness and without putting any personal feeling into it, but as though he were reading a table of figures,—in these circumstances it is natural, I think, that it should make an indifferent impression upon its hearers. And these are the very circumstances which may detract most seriously also from the discourse which is now presented to you and cause it to impress you as a very indifferent performance; the more so since I have not adorned it with the rhythmic flow and manifold graces of style which I myself employed when I was younger and taught by example to others as a means by which they might make their oratory more pleasing and at the same time more convincing. For I have now no longer any capacity for these things because of my years; it is enough for me if I can only set before you in a simple manner the actual facts. And I think it becomes you also to ignore all else and give your attention to the facts alone. But you will be in the best position to discover with accuracy whether there is any truth in what I say if you put aside the prejudices which are held against the Sophists and against speeches which are composed to be read, and take them up one by one in your thought and scrutinize them, not making it a casual task, or one to be attacked in a spirit of indifference, but with the close reasoning and love of knowledge which it is common report that you also share. For if you will conduct your inquiry with these aides instead of relying upon the judgment of the masses, you will form a sounder judgment about such discourses" (To Philip, 25–30).

15. Norlin, "Introduction," *xxx, xxxiv*.

16. Jaeger, *Paideia* 3: 129.

17. Gagarin and Woodruff, *Early Greek Political Thought*, DK5b.

18. According to McLuhan, "the 'message' of any medium or technology is the change of scale or pace or pattern that it introduces into human affairs. The railway did not introduce movement or transportation or wheel or road into human society, but it accelerated and enlarged the scale of previous human functions, creating totally new kinds of cities and new kinds of work and leisure" (*Understanding Media*, 8). Similarly, the "message" of the spoken word (to a non-speaking species) is inclusive, tribal unity. Because of the inclusive and highly participatory nature of orality which binds its

hearers together in common language, "each mother tongue teaches its users a way of seeing and feeling the world, and of acting in the world, that is quite unique" (80). By contrast, the "message" of the written word is the beginning of the tribal separation and action from a distance: "the phonetic alphabet, alone, is the technology that has been the means of creating 'civilized man'—the separate individuals equal before a written code of law. Separateness of the individual, continuity of space and of time, and uniformity of codes are the prime marks of literate and civilized societies" (84). It was Isocrates's ability to interpret the "message" of writing that makes him so central to understanding the relationship between rhetoric and power.

19. Poulakos, *Sophistical Rhetoric in Classical Greece*, 137.

20. Ibid.

21. Jaeger, *Paideia* 3: 72.

22. Ibid., 73.

23. Ibid., 80.

24. Ibid.

25. In many ways, this new paradigm of power as a form of cultural hegemony fabricated and guided by Logos appears as a more civilized framework than the old paradigm of power as persuasion backed by violence. In contemporary usage, all culture is generally thought to be a mark of civilization, not of savagery. According to Hannah Arendt, the modern word "culture" generally combines two notions, one of Greek origin and the other of Roman. From the Roman, "culture" has its root in the word *colere,* meaning "to cultivate, to dwell, to take care, to tend and preserve." Being agricultural in origin and connected to Roman life in the countryside, *colere* "relates primarily to the intercourse of man with nature in the sense of cultivating and tending nature until it becomes fit for human habitation. As such, it indicates an attitude of loving care and stands in sharp contrast to all efforts to subject nature to the domination of man." In the Greek, by contrast, the word "culture" is the translation of *paideia,* which means "the mode of intercourse prescribed by civilizations with respect to the least useful and most worldly of things, the works of artists, poets, musicians, philosophers, and so forth." In this case, culture refers not to the cultivation of the land but the cultivation of "taste," or the capacity to discriminate between what is truly beautiful and what is only superficially so. Yet in both senses culture stands opposed to the sphere of brute force and strategic manipulation which seeks to attain narrowly practical ends; for the Roman, Greek, and Modern alike, culture represents an achievement of loving care for things, people, and environments worthy of respect and cultivation (*Between Past and Future,* 208, 210).

26. The term "representative publicity" is borrowed from Jurgen Habermas. Although he originally uses the phrase to refer to the representation of feudal authority in the body of the king, he later says that it in a more developed public sphere it eventually takes the form of public relations work. Thus "publicity work is aimed at strengthening the prestige of one's own position without making the matter on which a compromise is to be achieved itself a topic of public discussion. Organizations and functionaries display representation. . . . Representative publicity of the old type [i.e., the feudal king] is not thereby revived; but it still lends certain traits to a refeudalized public sphere of civil society whose characteristic feature . . . is that the large-scale organizers in

state and society 'manage the propagation of their positions.' The aura of personally represented authority returns as an aspect of publicity; to this extent modern publicity indeed has affinity with feudal publicity. Public relations do not genuinely concern public opinion but opinion in the sense of reputation. The public sphere becomes the court *before* whose public prestige can be displayed—rather than *in* which public critical debate is carried on." The larger point is that Habermas implies this kind of publicity is a relatively modern invention, when in fact its basic premises were already established by Isocrates in Classical Greece. Rather than being invented in the modern age it was simply revived with the passing of feudalism (*The Structural Transformation of the Public Sphere*, 200–201).

27. Poulakos, *Sophistical Rhetoric in Classical Greece*, 136.

28. Derrida, "*Dissemination: The Pharmakon*," 78.

29. Ibid., 78–79.

30. Ibid., 79.

31. Poulakos, "Rhetoric and Civic Education," 73.

32. Ibid.

33. Jaeger, *Paideia* 3: 90.

34. Ibid., 80–81.

35. Ibid., 80.

36. Weaver, *The Ethics of Rhetoric*, 9.

37. As John Peters explains, Plato felt that writing allows conception to "occur between anonymous partners whose junction can be manipulated across great distances of space and time. The written word unleashes a cloud of idea spores that float through space, waiting to germinate and take root wherever they can." See Peters, *Speaking into the Air*, 49.

38. Neel, *Plato, Derrida, and Writing*, 22–23.

39. Nehamas and Woodruff, "Introduction," xxxv.

40. Haskins, *Logos and Power in Isocrates and Aristotle*, 136; Vitanza, *Negation, Subjectivity, and the History of Rhetoric*, 140.

41. Poulakos, *Speaking for the Polis*, 25.

Chapter 10: Aristotle on Rhetoric and Civilization

1. Aristotle, *On Rhetoric*, 1355a22–1355b5. This citation is from the W. Rhys Roberts translation. All future citations will be from George Kennedy.

2. Hamilton, *The Echo of Greece*, 59.

3. Ibid., 60.

4. See Kennedy, *A New History of Classical Rhetoric*, 53.

5. Aristotle, *On Rhetoric*, 37.

6. Randall, *Aristotle*, 1.

7. Lear, *Aristotle*, 7–8.

8. Also see Aristotle's comment in the *Nichomachean Ethics*, in which practical wisdom is said to be "concerned with the things human and things about which it is possible to deliberate; for we say this is above all the work of the man of practical wisdom, to deliberate well, but no one deliberates about things invariable, nor about things which have not an end, and that a good that can be brought about by action" (1141b12).

9. This attitude is precisely the underlying premise of Lloyd Bitzer's conception of rhetoric and the rhetorical situation in "The Rhetorical Situation."

10. Wardy, "Mighty Is the Truth and It Shall Prevail?"

11. Long, *Aristotle on the Nature of Truth*, 161.

12. Jaeger, *Paideia* 3: 266.

13. Ibid., 266, 268.

14. Nietzsche, *The Birth of Tragedy*, 55.

15. Ibid., 56.

16. Dewey describes the difference between Plato and Aristotle this way: "The so-called transcendentalism of Plato, his insistence upon pure forms apart from concrete incarnation as standards of existence, is directly associated with his desire for thorough-going reform. To change the actual he required leverage outside of the actually existent, an independent realm of possibilities higher in value and potency than anything found in existence. Aristotle's insistence that forms have no existence apart from their actual embodiment corresponds, on the other hand, with his general tendency to rationalize the existent world by exhibiting it as containing upon the whole (special aberrations excepted) all the meaning and value that the nature of the case permits" ("Philosophy," 30–31).

17. Arendt, *Between Past and Future*, 188.

18. Dewey, "Logic," 5.

19. Frederick Woodbridge summarizes his attitude: "Nature in its own right must possess such a realm of being, or man could not think at all, just as he could not see at all if nature in its own right were never visible. For the exercise of reason is a life, and every life involves a world to live in, a world appropriate to the exercise of that life" (*Aristotle's Vision*, 47).

20. Randall, *Aristotle*, 66–67.

21. Arendt, *The Human Condition*, 206.

22. Gadamer, *Truth and Method*, 279.

23. Aristotle's naturalism does without the Platonic notions that the soul is rewarded in some afterlife. Aristotle wishes to rid philosophy of any sentimental notions such as the tragic idea that "a man is happy when he is dead" and the Platonic suggestion that suffering injustice is preferable to committing it (*Nichomachean Ethics*, 1100a10, 1055b19). As he makes clear, "those who say that the victim on the rack or the man who falls into great misfortunes in happy if he is good, are, whether they mean to or not, talking nonsense" (1153b20). For this naturalistic perspective, it is obvious that the end of life cannot be identified with something that exists outside of lived experience, whether metaphysically or temporally.

24. Randall, *Aristotle*, 170.

25. Arendt, *The Life of the Mind*, 60.

26. By "discovering" *proairesis*, then, Aristotle gives to human beings what Arendt calls the "first, small restricted space for the human mind, which without it was delivered to two opposed compelling forces: the force of self-evident truth, with which we are not free to agree or disagree on one side; on the other, the force of passions and appetites, in which it is as though nature overwhelms us unless reason 'forces' us away." *Proairesis*

thus emancipates us from the tyrannies of tragic fate, absolute reason, and irresistible appetite and gives to them the responsibility to use rhetoric to advocate choices in a moment of contingency (*The Life of the Mind*, 62).

27. Gadamer, "Aristotle and the Ethic of Imperatives," 62.

28. With its emphasis on deliberation, conflict, choice, and rational desire, *proairesis* represents a distinctly rhetorical attitude toward human action that stands in stark contrast to the more tragic spirit of *prometheus*, its fifth-century counterpart. The term *prometheus*, anthropomorphized in the character of the god, had represented the prophetic capacity to foresee or think ahead, thus implying the existence of a linear sequence of events already written into the future. The tragedy underlying this notion was that this writing was barely legible and frequently misread, thus leading those most virtuous souls to suffering or ruin, just as Odysseus spends years wandering in the wilderness while Prometheus gets tortured and bound to a crag. With *proairesis* the problematic is different. In the *Rhetoric*, Aristotle remarks that "most of the things about which we make decisions, and into which therefore we inquire, present us with alternative possibilities. For it is about our actions that we deliberate and inquire, and all our actions have a contingent character; hardly any of them are determined by necessity" (1357a25). Here is the naturalistic basis for *proairesis*. For what distinguishes *proairesis* from *prometheus* is that it is a dialectical rather than a unitary term; it thus signals a prior deliberation to a choice between two or more alternatives rather than a prophetic vision of a determinate future. In this sense, *proairesis* is exactly the opposite of *prometheus*, for the latter deals with things that are invariable but hidden from us, while the former addresses matters that are amenable to being altered by humans having "desire and reasoning with a view to an end" (*Nichomachean Ethics*, 1139a32).

29. Nussbaum, *The Fragility of Goodness*, 242.

30. Ibid., 258.

31. Arendt, *The Life of the Mind*, 140.

32. Farrell, *Norms of Rhetorical Culture*, 32.

33. Ibid., 33.

34. Jaeger remarks that it was the significant recalcitrance Aristotle was up against in his time that necessitated such a rhetorical exhibition: "To us moderns the scientific study of minutiae is no longer unfamiliar. . . . It needs a lively historical sense, such as is not often found, to realize vividly at this time of day how strange and repellent this mode of procedure was to the average Greek of the fourth century, and what a revolutionary innovation Aristotle was making. . . . It cost him many efforts of persuasion and many biting reprimands to teach the young men, who were accustomed to the abstract lay of ideas in Attic verbal dueling, and understood by a liberal education with formal capacity to handle political questions with the aid of rhetoric and logic, or at best perhaps knowledge of "higher things"—to teach them to devote themselves to the inspection of insects and earth-worms, or to examine the entrails of dissected animals without aesthetic repugnance. In the introduction to his *On the Parts of Animals* he initiates his hearers into his work with an acute exposition of the method, and depicts in an impressive manner his new joy in the art of nature and in the newly discovered world of secret orderliness." See Jaeger, *Aristotle*, 336–38.

35. As Newman explains, "'bringing-before the eyes' is that form of *energeia* that has the potential to actualize the imagistic force within metaphors and thus prompt sensory response in their audiences" (17). It is thus a "lexical species of *energeia* which prompts the audience to visualize images within the persuasive process, making possible though not yet activating human understanding and reflection on the issues these images involve" (22). Thus metaphors do more than convey ideas; they actively engage the audience in the process of meaning-creation based on their own perceptual knowledge (*gnosis*). Consequently, she argues that "capturing audience attention through style is a significant element of successful argument" insofar as the visualization of images "enables those individuals to participate in the persuasive process as more than the passive aim of emotional appeals" ("Aristotle's Notion," 23).

36. Walker, "The Body of Persuasion," 53.

37. Goodnight, "The Personal, Technical, and Public Spheres of Argumentation," 253.

38. More specifically, Goodnight identifies three spheres, the personal, the technical, and the public. According to Goodnight: "some disagreements are created in such a way as to require only the most informal demands for evidence, proof sequences, claim establishment, in language use. These may typify arguments in the personal sphere where the subject matter and consequences of the dispute are up to the participants involved. Other disagreements are created in such a way as to narrow the range of permissible subject matter while requiring more specialized forms of reasoning. These typify the technical sphere where more limited rules of evidence, presentation, and judgment are stipulated in order to identify arguers of the field and facilitate the pursuit of their interests. Transcending the personal and technical spheres is the public, a domain which, while not reducible to the argument practice of any group of social customs or professional communities, nevertheless may be influenced by them. But the public realm is discreet insofar as it provides forums with customs, traditions, and requirements for arguers in the recognition that the consequences of dispute extend beyond the personal and technical spheres" ("The Personal, Technical, and Public Spheres of Argumentation," 255–56).

Conclusion

1. Aristotle, *Politics*, 1286b9 22.

2. Shipley and Hansen, "The Polis and Federalism," 68.

3. Kagan, *The Great Dialogue*, 234.

4. McLuhan, *Understanding Media*, 99.

5. Shipley and Hansen, "The Polis and Federalism," 62.

6. Ibid., 68.

7. Ober, *Mass and Elite in Democratic Athens*, 114.

8. Zeller, *The Stoics, Epicureans, and Sceptics*, 16.

9. Ibid., 17.

10. Poulakos, *Sophistical Rhetoric in Classical Greece*, 58.

11. Ibid.

12. Long, *Hellenistic Philosophy*, 205.

BIBLIOGRAPHY

Works Cited

Aeschylus. *The Persians.* Trans. Alan H. Sommerstein. In *The Persians and Other Plays,* 13–48. New York: Penguin, 2009.

———. *Prometheus Bound.* Trans. James Scully and C. J. Herington, 3–22. London: Oxford University Press, 1975.

Arendt, Hannah. *Between Past and Future.* New York: Penguin, 1968.

———. *The Human Condition.* 2nd ed. Chicago: University of Chicago Press, 1998.

———. *The Life of the Mind.* New York: Harcourt, 1978.

———. *On Violence.* New York: Harcourt, 1970.

———. *The Origins of Totalitarianism.* New York: Harcourt, 1968.

———. *The Promise of Politics.* New York, Shocken Books, 2005.

Aristophanes. *Birds.* Trans. William Arrowsmith. In *Aristophanes: Three Comedies: Birds, The Clouds, The Wasps,* ed. William Arrowsmith. Ann Arbor: University of Michigan Press, 1969.

Aristotle. *Metaphysics.* Trans. W. D. Ross. Rev. J. Barnes. In *A New Aristotle Reader,* ed. J. L. Ackrill. Princeton, N.J.: Princeton University Press, 1987.

———. *Nichomachean Ethics.* Trans. W. D. Ross. Rev. J. Barnes. In *A New Aristotle Reader,* ed. J. L. Ackrill. Princeton, N.J.: Princeton University Press, 1987.

———. *On Rhetoric: A Theory of Civic Discourse.* Trans. George Kennedy. 2nd ed. Oxford, U.K.: Oxford University Press, 2007.

———. *On the Parts of Animals.* Trans. D. M. Balme. In *A New Aristotle Reader,* ed. J. L. Ackrill. Princeton, N.J.: Princeton University Press, 1987.

———. *On the Soul.* Trans. D.W. Hamlyn. In *A New Aristotle Reader,* ed. J. L. Ackrill. Princeton, N.J.: Princeton University Press, 1987.

———. *Politics.* Trans. Benjamin Jowett. In *The Basic Works of Aristotle,* ed. Richard McKeon. New York: Random House, 1941.

———. *The Rhetoric and the Poetics of Aristotle.* Trans. Roberts, W. Rhys. Ed. Edward P. J. Corbett. New York: Modern Library, 1984.

———. *Topics.* Trans. W. A. Pickard-Cambridge. Rev. J. Barnes. In *A New Aristotle Reader,* ed. J. L. Ackrill. Princeton, N.J.: Princeton University Press, 1987.

Arrowsmith, William. "Aristophanes' Birds: The Fantasy Politics of Eros." *Arion* 1, no. 1 (1973): 119–67.

———. Introduction to *Birds.* In *Aristophanes: Three Comedies,* 1–10.

Atwill, Janet. *Rhetoric Reclaimed: Aristotle and the Liberal Arts Tradition*. Ithaca, N.Y.: Cornell University Press, 1998.

Bakhtin, Mikhail. *The Dialogic Imagination: Four Essays*. Ed. Michael Holquist. Trans. Carol Emerson and Michael Holquist. Austin: University of Texas Press, 1981.

———. *Rabelais and His World*. Bloomington: Indiana University Press, 1984.

Benjamin, Walter. "Fate and Character." In *Walter Benjamin: Selected Writings*, vol. 1: *1913–1926*, ed. Marcus Bullock and Michael W. Jennings, 201–6. Cambridge, Mass.: Harvard University Press, 1996.

Bitzer, Lloyd. "The Rhetorical Situation." *Philosophy and Rhetoric* 1, no. 1 (1969): 1–14.

Burke, Kenneth. *Attitudes toward History*. Berkeley: University of California Press, 1959.

———. *Counter-Statement*. Berkeley: University of California Press, 1968.

———. *Essays toward a Symbolic of Motives, 1950–1955*. Ed. William H. Rueckert. West Lafayette, Ind.: Parlor Press, 2007.

———. *A Grammar of Motives*. Berkeley: University of California Press, 1969.

———. *Language as Symbolic Action: Essays on Life, Literature, and Method*. Berkeley: University of California Press, 1966.

———. *On Symbols and Society*. Ed. Joseph Gusfield. Chicago: University of Chicago Press, 1989.

Cole, Thomas. *The Origins of Rhetoric in Ancient Greece*. Baltimore: Johns Hopkins University Press, 1991.

Conacher, D. J. *Aeschylus' Prometheus Bound: A Literary Commentary*. Toronto: University of Toronto Press, 1980.

Cornford, Francis Macdonald. *The Origin of Attic Comedy*. Garden City, N.Y.: Doubleday, 1961.

Consigny, Scott. *Gorgias: Sophist and Artist*. Columbia: University of South Carolina Press, 2001.

Crick, Nathan. *Democracy and Rhetoric: John Dewey on the Arts of Becoming*. Columbia: University of South Carolina Press, 2010.

———. "Rhetoric, Philosophy, and the Public Intellectual." *Philosophy and Rhetoric* 39, no. 2 (2006): 127–39.

———, and John Poulakos. "Go Tell Alcibiades: Tragedy, Comedy, and Rhetoric in Plato's *Symposium*." *Quarterly Journal of Speech* 94, no. 1 (2008): 1–22.

Derrida, Jacques. "Dissemination: The Pharmakon." In *Jacques Derrida: Basic Writings*, ed. Barry Stocker, 56–83. New York: Routledge, 2007.

Dewey, John. *Art as Experience*. 1934. New York: Perigee, 1980.

———. "From Absolutism to Experimentalism." In *John Dewey: The Later Works*, ed. JoAnn Boydston, vol. 5: 147–60. 1930. Rpt. Carbondale: Southern Illinois University Press, 1986.

———. "Logic." In *John Dewey: The Later Works*, ed. Jo Ann Boydston, vol. 8: 3–12. 1933. Rpt. Carbondale: Southern Illinois University Press, 1987.

———. "Philosophy." In *John Dewey: The Later Works*, ed. Jo Ann Boydston, vol. 8: 19–42. 1933. Rpt. Carbondale: Southern Illinois University Press, 1987.

———. "Philosophy and Education." In *John Dewey: The Later Works*, ed. JoAnn Boydston, vol. 5: 289–98. 1930. Rpt. Carbondale: Southern Illinois University Press, 1986.

——. "The 'Socratic Dialogues' of Plato." In *John Dewey: The Later Works,* ed. Jo Ann Boydston, vol. 2: 124–40. 1925. Rpt. Carbondale: Southern Illinois University Press, 1984.

Emerson, Ralph Waldo. "The Comic." In *The Portable Emerson,* ed. Mark Van Doren, 204–15. New York: Viking Press, 1946.

Farrar, Cynthia. *The Origins of Democratic Thinking: The Invention of Politics in Classical Athens.* Cambridge, U.K.: Cambridge University Press, 1988.

Farrell, Thomas. *Norms of Rhetorical Culture.* New Haven, Conn.: Yale University Press, 1993.

Foucault, Michel. "The Subject and Power." In *Essential Foucault: Selections from the Essential Works of Foucault,* ed. Paul Rabinow and Nikolas Rose, 126–44. New York: New Press, 1994.

Gadamer, Hans-Georg. "Aristotle and the Ethic of Imperatives." In *Action and Contemplation: Studies in the Moral and Political Thought of Aristotle,* ed. Robert C. Bartlett and Susan D. Collins, 53–58. Albany: State University of New York Press, 1999.

——. *Truth and Method.* New York: Crossroad, 1975.

Gagarin, Michael. *Aeschylean Drama.* Berkeley: University of California Press, 1976.

——, and Paul Woodruff, eds. *Early Greek Political Thought from Homer to the* Sophists. Cambridge, U.K.: Cambridge University Press, 1995.

Gonzalez, Francisco J. "Introduction: A Short History of Platonic Interpretation and the 'Third Way.'" In *The Third Way: New Directions in Platonic Studies,* ed. Francisco J. Gonzalez. Lanham, Md.: Rowman & Littlefield, 1995.

Goodnight, G. Thomas. "The Personal, Technical, and Public Spheres of Argumentation: A Speculative Inquiry in the Art of Public Deliberation." In *Contemporary Rhetorical Theory: A Reader,* ed. John Louis Lucaites, Celeste Michelle Condit, and Sally Caudill, 251–64. New York: Guilford Press, 1999.

Gorgias. *Defense of Palamedes.* Trans. Michael Gagarin and Paul Woodruf. In Michael Gagarin and Paul Woodruf, eds. *Early Greek Political Thought from Homer to the Sophists.* Cambridge, U.K.: Cambridge University Press, 1995.

——. Encomium of Helen. Trans. Michael Gagarin and Paul Woodruf. In Michael Gagarin and Paul Woodruf, eds. *Early Greek Political Thought from Homer to the Sophists.* Cambridge, U.K.: Cambridge University Press, 1995.

Guthrie, W. K. C. *The Sophists.* Cambridge, U.K.: Cambridge University Press, 1971.

Habermas, Jürgen. *The Structural Transformation of the Public Sphere: An Inquiry into a Category of Bourgeois Society.* Trans. Thomas Burger. Cambridge, Mass.: MIT Press, 1989.

Hamilton, Edith. *The Echo of Greece.* New York: Norton, 1957.

——. *The Greek Way.* New York: Norton, 1943.

Hariman, Robert. "Civic Education, Classical Imitation, and Democratic Polity." In *Isocrates and Civic Education,* ed. Takis Poulakos and David Depew, 217–34. Austin: University of Texas Press, 2004.

Haskins, Ekaterina V. *Logos and Power in Isocrates and Aristotle.* Columbia: University of South Carolina Press, 2004.

Havelock, Eric A. *The Liberal Temper in Greek Politics.* New Haven, Conn.: Yale University Press, 1957.

——. *Preface to Plato.* Cambridge, U.K.: Cambridge University Press, 1963.

Herington, C. J. *Aeschylus.* New Haven, Conn.: Yale University Press, 1986.

——. "Introduction." In Aeschylus, *Prometheus Bound,* trans. Scully and Herington, 3–22.

Herodotus. *The Histories.* Trans. Aubrey De Selincourt. New York: Penguin, 1954.

Hesiod. *Theogony, Works and Days, Shield.* Trans. Apostolos N. Athanassakis. 2nd ed. Baltimore: Johns Hopkins University Press, 2004.

Homer. *The Iliad.* Trans. Robert Fagles. New York: Penguin, 1990.

——. *The Odyssey.* Trans. Robert Fitzgerald. New York: Vintage, 1989.

Hurwit, Jeffrey. *The Athenian Acropolis: History, Mythology, and Archaeology from the Neolithic Era to the Present.* Cambridge, U.K.: Cambridge University Press, 2000.

Innis, Harold A. *Empire and Communications.* Lanham, Md.: Rowman and Littlefield, 2007.

——. *Isocrates: To Demonicus. To Nicocles. Nicocles or the Cyprians. Panegyricus. To Philip. Archidamus.*

Jaeger, Werner. *Aristotle: Fundamentals of the History of His Development.* Trans. Richard Robinson. Oxford, U.K.: Clarendon Press, 1948.

——. *Paideia: The Ideals of Greek Culture.* Trans. Gilbert Highet. Vol. 1: *Archaic Greece: The Mind of Athens.* Oxford, U.K.: Basil Blackwell, 1946.

——. *Paideia: The Ideals of Greek Culture.* Trans. Gilbert Highet. Vol. 2: *In Search of the Divine Centre.* Oxford, U.K.: Oxford University Press, 1971.

——. *Paideia: The Ideals of Greek Culture.* Trans. Gilbert Highet. Vol. 3: *The Conflict of Cultural Ideals in the Age of Plato.* Oxford, U.K.: Oxford University Press, 1971.

——. *The Theology of the Early Greek Philosophers.* Oxford, U.K.: Clarendon Press, 1947.

Kagan, Donald. *The Great Dialogue: History of Greek Political Thought from Homer to Polybius.* New York: Free Press, 1965.

Kennedy, George. *A New History of Classical Rhetoric.* Princeton, N.J.: Princeton University Press, 1994.

Kerferd, G. B. *The Sophistic Movement.* Cambridge, U.K.: Cambridge University Press, 1981.

Kierkegaard, Søren. *The Essential Kierkegaard.* Ed. Howard Hong and Edna Hong. Princeton, N.J.: Princeton University Press, 2000.

King, Andrew. *Power and Communication.* Prospect Heights, Ill.: Waveland, 1987.

King, Martin Luther, Jr. *I Have a Dream: Writings and Speeches That Changed the World.* Ed. James M. Washington. San Francisco: Harper, 1992.

Kirk, G. S., J. E. Raven, and M. Schofield. *The Presocratic Philosophers.* 2nd ed. Cambridge, U.K.: Cambridge University Press, 1983.

Konstan, David. *Greek Comedy and Ideology.* Oxford, U.K.: Oxford University Press, 1995.

Lattimore, Richmond. "Introduction." In *Aeschylus,* vol. 1: *Oresteia,* trans. Richmond Lattimore, 1–31. Chicago: University of Chicago Press, 1953.

Lear, Jonathan. *Aristotle: The Desire to Understand.* Cambridge, U.K.: Cambridge University Press, 1988.

LeBow, Richard Ned. *The Tragic Vision of Politics: Ethics, Interests and Orders.* Cambridge, U.K.: Cambridge University Press, 2003.

Long, A. A. *Hellenistic Philosophy: Stoics, Epicureans, Skeptics.* Berkeley: University of California Press, 1986.

Long, Christopher P. *Aristotle on the Nature of Truth.* Cambridge, U.K.: Cambridge University Press, 2010.

MacIntyre, Alasdair. *After Virtue: A Study in Moral Theory.* Notre Dame, Ind.: University of Notre Dame Press, 2007.

Martin, Thomas R. *Ancient Greece: From Prehistoric to Hellenistic Times.* New Haven, Conn.: Yale University Press, 1996.

Matthews, William "Translator's Preface." In *Aeschylus,* vol. 2: *The Persians, Seven Against Thebes, The Suppliants, Prometheus Bound,* ed. David R. Slavitt and Palmer Bovie, 153–55. Philadelphia: University of Pennsylvania Press, 1999.

McLuhan, Marshall. *The Gutenberg Galaxy: The Making of Typographic Man.* Toronto: University of Toronto Press, 1962.

——. *Understanding Media: The Extensions of Man.* Boston: MIT Press, 1994.

Neel, Jasper. *Plato, Derrida, and Writing.* Carbondale: Southern Illinois University Press, 1988.

Nehamas, Alexander, and Paul Woodruff. "Introduction." In *Plato: Phaedrus,* ix–xlviii. Indianapolis: Hackett Publishing, 1995.

Newman, Sara. "Aristotle's Notion of 'Bringing-Before-the-Eyes': Its Contributions to Aristotelian and Contemporary Conceptualizations of Metaphor, Style, and Audience." *Rhetorica: A Journal of the History of Rhetoric* 20, no. 1 (2002): 1–23.

Niebuhr, Reinhold. *The Essential Reinhold Niebuhr: Selected Essays and Addresses.* Ed. Robert McAffee Brown. New Haven, Conn.: Yale University Press, 1986.

——. *Moral Man and Immoral Society: A Study in Ethics and Politics.* Louisville, Ky.: Westminster John Knox Press, 1932.

Nietzsche, Friedrich. *The Birth of Tragedy and Other Writings.* Trans. Robert Speirs. Cambridge, U.K.: Cambridge University Press, 1999.

——. *Human, All-too-Human: A Book for Free Spirits.* Trans. R. J. Hollingdale. Cambridge, U.K.: Cambridge University Press, 1996.

——. *Philosophy in the Tragic Age of the Greeks.* Washington, D.C.: Regnery, 1962.

——. *Twilight of the Idols.* In *The Portable Nietzsche,* trans. and ed. Walter Kaufmann, 463–564. New York: Penguin, 1982.

Norlin, George. "Introduction." In *Isocrates,* trans. George Norlin, vol. 1: ix–li. Cambridge, Mass.: Harvard University Press, 1928.

Nussbaum, Martha. *The Fragility of Goodness: Luck and Ethics in Greek Tragedy and Philosophy.* Cambridge, U.K.: Cambridge University Press, 1986.

Ober, Josiah. *Mass and Elite in Democratic Athens: Rhetoric, Ideology, and the Power of the People.* Princeton, N.J.: Princeton University Press, 1989.

Ong, Walter. *Orality and Literacy: The Technologizing of the Word.* New York: Routledge, 2002.

Peters, John. *Speaking into the Air: A History of the Idea of Communication.* Chicago: University of Chicago Press, 1999.

Plato. *Apology.* Trans. G. M. A. Grube. In *Plato: Complete Works,* ed. John M. Cooper. Indianapolis: Hackett Publishing, 1997.

———. *Gorgias.* Trans. Donald J. Zeyl. In *Plato: Complete Works*, ed. John M. Cooper. Indianapolis: Hackett Publishing, 1997.

———. *Meno.* Trans. G.M.A. Grube. In *Plato: Complete Works*, ed. John M. Cooper. Indianapolis: Hackett Publishing, 1997.

———. *Phaedrus.* Trans. Alexander Nehamas and Paul Woodruff. In *Plato: Complete Works*, ed. John M. Cooper. Indianapolis: Hackett Publishing, 1997.

———. *Protagoras.* Trans. Stanley Lombardo and Karen Bell. In *Plato: Complete Works*, ed. John M. Cooper. Indianapolis: Hackett Publishing, 1997.

———. *Symposium.* Trans. Alexander Nehamas and Paul Woodruff. In *Plato: Complete Works*, ed. John M. Cooper. Indianapolis: Hackett Publishing, 1997.

———. *Theaetetus.* Trans. M. J. Levett. Rev. Myles Bernyeat. In *Plato: Complete Works*, ed. John M. Cooper. Indianapolis: Hackett Publishing, 1997.

Podlecki, Anthony J. *The Political Background of Aeschylean Tragedy.* Ann Arbor: University of Michigan Press, 1966.

Poulakos, John. "Rhetoric and Civic Education: From the Sophists to Isocrates." In *Isocrates and Civic Education*, ed. Takis Poulakos and David Depew, 69–83. Austin: University of Texas Press, 2004.

———. *Sophistical Rhetoric in Classical Greece.* Columbia: University of South Carolina Press, 1995.

———. "Toward a Sophistic Definition of Rhetoric." *Philosophy and Rhetoric* 16, no. 1 (1983): 35–48.

Poulakos, Takis. *Speaking for the Polis: Isocrates' Rhetorical Education.* Columbia: University of South Carolina Press, 1977.

Press, Gerald A. "Plato's Dialogues as Enactment." In *The Third Way: New Directions in Platonic Studies*, ed. Francisco J. Gonzalez. Lanham, Md.: Rowman & Littlefield, 1995.

Randall, John Herman, Jr. *Aristotle.* New York: Columbia University Press, 1960.

Roseman, Norman. "Protagoras and the Foundations of His Educational Thought." *Padeagogica Historica* 11, no. 1 (1971): 75–89.

Rothwell, Kenneth, Jr. *Nature, Culture, and the Origins of Greek Comedy: A Study of Animal Choruses.* Cambridge, U.K.: Cambridge University Press, 2007.

Schiappa, Edward. *The Beginnings of Rhetorical Theory in Classical Greece.* New Haven, Conn.: Yale University Press, 1999.

———. *Protagoras and Logos: A Study in Greek Philosophy and Rhetoric.* Columbia: University of South Carolina Press, 2003.

Shipley, Graham, and Mogens Hansen. "The Polis and Federalism." In *The Cambridge Companion to the Hellenistic World*, ed. Glenn Bugh, 52–72. Cambridge, U.K.: Cambridge University Press, 2006.

Sprague, Rosamond Kent. *The Older Sophists.* Cambridge, Mass.: Hackett Publishing, 1972.

Thucydides. *History of the Peloponnesian War.* Trans. Rex Warner. New York: Penguin, 1972.

Too, Yun Lee. *The Rhetoric of Identity in Isocrates: Text, Power, Pedagogy.* Cambridge, U.K.: Cambridge University Press, 1995.

Virgil. *The Aeneid.* Trans. Robert Fitzgerald. New York: Random House, 1983.

Vitanza, Victor. *Negation, Subjectivity, and the History of Rhetoric.* Albany: State University of New York Press, 1997.

Walker, Jeffrey. "The Body of Persuasion: A Theory of the Enthymeme." *College English* 56, no. 1 (1994): 46–65.

Wardy, Robert. "Mighty Is the Truth and It Shall Prevail?" In *Essays on Aristotle's Rhetoric,* ed. Amélie Rorty, 56–87. Berkeley: University of California Press, 1996.

Waterfield, Robin. *The First Philosophers: The Presocratics and Sophists.* Oxford, U.K.: Oxford University Press, 2000.

Weaver, Richard. *The Ethics of Rhetoric.* Davis, Calif.: Hermagoras Press, 1985.

West, Cornel. *The American Evasion of Philosophy: A Genealogy of Pragmatism.* Madison: University of Wisconsin Press, 1989.

West, M. L. *Studies in Aeschylus.* Stuttgart: B. G. Teubner, 1990.

West, Willis Mason. *The Ancient World from the Earliest Times to 800 A.D.* Boston: Allyn & Bacon, 1913.

White, E. C. *Kaironomia: On the Will to Invent.* Ithaca, N.Y.: Cornell University Press, 1987.

Woodbridge, Frederick. *Aristotle's Vision of Nature.* Ed. John Hermann Randall. New York: Columbia University Press, 1965.

Zeller, Eduard. *Outlines of the History of Greek Philosophy.* New York: Meridian, 1964.

———. *The Stoics, Epicureans, and Sceptics.* Trans. Oswald Reichel. London: Longmans, Green, and Co., 1880.

Further Readings by Topic
Aristophanes

Hall, Edith, and Amanda Wrigley, eds. *Aristophanes in Performance 421 BC–AD: Peace, Birds and Frogs.* London: Legenda, 2007.

Reckford, Kenneth J. *Aristophanes' Old-and-new Comedy.* Chapel Hill: University of North Carolina Press, 1987.

Segal, Erich. *Oxford Readings in Aristophanes.* Oxford, U.K.: Oxford University Press, 1996.

Silk, M. S. *Aristophanes and the Definition of Comedy.* Oxford, U.K.: Oxford University Press, 2001.

Vickers, Michael. *Pericles on Stage: Political Comedy in Aristophanes' Early Plays.* Austin: University of Texas Press, 1997.

Aristotle

Enos, Richard Leo, and Lois Peters Agnew, eds. *Landmark Essays on Aristotelian Rhetoric.* Mahwah: Lawrence Erlbaum / Hermagoras Press, 1998.

Furley, David J., and Alexander Nehamas, eds. *Aristotle's Rhetoric: Philosophical Essays.* Princeton, N.J.: Princeton University Press, 1994.

Garver, Eugene. *Aristotle's Rhetoric: An Art of Character.* Chicago: University of Chicago Press, 1994.

Grimaldi, William M. *Aristotle, Rhetoric I: A Commentary.* New York: Fordham University Press, 1980.

Gross, Alan G., and Arthur E. Walzer, eds. *Rereading Aristotle's Rhetoric.* Carbondale: Southern Illinois University Press, 2000.

Modrak, Deborah K. *Aristotle's Theory of Language and Meaning.* New York: Cambridge University Press, 2001.

Rorty, Amelie Oksenberg, ed. *Essays on Aristotle's Rhetoric.* Berkeley: University of California Press, 1996.

Heraclitus

Barnes, Jonathan. *The Presocratic Philosophers.* London: Routledge & Kegan Paul, 1982.

Graham, Daniel W. "Heraclitus' Criticism of Ionian Philosophy." *Oxford Studies in Ancient Philosophy* 15 (1997): 1–50.

Hussey, Edward. "Epistemology and Meaning in Heraclitus." In *Language and Logos,* ed. Malcolm Schofield and Martha Nussbaum, 33–59. Cambridge, U.K.: Cambridge University Press, 1982.

Kahn, Charles H. *The Art and Thought of Heraclitus.* Cambridge, U.K.: Cambridge University Press, 1979.

Kirk, George S. *Heraclitus: The Cosmic Fragments.* Cambridge, U.K.: Cambridge University Press, 1954.

Wheelwright, Philip. *Heraclitus.* New York: Atheneum, 1974.

History of Greek Rhetoric

Ober, Josiah. *Political Dissent in Democratic Athens: Intellectual Critics of Popular Rule.* Princeton, N.J.: Princeton University Press, 1998.

Pollitt, J. J. *Art and Experience in Classical Greece.* Cambridge, U.K.: Cambridge University Press, 1972.

Schiappa, Edward, ed. *Landmark Essays on Classical Greek Rhetoric.* Davis, Calif.: Hermagoras Press, 1994.

Sinclair, R. K. *Democracy and Participation in Athens.* Cambridge, U.K.: Cambridge University Press, 1988.

Sipiora, Phillip, and James S. Baumlin, eds. *Rhetoric and Kairos: Essays in History, Theory, and Praxis.* Albany: SUNY University Press, 2002.

Vickers, Brian. *In Defense of Rhetoric.* Oxford, U.K.: Oxford University Press, 1988.

Walker, Jeffrey. *The Genuine Teachers of This Art: Rhetorical Education in Antiquity.* Columbia: University of South Carolina Press, 2011.

——. *Rhetoric and Poetics in Antiquity.* New York: Oxford University Press, 2000.

Yunis, Harvey. *Taming Democracy: Models of Political Rhetoric in Classical Athens.* Ithaca, N.Y.: Cornell University Press, 1996.

Homer and Orality

Goody, Jack. *The Logic of Writing and the Organization of Society.* Cambridge, U.K.: Cambridge University Press, 1986.

——. *Myth, Ritual and the Oral.* Cambridge, U.K.: Cambridge University Press, 2010.

Havelock, Eric A. *The Literate Revolution in Greece and Its Cultural Consequences.* Princeton, N.J.: Princeton University Press, 1982.

———. *The Muse Learns to Write: Reflections on Orality and Literacy from Antiquity to the Present.* New Haven. Yale University Press, 1986.

Lentz, Tony M. *Orality and Literacy in Hellenic Greece.* Carbondale, Ill.: Southern Illinois University Press, 1989.

Martin, Richard P. *The Language of Heroes: Speech and Performance in the Iliad.* Ithaca, N.Y.: Cornell University Press, 1989.

Thomas, Rosalind. *Oral Tradition and Written Record in Classical Athens.* Cambridge, U.K.: Cambridge University Press, 1989.

Isocrates

Cahn, Michael. "Reading Rhetoric Rhetorically: Isocrates and the Marketing of Insight." *Rhetorica* 7, no. 2 (1989): 121–44.

Flower, Michael A. "From Simonides to Isocrates: The Fifth-Century Origins of Fourth-Century Panhellenism." *Classical Antiquity* 19, no. 1 (2000): 65–101.

Heilbrunn, G. "Isocrates on Rhetoric and Power." *Hermes* 103, no. 2 (1975): 154–78.

Lentz, Tony M. "Writing as Sophistry: From Preservation to Persuasion." *Quarterly Journal of Speech* 68, no. 1 (1982): 60–68.

Moysey, Robert A. "Isokrates and Chares: A Study in the Political Spectrum of Mid-4th Cent. Athens." *Ancient World* 15, no. 3 (1987): 81–86.

Rummel, E. "Isocrates' Ideal of Rhetoric: Criteria of Evaluation." *Classical Journal* 75, no. 1 (1979): 25–35.

Plato

Benardete, Seth. *The Rhetoric of Morality and Philosophy: Plato's* Gorgias *and* Phaedrus. Chicago: University of Chicago Press, 1991.

Kahn, Charles H. *Plato and the Socratic Dialogue: The Philosophical Use of a Literary Form.* New York: Cambridge University Press, 1998.

Kastely, James L Plato's *Protagoras:* Revisionary History as Sophisticated Comedy." *Rhetoric Review* 15, no. 1 (1996): 26–43.

Marback, Richard. *Plato's Dream of Sophistry.* Columbia: University of South Carolina Press, 1999.

Nehamas, Alexander "Eristic, Antilogic, Sophistic, Dialectic: Plato's Demarcation of Philosophy from Sophistry." *History of Philosophy Quarterly* 7, no. 1 (1990): 3–16.

Neinkamp, Jean. *Plato on Rhetoric and Language.* Mahwah, N.J.: Lawrence Erlbaum / Hermagoras Press, 1999.

Petruzzi, Anthony P. "Rereading Plato's 'Rhetoric.'" *Rhetoric Review* 15, no. 1 (1996): 5–25.

Vlastos, Gregory. *Socrates, Ironist and Moral Philosopher.* Ithaca, N.Y.: Cornell University Press, 1991.

Wardy, Robert. *The Birth of Rhetoric: Gorgias, Plato and Their Successors.* London: Routledge, 1996.

Sophists

Bett, Richard, "The Sophists and Relativism." *Phronesis* 34, no. 1 (1989): 139–69.

Crockett, Andy. "Gorgias' Encomium of Helen: Violent Rhetoric or Radical Feminism?" *Rhetoric Review* 13, no. 1 (1994): 71–90.

Crowley, Sharon. "A Plea for the Revival of Sophistry." *Rhetoric Review* 7, no. 2 (1989): 318–34.

De Romilly, Jacqueline. *The Great Sophists in Periclean Athens.* New York: Clarendon Press, 1991.

Gronbeck, Bruce. "Gorgias on Rhetoric and Poetic: A Rehabilitation." *Southern Speech Communication Journal* 38, no. 1 (1972): 27–38.

Hunt, Everett Lee. "On the Sophists." In *The Province of Rhetoric,* ed. J. Rycenga, 69–84. New York: Ronald, 1965.

Mailloux, Steven, ed. *Rhetoric, Sophistry, Pragmatism.* Cambridge, U.K.: Cambridge University Press, 1995.

Mayhew, Robert. *Prodicus the Sophist: Texts, Translations, and Commentary.* Oxford, U.K.: Oxford University Press, 2011.

McComiskey, Bruce. *Gorgias and the New Sophistic Rhetoric.* Carbondale: Southern Illinois University Press, 2002.

Schiller, F. C. S. *Plato or Protagoras?* Oxford, U.K.: Basil Blackwell, 1908.

Untersteiner, Mario. *The Sophists.* Trans. Kathleen Freedman. Oxford, U.K.: Basil Blackwell, 1954.

Thucydides

Cogan, Marc. *The Human Thing: The Speeches and Principles of Thucydides' History.* Chicago: University of Chicago Press, 1981.

Connor, W. Robert. *Thucydides.* Princeton, N.J.: Princeton University Press, 1984.

Crane, Gregory. *Thucydides and the Ancient Simplicity: The Limits of Political Realism.* Berkeley: University of California Press, 1998.

Dover, Kenneth. *Thucydides.* Oxford, U.K.: Clarendon Press, 1973.

Edmunds, L. *Chance and Intelligence in Thucydides.* Cambridge, Mass.: Harvard University Press, 1975.

Finley, John. "The Origins of Thucydides' Style." *Harvard Studies in Classical Philology* 50 (1939): 35–84.

Gomme, A. W. *A Historical Commentary on Thucydides.* Ed. A. Andrewes and K. J. Dover. Oxford, U.K.: Clarendon Press, 1970.

Rawlings, H. R. *The Structure of Thucydides' History.* Princeton, N.J.: Princeton University Press, 1981.

INDEX

ABOUT THE AUTHOR

NATHAN CRICK is an associate professor of communication at Texas A&M University and author of *Democracy and Rhetoric: John Dewey on the Arts of Becoming* (University of South Carolina Press) and *Rhetorical Public Speaking.*